C0-AAU-290
3 1611 00108 3374

MEASUREMENT OF NURSING OUTCOMES

VOLUME FOUR

Measuring Client Self-Care and Coping Skills

Ora L. Strickland, Ph.D., R.N., F.A.A.N., is the Independence Foundation Research Chair and Professor at Emory University Nell Hodgson Woodruff School of Nursing. Dr. Strickland earned a doctoral degree in child development and family relations from the University of North Carolina, Greensboro. She took a master's degree in maternal and child health nursing from Boston University, Massachusetts, and received a bachelor's degree in nursing from North Carolina Agricultural and Technical State University. As a nationally known specialist in nursing research, measurement, evaluation, maternal and child health, and parenting, Dr. Strickland is frequently called upon as a consultant by universities, health care agencies, community organizations, and governmental agencies. She has presented more than 100 public lectures, speeches, and workshops, and her research has been featured in newspapers and on radio and television. Dr. Strickland is on the editorial boards of several professional journals.

Carolyn F. Waltz, Ph.D., R.N., F.A.A.N., is a professor and coordinator of evaluation at the University of Maryland School of Nursing and was Program Director of the Measurement of Clinical and Educational Nursing Outcomes grants funded by the Division of Nursing 1983–1985 and 1985–1988. She was Program Director of the Accreditation Outcomes Project, National League for Nursing, which was funded by the Helene Fuld Health Trust Fund. She received her B.S. and M.S. degrees from the University of Maryland and her Ph.D. from the University of Delaware. She has published numerous books, chapters, and journal articles on nursing research, measurement, nursing outcomes, and evaluation, including the well-received Volumes 1 and 2 of the Measurement of Nursing Outcomes books co-authored with Dr. Strickland. To date, she has served as a consultant to more than 100 universities and institutions nationally and internationally regarding topics such as measurement, program evaluation, and nursing outcomes.

MEASUREMENT OF NURSING OUTCOMES

Volume Four
Measuring Client Self-Care and Coping Skills

Ora L. Strickland
R.N., Ph.D., F.A.A.N.
Carolyn F. Waltz
R.N., Ph.D., F.A.A.N.
Editors

SPRINGER PUBLISHING COMPANY
New York

Springer Publishing Company, Inc.
536 Broadway
New York, NY 10012-3955

90 91 92 93 94 / 5 4 3 2 1

Library of Congress Cataloging-in-Publication Data

Revised for (vol. 3 & 4)

Measurement of nursing outcomes.

Includes bibliographies and indexes.
Contents: v. 1. Measuring client outcomes — [etc.] — v. 3. Measuring nursing performance — v. 4. Measuring client self-care and coping skills.
0-8261-5273-2 (v.3) 0-8261-5274-0 (v.4)
1.Nursing audit. 2. Nursing—Standards.
I. Waltz, Carolyn Feher. II. Strickland, Ora.
[DNLM: 1. Nursing—methods. 2. Nursing—standards.
3. Personnel Management, WY 16 M484]
RT85.5.M434 1988 362.1'73'068 88-19961

Printed in the United States of America

CONTENTS

PREFACE

The major purpose of this publication and its companion volumes is to disseminate information about the measurement of clinical and educational nursing outcomes. More specifically, these volumes include nursing measurement tools, comprehensive measurement protocols for the tools, presentation of results in testing the tools (including reliability and validity assesssment), discussion of results, and conclusions (including the utility of the instruments for measuring outcomes of nursing education and practice).

The tools and other methods resulted from the efforts of selected participants in the second Measurement of Clinical and Educational Nursing Outcomes Project, a two-and-one-half-year continuing education project administered by Drs. Carolyn F. Waltz, and Ora L. Strickland at the University of Maryland School of Nursing and funded by the Division of Nursing, Special Projects Branch. The project, offered for the first time in 1983–1985, was so highly successful that it was offered a second time, from 1985 to 1988, in response to requests by potential participants. Nurse researchers, clinicians, and educators from across the nation were provided the opportunity to refine their skills in nursing measurement through a series of three intensive workshops and individualized consultations. The project focused on the development and testing of clinical and educational outcome measurement tools in nursing. Enrollment was limited to nurses actively involved in research or education, and selection for participation was on a competitive basis.

The objectives of the project were to

1. Introduce participants to new and expanded measurement theories and practices germane to the measurement of clinical and educational outcomes in nursing.
2. Provide opportunities for participants to scrutinize measurement tools and devices currently utilized in nursing to measure outcomes in terms of new advances in measurement theory and practices.

3. Provide opportunities for participants to apply new and expanded measurement principles and practices to the development and testing of sound tools for the measurement of clinical and educational outcomes in nursing.
4. Provide for the dissemination of information about measurement of clinical and educational outcomes in nursing through the publication of workshop proceedings and outcome measures developed and/or tested by participants.

The workshops were led and facilitated by experts in measurement, nursing education, and nursing research. Each participant developed and/or modified and tested a tool to measure a nursing outcome variable. In addition to Drs. Waltz and Strickland, the consultants involved in the workshops and in providing consultation to participants were:

Jan Atwood, R.N., Ph.D., F.A.A.N.
University of Arizona

Ada Sue Hinshaw, R.N., Ph.D., F.A.A.N.
National Institutes of Health, National Center for Nursing Research

Wealtha C. McGurn, R.N., Ph.D.
University of Texas at San Antonio

Geraldine Padilla, Ph.D.
University of California at Los Angeles

One hundred fifteen participants were selected by a committee composed of nursing leaders located throughout the United States. Of these, 104 of the participants continued with the project for the whole two-and-one-half-year period. A listing of the participants, their degrees, affiliations, and project titles is included in the Appendix.

The papers published here were selected from those developed through the project; they include tools developed, modified, and/or tested by project participants, as well as presentations by other nurses who have developed tools to measure nursing outcome variables. These were presented at a conference open to the profession at large, and attended by approximately 200 individuals.

In essence, Volume 3 is a compendium of tools applicable to measuring nursing performance—clusters of topic areas that address professional roles, clinical performance and decision making, and organizational climate and other factors affecting student outcomes. Some of the major areas include, but are not limited to, faculty teaching role preparation, quality of nursing care performance, clinical competence, diagnostic reasoning, critical thinking, nursing attitudes toward cost-effectiveness, computing, fear of success, factors affecting student outcomes such as English language competency, course participation, and integrated and nonintegrated baccalaureate nursing curriculums. Volume 4 presents tools that focus on client-centered outcomes, also resulting from the project. For example, some of the major topic areas include, but are not limited to, coping, social support, empathy, client outcomes related to long-term health problems, and outcomes of self-care and nursing care.

The measurement protocol for each tool includes the following:

1. A critical review and analysis of the literature related to the outcome variable/concept selected.
2. A review and analysis of existing tools and procedures for measuring the selected outcome variable.
3. The conceptual basis of the measure.
4. Purpose and/or objectives of the measure.
5. Procedures for construction, revision, or further development of the measure.
6. Procedure for administration and scoring.
7. Methodology for testing the reliability and validity of the measure, including approach to data collection, procedure for protection of human subjects where appropriate, and statistical analysis procedures.

The reader will find in these volumes a collection of tools for the measurement of clinical and educational outcome variables that represents some of the finest work to date.

A variety of substantive topic areas are addressed, and in addition, prototypes of methodologies for the measurement of outcome variables whose utility extends well beyond a given topic area are provided. Other benefits to the reader result from the following: all tools are conceptually based; extensive reviews of the literature and bibliographies provide state-of-the-art information regarding measurement of nursing outcomes; all tools and methods are well grounded in sound measurement theory and practices; both norm-referenced and criterion-referenced measurement frameworks are used, and varied types of instrumentation, including, but not limited to, clinical simulations and magnitude estimation scaling, are represented; newly developed measures as well as modifications of existing methods are included; reliability and validity data are provided for all tools, often in cases where such information was not available before; and varied methods for determining reliability and validity with unrealized potential in nursing measurement, such as confirmatory factor analysis and the multitrait–multimethod approach, are applied in an easily understood and replicable manner.

ORA L. STRICKLAND, R.N., PH.D., F.A.A.N.
Project Director
Measurement of Clinical and Educational Nursing Outcomes Project,
Independence Foundation Research Chair and Professor,
Nell Hodgson Woodruff School of Nursing, Emory University, Atlanta, Georgia

CAROLYN F. WALTZ, R.N., PH.D., F.A.A.N.
Program Director
Measurement of Clinical and Educational Nursing Outcomes Project, and Professor and Coordinator for Evaluation,
University of Maryland, School of Nursing

CONTRIBUTORS

Elizabeth Ann Manhart Barrett, R.N., Ph.D.
Associate Professor
Hunter-Bellevue School of Nursing
Hunter College of The City University of New York
New York, New York

Marci Catanzaro, R.N., Ph.D.
Associate Professor
Department of Physiological Nursing
School of Nursing
University of Washington
Seattle, Washington

Judith Haber, R.N., C.S., Ph.D.
Director, Department of Nursing
College of Mount Saint Vincent
Riverdale, New York

Gloria Hagopian, R.N., Ed.D.
Assistant Professor of Oncologic Nursing
School of Nursing
University of Pennsylvania
Clinician Educator
Department of Radiation Oncology
Hospital of the University of Pennsylvania
Philadelphia, Pennsylvania

Gail A. Hilbert, R. N., D.N.Sc.
Professor and Assistant Dean for Graduate Studies
School of Nursing
Widener University
Chester, Pennsylvania

Alicia Huckstadt, R.N., Ph.D.
Associate Professor
Department of Nursing
The Wichita State University
Wichita, Kansas

Ann C. Hurley, R.N., D.N.Sc.
New England Deaconess Hospital
Boston, Massachusetts

Debra P. Hymovich, R.N., Ph.D., F.A.A.N.
Postdoctoral Fellow
School of Nursing
University of Pennsylvania
Philadelphia, Pennsylvania

Linda Corson Jones, R.N., Ph.D.
Associate Professor
School of Nursing, Graduate Program
Louisiana State University Medical Center
New Orleans, Louisiana

Patricia L. Lane, R.N., Ph.D.
Associate Professor
Graduate Nursing Program
School of Nursing
Louisiana State University Medical Center
New Orleans, Louisiana

Anna M. McDaniel, R.N., C.S., M.A.
Assistant Professor of Nursing Education
Division of Nursing
Indiana Wesleyan University
Marion, Indiana

Margaret Chamberlain Metcalfe, R.N., M.S.
Assistant Professor
College of Nursing
University of Delaware
Newark, Delaware

Ngozi O. Nkongho, R.N., Ph.D.
Assistant Professor
Lehman College, Department of Nursing
The City University of New York
New York, New York

Michael Perlow, R.N., D.N.S.
Assistant Professor
Department of Nursing
College of Science
Murray State University
Murray, Kentucky

Kathleen J. Sawin, R.N., D.N.S.
Assistant Professor
School of Nursing
Virginia Commonwealth University
Richmond, Virginia

Sarah S. Strauss, R.N., Ph.D.
Associate Professor
School of Nursing
Virginia Commonwealth University
Richmond, Virginia

Nancy Wells, R.N., D.N.Sc.
Robert Wood Johnson Clinical Nurse Scholar
School of Nursing
University of Rochester
Rochester, New York

Kathleen Wheeler, R.N., Ph.D.
Assistant Professor
Hunter-Bellevue School of Nursing
Hunter College of the City University of New York
New York, New York

Joan Ramsey Wilk, R.N., Ph.D.
Assistant Professor
School of Nursing
University of Wisconsin-Milwaukee
Milwaukee, Wisconsin

PART I
Caring and Self-Care Measures

1
The Caring Ability Inventory

Ngozi O. Nkongho

This chapter discusses the Caring Ability Inventory, a tool which measures one's ability to care when involved in a relationship with others.

The purpose of this study was to develop an instrument to measure caring ability (the Caring Ability Inventory) and to develop initial reliability and validity evidence for the inventory. The concept of care is of interest to philosophers, psychologists, nurses, and other students of human relations.

It is generally recognized that people feel and behave differently in varied relationships with others. One possible explanation for this difference relates to the amount of caring present and felt by those involved. Not only do we need to be able to measure the ability of health care providers to care, but also we may want to know the ability of patients to care. This measure may be used to assess the degree to which abusive parents, clients unable to maintain relationships, or nurses and other health care providers who work with patients have the ability to care. To increase our understanding of human relationships, it is essential that people's caring ability be analyzed and quantified. With this knowledge, it is possible to identify areas of weakness and strength in a person's ability to care. Intervention strategies can be planned based on these findings.

The purpose of the Caring Ability Inventory (CAI) is to quantify a person's degree of caring ability relative to others.

REVIEW OF RELATED LITERATURE

A review of the literature pertinent to caring indicates that this concept has been described in multiple ways by varied authors in different fields. The following brief discussion of the literature on caring is divided into the discipline of nursing and other disciplines.

Nursing

Leininger (1984, 1986) has devoted much effort to studying caring. She states that caring is essential for health, human development, and human survival. Leininger (1981) defines care as "cognitively learned, culturally specific modes of helping others to receive personalized services to improve, maintain a healthy state for life or death" (p. 9). Leininger further differentiates curing and caring activities and asserts that nursing's central domain is on caring. For Leininger, "professional caring embodies the cognitive and deliberate goals, processes, and acts of professional persons or groups providing assistance to others, and expressing attitudes and actions of concern for them, in order to support their well-being, alleviate undue discomforts, and meet obvious or anticipated needs" (1981, p. 46). She provides evidence from cross-cultural studies indicating that elements of caring vary among cultures. Twenty-eight caring constructs were identified from the study of 30 different cultural groups.

Watson (1979) views nursing as a science of caring with a balance between the scientific and the humanistic aspects of care. Caring is described as "an interpersonal process involving concern and the desire to assist the other person to achieve mental, physical, sociocultural and spiritual well-being" (p. 9).

Watson (1979) believes that caring components can be identified, studied, and researched. Ten factors that should form the structure for the study of the science of caring are identified. Two of these factors are establishing a humanistic–altruistic value system and using scientific problem-solving methods in decision making. Methods that could be employed to facilitate the acquisition of these factors are discussed at length by Watson.

Monea (1979) discusses caring as a characteristic of a helping relationship. Important elements in caring are commitment, responsibility, and establishing an "I–thou" relationship. Commitment provides meaning to life as one finds something worth living for and is open to changing ideas, values, and attitudes. Being responsible in a caring relationship includes knowing oneself and the other, as well as having the courage to accept the consequences of one's actions. The I–thou relationship means relating to people on a humanistic level. Such a relationship improves the quality of the interaction, and the person being cared for feels accepted and respected. This type of relationship facilitates the development of trust.

Gaut (1984) provides a framework for caring as an ordered series of actions by the nurse beginning with goal setting and ending with implementation. Gaut states that the caring nurse must meet three criteria: have an awareness of the needs, rights, and dignity of the other; have the knowledge to choose and implement actions; and through her or his actions bring about positive change in the other.

To summarize, nurse theorists address the importance of caring as a major component of nursing. They define care, identify essential caring behavior by nurses, and encourage research regarding the phenomenon of care.

Few studies have explored nursing behaviors that convey caring to patients. Henry (1975) interviewed a sample of 50 home-care patients on what they perceived as caring behaviors of the nurse. She classified responses obtained into what the nurse does, how the nurse does, and how much the nurse does.

Brown (1982) interviewed hospitalized patients and identified nursing behaviors that indicate caring. Two categories emerged: task and affective dimensions. The dimension of task includes surveillance, availability and accessibility, nursing procedures, providing information, demonstrating professional knowledge, and supporting individuality. The affective dimension addressed the personal and professional qualities of the nurse.

Ford (1981) studied nurses' descriptions of caring to identify behaviors associated with caring. The result revealed that nurses defined caring as having genuine concern for the other and considered listening as the behavior most indicative of caring.

Larson (1984) studied hospitalized patients' perceptions of nurses' caring behaviors, using the CARE-Q instrument. This instrument addressed six areas: accessibility, explanation and facilitation, comfort, anticipation, trusting relationship, and monitoring and following through. The patients ranked "being accessible" and "monitoring and following through" as the most important caring behaviors for the nurse.

From the results of these studies it seems that perception of care varies according to the provider and the recipient. Nurses identified the affective component of caring as more important, and patients focused more on the tasks performed by the nurse. This difference in perception may reflect the immediate needs of patients as opposed to long-range goals that nurses may have for patients.

Other Disciplines

Gaylin (1976) discusses caring as being intrinsic to human nature. Caring is essential for human survival, and human survival is dependent on our continued ability to care. Gaylin believes that the violence, depression, and sense of helplessness so prevalent in society can be ameliorated through caring because the degrees to which people are nurtured and cared for determine the degree to which they are capable of nurturing and caring.

The concept of caring is prominent in Rogers's (Meador & Rogers, 1979) person-centered therapy. The goal of this approach is that the "growthful potential of any individual will tend to be released in a relationship in which the helping person is experiencing and communicating realness, caring, and a deeply sensitive, non-judgmental understanding" (p. 131). For change and growth to occur in the other, Rogers states that three critical elements of the helping process must be present. The first is genuineness, realness, or congruence by the helper. The second element is an "unconditional positive regard" for the other person. This involves a willingness to accept whatever feelings are expressed by the other as real to that person at that moment. The third element is empathic understanding, which is a combination of active listening and accurately sensing the feeling and personal meanings of what the other is trying to communicate. For Rogers, these conditions must be present for a climate to be growth-promoting, and they can be seen in many types of relationships, such as parent–child, teacher–student, administrator–staff, and therapist–client relationships.

Mayeroff (1971) defines caring as helping another person to grow and self-actualize. Caring for another allows for growth in the person being cared for. Critical elements necessary in a caring relationship are knowing, alternating rhythm, patience, honesty, trust, humility, hope, and courage. A caring person experiences a sense of belonging and connectedness, is stable, and is more resilient to stress. Mayeroff's conceptualization of caring provides the theoretical framework on which the development of the CAI is based.

CONCEPTUAL FRAMEWORK OF THE MEASURE

The conceptual framework for the CAI was derived from the literature on caring. Four theoretical assumptions were identified. Specifically, these were (1) caring is multidimensional, with cognitive and attitudinal components; (2) the potential to care is present in all individuals; (3) caring can be learned; and (4) caring is quantifiable.

Further development of the conceptual basis is based on Mayeroff's (1971) discussion of caring. He defines caring as "helping another grow and actualize himself, . . . a process, a way of relating to someone that involves development" (p. 1). He identified eight indicators of caring: knowing, alternating rhythm, patience, honesty, trust, humility, hope and courage.

Knowing involves an awareness of the other as separate, with unique needs. It implies understanding who the person cared for is, his or her needs, strengths and weaknesses, and what enhances his or her well-being. Knowing can be explicit or implicit, direct or indirect; it includes both general and specific knowledge of the person cared for. An important aspect of knowing is knowing one's own strengths and limitations.

Alternating rhythms refers to fluctuations in the scope of caring. At times caring involves "doing" for the other, and at times it may involve doing "nothing." The caregiver needs to be aware of when doing and not doing represent caring. Alternating rhythm provides a basis for identifying patterns of caring. Patterns make it possible to learn from past experience what behaviors were helpful or not helpful and to modify one's actions to facilitate growth.

Patience is essential in caring because it allows time and room for self-expression and exploration. Being patient includes being tolerant of some degree of confusion and disorganization, which characterizes growth for self and others.

Honesty involves seeing others as they are instead of as the caregiver wishes them to be. The changing needs of the individual over time are visible when that person is seen as he or she is at a given time. Honesty in caring also implies being genuine or real to oneself. When one is genuine, there is congruence between what is said and what is felt. When honesty is present, the caregiver is available and open to the other, and energy is not wasted on pretending to be what one is not.

Trust is present in caring as it allows others to grow in their own time and their own way. Trust involves having confidence in one's abilities and in the other person's abilities as well. A trusting relationship encourages and fosters independence.

Humility involves continuous learning about the other and is never completed. Different people can care for others without any particular kind of caring being more important than another. With humility there is genuineness without the need to pretend what one is not or to conceal aspects of self. Without pretense one can be seen truly, as a person with both strengths and limitations.

Hope is present in caring and is associated with the anticipation of growth with caring. With hope in caring the present becomes alive and significant as the possibilities to be realized in the future are recognized.

Courage is present in caring when the direction of growth and its outcome are largely unknown. The courage to care is gained from past experience and by being sensitive and open to the needs of the present.

PURPOSE OF THE INVENTORY

The ethnographic approach—using such strategies as participant observation and interview—has been widely used to identify and describe caring behaviors of people from varied cultures. The phenomenological method has also been suggested and used to study caring. The researcher using this method approaches the study with no preconceived categories, expectations, or operational definitions. This method seeks to uncover the meaning of caring through the analysis of subjects' descriptions. These two methods of studying caring have identified and discussed constructs essential in a caring relationship.

No other instrument that measures an individual's ability to care was found. But it is essential that both qualitative and quantitative approaches be used in order to fully understand and carry out the concept of caring in practice. The development of the CAI fills this gap. Specifically, the purpose of CAI is to measure the degree of a person's ability to care for others.

PROCEDURES FOR DEVELOPMENT

The work of Mayeroff (1971), in which the eight critical elements of caring were identified (knowing, alternating rhythm, patience, honesty, trust,

TABLE 1.1 Open-ended Interview Questions that Aided Item Construction

1. What does "care" mean to you? (Define or describe "caring.")
2. What are the indicators (ingredients) of caring?
3. How would you distinguish between a caring and a noncaring person?
4. What groups of people do you find most caring?
5. What groups of people are the least caring?
6. Describe a situation in which you really cared for another person.
7. What made this situation different?
8. How does giving care to another person make you feel? (How do you feel after caring for another person?)
9. How do you think the other person feels?
10. Describe a situation in which you were cared for by another person.

humility, hope, courage), provided the theoretical framework for formulating the CAI. Items were derived in two ways. First, from the review of the literature on caring and related concepts, 61 items were constructed. The second method involved interviewing 15 consenting adults on their thoughts on caring, using 10 open-ended questions, which are presented in Table 1.1. From these interviews 19 additional items were derived. A total of 80 items were constructed: 34 positive statements and 46 negatively worded statements. The initial inventory consisted of 80 items using a 7-point Likert scale.

The responses of 543 participants were subjected to a principal-axis factor analysis. On the basis of the Scree test, as well as the interpretability of factors, it was decided that a three-factor analysis was appropriate for these data. Both orthogonal and oblique solutions were used. The correlations among factors were so low in the oblique solution that an orthogonal solution was used. Items that loaded on Factor 1 appeared to deal with understanding of self and others. This factor was therefore named Knowing because it approximates Mayeroff's original description of the element. Factor 2 seemed to tap ability to deal with the unknown and is named Courage. Factor 3 included items characterized by toleration and persistence and was therefore named Patience. Items were chosen for inclusion in the final three subscales only if they loaded above .30 on a given factor and did not load at the .30 level on the other factors. The Knowing subscale consists of 14 items, Courage consists of 13 items, and Patience has 10 items. So the total CAI consists of 37 items (see CAI instrument at the end of this chapter). Intercorrelation of the subscales is moderate in size and reflects separate domains within the overall concept of caring (see Table 1.2).

TABLE 1.2 Intercorrelation of CAI Subscales

Subscale	Courage	Patience
Knowing	.42	.35
Courage		.19

ADMINISTRATION AND SCORING

The CAI is self-administered and requires no instructions beyond that indicated at the beginning of the inventory. The Likert-type responses range from 1 to 7, with higher scores indicating greater degree of caring for a positively phrased item. For negatively worded items, the scoring is reversed. Item responses are then summed for each subscale, yielding a total score for each subscale. Since the Knowing subscale has 14 items, the possible range of scores is from 14 to 98. The Courage subscale has 13 items, with a possible range of scores from 13 to 91. The Patience subscale has 10 items; its scores can range from 10 to 70. See "Scoring Information" (at the end of this chapter) for items in each subscale, items to be reverse-scored, and norms for nurses and college female and male students.

RELIABILITY AND VALIDITY

Sample

The sample consists of two groups: (1) 462 students, with varied majors, attending a large metropolitan university located in New York City and (2) 75 nurses who were attending a national professional conference. The purpose of the study was explained to the students and nurses and their participation sought. All who participated signed a consent form prior to completing the scale(s). The students responded to two scales: the CAI and the Tennessee Self-Concept Scale (Fitts, 1986). The nurses completed only the CAI. A total of 537 participants completed the CAI; almost 20% of them were male and 80% were female. Slightly over 61% of the participants were under 33 years of age, and 5.3% were over 53 years. The sample included people from varied ethnic backgrounds.

The means and standard deviations of the subscales obtained from this sample are shown in Table 1.3.

Reliability

Reliability was assessed in two ways. The internal consistency of each subscale was determined by computing Cronbach's alphas. In addition, a

TABLE 1.3 Means and Standard Deviations of CAI and Its Subscales (*N* = 537)

Subscales	*M*	*SD*
Knowing	73.36	10.78
Courage	64.22	11.18
Patience	60.53	6.65
Total CAI	198.16	21.53

TABLE 1.4 Reliabilities of CAI and Its Subscales

Subscales	Alpha Coefficient (n = 537)	Test–Retest r (n = 38)
Knowing	.79	.80
Courage	.75	.64
Patience	.71	.73
Total CAI	.84	.75

subsample of 38 participants took the CAI on two occasions, 2 weeks apart. Scores on the two administrations were correlated for each subscale to obtain test–retest reliability. The reliabilities, reported in Table 1.4, are within the acceptable range for research purposes.

Validity

Two experts in the content area analyzed the items for clarity and to see if they adequately represented the concept of caring as described conceptually by the tool's developer. Their suggestions were used to make changes. Revised items were resubmitted to the reviewers to assess clarity, consistency, and relevancy. The content validity index (CVI) was computed using the method outlined by Waltz, Strickland, and Lenz (1984). Percentage of agreement was .80.

For construct validity, two approaches were taken. The first was discrimination between groups, and the second was correlation with the Tennessee Self-Concept Scale.

The literature on caring suggests that caring is partly learned. It is expected that practicing nurses will exhibit more of this attribute than would college students. The t-test on the mean scores of the two groups was statistically significant at the $p \leq .001$ level (see Table 1.5).

A comparison of the mean scores of female and male participants also was found to be significant. This finding is not surprising because in this society women are socialized to be more expressive and caring; therefore, it

TABLE 1.5 Comparison of Nurses with College Students on CAI (df = 535)

	Nurses (n = 75)		Students (n = 462)		
Subscales	M	SD	M	SD	t
Knowing	80.22	7.56	72.24	10.78	7.95*
Courage	68.25	11.57	63.57	11.05	3.43*
Patience	63.11	4.19	60.11	6.88	5.16*
Total CAI	211.67	17.21	195.97	21.39	7.06*

*$p \leq .001$.

TABLE 1.6 Comparison of Females and Males on CAI (*df* = 525)

	Females (n = 424)		Males (n = 103)		
Subscales	*M*	*SD*	*M*	*SD*	*t*
Knowing	74.22	10.64	69.86	10.53	3.73*
Courage	65.24	10.92	60.97	11.18	3.57*
Patience	61.24	6.30	57.88	6.98	4.74*
Total CAI	200.70	20.83	188.68	21.35	5.22*

*$p \leq .001$.

TABLE 1.7 Correlations between CAI, Its Subscales, and Self-Concept (*n* = 418)

Subscale	*r*
Knowing	.55**
Courage	.42**
Patience	.12*
Total CAI	.53**

*$p \leq .01$.
**$p \leq .001$.

was expected that female students would score significantly higher than male students, as indicated in Table 1.6.

According to Mayeroff (1971), a sense of identity—"who I am" and "what I am about"—is necessary in order to understand and permit expressions of individuality. It seems that persons with a strong and secure sense of themselves might be expected to be more caring than those who have a lesser sense of who they are. In this study a positive correlation between the CAI and self-concept was obtained, as noted in Table 1.7.

DISCUSSION AND CONCLUSIONS

The development of the CAI represents an initial attempt to measure a person's ability to care. The CAI is based on Mayeroff's (1971) conceptualization of caring and the eight critical elements identified. If the ability to care is necessary for human survival, it is important to assess the degree to which this ability is present for people in general and to identify situations under which their ability to care changes.

The CAI consists of 37 items representing three of the elements cited by Mayeroff (1971): Knowing, Courage, and Patience. Reliabilities for the subscales were established by test–retest and by computing Cronbach's alpha. The correlations and alpha coefficients are listed in Table 1.4. These findings indicate that the CAI is a reliable measure.

Assessment of content validity by two content experts yielded a CVI of .80. Criterion-related validity was not possible because of the lack of a comparable measure. Construct validity was established by discrimination between students and nurses and between females and males. Differences between means are statistically significant at the $p \leq .001$ level. Pearson correlations between self-concept and CAI subscales are moderately high, reflecting that persons who were high on self-concept were also high in caring. This is evidence for the construct validity of the CAI.

Further validation efforts may proceed in different areas. The CAI may be administered to different professional groups (e.g., engineers, social workers, physicians). Patients' rating of a nurse on caring can be correlated to the CAI scores of the nurse. A high correlation between the two scales will indicate that the scales are measuring the same concept. Because it is postulated that people who are more mature will be more caring, further approaches to validation of this scale may include evaluation of an individual's ego development level and the extent to which this relates to CAI scores.

The development of the CAI has many implications for the nursing and other professions. The ability to care is multidimensional, with cognitive and affective domains. The CAI can be used to identify persons who are high or low on these dimensions. Individuals who are high may serve as models or mentors for those who are low on caring. The ability to care is more important in some situations and in some professions than in others. Therefore, the CAI may be used in counseling and vocational guidance.

In the care of the aged parent, a family member who is high on caring might be encouraged to assume the care of the parent, rather than a person who is less caring. The CAI may be administered at specific intervals to determine if and when changes occur. Changes in CAI scores might be an early indication of stress or burden in this relationship.

The CAI has potential implications for education. Can the dimensions of the CAI be taught? What teaching methods are appropriate? Are the dimensions of caring included as learning objectives? The CAI can be administered to new students and at each level to determine their mastery of caring constructs as students advance in their studies. In addition, the CAI can be used as a pre–post measure for assessing the success of new programs or courses designed to foster caring behaviors.

REFERENCES

Brown, L. (1982). Behaviors of nurses perceived by hospitalized patients as indicators of care. *Dissertation Abstracts International, 42*:4361B.

Fitts, W. H. (1986). *Tennessee Self-Concept Scale.* Nashville, TN: Counselor Recordings and Tests.

Ford, M. (1981). Nurse professionals and the caring process. *Dissertation Abstracts International, 43*:967B–968B.
Gaut, D. (1984). A theoretic description of caring as action. In M. Leininger (Ed.), *Care: The essence of nursing and health* (pp. 27–44). Thorofare, NJ: Charles B. Slack.
Gaylin, W. (1976). *Caring*. New York: Alfred A. Knopf.
Henry, O. (1975). Nurse behaviors perceived by patients as indicators of caring. *Dissertation Abstracts International, 36*:02652B.
Larson, P. J. (1984). Important nurse caring behaviors perceived by patients with cancer. *Oncological Nursing Forum, 11*(6), 46–50.
Leininger, M. (1981). The phenomenon of caring: Importance, research questions and theoretical considerations. In M. Leininger (Ed.), *Caring: An essential human need* (pp. 3–15). Thorofare, NJ: Charles B. Slack.
Leininger, M. (1984). Caring: A central focus of nursing and health care services. In M. Leininger (Ed.), *Care: The essence of nursing and health* (pp. 45–60). Thorofare, NJ: Charles B. Slack.
Leininger, M. (1986). Care facilitation and resistance factors in the culture of nursing. *Holistic Nursing Practice, 8*(2), 1–12.
Mayeroff, M. (1971). *On caring*. New York: Harper & Row.
Meador, B., & Rogers, C. (1979). Person-centered therapy. In R. Cosini (Ed.), *Current psychotherapies* (pp. 131–184). Itasca, IL: F. E. Peacock.
Monea, H. E. (1979). The development of caring and care-giving roles. In I. M. Burnside, P. Ebersole, H. E. Monea (Eds.), *Psychosocial caring throughout the life span* (pp. 4–17). New York: McGraw-Hill.
Waltz, C. F., Strickland, O. L., & Lenz, E. R. (1984). *Measurement in Nursing Research* (pp. 198–199). Philadelphia: F. A. Davis.
Watson, J. (1979). *Nursing: The philosophy and science and caring*. Boston: Little, Brown.

Caring Ability Inventory

Please read each of the following statements and decide how well it reflects your thoughts and feelings about other people in general. There is no right or wrong answer. Using the response scale, from 1 to 7, circle the degree to which you agree or disagree with each statement directly on the booklet. Please answer all questions.

1	2	3	4	5	6	7
strongly disagree					strongly agree	

	Strongly Disagree 1	2	3	4	5	6	Strongly Agree 7
1. I believe that learning takes time.	1	2	3	4	5	6	7
2. Today is filled with opportunities.	1	2	3	4	5	6	7
3. I usually say what I mean to others.	1	2	3	4	5	6	7
4. There is very little I can do for a person who is helpless.	1	2	3	4	5	6	7
5. I can see the need for change in myself.	1	2	3	4	5	6	7
6. I am able to like people even if they don't like me.	1	2	3	4	5	6	7
7. I understand people easily.	1	2	3	4	5	6	7
8. I have seen enough in this world for what I need to know.	1	2	3	4	5	6	7
9. I make the time to get to know other people.	1	2	3	4	5	6	7
10. Sometimes I like to be involved and sometimes I do not like being involved.	1	2	3	4	5	6	7
11. There is nothing I can do to make life better.	1	2	3	4	5	6	7
12. I feel uneasy knowing that another person depends on me.	1	2	3	4	5	6	7
13. I do not like to go out of my way to help other people.	1	2	3	4	5	6	7
14. In dealing with people, it is difficult to let my feelings show.	1	2	3	4	5	6	7
15. It does not matter what I say, as long as I do the correct thing.	1	2	3	4	5	6	7
16. I find it difficult to understand how the other person feels if I have not had similar experiences.	1	2	3	4	5	6	7
17. I admire people who are calm, composed, and patient.	1	2	3	4	5	6	7
18. I believe it is important to accept and respect the attitudes and feelings of others.	1	2	3	4	5	6	7

19. People can count on me to do what I say I will.	1	2	3	4	5	6	7
20. I believe that there is room for improvement.	1	2	3	4	5	6	7
21. Good friends look after each other.	1	2	3	4	5	6	7
22. I find meaning in every situation.	1	2	3	4	5	6	7
23. I am afraid to "let go" of those I care for because I am afraid of what might happen to them.	1	2	3	4	5	6	7
24. I like to offer encouragement to people.	1	2	3	4	5	6	7
25. I do not like to make commitments beyond the present.	1	2	3	4	5	6	7
26. I really like myself.	1	2	3	4	5	6	7
27. I see strengths and weaknesses (limitations) in each individual.	1	2	3	4	5	6	7
28. New experiences are usually frightening to me.	1	2	3	4	5	6	7
29. I am afraid to be open and let others see who I am.	1	2	3	4	5	6	7
30. I accept people just the way they are.	1	2	3	4	5	6	7
31. When I care for someone else, I do not have to hide my feelings.	1	2	3	4	5	6	7
32. I do not like to be asked for help.	1	2	3	4	5	6	7
33. I can express my feelings to people in a warm and caring way.	1	2	3	4	5	6	7
34. I like talking with people.	1	2	3	4	5	6	7
35. I regard myself as sincere in my relationships with others.	1	2	3	4	5	6	7
36. People need space (room, privacy) to think and feel.	1	2	3	4	5	6	7
37. I can be approached by people at any time.	1	2	3	4	5	6	7

Scoring Information

Items to be summed for each subscale:

Knowing: 2, 3, 6, 7, 9, 19, 22, 26, 30, 31, 33, 34, 35, 36.

Courage: 4, 8, 11, 12, 13, 14, 15, 16, 23, 25, 28, 29, 32.

Patience: 1, 5, 10, 17, 18, 20, 21, 24, 27, 36.

Items to be reverse-scored: 4, 8, 11, 12, 13, 14, 15, 16, 23, 25, 28, 29, 32.

The nurse group comprised 75 practicing nurses attending a national conference. Participants came from all areas of the country. To determine ranges for low, medium, and high norm scores, .5 standard deviation on either side of the mean was considered to be in the middle range of scores. Scores above this were considered high, and scores below this were considered low. See Table 1.8 for low, medium, and high norms for the nurse group.

The college students group consisted of 424 females and 103 males attending a large university in metropolitan New York. The students represented a wide variety of ability, ethnic, and socioeconomic groups. Low, medium, and high groups were determined in the same way as above. See Table 1.9 for low, medium, and high norms for female and male college students.

TABLE 1.8 Low, Medium, High Norms for CAI and Its Subscales for Nurses

Subscale	Low	Medium	High
Knowing	Below 76.4	76.4–84.0	Above 84.0
Courage	Below 62.5	62.5–74.0	Above 74.0
Patience	Below 61.0	61.0–65.2	Above 65.2
Total CAI	Below 203.1	203.1–220.3	Above 220.3

TABLE 1.9 Low, Medium, High Norms for CAI and Its Subscales for Female and Male College Students

	Females (n = 424)			Males (n = 103)		
Subscale	Low	Medium	High	Low	Medium	High
Knowing	< 68.8	68.8 – 79.5	> 79.5	< 64.6	64.6 –75.1	> 75.11
Courage	< 62.14	62.14– 73.06	> 73.06	< 54.41	54.41–66.56	> 66.56
Patience	< 58.05	58.05– 64.35	> 64.35	< 53.4	53.4 –62.4	> 62.4
Total CAI	<190.29	190.29–211.12	>211.12	<178.00	178.00–199.36	>199.36

2

The Caring Process in Nursing: Two Instruments for Measuring Caring Behaviors

Anna M. McDaniel

This chapter discusses the Caring Behavior Checklist and the Client Perception of Caring Scale, two measures of caring behaviors of nurses as they care for clients.

Caring has been traditionally viewed by nurses and the public as the basis for the nursing profession. However, increases in technology and specialization have contributed to the depersonalization of health care in our society today (Carper, 1979). Perhaps in response, current nursing literature has shown an increase in theoretical and scientific exploration of the phenomenon of caring. This study was proposed to develop valid methods for the investigation of the components of the caring process.

REVIEW OF RELATED LITERATURE

The concept of care is inherent to the process of nursing. The word *care* can scarcely be separated from any discussion of nursing. Leininger (1981b), Watson (1985), and others suggest that care is the essence of nursing, yet the meaning of care in nursing remains implicit. Nurses and patients alike have difficulty describing caring. Often people respond when asked, "What is caring in nursing?" by stating, "I can't describe it—but I know it when I see it."

Dunlop (1986) states that caring is an emerging construct. She traces the meanings of the word *care* from its Anglo-Saxon origins to current meanings of care as a form of love. Gaut (1983) also explores the multiple meanings of caring from philosophical, behavioral, and nursing literature. She describes a family of meanings related to three concepts of caring as attention to or concern for responsibility for, or providing for, and regard, fondness, or attachment.

Because of the multiplicity of definitions of caring and the qualitative nature of caring relationships, nursing research on caring remains limited. Leininger (1981a) has studied caring from a cross-cultural perspective and has developed a taxonomy of caring constructs. Bevis (1981) describes the variables affecting caring behaviors, including culture, values, cost, time, stress, and maturational level.

Ford (1981), using an open-ended survey, explored the definition of caring and caring behaviors as described by professional nurses. "Genuine concern" and "giving of self" were identified by 81 nurses when defining caring. Listening was the behavior most frequently associated with caring by these nurses. Ray (1984) investigated perceptions of caring in hospital nurses and other employees to analyze the impact of the hospital as an institution for caring.

Weiss (1984) found gender-related differences in client perceptions of verbal and nonverbal caring behaviors of the nurse. Field (1984) studied client care-seeking behaviors and outcomes of nurse–client interactions. Feeling listened to and understood was an important factor in patient satisfaction with care. Henry (1975) used an open-ended interview to study home-care patients' perception of nurse caring behaviors. The responses were classified into three categories, with the largest number of responses in the category "How the Nurse Does." Brown (1981) identified two aspects of care that were perceived by hospitalized patients as indicators of caring. These were "What the Nurse Does" and "How the Nurse Does." Themes found in "What the Nurse Does" were surveillance, demonstration of professional knowledge, providing information, and assisting with pain. "How the Nurse Does" was described by patients as amount of time spent, reassuring presence, recognition of individual qualities, and promotion of autonomy.

Larson (1987) developed a Q-sort instrument to compare nurses' and cancer patients' perceptions of caring behaviors. She found differences in the ranking of important nurse caring behaviors between nurses and patients. Reiman (1986) researched the phenomenon of caring from the client's perspective. She described the essential structure of a caring nurse–client transaction through analysis of interviews of both male and female clients. She identified a cluster of common themes from clients' descriptions of caring on the part of the nurse and the consequences or feelings that resulted from a caring interaction.

CONCEPTUAL BASIS OF THE MEASURE

A dichotomy exists in the definitions of care in nursing. In the ANA Position Paper of 1965 (American Nurses' Association, 1965), nursing is described as caring *for* and caring *about.* From a nursing perspective, caring for incorporates the activities involved in taking care of. Much effort in nursing and nursing education is directed toward this aim. Nurses give back care, hygienic care, and catheter care. However, it cannot be assumed from the performance of such caregiving activities that the nurse cares about.

In discussing *caring about,* nursing authors draw heavily on the existential philosophers Marcel and Buber (Reiman, 1986; Valliot, 1966; Watson, 1985). Caring *about* involves the sharing of human experiences and existence. It requires that the nurse adopt an attitude of regard for the being of the individual. However, unless this motivates the nurse to act or care *for,* caring has not actually taken place.

According to Bevis (1981), "caring demands that feelings be converted into behaviors and that the behaviors and feelings be accompanied by thoughts" (p. 50). True caring must encompass both concepts: caring for and caring about. When developing a theoretical definition of caring, one needs to examine the relationship between the philosophical context of caring about and the behavioral context of caring for. This can be accomplished by conceptualizing caring as a process or series of actions intended to achieve a certain result.

Care is the investment of oneself for the benefit of another (person, group, or institution) without regard for personal gain. In nursing, care is the investment of one's personal resources in another in order to promote well-being. The nurse's personal resources may include, but are not limited to, knowledge, expertise, time, and emotional energy.

The process of caring in nursing can be conceptualized in four levels (Figure 2.1). Acknowledgment of the need for care is the first stage. This involves the nurse's awareness of the human experiences of the other. From an existential perspective, this is described as the I–Thou" relationship (Reiman, 1986; Valliot, 1966). The I–Thou relationship, in contrast to an "I–It" relationship, involves the sharing of experiences with the other person as a human being. One could postulate that the widespread use of the nursing process has encouraged nurses to adopt an objective I–It view of patients, thus hindering nurses' potential to care.

Once the need for care has been recognized in the other, a decision to care is the next phase. Self-assessment of personal resources within the nurse is necessary. The choice to commit these resources solely to the

ACTUALIZATION

↑

CARING ACTS

↑

DECISION

↑

ACKNOWLEDGMENT

FIGURE 2.1 Conceptual model of the caring process in nursing.

well-being of the other completes this phase. Gadow (1980) describes this as "unifying and directing of one's entire self in relation to another's need" (p. 90). This involves a willingness by the nurse to risk the cost of caring for the benefit of the other.

The third level in the caring process includes the actions and behaviors of the nurse intended to promote the welfare of the other. As Watson (1985) states, the "essence of the value of human care and caring may be futile unless it contributes to a philosophy of action" (p. 32). Gaut (1984) describes caring as a series of actions. Yet, as Mayeroff (1971) notes, "the process rather than the product is primary in caring" (p. 31). Actions taken on behalf of the other are the external manifestation of the internal cognitive and affective processes of the nurse that have taken place at prior levels.

Actualization of the caring experience is the ultimate result of the caring process. The perception of the other as being cared for and about is the fulfillment of the caring interaction. The realization that caring has occurred promotes growth and satisfaction in both the nurse and the other. Noddings (1984) describes an intangible transformation that takes place in the cared-for and the one caring. Benner (1984) describes this as the transformative power of caring.

PURPOSE OF THE MEASURE

The purpose of this study was to develop valid methods for the investigation of the components of the caring process. A norm-referenced measurement framework was used to measure caring behaviors and the effect of these actions on the client. The outcome variables of intent were caring behaviors and the client perception of caring. In this study, caring behaviors were defined as those verbal and nonverbal actions denoting care performed by the nurse. The operational definition of the client's perception of caring was based on the subjective, affective response of the client to the nurse's caring behaviors.

PROCEDURE FOR DEVELOPMENT

From analysis of current research findings, two tools have been developed to examine the caring process in nursing. The first tool is the Caring Behavior Checklist (see instrument at the end of this chapter). Specific verbal and nonverbal behaviors have been identified a priori as significant indicators of caring (Field, 1984; Gardner & Wheeler, 1981; Larson, 1984; Reiman, 1986; Weiss, 1984). The tool is designed to measure the presence or absence of specific actions denoting care, not to quantify the degree or amount of care.

The second tool, The Client Perception of Caring Scale (see instrument at the end of this chapter), is a questionnaire designed to measure the client's response to the caring behaviors of the nurse. Reiman (1986) suggests that to study "only empirical indicators of caring from the nurse's perspective would not get at the essential structure of the caring interaction as experienced by the client" (p. 86). The items were developed from studies describing the reactions of clients to nurse–client interactions (Field, 1984; Reiman, 1986; Weiss, 1984).

ADMINISTRATION AND SCORING

The two instruments are designed to be used together to measure the caring process. The instruments are intended for use in a hospital setting with patients who possess the cognitive skills necessary to complete the instrument. A trained observer scores the Caring Behavior Checklist while observing a nurse–patient interaction for a period of 30 minutes. As noted in Waltz, Strickland, and Lenz (1984), no data should be recorded for the first 10 minutes in order to reduce subject reactivity. Each behavior on the checklist is to be scored dichotomously as present or absent. The checklist consists of 12 items representing the behaviors indicative of caring. The potential range of scores for the instrument is from 0 to 12. High scores indicate a high number of behaviors was observed; low scores indicate few behaviors were observed.

The Client Perception of Caring Scale is to be administered to the client following the observation period. The tool consists of 10 items that are rated on a 6-point summated rating scale. Each item value is to be summed to obtain the score. Items 5 and 8 are perceptions associated with noncaring behaviors of the nurse, and the item value is reversed before being summed. The scores for the Client Perception of Caring Scale have a potential range of 10 to 60. High scores indicate a high degree of caring as perceived by the client. Low scores mean that the client perceived low caring behavior in the nurse.

RELIABILITY AND VALIDITY ASSESSMENT

Both tools have been submitted to two doctorally prepared nurse researchers with experience in the field of caring. The method for determining content validity described in Waltz, Strickland, and Lenz (1984) was used. The content validity index (CVI) for the Caring Behaviors Checklist was calculated as .80. The CVI for the Client Perception of Caring Scale was determined to be 1.00.

A time sampling of student nurse–patient interactions was used to collect data to determine reliability and validity of the measures. Following approval from the Research Review Committee, a convenience sample of junior-level nursing students from a baccalaureate nursing program was selected. Clients assigned to these participating students for clinical laboratory experience were randomly selected as the client sample. Although students were observed more than once, a total of 21 different student nurse–patient interactions were observed for data collection. Both the students and the clients participating received a verbal explanation of the purpose and procedures of the study before signing a written consent form.

Reliability of the Client Perception of Caring Scale was determined by the internal consistency approach. The standardized item alpha coefficient was calculated at .81. Item-to-total correlation averaged .41 for this scale.

Reliability of the Caring Behavior Checklist was estimated using interrater agreements. Each of the 21 interactions was simultaneously observed by two trained raters, who scored the items independently. The interrater reliability of the Caring Behavior Checklist was determined as a function of agreements between observers. This was calculated by using the following formula: number of agreements divided by total number of agreements and disagreements (Polit & Hungler, 1987). This was first calculated after nine observations and determined at .82. Items 10 and 12 were further clarified, and the raters were given additional instructions. Interrater agreements for the remaining 12 observations was .99. Overall interrater reliability was .92. Agreements for each of the 12 items are displayed in Table 2.1.

The measure used to estimate construct validity of the two caring instruments was the LaMonica Empathy Profile. This tool, formerly known as the LaMonica Empathy Construct Rating Scale, is a 30-item self-report using a forced-choice format. Scores are obtained on five subscales:

TABLE 2.1 Caring Behavior Checklist: Interrater Agreement per Item

Caring behaviors	Agreement
Verbal	
Verbally responds to an expressed concern.	.90
Explains procedure prior to initiation.	.76
Verbally validates patient's physical status.	.95
Verbally validates patient's emotional status.	.95
Shares personal observations or feelings (self-disclosing) in response to patient's expression of concern.	.95
Verbally reassures patient during care.	.86
Discusses topics of patient's concern other than current health problems.	1.00
Nonverbal	
Sits down at bedside.	1.00
Touches patient exclusive of procedure.	1.00
Sustains eye contact during patient interaction.	.86
Enters patient room without solicitation.	.90
Provides physical comfort measures.	.86

responding verbally; nonverbal behavior; respect of self and others; openness, honesty, and flexibility; and perceiving feelings and listening. The reliability index for this tool as a self-report was estimated by a coefficient alpha of .96 (LaMonica, 1981). Discriminant validity of this instrument was determined by the multitrait–multimethod approach with $r = .20$ ($p < .001$) (LaMonica, 1981).

A measure of empathy was considered appropriate to estimate construct validity because conceptually it is closely related to caring, and tools measuring the two concepts should be significantly correlated. LaMonica (1981) defines empathy as signifying "a central focus and feeling with and in the client's world by the helper, communication of this understanding to the client, and the client's perception of the helper's understanding" (p. 398). This definition of empathy as a process is similar to the theoretical definition of caring presented here. Empathy is a necessary part of caring, particularly at the acknowledgment level. Indeed, without empathy the caring process would not take place. Noddings (1984) describes the relationship between empathy, feeling with and in, and caring when she states: "Apprehending the other's reality, feeling what he feels as nearly as possible, is the essential part of caring from the view of the one-caring. For if I take on the other's reality as possibility and begin to feel its reality, I feel also that I must act accordingly" (p. 16).

To estimate construct validity, the results of the Client Perception of Caring Scale were correlated with the subscale scores on the Empathy Profile. This yielded no significant results at the .05 level. This could be attributed in part to the low number of subjects.

As an additional method to evaluate content validity of the Caring Behavior Checklist, each client was asked to respond to the question "What is the one thing that a nurse does that shows you that he/she really cares about you?" Of the 18 clients responding to this question, 17 identified behaviors that were described in the 12 items on the tool. The one behavior not included on the tool, "Has a soft tone of voice," was identified by a blind client.

DISCUSSION AND CONCLUSIONS

The analysis of the reliability estimate of the Client Perception of Caring Scale yielded satisfactory results with a standardized alpha coefficient of .8144. Bcause of low item-to-total correlation, revision of items 6 ($r = -.1529$) and item 3 ($r = .1726$) is indicated. Increasing the length of the scale would result in a higher alpha for the tool. Although the construct validity assessment in this study did not support the tool's validity, criterion-related validity may be established in replicative studies using a more appropriate instrument, such as the Trusting Relationship Scale of Risser's Patient Satisfaction Instrument as revised by Hinshaw and Atwood (1982), and a larger number of subjects.

By analysis of the interrater reliability of the Caring Behavior Checklist, one can infer that there is agreement between observers when using this tool; that is, the two observers identified the same caring behaviors. Use of this tool as an observation guide to categorize behaviors may be appropriate. However, a limitation of the tool is that the items are dichotomously scored, which reduces score variance. Results obtained from using this tool may be improved by increasing the potential for item variability.

Implications for further study would include observation of a different population of nurses to see if a significant difference in behaviors is found compared to those observed in this study. Prolonging the observation period and standardizing the circumstances of the observation—for example, around specific types of nurse–patient interactions or procedures—may also be indicated.

REFERENCES

American Nurses' Association Committee on Education. (1965). *A position paper.* New York: Author.

Benner, P. (1984). *From novice to expert: Excellence and power in clinical nursing practice.* Menlo Park, CA: Addison-Wesley.

Bevis, E. (1981). Caring: A life force. In M. Leininger (Ed.), *Caring: An essential human need* (pp. 49–59). Thorofare, NJ: Charles B. Slack.

Brown, L. (1981). Behaviors of nurses perceived by hosptialized patients as indicators of care. *Dissertation Abstracts Internationl, 43,* 436iB.

Carper, B. (1979). The ethics of caring. *Advances in Nursing Science, 1*(3), 11–19.

Dunlop, M. (1986). Is a science of caring possible? *Journal of Advanced Nursing, 11,* 661–670.

Field, P. (1984). Client care-seeking behaviors and nursing care. In M. Leininger (Ed.), *Care: The essence of nursing and health* (pp. 249–262). Thorofare, NJ: Charles B. Slack.

Ford, M. (1981). Nurse professionals and the caring process. *Dissertation Abstracts International, 43,* 967B-968B.

Gadow, S. (1980). Existential advocacy: Philosophical foundations of nursing. In S. Spicker & S. Gadow (Eds.), *Nursing: Images and ideals—opening dialogue with the humanities* (pp. 79–101). New York: Springer Publishing Co.

Gardner, K., & Wheeler, E. (1981). The meaning of caring in the context of nursing. In M. Leininger (Ed.), *Caring: An essential human need* (pp. 69–79). Thorofare, NJ: Charles B. Slack.

Gaut, D. (1983). Development of a theoretically adequate description of caring. *Western Journal of Nursing Research, 5,* 313–324.

Gaut, D. (1984). A theoretical description of caring as action. In M. Leininger (Ed.), *Care: The essence of nursing and health* (pp. 27–44). Thorofare, NJ: Charles B. Slack.

Henry, D. (1975). Nurse behaviors perceived by patients as indicators of caring. *Dissertations Abstracts International, 36,* 02-652B.

Hinshaw, A., & Atwood, J. (1982). A patient satisfaction instrument: Precision by replication. *Nursing Research, 31*(3), 170–175.

LaMonica, E. (1981). Construct validity of an empathy instrument. *Research in Nursing and Health, 4,* 389–400.

Larson, P. (1984). Important nurse caring behaviors perceived by patients with cancer. *Oncology Nursing Forum, 11*(6), 46–50.

Larson, P. (1987). Comparison of cancer patients' and professional nurses' perceptions of important nurse caring behaviors. *Heart and Lung, 16*(2), 187–193.

Leininger, M. (1981a). Cross-cultural hypothetical functions of caring. In M. Leininger (Ed.), *Caring: An essential human need* (pp. 95–102). Thorofare, NJ: Charles B. Slack.

Leininger, M. (1981b). The phenomenon of caring: Importance, research questions, and theoretical considerations. In M. Leininger (Ed.), *Caring: An essential human need* (pp. 3–15). Thorofare, NJ: Charles B. Slack.

Leininger, M. (1981c). Some philosophical, historical, and taxonomic aspects of nursing and caring in American culture. In M. Leininger (Ed.), *Caring: An essential human need* (pp. 133–143). Thorofare, NJ: Charles B. Slack.

Mayeroff, M. (1971). *On caring.* New York: Harper and Row.

Noddings, N. (1984). *Caring: A feminine approach to ethics and moral education.* Berkeley, CA: University of California Press.

Polit, D., & Hungler, B. (1987). *Nursing research: Principles and methods* (3rd ed.). Philadelphia: J. B. Lippincott.

Ray, M. (1984). The development of a classification system of institutional caring. In M. Leininger (Ed.), *Care: The essence of nursing and health* (pp. 95–112). Thorofare, NJ: Charles B. Slack.

Reiman, D. (1986). The essential structure of a caring interaction: Doing phenomenology. In P. Munhall & C. Oiler (Eds.), *Nursing research: A qualitative perspective* (pp. 85–106). Norwalk, CT: Appleton-Century-Crofts.

Valliot, M. (1966). Existentialism: A philosophy of commitment. *American Journal of Nursing, 66,* 500–505.

Waltz, C., Strickland, O., & Lenz, E. (1984). *Measurement in nursing research.* Philadelphia: F. A. Davis.

Watson, J. (1985). *Nursing: Human science and human care.* Norwalk, CT: Appleton-Century-Crofts.

Weiss, C. (1984). Gender-related perceptions of caring in nurse-patient relationship. In M. Leininger (Ed.), *Care: The essence of nursing and health.* (pp. 161–181). Thorofare, NJ: Charles B. Slack.

Caring Behavior Checklist

Absent = 0
Present = 1

Verbal Caring Behaviors

Verbally responds to an expressed concern.	
Explains procedure prior to initiation.	
Verbally validates patient's physical status.	
Verbally validates patient's emotional status.	
Shares personal observations or feelings (self-disclosing) in response to patient's expression of concern.	
Verbally reassures patient during care.	
Discusses topics of patient's concern other than current health problems.	

Nonverbal Caring Behaviors

Sits down at bedside.	
Touches patient exclusive of procedure.	
Sustains eye contact during patient interaction.	
Enters patient room without solicitation.	
Provides physical comfort measures.	

Client Perception of Caring Scale

1. I felt that this nurse really listened to what I was saying.
/___1___/___2___/___3___/___4___/___5___/___6___/
Not at all Very Much

2. I felt reassured when this nurse cared for me.
/___1___/___2___/___3___/___4___/___5___/___6___/
Not at all Very Much

3. I felt that this nurse really valued me as an individual.
/___1___/___2___/___3___/___4___/___5___/___6___/
Not at all Very Much

4. I felt free to talk to this nurse about what concerned me.
/___1___/___2___/___3___/___4___/___5___/___6___/
Not at all Very Much

5. I felt the nurse was more interested in her "job" than my needs.
/___1___/___2___/___3___/___4___/___5___/___6___/
Not at all Very Much

6. I felt that this nurse could tell when something was bothering me.
/___1___/___2___/___3___/___4___/___5___/___6___/
Not at all Very Much

7. I felt secure with this nurse taking care of me.
/___1___/___2___/___3___/___4___/___5___/___6___/
Not at all Very Much

8. I felt frustrated by this nurse's attitude.
/___1___/___2___/___3___/___4___/___5___/___6___/
Not at all Very Much

9. I could tell this nurse really cared about me.
/___1___/___2___/___3___/___4___/___5___/___6___/
Not at all Very Much

10. I could tell that this nurse wanted to make me feel comfortable.
/___1___/___2___/___3___/___4___/___5___/___6___/
Not at all Very Much

3
Measuring Self-Care Ability in Patients with Diabetes: The Insulin Management Diabetes Self-Efficacy Scale

Ann C. Hurley

This chapter discusses the Insulin Management Diabetes Self-Efficacy Scale, a measure of individuals' beliefs in their ability to organize and implement their care related to insulin administration, monitoring, and management.

The Insulin Management Diabetes Self-Efficacy Scale (IMDSES) was designed to be used as an assessment guide to identify individuals who might benefit from individual and group competence-building exercises designed to complement traditional diabetes health education. The IMDSES may also be used as an outcome measure to evaluate a diabetes education program.

REVIEW OF RELATED LITERATURE

Diabetes Mellitus

Diabetes mellitus, a progressive, incurable, chronic illness is the seventh leading cause of death in the United States and affects approximately 10 million persons (Harris & Hamman, 1985). Strict metabolic control that maintains blood glucose levels close to the nondiabetic range is generally considered the best treatment outcome to prevent, minimize, or delay the

This project was supported in part by an individual National Research Service Award from the National Center for Nursing Research, National Institutes of Health (#5F31NR05933), a clinical research grant from Alpha Chi Chapter, Sigma Theta Tau International, scholarships from the Leroy E. Dettman Foundation and the Reserve Officers Association of the United States, and tuition assistance from the U.S Army.

Appreciation is expressed to Dr. M. Katherine Crabtree for her encouragement and advice during the scale augmentation process, and to the staffs of the Diabetes Treatment Units of the New England Deaconess Hospital and the Joslin Diabetes Center for their assistance in the data collection process.

onset of chronic complications that lead to morbidity and premature death. Every day, individuals must engage in 10 to 20 self-care practices—self-monitoring; insulin administration; deciding when and what to eat; preventing, detecting, and treating high or low blood glucose levels—to control their diabetes regimen. Decisions must be made, and individuals must always be disciplined, even on a special day, such as a birthday, when some dietary leniency and regimen flexibility is appropriate. Other days require additional vigilance. A feeling that the flu is coming on may mean the onset of diabetic ketoacidosis and may require the enactment of a set of self-care behaviors to prevent that complication.

The magnitude of morbidity and mortality related to uncontrolled diabetes, the difficulty that many individuals have in carrying out their diabetes activities of daily living, and the important role of self-care to forestall complications make this disorder a priority for nursing. Previous research has shown that, in general, neither demographic variables nor level of knowledge predict diabetes self-care behaviors or degree of metabolic control; although, when motivation has been made operational by application of various psychosocial models, some diabetes behaviors have been explained.

Self-Efficacy and Diabetes

Self-efficacy is one of the newer psychosocial theories (Bandura, 1977); it refers to personal beliefs of how well one can organize and implement patterns of behavior that may contain novel, unpredictable, and stressful elements (Bandura, 1982b). Bandura (in press) suggests that self-efficacy is a powerful psychosocial variable capable of predicting the enactment of health-related behaviors.

Bandura (in press) and O'Leary (1985) reviewed the literature relating self-efficacy to health behaviors and found that high levels of self-efficacy were positively associated with carrying out regimen-specific behaviors. Because the regimen required to control diabetes requires that individuals plan and carry out actions in diverse circumstances and settings, there is a pragmatic interconnection between perceived self-efficacy and self-care of diabetes mellitus. Two reported studies made self-efficacy operational for individuals who have diabetes: Crabtree (1986) concurred with O'Leary and Bandura and found that diabetes self-efficacy predicted diabetes behaviors of adults who self-managed their disorder; Grossman, Brink, and Hauser (1987) developed a scale for use with children and found that self-efficacy of adolescent girls was correlated with their metabolic state.

CONCEPTUAL BASIS OF THE MEASURE

Definitions

Self-efficacy is a sense of "I can do." "Perceived self-efficacy refers to beliefs in one's capabilities to organize and execute courses of action required to meet given situational demands" (Bandura, in press). Self-efficacy means individuals' judgments of their capability to monitor, plan, and carry out their diabetes activities of daily living. It is a concept that is oriented to behaviors, and as such it is concerned with the actions that people take rather than the outcomes that are expected to follow.

Assumptions

Analysis of some of Bandura's initial writing about self-efficacy (Bandura, 1977, 1978a, 1978b, 1982a, 1982b), reports published with colleagues (Bandura & Adams, 1977; Bandura, Adams, & Beyer, 1977; Bandura, Adams, Hardy, & Howells, 1980; Bandura, Reese, & Adams, 1982), subsequent conceptual clarification (Bandura, 1983, 1984), and the recent conclusive composition (Bandura, 1986) provided the literature base to describe the theoretical basis of self-efficacy.

The conceptualization of several beliefs about people that underlie social cognitive theory can be framed into six theoretical assumptions. Because people are able to process and store symbolic information, they can (1) anticipate consequences of actions, (2) represent goals in thought, (3) plan necessary steps to accomplish goals, and (4) weigh evidence from different sources. Additionally, (5) behavior is learned, and (6) it is influenced by social interactions. As a result, people have the capability for self-appraisals and can regulate their own environments and actions. The assumptions of social cognitive theory illustrate that instead of merely viewing learning through the effects of one's actions, the importance of *forethought* and *judgment* are recognized.

Theoretical Framework

These human capacities of self-regulation are an inherent operating force of social cognitive theory and have determined the conceptual model of the theory. There are three basic elements of the theory: environmental events, personal factors, and behavior. These core concepts act on and are acted on by each other. In this three-part model of human behavior, each element is a distinct concept, but singly or in combination, they have a dynamic interplay with one another. The conceptual model of social cognitive theory is an interactional model of causation. The dynamic interplay of the central concepts, known as reciprocal determinism, is shown in Figure 3.1.

Personal factors are conceptualized as being four transformational activities: (1) knowing and information processing, (2) learning from symbolic environments, (3) controlling oneself by more than external feedback, and (4) the distinctively human capability for self-reflection. People analyze their experiences, think about their own thought processes, and develop self-images. These global self-thoughts are (1) a composite view of self, (2) an evaluation of self-worth, and (3) self-efficacy, "a judgment of one's capability to accomplish a certain level of performance" (Bandura, 1986, p. 391), that is considered to be the most influential aspect of self-knowledge in everyday lives.

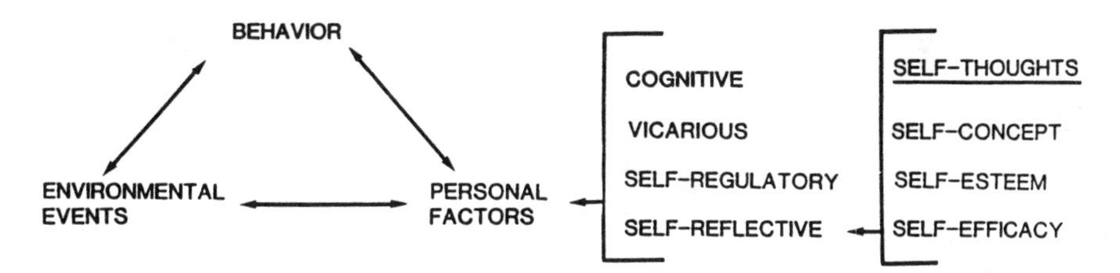

FIGURE 3.1 Model of reciprocal determinism. Self-efficacy is one of the three self-thoughts that comprise the self-reflective component of individuals' thought processes.

Conceptual Model

Antecedents of the concept self-efficacy provide the information that individuals cognitively process to make their efficacy judgments (Bandura, 1977, 1986). They include the following four sources of information:

1. Enactive attainment (EA) is a composite of past accomplishments. EA is the most influential determinant of efficacy because it is based on the individual's own mastery experiences (Bandura et al., 1977).
2. Vicarious experience (VE) is a comparison of self to an observed experience. VE is generally weaker than enactive experience (Bandura, 1986).
3. Verbal persuasion (VP) is a weaker efficacy source than either EA or VE, but it can contribute to successful performance when it is realistic (Bandura, 1986).
4. Physiological state (PS) means emotional arousal as identified by the interpretation of somatic symptoms (Bandura & Adams, 1977).

The consequences of self-efficacy are the behaviors that people undertake and the outcome that follows the behavior. Figure 3.2 illustrates the antecedents and consequences of self-efficacy.

The theoretical model of self-efficacy in social cognitive theory (see Figure 3.3) illustrates the role of knowledge, outcome expectations, and incentive to action, which collectively determine the behavior that follows and leads to the outcome. Knowledge is necessary, but alone it is an insufficient predictor of behavior. Outcome expectations refer to the belief that outcomes are determined either by one's actions or by forces beyond one's control (Rotter, 1966). The expectation that behavior will or will not be related to the outcome and the value of the outcome to the individual constitute an outcome expectation. When studies have made both self-efficacy and outcome expectations operational, self-efficacy was found to be more important than outcome expectations in predicting behavior (Barling & Abel, 1983; Godding & Glasgow, 1985; Lee, 1984; Schunk, 1985), and because outcome expectation is highly dependent on self-efficacy to enact behavior, outcome expectations may not add to the predic-

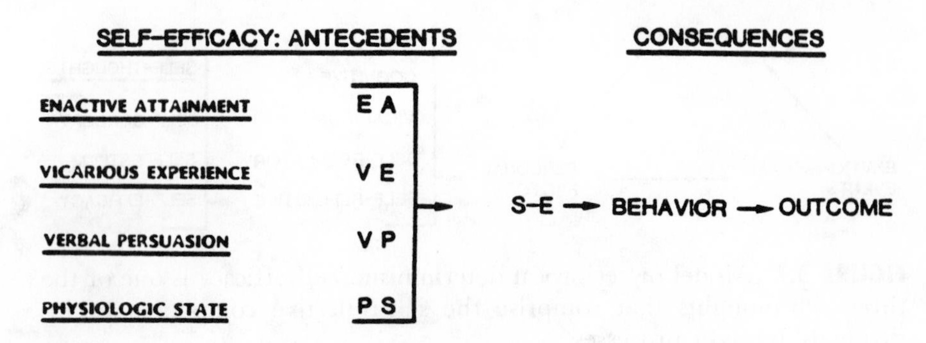

FIGURE 3.2 Four antecedents contribute to the development of self-efficacy beliefs. Self-efficacy is followed by the behavior of note, and the effects of the behavior illustrate the consequences.

tion of behavior once self-efficacy has been considered (Williams & Watson, 1985). No matter how capable one is of performing the behavior, motivation to do so or an action incentive variable is required to invoke self-efficacy (Bandura, 1986; Rosenstock, 1985).

Conceptual Measurement Issues

Judgments of efficacy are not generalized feelings of success or control but assessments of how well one can perform in specified settings (Cervone & Peake, 1986). Bandura and Adams (1977) advised investigators extending self-efficacy to the study of nonphobic behavior to precisely assess grada-

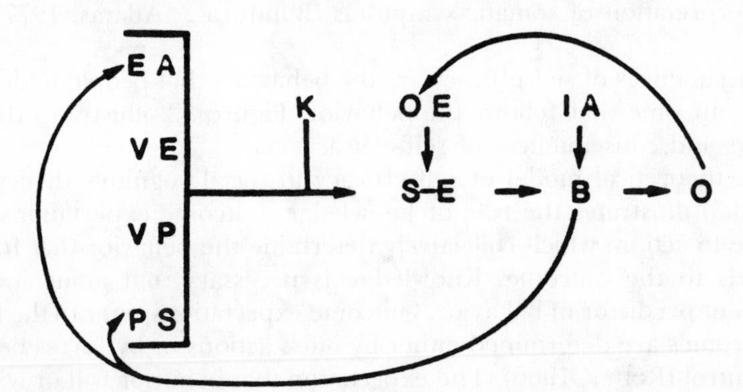

FIGURE 3.3 Theoretical model. The model illustrates the feedback loops from behavior to the antecedents of self-efficacy (SE) and from outcome to outcome expectations. EA = enactive attainment; VE = vicarious experience; VP = verbal persuasion; PS = physiologic state; K = knowledge; OE = outcome expectations; IA = incentive to action; B = behavior; S-E = self-efficacy; O = outcome.

tions in behavior by task-specific examination of the correspondence between self-efficacy and action. Therefore, scales that measure self-efficacy must be performance-specific and capable of being matched to subsequent behavior, a notion referred to as a microanalytic match.

The self-efficacy concept has three dimensions: magnitude, strength, and generality. Each dimension was clearly distinct in the scales used for the initial phobic research series conducted by Bandura and colleagues (Bandura & Adams, 1977; Bandura et al., 1977, 1980, 1982). The cluster of smoking investigations (Coelho, 1984; Colletti, Supnick, & Payne, 1985; Condiotte & Lichtenstein, 1981; DiClemente, 1981; DiClemente, Prochaska, & Gibertini, 1985; McIntyre, Lichtenstein, & Mermelstein, 1983; Prochaska, Crime, Lapsanski, Martel, & Reid, 1982) that followed the phobic studies combined the three dimensions in the measures used to make smoking self-efficacy operational. Crabtree (1986) had selected this latter format for the Diabetes Self-Efficacy Scale (DSES). Therefore, the IMDSES, building on the DSES, was also developed in the same format.

PURPOSE OF THE MEASURE

The Crabtree (1986) DSES was developed to be used with adults who have diabetes, regardless of type of diabetes or of whether or not individuals used insulin. With both the permission and advice of Dr. Crabtree, the IMDSES was developed from the DSES and modified for adults who use insulin. The IMDSES measures individuals' beliefs in their capability to plan, carry out, monitor, and adjust their diabetes activities of daily living.

PROCEDURES FOR DEVELOPMENT

The Crabtree 32-item DSES had been constructed with advice from Dr. Bandura and tested with a sample of 48 adults. The scale total demonstrated adequate estimates of measurement reliability by internal consistency (alpha = .79) and retest stability (r = .87) after a 10 day interval. Self-efficacy was moderately correlated with self-esteem ($r = .50$, $n = 40$, $p < .001$), evidence to support construct validity. The revised scale (25 items) had a coefficient alpha of .71 when used in a predictive study. Preliminary evidence of construct validity was provided when four factors representing the hypothesized subscales emerged and accounted for 44% of the variance.

For the IMDSES, a scale development blueprint for writing new items and revising some of the Crabtree (1986) items was developed so that individuals would interpret the statements as being specific to their diabetes activities of daily living. Items were constructed to reflect only the self-efficacy concept and not related concepts. Other item characteristics were that (1) the action word was an act, not an outcome; (2) items contained only one behavior; (3) "I can" or a negative wording of "I can" was the verb used to anchor the assertion in the present; (4) the word *diabetic* was used as an adjective, not a noun; (5) circumstances to reflect different situations, such as daily tedium or feeling sick, were used; and (6) the word *insulin* replaced the generic term *medication.* Sample items are "I can stay on my diabetic diet when I eat in unfamiliar places" and "I'm not sure I can recognize when my blood sugar is low."

The 28-item IMDSES was developed within a norm-referenced framework to test for varying levels of efficacy. Ten items were negatively worded. Seven types of diabetes behaviors were represented: (1) general, (2) diet, (3) exercise, (4) foot care, (5) monitoring, (6) insulin administration, and (7) detecting, preventing, or treating high and low blood glucose reactions. Four general items were placed at the beginning and two at the end of the scale. The other items were arranged in like clusters in a sequence determined by the diabetes content experts. (Subject instructions for taking the scale, sequential listing of items, and identification of item subscales and those items that are reverse-scored can be found at the end of this chapter.)

ADMINISTRATION AND SCORING

Efficacy assertions are made privately to avoid the possible influence of public disclosure on the target behavior (Telch, Bandura, Vinciguerra, Agras, & Stout, 1982). The IMDSES is a paper-and-pencil test with items and response selection on a Likert scale ranging from 1 (strongly agree) to 6 (strongly disagree). A "not applicable" category is provided and was coded as missing data for computing measurement reliability estimates. The 18 positively worded items are reverse-scored, so higher scores are interpreted as meaning the individual tested has a higher level of self-efficacy. The range of possible score means is 1 to 6. Scale total scores or the three subscales—general, diet, and insulin—can be used. There are two items each on foot care and exercise, too small a number to have subscales for those behaviors.

RELIABILITY AND VALIDITY ASSESSMENTS

A sequence of steps was followed to examine and adjust the IMDSES to assure that the scale would have reliability and validity estimates considered adequate for a new measure. The initial DSES, developed with the advice of content specialists and using the results of two phases of empirical testing, was considered to be a reliable and valid new instrument (Crabtree, 1986).

The IMDSES used some of the DSES items, but others were slightly modified to be consistent with the table of specifications. The *Diabetes*

TABLE 3.1 Reliability and Content Validity Steps, IMDSES

Sequence	Expert Panel	Purpose
1	Crabtree, Hurley, literature review	Initial revision to develop the second-generation instrument
2	Diabetes content experts	Assure representation of diabetes domain in instrument
3	5 patients	Review for clarity and meaning
4	Diabetes content experts	Evaluate instrument after patient input
5	Self-efficacy construct experts	Assure that statements contain only self-efficacy (construct validity index)
6	38 outpatients	Internal consistency
	27 outpatients	Retest stability
7	89 inpatients	Internal consistency
8	127 patients	Exploratory factor analysis; construct validity

Teaching Guide (Joslin Diabetes Center, 1986) provided the diabetes content domain for additional items that were added. Three diabetes educator nurses served as content specialists, and five patients reviewed and edited the items for understanding and clarity from the subject viewpoint. Then six self-efficacy judges rated the items for conceptual distinction, relevance, and clarity. Level of agreement provided quantification that a content validity index beyond the .05 level of significance had been achieved (Lynn, 1986). Finally, two phases of empirical testing provided evidence of reliability by test stability, internal consistency, preliminary factor structure, and convergent validity. The sequence of steps undertaken to assure measurement reliability and validity is shown in Table 3.1.

Sample and Setting

Empirical testing was conducted in two phases: (1) An outpatient sample of 38 subjects from a diabetes clinic provided data for the reliability estimates; 27 of those subjects participated in the retest phase; (2) an inpatient sample from a diabetes treatment unit located in the same large metropolitan New England city provided additional data for computing reliability estimates. The combined sample of 127 subjects (38 outpatients and 89 inpatients) provided evidence for convergent validity and preliminary factor structure.

To be considered for inclusion in the study, subjects had to meet the following 11 criteria: (1) be diagnosed as having diabetes mellitus, (2) require insulin to control their diabetes, (3) be a patient of the Diabetes Center, (4) be free of other serious disorders and severe debilitating diabetic sequelae (blindness, marked neuropathy, incapacitating renal or cardiovascular problems), (5) currently be in a nonacute phase of diabetes and free of potential complications (not in acidosis, initiating hemodialysis), (6) have sufficient English language, reading, and cognitive capacities to participate in the investigation, (7) be free of any mental impairment, (8) be 18 to 73 years of age, (9) not be known to be pregnant, (10) not be recommended for exclusion by their nurse or physician, and (11) be willing to provide informed consent. Outpatients had to meet an additional criterion of currently being in a stable state of diabetes management. That was defined as having documentation in the medical record that the patient had been examined within the past 6 months and was not being scheduled for an inpatient admission because of uncontrolled diabetes.

There were no statistically significant differences in the demographic variables or diabetes characteristics between the outpatient subjects who participated in the retest phase (n = 27) and those who did not (n = 11). The combined sample of outpatient subjects (n = 38) was similar to the sample of inpatient subjects (n = 89) except that outpatients were older—M = 47.92), $t(124)$ = 2.43, $p < .017$—than the inpatients (M = 40.28). Therefore, the demographic and diabetes characteristics of the combined data set (N = 127) were used to describe the sample.

Subjects were middle-aged and had many years of experience in managing diabetes and using insulin. The average duration of diagnosed diabetes was 12 years (SD = 8.1), and subjects had required insulin for 10.2 years (SD = 8.3). More females (n = 71) than males (n = 56) participated in the study. Most subjects were married (n = 75). More subjects lived with someone else (n = 109), such as parents (n = 19), spouse or one good adult friend (n = 48), or one adult and a child or children (n = 42) than lived alone (n = 17). The sample was considered well educated. Only seven subjects had less than a high school education, the most common educational level of the majority (n = 47). Other subjects had a postsecondary technical or vocational education (n = 19), college or university degree (n = 33), or graduate degree (n = 16). The majority (n = 75) were out of the house for over 40 hours a week holding a full-time job or were volunteers or full-time students. Subjects were employed in a variety of positions that were categorized as professional (n = 20), technical (n = 12), clerical (n = 20), laborer (n = 8), or supervisor (n = 6). The remaining subjects were at home (n = 34) or were full-time students (n = 12), or data were missing (n = 15).

In general, most subjects had complex diabetes regimens that they were required to manage. Sixty-nine percent of the sample required two daily injections of insulin to control their diabetes. The number and type of daily insulin injections were as follows: (1) one daily injection of a single type of insulin (n = 25); (2) one daily injection and two types of insulin (n = 14); (3) two daily injections, each with a single type of insulin (n = 16); (4) two daily injections: one with a single insulin and one with two types of insulin (n = 17); (5) two daily injections of two types of insulin (n = 39); and (6) three or more daily injections of insulin (n = 15).

The empirical testing for scale reliability was conducted among a sample of subjects whose diabetes was difficult to control (89 subjects required intensive inpatient diabetes management), and the findings must be interpreted in that light. Another diabetes characteristic, degree of metabolic control at the time subjects were administered the IMDSES, indicates that half of the sample could be defined as having uncontrolled diabetes.

Glycosylated hemoglobin (GH) is a minor hemoglobin fraction that is interpreted as a "marker" for the average blood glucose level during the past few months. GH develops slowly throughout the 120-day life span of the red blood cells. The measurement of GH represents the average amount of GH in the red cells, and GH levels have demonstrated reliability as a measure of overall blood glucose levels over a 2- to 3-month period (Grossman et al., 1987). High GH levels are associated with high blood glucose levels. All GH levels were measured by use of the Glytrac system, distributed by Corning Medical, Corning Glass Works. The nondiabetic range is 5.4% to 7.4%.

Patients who use insulin and are cared for at the setting used for this study are encouraged to maintain their GH below 11%. Of the subjects who had a recent report of GH in their medical record ($n = 127$), half were in a state of metabolic control that required correction. Both the median and the mean GH were 10.9 ($SD = 2.36$). The range of values was 6.5 to 18.9.

Descriptive Data: Subscales and Scale Total

To compute the means for the subscales, if subjects had answered all but two items on a subscale, their mean score for the other items was substituted for the missing value(s). Likewise, for the scale total, if subjects had responded to 20 of the 28 items, their total mean score was substituted for the missing value(s) to compute the scale total mean for the sample. Otherwise, subjects were not included in the descriptive data reported. Comparisons of the scale and subscale means between the outpatient and inpatient subjects revealed that there were no differences between the scores (all t tests were small and statistically not significant). (See Table 3.2 for actual scale and subscale means.)

Internal Consistency

Cronbach's alpha for the scale total (.82) revealed that the IMDSES achieved a reliability estimate considered adequate for a new scale (Nunnally, 1978). (See Table 3.2.) The diet subscale had the highest alpha coefficients across the samples. The general subscale for the inpatient sample had an alpha over .70, but it was only .68 for the combined sample. The insulin subscale, consisting of items dealing with monitoring, insulin administration and dose adjustment, and prevention, detection, and treat-

TABLE 3.2 IMDSES Means and Internal Consistency: Subscales and Scale Total by Sample

Scale	Descriptive statistics			Internal consistency	
	N	*M*	*SD*	*N*	Alpha
General subscale (6 items)					
Outpatients	37	5.000	0.706	34	.49
Inpatients	89	4.899	0.833	84	.73
Combined	126	4.929	0.796	118	.68
Diet subscale (7 items)					
Outpatients	38	4.420	1.052	34	.78
Inpatients	88	4.592	0.903	84	.78
Combined	126	4.540	0.949	118	.78
Insulin subscale (11 items)					
Outpatients	36	5.382	0.462	33	.38
Inpatients	88	5.094	0.632	80	.63
Combined	122	5.179	0.599	113	.62
Scale total (28 items)					
Outpatients	37	4.995	0.509	19	.68
Inpatients	88	4.889	0.585	60	.85
Combined	125	4.921	0.563	79	.82

ment of high and low blood sugars, had the lowest alpha coefficients. This can be explained by the range and complexity of behaviors that constitute the subscale. All items were considered essential to maintain content validity and were retained.

Retest Stability

Self-efficacy is a dynamic concept that theoretically can be altered by interventions that change any of its antecedents. Therefore, a homogeneous and stable group of subjects was hypothesized to provide a moderate coefficient of stability, evidence for instrument stability. A convenience sample of 130 outpatients was identified through a medical records review. Potential subjects were mailed a packet of information consisting of a letter of introduction and instructions, informed consents, and survey materials. Thirty-eight subjects (29%) chose to participate in the study, and 27 of those (71%) provided data for the examination of retest stability. Two weeks after subjects returned the initial packet, a second was mailed; there was a mean duration of 22 days between test and retest. Given a dynamic concept but a stable sample, the Pearson correlation (r = .58, $p < .002$) was considered evidence of instrument stability. Paired t tests, t (24) = .59, $p < .56$, revealed that the scale means and variance were unchanged from the test (M = 4.95) to the retest (M = 5.007), providing additional confirmation of instrument stability.

Preliminary Factor Analysis

Data from the 127 subjects in the combined sample (4.5 subjects per item) revealed that there were nine factors with an eigenvalue equal to or greater than 1 and that they explained 69% of the variance. The first-factor eigenvalue of 6.14 provided the scale with a theta coefficient of .87, interpreted as a maximized alpha coefficient (Carmines & Zeller, 1979) and additional evidence of internal consistency. Five of the factors were interpretable and were labeled dietary control, insecurity, general confidence, treatment decisions, and discipline. Data from an additional sample of inpatient subjects will be combined with this data set so that future examination of the IMDSES factor structure will be conducted with 10 subjects per item.

Convergent Validity

Two measures, the Insulin Management Diabetes Self Care Scale (IMDSCS) and GH, provided evidence to support the convergent validity of the IMDSES. During the initial revision and testing of the IMDSES, an item-for-item self-report measure, the IMDSCS, was developed. If the self-efficacy item was "I can follow my diet plan when I go to parties," the corollary self-care item in the IMDSCS was "I followed my diet plan when I went to parties." The 28-item IMDSCS (the care scale) was administered to all subjects, before they responded to the IMDSES (the efficacy scale), as part of the pilot test for all of the measures and procedures that would then be used in a prospective study.

The IMDSCS had been examined along with the IMDSES during the two phases of empirical testing, and that 28-item scale was also considered to have an adequate reliability estimate for a new scale. Cronbach's alpha was .96, $N = 48$. More of the 127 subjects provided data for computing the reliability estimates for the three subscales, and those alpha coefficients were: (1) six general items (.91, $n = 120$), (2) seven diet items (.93, $n = 110$), and (3) 11 insulin items (.88, $n = 92$). Retest stability of the IMDSCS indicated that it was a stable measure ($r = .859$, $n = 27$, $p = .000$) and that the means were unchanged from the test (M = 4.84) to the retest (M = 4.86) 22 days later, t (26) = 0.32, $p = .751$.

There is not a direct correspondence between GH levels and self-care behaviors, especially in individuals who have Type I diabetes, with fluctuating extremes of high and low blood glucose levels or a regimen in need of adjustment in order to promote good metabolic control. Because a study criterion specified that all subjects must use insulin to manage their diabetes, it was known that this sample did not contain individuals who required insulin but had not been using it for the month before their GH level was drawn. For subjects who had been following a regimen that was correct for meeting their metabolic needs, if they were also correct in making their assessment of previous diabetes behaviors and if the IMDSCS accurately captured that information, then reported self-care behaviors should be negatively associated with the biochemical marker of "good control."

Therefore, the IMDSCS, IMDSES, GH, and two additional variables that had been a part of the sociodemographic scale—perception of previous metabolic control (CDB) and expectation for future metabolic control (CDA)—as well as GH levels, were examined in a correlation matrix. The CDB is scored so that high scores mean uncontrolled diabetes, and CDA is scored so that high scores mean an expectation of well-controlled diabetes in the future.

Pearson correlations revealed the following associations: (1) IMDSES/IMDSCS $r = +.376$, $n = 122$, $p = 000$; (2) IMDSCS/GH $r = -.1738$, $n = 113$, $p = .033$; (3) GH/CDB $r = +.2708$, $n = 116$, $p = .002$; (4) CDB/IMDSCS $r = -.4388$, $n = 123$, $p = .000$; and (5) CDA/IMDSES $r = +.1687$, $n = 121$, $p = .032$. The IMDSCS and IMDSES were positively correlated as expected, since past behavior may be cognitively interpreted as enactive attainment, an antecedent of efficacy. GH and IMDSCS had a small negative association, meaning that the higher the score on the IMDSCS, the lower or "better" the GH. Thus, the association between GH (the biochemical marker of diabetes control) and IMDSCS (reported self-care), and the association between IMDSCS (interpreted in this case as the primary antecedent of self-efficacy, enactive attainment) and the IMDSES, support the construct validity of the self-efficacy scale. CDB (perception of control before) was positively associated with GH, and both were negatively related to the IMDSCS. CDA (expectation for a positive outcome) had a weak positive correlation with the IMDSES. These associations, even though small, collectively provide evidence to support construct validity of the IMDSES.

DISCUSSION AND CONCLUSIONS

The IMDSES is considered to have adequate reliable estimates for a new instrument. Although the scale has demonstrated content and construct validity, predictive validity should be evaluated. The predictive validity analysis should examine the microanalytic match between the specific behavior of the efficacy assertion and subsequent behavior.

Self-efficacy is a dynamic concept that has well-identified antecedents that may be enhanced or decreased by nursing interventions. When actions specific for managing diabetes regimens change individuals' interpretations of self-efficacy antecedents in a positive direction, the relative level of self-efficacy should increase. This result should lead to individuals' engaging in increased effort and persistence in carrying out those behaviors associated with good metabolic control of diabetes. Once the IMDSES has been evaluated to assure that it has predictive validity, an intervention study should be conducted to manipulate the antecedents of self-efficacy and precisely measure the gradations in behavior that follow. Nurses could also use the IMDSES in clinical practice to aid in determining if there has been a positive change in patients' insulin management self-efficacy as a result of the implementation of teaching interventions.

REFERENCES

Bandura, A. (1977). Self-efficacy: Toward a unifying theory of behavior change. *Psychological Review, 84,* 191–215.
Bandura, A. (1978a). On paradigms and recycled ideologies. *Cognitive Therapy and Research, 2,* 79–103.
Bandura, A. (1978b). The self system in reciprocal determinism. *American Psychologist, 33,* 344–358.
Bandura, A. (1982a). Self-efficacy mechanism in human agency. *American Psychologist, 37*(2), 122–147.
Bandura, A. (1982b). The self and mechanisms of agency. In J. Suls (Ed.), *Psychological perspectives and the self* (Vol. 1, pp. 3–39). Hillsdale, NJ: Erlbaum.
Bandura, A. (1983). Self-efficacy determinants of anticipated fears and calamities. *Journal of Personality and Social Psychology, 45,* 464–469.
Bandura, A. (1984). Recycling misconceptions of perceived self-efficacy. *Cognitive Therapy and Research, 8* (3), 231–255.
Bandura, A. (1986). *Social foundations of thought and action: A social cognitive theory.* Englewood Cliffs, NJ: Prentice-Hall.
Bandura, A. (in press). Self-efficacy mechanism in physiological activation and health-promoting behavior. In J. Madden IV, S. Mattyhsse, & J. Barchas (Eds.), *Adaptation.* New York: Raven Press.
Bandura, A., & Adams, N. E. (1977). Analysis of self-efficacy theory of behavior change. *Cognitive Therapy and Research, 1,* 287–310.
Bandura, A., Adams, N., & Beyer, J. (1977). Cognitive processes mediating behavioral change. *Journal of Personality and Social Psychology, 35,* 125–139.
Bandura, A., Adams, N. E., Hardy, A. B., & Howells, G. N. (1980). Tests of the generality of self-efficacy theory. *Cognitive Therapy and Research, 4,* 39–66.
Bandura, A., Reese, L., & Adams, N. (1982). Microanalysis of action and fear arousal as a function of differential levels of perceived self-efficacy. *Journal of Personality and Social Psychology, 43,* 5–21.
Barling, J., & Abel, M. (1983). Self-efficacy beliefs and tennis performance. *Cognitive Therapy and Research, 7,* 265–272.
Carmines, E. G., & Zeller, R. A. (1979). *Reliability and validity assessment.* Beverly Hills, CA: Sage Publications.
Cervone, D., & Peake, P. K. (1986). Anchoring, efficacy, and action: The influence of judgmental heuristics on self-efficacy judgments and behavior. *Journal of Personality and Social Psychology, 50,* 492–501.
Coelho, R. J. (1984). Self-efficacy and cessation of smoking. *Psychological Reports, 54,* 309–310.
Colletti, G., Supnick, J. A., & Payne, T. J. (1985). The smoking self-efficacy questionnaire (SSEQ): Preliminary scale development and validation. *Behavioral Assessment, 7,* 249–260.
Condiotte, N. M., & Lichtenstein, E. (1981). Self-efficacy and relapse in smoking cessation programs. *Journal of Consulting and Clinical Psychology, 49,* 648–658.
Crabtree, M. K. (1986). *Self-efficacy and social support as predictors of diabetic self-care.* Unpublished doctoral dissertation, University of California, San Francisco.

DiClemente, C. C. (1981). Self-efficacy and smoking cessation maintenance: A preliminary report. *Cognitive Therapy and Research, 5,* 175–187.

DiClemente, C., Prochaska, J. O., & Gibertini, M. (1985). Self-efficacy and the stages of self-change of smoking. *Cognitive Therapy and Research, 9,* 181–200.

Godding, P. R., & Glasgow, R. E. (1985). Self-efficacy and outcome expectations as predictors of controlled smoking status. *Cognitive Therapy and Research, 9,* 583–590.

Grossman, H. Y., Brink, S., & Hauser, S. (1987). Self-efficacy in adolescent girls and boys with insulin-dependent diabetes mellitus. *Diabetes Care, 10,* 324–329.

Harris, M. I., & Hamman, R. F. (Eds.). (1985). *Diabetes in America.* Washington, DC: U.S. Department of Health and Human Services, National Institutes of Health, National Institute of Arthritis, Diabetes, and Digestive and Kidney Diseases.

Joslin Diabetes Center. (1986). *Diabetes teaching guide* (rev. ed.). Boston: Author.

Lee, C. (1984). Efficacy expectations and outcome explanations as predictors of performance in a snake handling task. *Cognitive Therapy and Research, 8,* 509–516.

Lynn, M. (1986). Determination and quantification of content validity. *Nursing Research, 35,* 382–385.

McIntyre, K. O., Lichtenstein, E., & Mermelstein, R. J. (1983). Self-efficacy and relapse in smoking cessation: A replication and extension. *Journal of Consulting and Clinical Psychology, 51,* 632–633.

Nunnally, J. C. (1978). *Psychometric theory.* New York: McGraw-Hill.

O'Leary, A. (1985). Self-efficacy and health. *Behavior Research and Therapy, 23,* 437–451.

Prochaska, J. O., Crimi, P., Lapsanski, D., Martel, L., & Reid, P. (1982). Self change processes, self-efficacy, and self concept in relapse and maintenance of cessation of smoking. *Psychological Reports, 51,* 983–990.

Rosenstock, I. M. (1985). Understanding and enhancing patient compliance with diabetic regimens. *Diabetes Care, 8,* 610–616.

Rotter, J. B. (1966). Generalized expectancies for internal versus external control of reinforcement. *Psychological Monographs, 80* (1, Whole No. 609).

Schunk, D. H. (1985). Self-efficacy and classroom learning. *Psychology in the Schools, 22,* 208–223.

Telch, M. J., Bandura, A., Vinciguerra, P., Agras, A., & Stout, A. L. (1982). Social demand for consistency and congruence between self-efficacy and performance. *Behavior Therapy, 13,* 694–701.

Williams, S. L., & Watson, N. (1985). Perceived danger and perceived self-efficacy as cognitive determinants of acrophobic behavior. *Behavior Therapy, 16,* 136–146.

Diabetes Beliefs Survey

Thank you for your continuing participation in the Diabetes Health Beliefs Study. There are 28 multiple-choice items. Please try to answer them all. THERE ARE NO RIGHT OR WRONG ANSWERS. This survey asks you to rate your degree of confidence for being able to carry out your diabetes-related activities. Please write the date that you actually completed the survey and place it in the envelope provided and leave it in the study box at the nurses station.

Date __________

The following statements describe what some people believe about their ability to take care of their diabetes. Please take the next few minutes to tell me what *you* believe about your ability to manage *your* diabetes. After reading each statement, circle the number that best expresses your beliefs. There are twenty-eight (28) statements; please answer each one. There are no right or wrong answers.

Circle 1 if you strongly agree with the statement,
2 if you moderately agree with the statement,
3 if you slightly agree with the statement,
4 if you slightly disagree with the statement,
5 if you moderately disagree with the statement,
6 if you strongly disagree with the statement,
or NA if the statement does not apply to you.

	STRONGLY AGREE					STRONGLY DISAGREE	
EXAMPLE. I can test my urine for sugar before meals when I am away from home.	1	2	3	4	5	6	NA

ANSWER. If you are confident in your ability to test your urine before meals whenever you eat out, you should circle 1 because that statement best expresses your belief. If you do not test urine, you should circle NA.

Insulin Management Diabetes Self-Efficacy Scale

When used with subjects, the 28 items are arranged as per the sample item; the Likert choice and scoring system is added in the right columns. The codes for identifying subscales (G = general, D = diet, I = insulin) are at the end of the item that constitutes the subscale. An asterisk (*) beside the number indicates items that are reverse-scored. Both should be removed before using the scale.

1.* I can carry out practically all of the self-care activities in my daily diabetes routine. (G)
2.* I am confident in my ability to manage my diabetes. (G)
3. I feel unsure about having to use what I know about diabetes self-treatment every day. (G)
4. I don't think I can follow my diabetes routines every single day. (G)
5.* I can eat my meals at the same time every day. (D)
6.* I can stay on my diabetic diet when I eat in familiar places away from home (such as at a friend's house). (D)
7.* I can stay on my diabetic diet when I eat in unfamiliar places. (D)
8. I'm not sure I'll be able to stay on my diabetic diet when the people around me don't know that I have diabetes. (D)
9. I'm not sure I'll be able to follw my diabetic diet every day. (D)
10.* I can correctly exchange one food for another in the same food group. (D)
11.* When I go to parties, I can follow my diet plan. (D)
12.* I can exercise several times a week.
13. I can't exercise unless I feel like exercising.
14.* I can figure out when to call my doctor about problems with my feet.
15.* I can routinely apply the recommended lotion to my feet R
16. I cannot test my blood or urine when I am away from home. (I)
17.* I can recognize when my blood sugar is too high. (I)
18.* When I feel sick, I can test my blood or urine more than I routinely do. (D)
19.* I can take my insulin using the recommended procedure. (I)
20. I may have difficulty taking my insulin when away from home. (I)
21.* I can adjust my insulin dose based on the results of my urine or blood tests. (I)
22. I'm not sure I can figure out what to do about my insulin dose when changes occur in my usual routine. (I)
23.* I can do what was recommended to prevent low blood sugar reactions when I exercise. (I)
24.* I can figure out what self-treatment to administer when my blood sugar gets higher than it should be. (I)
25. I'm not sure I can recognize when my blood sugar is low. (I)
26. I'm not sure I can adjust my diabetes self-treatments if I get a cold or the flu. (I)
27.* I can fit my diabetes self-treatment routine into my usual life style. (G)
28.* I think I'll be able to follow my diabetes plan even when my daily routine changes. (G)

Do you have any comments you wish to add about confidence in your ability to self-manage your diabetes?

Thank You

4
The Measurement of Self-Care Strategies of Patients in Radiation Therapy

Gloria Hagopian

This chapter discusses the Radiation Side Effects Profile, an instrument that measures the side effects of radiation therapy and the self-care approaches used by patients to deal with them.

The purpose of this study was to develop a tool to measure the self-care strategies used by patients to reduce the severity of the side effects of radiation therapy. While undergoing radiation therapy, patients usually experience a number of side effects of treatment, and they deal with these in a variety of ways. One way is to try to alleviate the side effects. This study measures the side effects experienced as a result of radiation therapy and the self-care strategies used to manage them.

CONCEPTUAL BASIS OF THE MEASURE

For the purposes of this study, side effects are defined as the symptoms experienced by patients as a result of radiation therapy. The number and severity of the side effects experienced by patients were determined. Self-care strategies are defined as activities that patients use to deal with the side effects of radiation therapy. They were measured by patients according to the degree of help afforded by the strategy employed. The side effects and self-care strategies were measured by the Radiation Side Effects Profile (RSEP), a tool developed for this study.

The concept of self-care selected for this study is based on Orem's (1971) conceptual model. According to Orem, "self-care is the practice of

The author wishes to thank Dr. Geraldine Padilla, consultant for this project, and Dr. Debra Hymovich, who did the data analysis.

This study was supported in part by an American Cancer Society Grant IN-135 and the Center for Nursing Research, University of Pennsylvania.

activities that individuals personally initiate and perform on their own behalf in maintaining life, health, and well-being" (p. 13). Adults normally take care of their own health needs, and self-care is a contribution to one's own health. When a person becomes ill, self-care demands may exceed the individual's ability to meet them, and there may be a need for nursing to help the person regain a steady state. Orem's model indicates three goals for nursing actions. First, one must meet the patient's self-care needs. Next, one must move the patient toward responsible action in matters of self-care. The movement can be in several directions: In some instances, the patient may move toward increased independence; at other times, the patient must adapt to steadily declining capacities. The third goal is the involvement and transfer of responsibility to the patient's family, thus decreasing the amount of nursing supervision.

Nursing is based on the values of self-help and help to others. To engage in self-care activities, the individual must have the ability and skills to initiate and sustain self-care efforts as well as the knowledge and understanding of the necessary self-care practices. Orem (1971) believes that when there is a self-care deficit, the patient needs assistance in learning and performing self-care activities. The role of the nurse is to provide the necessary assistance.

REVIEW OF RELATED LITERATURE

Radiation therapy employs the use of ionizing radiation to destroy malignant cells. The DNA of the cell, responsible for storing, duplicating, and transmitting information needed for cell function, is the target of the radiation's effect. The principal insult produced by the radiation is a single chromosomal strand break. Cell death after exposure to radiation can occur in three ways: (1) immediately, when a cell experiences a chromosomal strand break that it can not repair (in this instance, the cells die within 2 hours after exposure to radiation); (2) at the time of cell division, which may be several days to several months after exposure to radiation; and (3) as a result of cellular degeneration (Yasko, 1982).

Radiation therapy is usually delivered in a series of treatments administered over a period of 2 to 8 weeks on a Monday through Friday schedule. The rad (radiation absorbed dose) is the unit of measurement of radiation. Because most tumors require a dose of between 4500 and 7500 rads, patients usually receive a daily fractionated dose of 180 to 200 rads. The immediate effect occurs within the first 2 hours after exposure to the radiation. The effect of radiation is progressive in nature, and as the cumulative dose of radiation increases, so do the side effects. Because radiation has the same effect on normal cells that it has on cancer cells, the objective of radiation therapy is to maximize tumor cell destruction while minimizing destruction of neighboring normal cells, by making the area to be treated as focused as possible. The effects of radiation are generally related to the field of treatment (Yasko, 1982). Radiation therapy is a local cancer treatment modality, and only the cells located in the particular anatomical site being treated will experience the effects of radiation therapy. When normal cells in the radiation field are destroyed or altered, the patient will experience predicatable side effects. In some patients the side effects will be minimal and hardly noticed, but in others, the side effects will seriously alter the usual life-style.

Burrish and Lyles (1983) discussed coping with the effects of cancer treatment and concluded that few therapeutic modalities produce more misunderstanding, confusion, and apprehension than radiation therapy. They suggest that research is needed to develop ways of helping patients to cope with their side effects or to comply with the successful treatment techniques that already have been developed. They state that approaches used with other medical treatments may be effective in the radiation area, or new treatment techniques may be needed. "In either case, the severity and frequency of radiation induced side effects warrant considerable increased research efforts" (p. 182).

McCorkle (1983) believes that people living with cancer and receiving medical therapy often must meet a new set of demands that are not among their usual knowledge and skills. She believes that knowledge of self-care is necessary to prevent patients from becoming passive recipients of care. It is the responsibility of all nurses to give patients the knowledge and skills they need to maintain their own health. McCorkle further believes that the type of information that nurses should give to patients with cancer, and its effect on increasing self-care practices and quality of life, has not yet been determined.

There have been few studies in the area of self-care related to chronic illness. Some work has been done in the area of self-care related to hypertension (Cadwell, Cobb, & Dowling, 1970; Finnerty, Mattie, & Finnerty, 1973) and diabetes (Backshieder, 1974; Bruhn, 1977). However, these studies are not related to side effects associated with radiation therapy and are not useful with patients undergoing radiation therapy.

The most significant work in the area of self-care related to patients with cancer has been done by Dodd. She first studied self-care activities in patients undergoing chemotherapy (Dodd, 1982a, 1982b, 1983). Her later work has been with patients undergoing radiation therapy (Dodd, 1984).

Review of Existing Tools

An important role of the nurse in radiation therapy is assessing the client for side effects of treatment and suggesting self-care activities the patient can perform to minimize the side effects. It is important to do the assessment systematically, and one way to obtain systematic information is to use a tool to measure the side effects. Three existing tools that measure symptoms or side effects in patients with cancer include McCorkle and Young's Symptom Distress Scale (McCorkle & Young, 1976), Dodd's Self-Care

Behaviors Log (Dodd, 1982a), and a Symptoms Profile developed by King and her colleagues (King, Nail, Kreamer, Strohl, & Johnson, 1985).

McCorkle and Young (1976) developed a 10-item symptom distress scale. Included were the symptoms of nausea, mood, insomnia, pain, mobility, fatigue, bowel pattern, concentration, and appearance. It was tested on 53 patients with advanced medical conditions (48 of the patients had cancer). Using 10 cards with a symptom listed on each card, the patients were asked to indicate the degree of distress on a 1–5 scale. Test–retest reliability, using Cronbach's alpha, was reported to be .82, indicative of good reliability. Content validity was established in a previous study in which patients themselves indicated the major symptoms that concerned them. Although this study is important because it generated a list of symptoms causing distress in cancer patients, not all of the symptoms are specific to patients undergoing radiation therapy, and therefore it is not useful in a radiation therapy setting.

Currently, there is only one tool to measure both the number and severity of side effects experienced by patients undergoing radiation therapy and the self-care activities used to deal with the side effects. This exists in the form of a self-care log developed by Dodd (1982a). It was originally used with patients undergoing chemotherapy. A patient experiencing a side effect recorded the date of onset, the type of side effect, and the severity of the side effect, using a 5-point scale. The patient also indicated on a 5-point scale how distressing the side effect was. In the third section the patient was asked to write in the self-care activities employed to alleviate the side effect, followed by the date the activity was undertaken. Next, the effectiveness of the self-care activity was indicated on a 5-point scale. In the last section, the patient was asked for the source of information for the self-care activity.

The reliability of the self-care behaviors log was determined by test–retest with a control group. No statistical difference was reported on pre- and postinterviews conducted 6 to 9 weeks apart. The self-care performance variable scores were correlated at a low level, $r = 0.21$ (Dodd, 1983). The reliability coefficient used was not specified. The content validity of the log was established by two groups of medical oncologists and four clinical nurse specialists. Both reliability and validity were checked in the original study done in 1982 with patients in a chemotherapy setting. The tool was modified after the initial chemotherapy study and then used in a radiation therapy setting. The chemotherapy setting varies from that of a radiation therapy department, and, of course, the side effects are different. However, the reliability and validity were not rechecked in the radiation therapy study.

In addition to Dodd's work, there is only one other important study to consider. Although not related to self-care, it dealt with the side effects patients experienced while undergoing radiation therapy. King and her colleagues (1985), using a Symptoms Profile (SP), documented the presence and severity of symptoms experienced by 96 patients while undergoing treatment. A list of 15 possible side effect symptoms was compiled by a clinical nurse specialist. Subjects were interviewed each week and asked if they had experienced any of the symptoms. If the subject experienced the side effect, details about the symptom were obtained, including information about the time of onset, frequency, duration, and severity. The severity of the symptom was obtained by using a 5-point Likert-type scale. Although the list of symptoms for the SP was compiled by a clinical nurse specialist, content validity cannot be inferred from this statement. The authors further indicated that no formal assessment of the reliability or validity of the Symptoms Profile was performed.

As mentioned earlier, it is important for the nurse to assess patients for side effects of radiation therapy, and the use of a tool allows the nurse to perform that assessment more systematically. Such a tool should include all possible side effects that a patient may experience and allow for increases in the severity of side effects over time and for individual differences. There should be a way for clients to indicate when the side effect begins and how long it lasts. Information should be obtained about what type of self-care measures were tried and the helpfulness of those measures. The Radiation Side Effects Profile (RSEP) is a tool designed to obtain the above information.

PURPOSE AND OBJECTIVES OF THE MEASURE

The overall purpose of this study was to develop and test the RSEP to be used with patients undergoing radiation therapy. The objectives of the RSEP were to determine the following:

1. Side effects experienced by patients undergoing radiation therapy.
2. Severity of the side effects.
3. Self-care strategies used to relieve the side effects.
4. Effectiveness of the self-care strategy used.

PROCEDURES FOR DEVELOPMENT OF TOOL

Construction

The RSEP, building on the work of previous researchers, is a one-page tool that takes about 3 minutes to complete (see instrument at the end of this chapter). It is a norm-referenced measurement tool with two separate interval scales. There are five sections. In the first section there is a list of common side effects experienced by patients undergoing radiation therapy. They include tiredness, skin changes, loss of appetite, nausea, hair loss, trouble swallowing, taste changes, sore throat or mouth, urinary frequency, diarrhea, sleep problems, and other. Most of the side effects listed were those generated by the research of King and her colleagues (King et al., 1985). In the next section, patients are asked to rate the severity of the side effects they experienced on a 4-point scale, from 0 (none) to 3 (very bad). Next, patients are asked to write in the self-care measures they have tried in an attempt to relieve their side effects. In the last section, patients are asked to rate the effectiveness of their measures on a 4-point scale from 0 (not at all helpful) to 3 (very helpful). Also, patients are asked who provided the information to them on what to do about their side effects. This question and the last two sections were influenced by Dodd's Self-Care Behaviors Log.

On several occasions during the construction of the tool, patients were asked to fill out the RSEP and comment on its readability, ease of use, and completeness. Although some patients had no difficulty with the tool, it did present problems for others, who did not understand some of the terminology used, especially in the list of side effects. Some words in the original list of side effects were changed; for example, "fatigue" and "anorexia" were changed to "tiredness" and "loss of appetite." The form was rearranged to give the patient more room to write in the self-care measures tried, and the code for the rating scales was listed just above the columns to be checked, rather than at the bottom of the page. Using the Fog Index of reading level, it was determined that the tool was written at a fourth-grade level (Gunning, 1968).

The RSEP is a self-report measure. Some researchers have expressed serious doubts concerning the reactivity effects and potential inaccuracies associated with self-monitored measures of behavior. However, Waltz and her colleagues (Waltz, Strickland, & Lenz, 1984) state that self-report offers the most valid approach currently available. For that reason and because many of the side effects experienced by patients are subjective and must be reported by the patients themselves, the self-report was chosen for this project.

ADMINISTRATION AND SCORING

The RSEP is a self-administered tool, from which two scores can be obtained. The Severity Index is obtained by summing the scores in the first column. On this scale, higher scores represent greater severity of side effects. The Helpfulness Index is obtained by summing the scores in the third column. A high score on this scale indicates that the self-care activities undertaken were perceived to be helpful. The responses to what subjects might do to relieve the side effects were analyzed and classified into eight categories: conservation of energy, taking medications, stress-reduction activities, skin care, diet modification, mouth care regimen, body image modification, and other. Conservation of energy consists of measures taken to minimize fatigue and includes activities like rest, nap, and sleep. Taking medications includes making adjustments in both prescription and over-the-counter medication regimens. Stress reduction is defined as any activity designed to decrease stress, such as relaxation, distraction, and ignoring the problem. Skin care, defined as any activity to protect the skin, includes applying ointment and staying out of the sun. Diet modification, or measures taken to improve nutrition, includes using different foods, eating slowly, and trying different seasonings. Mouth care regime is defined as measures to improve the condition of the mouth and includes keeping the mouth moist, using rinses, and gargling. Body image modification is defined as measures to improve appearance, like wearing a wig, cutting hair, or wearing a scarf. The "other" category includes all other measures that do not fit into the above categories. The categories, definitions, and a complete listing of examples for each category are shown in Table 4.1. The categories were reviewed by two experts, and there was 100% agreement between the two raters for content.

TABLE 4.1 Categories, Definitions, and Examples of Activities to Relieve Side Effects

Category	Definition	Examples of activities
Conservation of energy	Measures taken to minimize fatigue	Rest, nap, sleep, stay home, go to bed earlier
Taking medications	Making adjustments in prescription and/or over-the-counter medications	Reduce medications, increase medications, take aspirin, drink alcohol
Stress reduction	Activities to decrease stress	Relaxation, see family, imagination, distraction, watch TV, listen to music, read, accept it, ignore
Skin care	Activities to protect skin	Peel it, use topical medication, use lotion, stay out of sun, avoid ointment
Diet modification	Measures to improve nutrition	Increase eating, decrease eating, try different foods, use different seasonings, eat crackers, eat more frequently, avoid sweets, eat slowly, drink warm milk
Mouth care regimen	Measures to improve	Keeping mouth moist, chew food more, drink fluids, remove dentures, drink more, gargle, take lozenges
Body image modification	Measures to improve appearance	Wear wig, wear scarf, wear hat, don't look, cut hair, use wide-toothed comb, pull hair out
Other		Voided more, forced self to do things.

RELIABILITY AND VALIDITY ASSESSMENTS

The tool was tested for reliability and validity in the radiation therapy department of a university hospital, where approximately 125 patients were treated daily. Fifty-six subjects participated in the testing. Subjects who were 18 years or older and were undergoing radiation therapy for cure were admitted to the study. After an explanation of the purpose of the tool and the reason for reliability and validity testing, the RSEP was given to the subjects. The subjects either filled out the form as they waited for their treatment and returned it immediately, or they took it home to fill out and returned it the next day at their scheduled treatment time. The tool was administered several times over the course of treatment, usually a 4- to 6-week period. Prior to data collection, the Institutional Review Board approved the study protocol. Each subject gave informed written consent prior to participating in the study.

Sample

Fifty-six subjects participated in the reliability and validity testing of the RSEP. The majority of the subjects (71%) were female. They ranged in age from 19 to 82, with a mean age of 54 years. Forty-eight (86%) of the subjects were Caucasian, and 8 (14%) were black. Thirty-seven (66%) were married, 8 (14%) were single, and the remainder were either separated, divorced, or widowed. The specific diagnoses of the subjects are presented in Table 4.2.

Reliability

Because the side effects experienced by patients depend on exactly where the radiation therapy is given and are therefore very individual, measures of internal consistency were not deemed appropriate. A score on one item of the RSEP does not necessarily indicate that a subject would score on any

TABLE 4.2 Number and Percentage of Subjects by Diagnosis (*N* = 56)

Diagnosis	No.	%
Breast	22	39
Head and neck	9	16
Lung	7	13
Gynecologic	4	7
Hodgkins	4	7
Genitourinary	4	7
Brain	3	4
Gastrointestinal	3	4

TABLE 4.3 Test–Retest Reliability for Severity and Helpfulness Indices

	n	*r*	*p*
Severity Index			
Weeks 1, 2	56	.59	.001
Weeks 4, 5	28	.83	.001
Helpfulness Index			
Weeks 1, 2	56	.46	.0007
Weeks 4, 5	28	.56	.001

other item on the tool. Neither interrater nor intrarater reliability were appropriate for this study.

To test for consistency of the RSEP, test–retest reliability, the most appropriate approach to reliability assessment, was determined for both the Severity Index and the Helpfulness Index, using the Pearson product-moment correlation. This was selected because the data are measured at the interval level. Testing occurred at 1-week intervals during the first and second weeks of treatment and again during the fourth and fifth weeks of treatment, when a greater number and severity of side effects were anticipated. Using 56 subjects, the correlation coefficient between Week 1 and Week 2 on the Severity Index was .59, significant beyond the .001 level (see Table 4.3). By the fourth and fifth weeks, only 28 subjects were still under treatment, and the test–retest correlation coefficient at this time was .83, significant beyond the .001 level. For the Helpfulness Index, using 56 subjects, the correlation coefficient between Week 1 and Week 2 was .46, significant at the .0007 level; for Weeks 4 and 5, with 28 subjects, it was .56, significant beyond the .001 level (see Table 4.3).

Validity

Validity refers to the ability of a tool to measure what it purports to measure. Content validity of the RSEP was determined by asking one physician and one nurse expert in the area of radiation therapy to serve as judges to determine if the side effects listed on the RSEP were accurate. Using the methods described by Waltz, Strickland, and Lenz (1984), the judges were asked to rate the relevance of the side effects on a scale of 1 to 4, where 1 indicated that the item was irrelevant and 4 indicated that the item was extremely relevant. The index of content validity (ICV), or proportion of items receiving a 3 or 4, indicating interrater agreement, was then determined. An acceptable ICV ranges from 0.80 to 1.0. The ICV for the RSEP was 0.84, an acceptable score.

Construct validity for the Severity and Helpfulness indices was established using a contrasted-groups approach with *t*-test analysis. The subjects were tested during the first and fourth weeks of treatment. Twenty-one subjects in the group with cancer of the breast were compared with the nine subjects who had cancer of the head and neck, with the expecta-

TABLE 4.4 Construct Validity for Severity and Helpfulness Indices Using t tests of Contrasted Groups for Weeks 1 and 4

	X	*t*	*df*	*p*
Severity Index				
Week 1				
Breast (n = 21)	1.76	1.78	28	.04
Head and neck (n = 9)	4.6			
Week 4				
Breast (n = 21)	2.5	1.71	28	.05
Head and neck (n = 9)	10.0			
Helpfulness Index				
Week 1				
Breast (n = 21)	2.0	.47	28	NS
Head and neck (n = 9)	1.4			
Week 4				
Breast (n = 21)	2.3	1.97	28	NS
Head and neck (n = 9)	1.3			

tion that those with cancer of the head and neck would have higher severity scores due to the nature of the cancer sites. A one-tailed paired *t* test was done for Week 1 and Week 4 with Severity scores and Helpfulness scores. For Week 1, the mean severity score for the subjects with cancer of the breast was 1.76, and the mean Severity score for subjects with cancer of the head and neck was 4.6 (see Table 4.4). A higher score reflects greater severity of side effects. The difference between the two groups was significant at the .04 level. Differences were also found at Week 4, when the mean score for subjects with breast cancer was 2.5, and the subjects with cancer of the head and neck had a mean score of 10.1, significant beyond the .001 level. These results indicate that the tool was sensitive to variations in the severity of side effects of specific diagnostic groups.

On the Helpfulness scale, the same procedure was followed, but, as expected, there were no significant differences between the group mean scores for Week 1 nor for Week 4. The mean Helpfulness score for subjects with breast cancer was 2.0 for Week 1, while the mean Helpfulness score of patients with head and neck cancer was 1.4; for Week 4, the mean Helpfulness scores were 2.3 and 1.3, respectively (see Table 4.4). A higher score on this scale indicates that the self-care activities were more helpful.

DISCUSSION AND CONCLUSIONS

Preliminary results indicate general support for the initial reliability and validity of the RSEP. The RSEP seems to be relevant for clinical nursing practice. It is useful in obtaining vital, systematic information about patients' reactions to radiation therapy and the effectiveness of the self-care measures employed. There are, however, two major concerns. The first is with the timing of the reliability testing. Waltz and her colleagues (1984) indicate that when doing test–retest reliability, there should be no activities between the first and second testing that could affect the stability of the tool. Because the side effects are cumulative and increase in severity as the therapy progresses, the daily treatment is a significant event that could interfere with the results of the second administration of the tool. Because of lack of time and funds, the test was administered during the first and fourth weeks of treatment, with a retest during the second and fifth weeks. This meant that 1 week intervened between test and retest rather than 1 day. Although the results indicate that the tool was reliable, with correlation coefficients of .59 and .83, further testing of the tool should be done at 1-day intervals rather than 1-week intervals.

The second issue, of clinical interest, is that of the results of the validity testing on the Helpfulness scores. Although there were expected differences between contrasted groups on severity scores, it is not surprising that there were no significant differences between groups on the Helpfulness scores. This score on the tool indicates the patients' perceptions of the helpfulness of the attempted self-care measures. The lack of difference and very low Helpfulness indicates that neither group of patients obtained much relief from their side effects. Clinically, these scores indicate that the patients' self-care behaviors were only a little helpful to them, pointing out a need for nursing intervention. It is the role of the nurse to intervene at this point to suggest more helpful activities, and helpfulness scores can serve as a basis for determining the need for such intervention.

In summary, this chapter describes a measurement protocol related to the side effects and the concept of self-care behaviors of patients undergoing radiation therapy. Results indicate general support for the initial reliability and validity of the RSEP. It is anticipated that this tool will be used to identify side effects and to contribute to the knowledge of how to help patients use effective self-care strategies to reduce the side effects of radiation therapy. In clinical nursing practice, the RSEP can be used to assess patients' reaction to radiation therapy, to guide the nurse in teaching, and to evaluate the results of intervention.

REFERENCES

Backscheider, J. E. (1974). Self-care requirements, self-care capabilities and nursing systems in the diabetic nurse management clinic. *American Journal of Public Health, 64,* 1138–1146.

Bruhn, J. G. (1977). Self concept and control of diabetes. *American Family Practice, 15,* 93–97.

Burish, T. G., & Lyles, J. N. (1983). Coping with the adverse effects of cancer treatments. In T. G. Burish & L. A. Bradley (Eds.), *Coping with chronic disease* (pp. 159–187). New York: Academic Press.

Cadwell, J. R., Cobb, S., & Dowling, M. D. (1970). The dropout problem in antihypertensive therapy. *Journal of Chronic Disease, 22,* 579.

Dodd, M. J. (1982a). Assessing self-care for side effects of cancer chemotherapy. *Cancer Nursing, 5*(6), 447–451.
Dodd, M. J. (1982b). Cancer patients' knowledge of chemotherapy: Assessment and informational interventions. *Oncology Nursing Forum, 9*(3), 39–44.
Dodd, M. J. (1983). Self-care for side effects of cancer chemotherapy. *Cancer Nursing, 6*(1), 63–67.
Dodd, M. J. (1984). Patterns of self care in cancer patients receiving radiation therapy. *Oncology Nursing Forum, 11*(3), 23–27.
Finnerty, F. A. Jr., Mattie, E. C., & Finnerty, F. A. III. (1973). Hypertension in the inner city: Analysis of clinic dropouts. *Circulation, 47,* 73–75.
Gunning, R. (1968). The Fog Index after twenty years. *Journal of Business Communication, 6,* 3–13.
King, K. B., Nail, L. M., Kreamer, K., Strohl, R. A., & Johnson, J. (1985). Patients' descriptions of the experience of receiving radiation therapy. *Oncology Nursing Forum, 12*(4), 55–61.
McCorkle, R. (1983). Nurses as advocates for self care [Editorial]. *Cancer Nursing, 1*(1), 17.
McCorkle, R., & Young, K. (1976). Development of a symptom distress scale. *Cancer Nursing, 1*(5), 373–378.
Orem, D. E. (1971). *Nursing: Concepts of practice.* New York: McGraw-Hill.
Waltz, C. F., Strickland, O. L., & Lenz, E. R. (1984). *Measurement in nursing research.* Philadelphia: F. A. Davis.
Yasko, J. M. (1982). *Care of the patient receiving external radiation therapy.* Reston, VA: Reston Publishing.

Radiation Side Effects Profile

Some people have side effects during radiation therapy. From the side effects listed below, check the column that shows how severe your side effects were during the past week. Next, write in what you did to relieve the side effects. In the last column, check how helpful you found the things you did to relieve the side effects.

SIDE EFFECT	SEVERITY 0 = none 1 = a little bad 2 = somewhat bad 3 = very bad				WHAT YOU DID TO RELIEVE THE SIDE EFFECT(S)	HELPFUL 0 = not at all 1 = a little 2 = somewhat 3 = very			
	0	1	2	3		0	1	2	3
Tiredness									
Skin changes									
Loss of appetite									
Nausea									
Hair loss									
Trouble swallowing									
Taste changes									
Sore throat or mouth									
Urinary frequency									
Diarrhea									
Sleep problems									
Other ____________ Specify									

Where did you get the information for what to do about the side effect?

Self ____ Doctor ____ Nurse ____ Technician ____

Family ____ Friend ____ Other patient ____ Other ____

5

Measuring Guarding: A Self-Care Management Process Used by Individuals with Chronic Illness

Linda Corson Jones

This chapter describes the SCMP-G, an instrument that measures guarding, a self-care management process that individuals use in managing illness self-care.

The SCMP-G has been developed after several years of work, beginning with the discovery of self-care management processes (SCMP) by Jones and Preuett (1986) and continuing with the validation of SCMP (Jones, Hill, Honer, & McDaniels, 1986) and delineation of characteristics of guarding (Huffman, 1987). Although further testing and development of the SCMP-G is needed, the inductive methodology—moving from the discovery of phenomena through qualitative research to further research validation of the phenomena and specification of empirical indicators to develop a measure—may be helpful to others investigating new phenomena of interest to nursing. The SCMP-G is designed to be useful in assessing guarding as an SCMP in chronic illness.

Chronic illness has become a major health problem. From 1900 to 1979 the mortality and morbidity rates for acute illnesses declined, while increasing by 250% for individuals with chronic diseases (USDHEW, 1979). Following this trend, health care professionals working with individuals with chronic illness are changing their focus from episodic treatment of illness to assisting chronically ill individuals to achieve optimal health and take responsibility for self-care (Brugge, 1981; Miller, 1983).

Despite health professionals' recent interest in working with the chronically ill, they have only a limited understanding of how these individuals view their illnesses and deal with various aspects of their care (Chang,

1980; Davis, 1981). Frequently, a discrepancy exists between health professionals' perspective of illness and the illness experience of patients (Davis, 1981; Kleinman, 1978). Kleinman proposed that health care providers and patients have different "explanatory models" of disease and illness. Health professionals tend to view sickness from the perspective of disease and place emphasis on diagnosis, treatment, and cure. On the other hand, when patients experience an illness, they attempt to understand the meaning of and reasons for the illness, manage their lives in spite of the illness, and separate their identities from the illness. A number of studies confirm that patients form their own representation of illness, monitor symptoms, and modify treatments based on their perceptions of the disorder (Forsyth, Delaney, & Gresham, 1984; Kennison, 1983; Leventhal, Leventhal, & Nguyen, 1985; O'Brien, 1984).

Traditionally, health care providers have focused on the patient as a passive recipient of care and have viewed chronic illness management in terms of compliance, service utilization, and psychological reactions. (Chang, 1980; Forsyth et al., 1984). During recent years, however, health professionals have become more aware of the importance of recognizing the lay perspective of illness and how individuals manage their care (Bury & Wood, 1979; Chang, 1980; Copp, 1974; Reid, 1984; Strauss et al., 1984).

REVIEW OF RELATED LITERATURE

Several characteristics of chronic illness are important in understanding it from the patient's perspective. Chronic illnesses are long-term by nature. Although a major life crisis may be triggered by a diagnosis of any major illness, an individual must live with a chronic illness for an extended period, often years. The chronically ill must learn to manage a treatment regimen that is typically complex, multidimensional, and expensive. The prognosis and treatment of chronic illnesses may involve a great deal of uncertainty. The chronic illness trajectory may be characterized by a number of phases of exacerbations and remissions. Frequently, individuals seek out or are invited to participate in experimental treatments or new medical developments. Participation in these efforts may help in the long-term course of the illness, but it also adds to the uncertainty surrounding the illness.

Critical to an understanding of how the chronically ill view and deal with their illnesses are the concepts of coping and self-care. Coping is a term that has been defined in many ways by various disciplines. Cohen and Lazarus (1979) defined coping as efforts, both action-oriented and intrapsychic, to manage environmental and internal demands/conflicts that tax or exceed a person's resources. Ray, Lindop, and Gipson (1982) simply conceptualized coping as action directed toward the resolution of a problem. Beutel (1985) attempted to integrate the perspectives of cognition and behavior, defining coping as conscious, cognitive-experiential and behavioral-action-oriented processes used in stressful situations.

A number of concerns have been raised about the study of coping. The literature on coping has been characterized as diffuse, abstract, weak, internally inconsistent, and imprecise (Beutel, 1985; Fleming, Baum, & Singer, 1984; Stone & Neale, 1984). Taylor (1984), in a comprehensive review of the state of knowledge of coping, declared that the coping literature needs a rigorous housecleaning. In a similar vein, Singer (1984) argued that coping is the name of a file drawer encompassing many concerns, rather than a single concept.

The diversity in the conceptualization of coping is evident in the literature on chronic illness (Beutel, 1985; Bloom, 1982; Craig & Edwards, 1983; Dimond, 1980; Forsyth et al., 1984; Miller, 1983; Viney & Westbrook, 1982, 1984). Although there has been a great deal of interest in attempting to understand how individuals cope with chronic illness, there is no agreed upon typology of coping strategies nor a theory of coping with illness. Thus, the dimensions of coping used in each study have differed. A number of recommendations have been made for studying coping (Beutel, 1985; Fleming et al., 1984; Stone & Neale, 1984). Two recommendations are especially applicable to chronic illness research. First, research should strive to generate principles of adaptation common to chronic illness, rather than studying specific diseases. Second, more specific aspects or components of coping should be studied. One area for nursing to explore is how individuals with chronic illness cope with illness self-care.

The chronically ill make many decisions about self-care. Orem (1985) has presented a theoretical model of nursing that incorporates self-care. She defines self-care as the practice of activities that individuals personally initiate to maintain health and well-being. Self-care is voluntary, culturally embedded, informally organized, learned through socialization, and influenced by personal experiences (Levin, 1978). As a result, self-care is based on individuals' perceived needs and preferences and may not conform to health professionals' perceptions (Dean, 1981; Levin, 1978).

There has been tremendous interest in self-care for the promotion of health and the prevention of illness. In the past, however, lay decision making and self-treatment during illness have been criticized by professionals as dangerous and, until recently, were not widely accepted. Empirical evidence of the dangers of self-care during illness is lacking, and in fact, a great deal of research has validated that individuals generally make appropriate self-care decisions and take helpful self-care actions during illness (Dean, 1986). Woods (1985) pointed out, however, that although more research is beginning to address self-care, few studies have examined illness self-care beyond use of health services, use of medications, and days of bedrest and reduced activity.

The recent movement away from interpreting behavior of ill individuals as possible interference with medical care (e.g., noncompliance and resistance) is being replaced with an appreciation that individuals living with a chronic illness make numerous self-care decisions and meet a number of challenges over time (Grieco & Kopel, 1983; Strauss et al., 1984). The chronically ill deal with a variety of complex tasks in order to maintain a positive concept of self and to function effectively in relationships and life roles (Miller, 1983).

Several authors have outlined self-care tasks that may be encountered during a chronic illness (Beutel, 1985; Craig & Edwards, 1983; Miller, 1983; Moos & Tsu, 1979; Strauss et al., 1984). Miller (1983) has presented the most complete description of self-care tasks of chronic illness. From the analysis of qualitative data from 56 chronically ill adults, she derived a taxonomy of self-care tasks, labeling them "coping tasks." The 13 tasks include various aspects of life, such as leisure and work, family interaction, role changes, and self-esteem. Miller noted that these tasks are necessary for chronically ill individuals to accomplish or maintain a positive self-concept and to function effectively in social relationships and life roles.

The self-care tasks confronting chronically ill individuals are multiple and complex. Individuals generally work on several tasks simultaneously and are unique in how they deal with self-care (Miller, 1983). For example, an individual with arthritis may be working on a number of tasks, such as modifying daily routines, dealing with role change and stigma, and maintaining hope. An individual newly diagnosed with diabetes may focus on modifying life-style, maintaining a positive self-concept, and adjusting to the treatment regimen. Little is known, however, about how individuals cope with the various self-care tasks.

In a beginning attempt to understand how patients manage self-care, Jones and Preuett (1986) interviewed 25 hemodialysis patients to determine self-care used in dealing with stressors related to dietary and fluid restrictions and hemodialysis treatments. During the analysis of patients' responses, Jones and Preuett noted a recurring theme, which they termed self-care management processes, or SCMP. Whereas self-care activities were defined as specific patient acts for dealing with treatment-related stressors, Jones and Preuett conceptualized SCMP as ongoing adaptive mechanisms that individuals used in performing a variety of self-care acts. Four patterns of SCMP were identified and defined as (a) equalizing—weighing, juggling, and shifting competing demands for time, energy, finances, desires, and requirements; (b) substituting—replacing and exchanging desires and activities; (c) withdrawing—moving away from events, people, and ideas; and (d) guarding—maintaining vigilance over the body and the delivery of care.

Jones and her colleagues (1986) conducted a second study to validate that individuals representing a variety of chronic illnesses use SCMP. In addition, they were interested in determining if the chronically ill use SCMP in self-care tasks other than managing their treatment regimen. This study will be reported in detail because its data were used to ground the development of the SCMP-G measure.

The primary source of data was taped interviews with 32 chronically ill individuals. A second source of data was the analysis of three written personal accounts by individuals with chronic illnesses. Respondents were obtained through a variety of outpatient and community settings in two large cities and several rural communities in the south. The final sample size was determined by data saturation, the point of data collection where the information obtained was redundant (Bogdan & Biklen, 1982).

The 35 individuals represented diverse backgrounds and illness conditions. The sample consisted of 23 females and 12 males. The main ethnic identification was white: 30 were white and 5 were black. Ages ranged from 25 to 82 years, with a mean age of 49. Ten were diagnosed with cardiac disease, nine with cancer, seven with diabetes, and one for each of the other diagnoses (thalassemia, hypertension, myasthenia gravis, asthma, arthritis, chemical dependency, and cerebral vascular accident). The time since diagnosis ranged from less than 6 months to 21 years. Eleven individuals had had their illness for about 1 year, while four reported having had their illness over 10 years.

Each respondent participated in a focused interview at least once. During the initial interview, the investigators obtained demographic and background information, overviews of the illnesses; the professional and self-care the illnesses required; and ways the respondents managed their care. The published personal accounts were read several times by one investigator, and themes related to self-care were extracted for analysis.

After conducting several initial interviews, data were analyzed and themes identified. The investigators reinterviewed nine respondents to further explore the use of SCMP, verify the use of SCMP over time, and allow the respondents time to develop further trust, confidence, and feelings of ease. Collecting and analyzing data at the same time allowed modification of interviews so that verification of themes could be incorporated. Data collection stopped when the research team believed that no new themes could be identified.

Various strategies for dealing with reliability and validity in qualitative research have been decribed (Campbell, 1979; Lincoln & Guba, 1985; Miles & Huberman, 1984). This study incorporated a number of strategies to increase the trustworthiness of the findings: checking for representativeness of the data among respondents, independently identifying themes by each interviewer, keeping a record of rival explanations considered, including a variety of respondents in the study, and reinterviewing some respondents.

Data analysis proceeded in several steps. The transcripts and personal accounts were read several times by each member of the research team. Particular words, phrases, ways of thinking, and events were noted. Patterns and themes related to SCMP were identified and verified by the total research team. As a final step, data for each process were examined to delimit instances, characteristics, and conditions of SCMP.

More than 400 pages of typewritten transcripts and excerpts from the published accounts were collected. Data validated the four types of SCMP discovered in the original study. Definitions of the processes were revised, and subcategories of three of the processes that emerged from the data were defined. In addition, two additional SCMP, shaping and receiving, were identified. Definitions and subcategories of the SCMP are displayed in Table 5.1.

To examine whether SCMP were used in managing illness self-care tasks other than management of the treatment regimen, instances of SCMP

TABLE 5.1 Self-Care Management Processes—Subcategories and Definitions

Process/subcategory	Definition
Equalizing	Weighing, juggling, and shifting competing demands for time, energy, finances, desires, and requirements
Adjusting: effective action vs. ineffective action	Correcting self-care actions that are not working
Pacing: energy vs. requirements	Arranging or changing activities and routines to set a tempo and conserve energy
Scheduling: time vs. demands	Constructing a time plan to deal with self-care actions
Rewarding: benefits vs. problems	Perceiving the positive benefits of having the illness
Guarding	Maintaining vigilance over self, the illness, the treatment regimen, the delivery of care, and important relationships
Self	Protecting self, checking on progress of illness, and exerting control over the treatment regimen and delivery of care
Social	Protecting social network from problematic aspects of the illness
Withdrawing	Moving away from events, people, and ideas
Illness idea	Separating from the idea of having an illness; ignoring illness signs
Regimen	Rejecting facets of the treatment regimen, especially prescribed medical regimen
People	Moving away from individuals in the social network
Activities	Cutting back or stopping usual activities
Receiving[a]	Seeking or taking in tangible, psychic, or informational resources
Accepted	Willingly and gratefully accepting support
Unaccepted	Recognizing that support is being offered but totally rejecting the support or only partially accepting it
Extracted	Perceiving the need for support that is not being offered and actively soliciting the support
Shaping	Directing efforts toward learning or practicing a desired outcome

[a]The definition and categories of receiving are based on Zabielski's (1984) typology of giving and receiving.

were noted for each self-care task identified by Miller (1983). SCMP were linked to a variety of self-care tasks. Guarding and equalizing were used in all 13 of Miller's tasks, and substituting and shaping were used in 9 of the 13 tasks.

Although there are plans to develop instruments to measure each of the SCMP, a decision was made to begin instrument development with one process. Of the five major SCMP, guarding was selected for initial instrument development for two reasons. Although respondents used a number of different SCMP, guarding was dominant, representing 30% of all instances of SCMP. In addition, limited striking evidence was collected that linked the use of guarding to health outcomes. A few respondents showed almost no evidence of self-guarding, a particular type of guarding identified in the validation study. In trying to understand this finding, attempts were made to schedule reinterviews with these individuals. Before second interviews could be scheduled, two of the respondents died, and one was hospitalized for an accidental injury.

CONCEPTUAL BASIS OF THE MEASURE

Self-care provides the broad conceptual framework for SCMP and development of an instrument to measure guarding. SCMP are adaptive behavioral, psychological, and cognitive mechanisms individuals use in performing a variety of illness self-care actions. Individuals have a repertoire of SCMP in coping with illness self-care, althouth they may use the processes to varying degrees. SCMP exist when individuals assume some responsibility for care of their illness and use mechanisms that make illness self-care more understandable, acceptable, or integral to their life. SCMP is distinct from compliance with a professionally prescribed treatment regimen. Some individuals use SCMP to adhere to a prescribed regimen; others use SCMP in developing their own regimen or avoiding the prescribed regimen.

Guarding, one of the SCMP, refers to the process of maintaining vigilance over self, the illness, the treatment regimen, the delivery of care, and important relationships. Empirical indicators of guarding are being alert and watchful to control the illness or effects of the illness. Two types of guarding can be identified: self and social guarding. Self-guarding refers to attempts to protect oneself, check on the progress of the illness, and exert control over the treatment regimen and delivery of care. Social guarding includes attempts by individuals to protect their social network members from the illness and the negative aspects of the illness.

The Critical Elements of Guarding

Four critical elements of guarding have been identified: (a) perceived vulnerability, (b) perceived controllability, (c) self-absorption, and (d) a sense of obligation. A description of each critical element will be defined and illustrated with actual respondent quotations from the Jones et al. (1986) study.

Vulnerability

Individuals who use guarding perceive that they or their social network are vulnerable to psychic, physical, and social threats. In the Jones et al. study (1986), individuals referred to parts of their bodies that "hurt" or were "sensitive." Some individuals shared fears that their illness might progress. They described themselves as "fragile," "real paranoid," "afraid of falling," and "afraid of getting hurt." A woman confided her fear of pain: "I'm scared to play with the kids the way I do or anything, because these legs being like that. I tell them all the time, 'Watch it, don't touch my legs, don't touch my legs!' I'm so scared it is going to hurt."

Fear of dying was referred to by most individuals. They cited being "scared to death" at times, afraid that their illness was "going to kill," and said that the "fear of dying," "the future catching up with you," and losing "the ball game" or "battle" motivated them. A woman with heart disease related her fear of a medical emergency: "I made my husband walk with me for two years, because it was beneficial for him too, but I did have that fear for almost close to one year. I wanted someone with me, and when I got over having someone with me, I then always let someone know where I was. If I left the house, I would tell a neighbor."

Frequently, individuals observed that certain foods or activities caused their illness to worsen or their regimen to be thrown off balance. A man with diabetes reported, "Anytime I eat red meat, I feel very sluggish and just feel bad." A woman stated, "I don't eat wheat; I have read that wheat tends to trigger [symptoms]." and "Arthritis is caused by stress—I believe a lot of it."

Individuals spoke of social relationship difficulties that their illness created. They expressed the following: "It makes people uncomfortable"; "People look at you like you might keel over"; "They put you in a category"; "They ask you a lot of questions"; and "People start to panic." Some people spoke of the need to "not jar" relationships and not to be a "constant, hourly bother," "nuisance," or "a pain in the neck." They cited the need to "accommodate to other people" and "allow each person to set his or her own boundaries." One individual said, "You tell somebody you've had a heart attack and, particularly at my age, being young, some people look at you like you've had leprosy."

Controllability

Individuals who use guarding believe and act as though they have the power and the capability to prevent, curb, diminish, or stop illness-related threats. Individuals spoke with a great deal of confidence about the central role they assumed in care of their illness (Jones et al., 1986). They used self-talk to remind themselves that they could "handle," "conquer," or "control" their illness. A woman stated: "It really has a lot to do with attitude, because when I feel myself getting sick, I say, 'Hey, you have too much, you have a job, a home to take care of. There is no way. I won't get sick.' And I don't. I really and truly don't." Another woman with diabetes explained about her decision to use guarding in managing her treatment regimen. "I just decided that it wasn't going to change my life. There was no reason it should. In order for it not to, then I had to be the one to control it." Another person said, "I just say to myself, 'Well, I had a bad night last night and tonight is going to be a better night, and if I'm that sick then I'm just right down the road [from the hospital].' "

Some people acknowledge that they, as opposed to health professionals, had the greater ability to direct their care. One person who made frequent trips to the hospital and endured numerous needle sticks explained, "If I have to be stuck every day, I'd rather do it myself." A man with asthma stated that although his doctor had instructed him not to run, he decided against medical advice to continue running. He noted, however, that he minimized his problems with asthma by always having the inhalant with him and "testing his limits every so often." A woman with diabetes asserted: "There is nothing that I feel I need to consult an endocrinologist about. I am getting regular checkups, regular blood work, regular eye exams. But as far as an endocrinologist telling or helping me control it, I've never really depended upon it." Another person explained: "He [physician] tells me to take my blood pressure, and I get actively involved in my own treatment. I'm actually doing almost 95% of it. Every now and then I go in and he tells me how I'm doing, although I already know before I get there."

Individuals described being able to influence threats to their social network. A woman with cardiac disease explained, "I feel like maybe I can break the chain of my children developing this by being able to tell them what they should to to care for themselves and my grandchildren now." Another woman who had been advised to lose weight because of her illness stated, "I don't try to diet and meet the public at the same time because I have a tendency to be grouchy as a bear when I diet, so I wouldn't want to inflict this on anybody I meet everyday."

Self-Absorption

Guarding is a self-absorptive process. Individuals are acutely aware of and sensitive to both internal body and external cues. In addition, they carefully think about what they can or should do, whereas before their illness they conducted daily activities without much conscious decision making. In the Jones et al. study (1986), a man said, "You've always got that [heart problems] in the back of your mind." Another person with cardiac problems stated, "Every time I want to do what I want to, I have to think—well, can I lift this or can I do that?"

This self-monitoring process can dominate people's thoughts and lives. One woman who had a mastectomy named the frequent need to examine her remaining breast for the recurrence of cancer a "self-examinational tic." She confided: "Twice a day I kneaded away. Each time I found no lump, I felt terrific. For a couple of hours. Then, later in the day, worry would build again, and I'd feel myself again and there wouldn't be anything there and I'd feel good again. For the next few hours. Until the next time or the next day." A man admitted: "Anything that causes my obsessive-compulsive components to come into play is a challenge. And my diabetes, I can get very obsessed with that. I can check my blood sugar and just sort of experiment on myself and see what makes the change in the blood sugar—what I eat or how much exercise, etc., and I enjoy doing that."

Individuals may become aware of situations and parts of themselves that previously were unknown. People described an awareness of body parts: "being protective of my veins," "if it stops ticking in a minute [heart], you will not be around in three minutes," and "my heart was so close to the surface now."

Tests and lab values were frequently cited as foremost in people's minds as they used guarding. Individuals cited: "lipid profile was getting better," "my cholesterol level was going downward, and it [cholesterol level] only has come down .6 after my heart attack." Individuals with diabetes cited the importance of home monitoring procedures in dealing with their illness: "Actually the blood tests hurt more than the shots [insulin]. But to me that is so important, because I couldn't stand the idea of not knowing exactly where the blood sugar was."

Sense of Obligation

Individuals view guarding as essential to adjustment and sometimes survival. This sense of obligation is expressed with language indicating a sense of both "must" (requirement) and "now" (urgency). A woman stated: "I always went [for cardiac rehabilitation]. I felt like I had made that commitment. That this is what I have to do for all lifetime."

This sense of obligation was evident also in people who used social guarding. A woman explained, "And I went home with the attitude (I still had three children at home when I went home) that if it [diet] was bad for me, then it was bad for them too." Another person with cardiac disease, a father, stated, "I'm so young that I just can't sit back. . . . gotta go on, if not for me, for my boys." A woman with diabetes remarked, "I have thought that any problem that you have, that will perhaps affect the way you interact with people, it is best to say it and talk about it." Another woman tried "desperately hard not to be a constant hourly bother."

PURPOSE OF THE MEASURE

The purpose of the SCMP-G is to determine the extent to which individuals use guarding in managing their chronic illness.

PROCEDURES FOR DEVELOPMENT

Although the process of guarding was confirmed and two types of guarding were identified during the validation study (Jones et al., 1986), the critical attributes of guarding had not been identified. Therefore, the first step in developing the SCMP-G consisted of delineating the characteristics of guarding. The data related to guarding from the Jones et al. (1986) study were reexamined. From the literature on theory construction (Chenitz & Swanson, 1986; Glaser, 1978; Glaser & Strauss, 1967; Walker & Avant, 1983), the following questions were formulated and used to identify from the data the critical elements of guarding as described above:

1. Under what conditions did individuals use guarding?
2. Under what conditions were individuals not able to use guarding?
3. In what context did guarding occur?
4. What were the consequences of using guarding?
5. What were the consequences of not using guarding?
6. What words or phrases referred to guarding?
7. What characteristics differentiated guarding from the other SCMP?

Development of an Item Pool

After the critical elements of guarding were identified, a blueprint was constructed to guide the development of items. The blueprint incorporated the characteristics of guarding and the two types of guarding. The number of items for the item pool was based on the need to write enough items for subscale scores of self- and social guarding (at least 10 items each) and possible item deletion in the stages of content validity testing and item analysis.

Data from the second SCMP study were used in developing items. Four guidelines were used in generating items. Items were generated that reflected each of the defining characteristics of guarding. In addition, only items applicable to a variety of chronic illnesses were included. Actual statements or phrases made by individuals in the Jones et al. (1986) study were used as much as possible. Items were stated at a third-grade reading level, using brief simple sentences or phrases of less than 15 words. A total of 65 items was initially written. Two subscales were developed, consisting of self-guarding and social guarding. Weak or questionable items were subsequently deleted from the item pool. The final 35-item blueprint for the SCMP-G is presented in Table 5.2.

ADMINISTRATION AND SCORING

The SCMP-G (see instrument at the end of this chapter) can be administered in either an individual or group setting, requiring about 15 to 20

TABLE 5.2 Blueprint for the SCMP-G

Critical Elements	Type	
	Self	Social
Vulnerability	3	4
Controllability	6	2
Self-absorption	5	5
Sense of obligation	6	4
Total items	20	15

minutes to complete. The SCMP-G has two subscales, consisting of self- (20 items) and social guarding (15 items). The self subscale includes items 2, 6, 8, 15, 18, 19, 22, 23, and 27–34. The social subscale includes items 1, 3–5, 7, 9, 10, 12–14, 16, 17, 21, 24, and 35. The response format for both subscales consists of a 5-point Likert format ranging from 5 (strongly agree) to 1 (strongly disagree). Responses to items indicating lack of guarding are reverse-scored: items 3, 15, 19, and 28. The possible range of scores is 15 to 60 for the social subscale and 20 to 80 for the self subscale. A high score indicates high use of guarding.

RELIABILITY AND VALIDITY ASSESSMENTS

Content validity of the SCMP-G was determined through review by two panels of experts. First, eight experts who were clinical nurse specialists or nursing researchers in the area of chronic illness were provided with a packet of materials describing SCMP and the defining characteristics of guarding. They rated the SCMP-G on a 4-point relevance scale recommended by Lynn (1986). The SCMP-G was revised based on their ratings, comments, and recommendations. The panel of experts recommended deleting 6 items and changing the wording of 34 items. With the deletion of questionable items, the resulting content validity index was 1.00.

Next, a second panel of five experts assessed the revised 59-item SCMP-G for item-to-subscale congruence, using information describing the defining characteristics of guarding. The experts categorized the SCMP-G items according to whether items reflected self- or social guarding. This process reduced the SCMP-G from 59 items to 48 items. The item-to-subscale congruence index for the 48-item instrument was .92.

Testing of the SCMP-G occurred in two phases. During the first phase, the instrument was administered to seven adults with chronic illness to check readability of the instrument and clarity of the instructions, identifying items that were unclear or difficult to understand. The subjects found all items understandable. Minor changes were made in four items.

During the second phase, the SCMP-G was tested for internal consistency. A total of 56 adults with chronic illnesses completed the SCMP-G and a set of demographic and illness background questions.

Individuals were recruited from outpatient clinics and a diabetic education program in the Gulf Coast area of Mississippi and Louisiana. All subjects had been diagnosed with an illness of at least 6 months duration that necessitated that they follow some type of treatment regimen. The sample consisted of 35 females and 21 males. The main ethnic identification was white; 51 were white and 5 were black. Subjects ranged in age from 26 to 84 years, with a mean of 58.5 years. Forty subjects were married, 10 were single, and 5 were widowed. A total of 44 had completed high school, and of these, 23 had completed at least 2 years of technical training or college. Subjects' family income ranged from less than $10,000 to $70,000 a year, with over 60% reporting incomes of less than $30,000. Although the majority of the subjects (n = 30) had diabetes, 17 subjects reported having diabetes and another major illness. Nine subjects reported having a chronic illness other than diabetes.

The time since diagnosis ranged from less than 1 year to 43 years. Only 5 subjects had had their illness for 1 year or less, and 38 individuals reported having had their illness for more than 6 years. Subjects rated the severity of their illnesses on a scale of 1 (mild) to 7 (severe), in comparison with other individuals with the same illness. Severity scores ranged from 1 to 7, with a mean of 4.09 and a standard deviation of 1.79.

The SCMP-G was refined through item analysis. During this step, items decreasing the reliability of the instrument through low correlations and items artificially inflating the internal consistency estimate because of item redundancy are identified (Hinshaw & Atwood, 1982; McIver & Carmines, 1981). Only items that demonstrated a large range of subject responses and had item-to-subscale and item-to-total correlations of .20 to .70 were retained. A total of 12 items were deleted (6 from each subscale) because item-to-subscale, item-to-total, and interitem correlations were below .20.

The mean, standard deviation, alpha reliability coefficient, and number of items for the toal SCMP-G and the social and self subscales are reported in Table 5.3. Nunnally (1978) cited the reliability criterion level of .70 for new psychosocial instruments and .80 for mature scales. Both subscales exceeded the criterion level for new instruments.

The self and social subscales were significantly positively related to the total SCMP-G scale. The two SCMP-G subscales, however, were slightly negatively correlated (–.03). This low correlation indicates that the two

TABLE 5.3 Means, Standard Deviations, and Alpha Coefficients of Modified SCMP-G and Subscales (n = 56)

Scale	Mean	*SD*	Alpha	No. of Items
SCMP-G	120.41	10.40	.75	35
Self	74.39	7.36	.78	20
Social	46.02	7.59	.78	15

SCMP-G subscales are more or less statistically independent, sharing less than 10% of the common variance.

DISCUSSION AND CONCLUSIONS

Initial reliability testing provides beginning evidence of the psychometric properties of self- and social guarding. The internal consistency coefficients for self- and social guarding indicate an acceptable stability. The very low negative correlation between these two scales suggests that combining them is not fruitful and that the subscales should be used as separate measures of self- and social guarding.

A great deal of additional psychometric research is needed. Work is underway to establish the test–retest reliability and construct validity through factor analysis of the SCMP-G. Further testing of the SCMP-G is critical for future research of guarding.

Several areas of inquiry concerning guarding seem particularly promising. For example, further exploration of the antecedents and consequences of guarding is needed. The Jones et al. (1986) study revealed that the vigilant monitoring and controlling nature of guarding requires a great deal of self-investment and mobilization of energy. Some individuals spoke of not being able to "police" their treatment or of "losing control" at times. These instances of "failed" guarding were most evident when individuals were very ill and lacked the energy to invest in guarding or when threats were perceived as too unpredictable or difficult to control. The number of instances of guarding was much higher for some individuals than for others with the same illness. Do individuals who exhibit high guarding overestimate potential harm from threats? Although some amount of guarding may help, the consequences of using too much guarding may exact a severe energy cost.

Self- and social guarding appear to serve different functions. Whereas some individuals in the Jones et al. (1986) study used both types of guarding, others used little social guarding. Does low use of social guarding result in high stress within the social network, eventually leading to low levels of social support being offered to the chronically ill individual? Conversely, does the use of social guarding protect the network from stress, thereby helping the network maintain the ability to return social support over a long period of time to the individual with chronic illness? Serious programmatic research efforts, as described in this chapter, are needed to advance clinical nursing knowledge.

REFERENCES

Beutel, M. (1985). Approaches to taxonomy and measurement of adaptation in chronic disease. *Psychotherapeutic Psychosomatics, 43,* 177–185.

Bloom, J. R. (1982). Social support, accommodation to stress and adjustment to breast cancer. *Social Science and Medicine, 16,* 1329–1338.

Bogdan, R. C., & Biklen, S. K. (1982). *Qualitative research for education.* New York: John Wiley

Brugge, P. A. (1981). *The relationship between family as a social support system, health status, and experience of self-care agency in the adult with a chronic illness.* Unpublished doctoral dissertation, Wayne State University, Detroit.

Bury, M. R., & Wood, P. (1979). Problems of communication in chronic illness. *International Rehabilitation Medicine, 1,* 130–134.

Campbell, D. T. (1979). Degrees of freedom and the case study. In T. D. Cook & C. S. Reichardt (Eds.), *Qualitative and quantitative research* (pp. 49–67). Beverly Hills, CA: Sage.

Chang, B. L. (1980). Evaluation of health care professionals in facilitating self-care: Review of the literature and a conceptual model. *Advances in Nursing Science, 3,* 43–58.

Chenitz, W. C., & Swanson, J. M. (1986). *From practice to grounded theory: Qualitative research in nursing.* Menlo Park, CA: Addison-Wesley.

Cohen, F., & Lazarus, R. (1979). Coping with the stresses of illness. In G. Stone, F. Cohen, & N. Adler, *Health Psychology* (pp. 217–254). San Francisco: Jossey-Bass.

Copp, L. A. (1974). The spectrum of suffering. *American Journal of Nursing, 74,* 491–495.

Craig, H. M., & Edwards, J. E. (1983). Adaptation in chronic illness: An eclectic model for nurses. *Journal of Advanced Nursing, 8,* 397–404.

Davis, A. J. (1981). Commentaries. *Western Journal of Nursing Research, 3,* 268.

Dean, K. (1981). Self-care responses to illness: A selected review. *Social Science and Medicine, 15A,* 673–687.

Dean, K. (1986). Lay care in illness. *Social Science and Medicine, 22,* 275–284.

Dimond, M. (1980). Patient strategies for managing maintenance hemodialysis. *Western Journal of Nursing, 2,* 555–573.

Fleming, R., Baum, A., & Singer, J. E. (1984). Toward an integrative approach to the study of stress. *Journal of Personality and Social Psychology, 46,* 939–949.

Forsyth, G. L., Delaney, K. D., & Gresham, M. L. (1984). Vying for a winning position: Management style of the chronically ill. *Research in Nursing and Health, 7,* 181–188.

Glaser, B. (1978). *Theoretical sensitivity.* Mill Valley, CA: Sociology Press.

Glaser, B., & Strauss, A. (1967). *The discovery of grounded theory: Strategies for qualitative research.* Chicago: Aldine.

Grieco, A. L., & Kopel, K. F. (1983). Self-help and self-care in chronic illness. *Southern Medical Journal, 76,* 1128–1130.

Hinshaw, A. S., & Atwood, J. R. (1982). A patient satisfaction instrument: Precision by replication. *Nursing Research, 31,* 170–175, 191.

Huffman, D. M. (1987). *Development of an instrument to measure use of self-care management processes—guarding (SCMP-G).* Unpublished master's thesis, Louisiana State University Medical Center, New Orleans.

Jones, L. C., Hill, K., Honer, K., & McDaniels, S. (1986). *Self-care management processes used by individuals with chronic illness.* Unpublished manuscript.

Jones, L. C., & Preuett, S. (1986). Self-care activities and processes used by hemodialysis patients. *American Nephrology Nurses Association Journal, 13,* 73–79.

Kennison, B. J. (1983). *Nurses and patients: The clinical reality of sickness.* Unpublished doctoral dissertation, University of Michigan, Ann Arbor.

Kleinman, A. (1978). Concepts and a model for the comparison of medical systems as cultural system. *Social Science and Medicine, 12,* 85–93.

Leventhal, H., Leventhal, E. A., & Nguyen, T. V. (1985). Reactions of families to illness: Theoretical models and perspectives. In D. C. Turks & R. D. Kerns

(Eds.). *Health, illness and families: A life-span perspective.* New York: John Wiley & Sons.

Levin, L. S. (1978). Patient education and self-care: How do they differ? *Nursing Outlook, 26,* 170–175.

Lincoln, Y. S., & Guba, E. G. (1985). *Naturalistic inquiry.* Beverly Hills, CA: Sage.

Lynn, M. R. (1986). Determination and quantification of content validity. *Nursing Research, 35,* 382–385.

McIver, J. P., & Carmines, E. G. (1981). *Unidimensional scaling.* Beverly Hills, CA: Sage.

Miles, M. G., & Huberman, A. M. (1984). *Qualitative data analysis.* Beverly Hills, CA: Sage.

Miller, J. F. (1983). Coping with chronic illness. In J. F. Miller (Ed.), *Coping with chronic illness: Overcoming powerlessness* (pp. 15–35). Philadelphia: F. A. Davis.

Moos, R. H., & Tsu, V. D. (1979). The crisis of physical illness: An overview. In R. H. Moos (Ed.), *Coping with physical illness* (pp. 3–21). New York: Plenum Medical Book.

Nunnally, J. C. (1978). *Psychometric theory.* New York: McGraw Hill.

O'Brien, M. E. (1984). *The courage to survive: The life career of the chronic dialysis patient.* New York: Grune & Stratton.

Orem, D. (1985). A concept of self-care for the rehabilitation client. *Rehabilitation Nursing, 10,* 33–36.

Ray, C., Lindop, J., & Gipson, S. (1982). The concept of coping. *Psychological Medicine, 12,* 385–395.

Reid, D. W. (1984). Participatory control and the chronic illness adjustment process. In H. M. Lefcourt (Ed.), *Research with the locus of control construct: Extensions and limitations* (Vol. 3, pp. 361–389) New York: Academic Press.

Singer, J. E. (1984). Some issues in the study of coping, *Cancer, 53,* 2303–2313.

Stone, A. A., & Neale, J. M. (1984). New measures of daily coping: Development and preliminary results. *Journal of Personality and Social Psychology, 46,* 892–906.

Strauss, A. L., Corbin, J., Fagerhaugh, S., Glaser, B. G., Maines, D., Suczek, B., & Wiener, C. L. (1984). *Chronic illness and the quality of life* (2nd ed.). Toronto: Mosby.

Taylor, S. E. (1984). Response. *Cancer, 53,* 2313–2315.

U.S. Department of Health, Education and Welfare (1979). *The surgeon general's report on health promotion and disease prevention* (PHS Publication No. 79–55071). Washington DC: U.S. Government Printing Office.

Viney, L. L., & Westbrook, M. T. (1982). Coping with chronic illness: The mediating role of biographic and illness-related factors. *Journal of Psychosomatic Research, 26,* 595–605.

Viney, L. L., & Westbrook, M. T. (1984). Coping with chronic illness: Strategy preferences, changes in preferences and associated emotional reactions. *Journal of Chronic Diseases, 37,* 489–502.

Walker, L. O., & Avant, K. C. (1983). *Strategies for theory construction in nursing.* Norwalk, CN: Appleton-Century-Crofts.

Woods, N. F. (1985). Self-care practices among young adult married women. *Research in Nursing and Health, 8,* 227–233.

Zabielski, M. T. (1984). Giving and receiving in the neomaternal period: A case of distributive inequity. *Maternal-Child Nursing Journal, 13,* 19–46.

SCMP-G Questionnaire

Directions:

An illness may require many changes in your life. The purpose of these questions is to find out how different people deal with their illness.

There are no right or wrong answers. For each statement, circle the answer that best describes your thoughts. Please answer all questions.

	Strongly Disagree				Strongly Agree
1. I worry about being a bother because of my illness.	1	2	3	4	5
2. I have made up my mind that I can control my illness.	1	2	3	4	5
3. My illness does not affect my family and friends.	1	2	3	4	5
4. Pleasing other people is more important than my health.	1	2	3	4	5
5. I worry that I am a bother to other people.	1	2	3	4	5
6. I must do all I can to control my illness.	1	2	3	4	5
7. I am responsible for making sure my illness does not worry other people.	1	2	3	4	5
8. I have to be careful with the way I live my life.	1	2	3	4	5
9. My illness has affected my relationships with friends.	1	2	3	4	5
10. I don't do certain things, because then people would worry about my health.	1	2	3	4	5
11. I worry that if I don't follow my treatment plan, my illness will worsen.	1	2	3	4	5
12. I am troubled that people treat me differently because of my illness.	1	2	3	4	5
13. Even though I think a lot about my illness, I try not to talk about it.	1	2	3	4	5
14. I try to convince other people to change the way they live so they won't develop my health problems.	1	2	3	4	5

15. It is hard to plan activities, because I never know whether my illness will keep me from doing things.	1	2	3	4	5
16. I must have a positive attitude about my illness for the sake of others.	1	2	3	4	5
17. My illness makes other people uncomfortable.	1	2	3	4	5
18. I only think about my illness when it causes me problems.	1	2	3	4	5
19. I don't think about my illness as I do daily activities.	1	2	3	4	5
20. I have changed the way I live to improve my health.	1	2	3	4	5
21. I tell people about my illness so they will understand if I'm out of sorts and they won't take it personally.	1	2	3	4	5
22. I can control my illness if I follow my treatment plan.	1	2	3	4	5
23. If I take care of myself, I can prevent further problems with my illness.	1	2	3	4	5
24. I am careful about how much I tell other people about my illness, because I don't want to trouble them.	1	2	3	4	5
25. I check myself for signs that my illness is changing.	1	2	3	4	5
26. When I make daily plans, I think about my illness.	1	2	3	4	5
27. I watch for signs that my illness is getting worse.	1	2	3	4	5
28. There is little I can do to control my illness.	1	2	3	4	5
29. I think about my health a great deal.	1	2	3	4	5
30. It is important to follow a routine so I can lead a normal life.	1	2	3	4	5
31. I manage my illness by learning all I can about it.	1	2	3	4	5
32. I have changed the way I live so that I can control my illness.	1	2	3	4	5
33. My life revolves around my treatment plan.	1	2	3	4	5
34. I must watch my health or it will get worse.	1	2	3	4	5
35. I go out of my way to make people feel comfortable with my illness.	1	2	3	4	5

PART II
Measuring Coping Ability in Patients with Chronic Illness

6

Measuring Social Support in Chronic Illness

Gail A. Hilbert

This chapter discusses the Social Support in Chronic Illness Inventory, a measure of the perceived satisfaction with social support received by chronically ill persons.

Social support is a concept that has received much attention in the literature in recent years because of its stress buffering and its direct effects on a variety of health-related outcomes. Nurses have intuitively involved the patient's support system when planning care, realizing that family and friends are important influences. If nurses are to involve the support system more effectively for patients with chronic illness, they need to know which behaviors are supportive, in which situations, and who is best able to provide those kinds of support.

However, there have been problems in designing research to provide that knowledge because of inadequate conceptualization and measurement of the support variable. This becomes increasingly important as experts in the field of social support (Gottlieb, 1985; Norbeck, 1985; Tilden, 1985b; Wortman & Conway, 1985) call for clinically focused social support studies with the use of situation-specific measures. Norbeck (1985) suggests that rather than having a series of instruments—one for each chronic illness—an instrument be developed that addresses the commonalities in the demands of coping with a chronic illness. Therefore, the purposes of this chapter are to review the literature in order to clarify the concept of social support and summarize the properties of existing instruments and to describe the development of a tool for the measurement of social support related to chronic illness.

This research was supported by a grant from Xi Chapter of Sigma Theta Tau.

REVIEW OF THE LITERATURE

Theoretical Considerations

Domain of Social Support

House and Kahn (1985) define the domain of social support by stating that it is necessary to consider three aspects of social relationships as part of the general domain of social support because they are logically and empirically interrelated: (1) the existence or quantity of relationships, (2) the structure of a person's social relationships, and (3) the functional content of relationships. Such terms as *social integration* and *social isolation* are most often used to refer to the existence or quantity of relationships. The term *social network* refers to the structures existing among a set of relations. In a specific sense, *social support* is most commonly used to mean the last of these three aspects, the functional content of relationships. However, social support encompasses all three aspects of social relationships, as the term is used to describe the global concept of support.

Definitions

There is a wide variety of definitions of social support in the literature, ranging from one sentence to complex typologies. Cobb's (1976) classic definition describes support as "information leading the subject to believe that he is cared for and loved, esteemed and member of a network of mutual obligations" (p. 300). Social support has also been defined in a less interpersonal way as "any input, directly provided by an individual (or group), which moves the receiver of that input toward goals which the receiver desires" (Caplan, Robinson, French, Caldwell, & Shinn, 1976, p. 221).

More complex definitions tend to enumerate the specific activities that provide support. Caplan (1974) outlined three broad themes involved in support: helping the individual mobilize psychological resources, helping in the mastery of emotional burdens, and sharing the individual's tasks and providing extra supplies (money, materials, skills, guidance) to improve handling of the situation.

Gottlieb (1978) has used one of the few inductive approaches to define social support. Based on a content analysis of 40 subjects, he identified four categories of helping behaviors: emotionally sustaining behaviors, problem-solving behaviors, indirect personal influence (perceived availability of help), and environmental advocacy (social advocacy on behalf of another). It is thought that this inductive approach lent credibility to the deductive definitions previously cited (House, 1981).

Using a deductive approach, Barrera and Ainlay (1983) reviewed the social support literature to that date in order to identify points of confluence that could be organized into a rational typology of support functions. The result was six categories of supportive behaviors:

1. Material aid: providing tangible materials in the form of money and other physical objects.
2. Behavioral assistance: sharing of tasks through physical labor.
3. Intimate interaction: traditional nondirective counseling behaviors such as listening and expressing esteem, caring, and understanding.
4. Guidance: offering advice, information, or instruction.
5. Feedback: providing individuals with feedback about their behavior, thoughts, or feelings.
6. Positive social interaction: engaging in social interactions for fun and relaxation.

Comparison of the previously cited definitions reveals many commonalities across definitions, even though the terminology varies. In addition to material resources, most definitions refer to an emotional component, such as love or attachment; an informational component, such as guidance; and an appraisal or positive feedback component. Barrera and Ainlay's (1983) typology separates tangible assistance into material aid and behavioral assistance. However, their factor analysis of the scale based on that typology indicated that these two items loaded together and essentially represented a single factor, which was termed tangible assistance. The original items relating to guidance and feedback also loaded together and formed a single factor termed directive guidance. This category of assistance is comparable to House's (1981) information and appraisal categories and Weiss's (1974) obtaining of guidance. Barrera and Ainlay's category of intimate interaction includes expressions of intimacy, unconditional availability, esteem, and trust. The last category, positive social interaction, represents a category of social support often missing in other conceptualizations. The authors state that support need not be restricted to crisis situations and that social interaction represents a growth-enhancing aspect of social support.

Assumptions

A review of the literature reveals a number of assumptions underlying the measurement of social support. First, it is assumed that the conceptualization of social support should be based on theory that is explicitly specified (Tilden, 1985b). This is of particular importance to nursing, a discipline that is in the beginning stages of theory development. Tilden noted that much social support research has failed to anchor definitions in any explanatory theory whatsoever and mentioned the possibility of using theories related to attachment, role, stress and coping, social exchange, interactionalism and ecology of host resistance, and vulnerability.

Second, there has long been the assumption that social support is always positive or beneficial (Antonucci & Depner, 1982). One is tempted to define support as behavior that is supportive or helpful (Wilcox & Vernberg, 1985). Not only is such a definition circular, but there are also indications that "behaviors which might appear to be supportive, which might seem to reflect empathy and understanding, may in fact be countertherapeutic under certain conditions" (p. 9). Support that is intended to be positive may be negative either because the objective outcome is negative or the recipient of the support perceives the support negatively (Antonucci, 1985).

Support attempts directed toward victims of life crises may be unhelpful because they discourage discussion of the victim's problems, encourage the victim to recover more quickly, or rely on scripted or automatic supportive behaviors, such as giving advice (Wortman & Lehman, 1985). Support providers for those who are physically ill may hold misconceptions about the process of coping with an illness, or they may lack understanding of the illness itself. Unlike healthy individuals, the physically ill are often thrust into relationships that are not egalitarian or reciprocal. Finally, "because illness often evokes negative feelings in others, the physically ill are likely to find that their closest and most important relationships are characterized by both positive and negative elements" (Wortman & Conway, 1985, p. 294).

Gottlieb (1983) comments on the negative aspects of the network, stating that a network may victimize a member, impose too much control, or fail to mobilize support. In addition, some bonds may have harmful side effects, such as the isolation and low prestige of the housewife role (Antonucci & Depner, 1982).

Several authors have commented on the cost of social support in terms of the expectation of reciprocity (Antonucci, 1985; Tilden, 1985a; Wortman & Conway, 1985). The one-sided giving of support may not only become overburdening for the provider but may also do a disservice to the recipient because it fosters dependency. Wortman and Conway (1985) suggest measuring behaviors perceived as negative along with those judged as positive. Tilden (1985a) reports the development of an instrument to measure cost, conflict, reciprocity, and equity in intimate relationships. As she so succinctly points out, "social support is neither free nor unilaterally benevolent" (Tilden, 1985b, p. 203).

Finally, there is an assumption in the literature that properties of the individual, as well as properties of the situation, jointly determine the need for social support (Norbeck, 1981). Bruhn and Philips (1984) concur, stating that environment and physical factors should be included, in addition to social, interpersonal, and cultural factors, in developing the concept of social support.

Tilden (1985b) delineates properties of the person to include such factors as social competence, introversion–extroversion, desire for stimulation, life stage, ego strength, and object relationships. She goes on to say that properties of the situation are such things as finances, family structure, and health status. Wilcox and Vernberg (1985), as well as Norbeck (1981), discuss individual differences in the need for support, the propensity to seek support, and the social competence necessary for attracting and maintaining a support network. In addition, there is much data to suggest that there are fundamental sex differences in both the nature and function of social support (Antonucci, 1985).

CONCEPTUAL BASIS OF THE MEASURE

The theoretical framework on which the development of the Social Support in Chronic Illness Inventory (SSCII) was based is twofold: the concept of the convoy (Kahn, 1979; Kahn & Quinn, 1976) and a model for stress, coping, and health (Hogue, 1977; Kahn, 1979).

Kahn and Quinn (1976) define the convoy as a metaphorical term implying "that each person can be thought of as moving through life surrounded by a set of significant other people to whom that person is related by giving or receiving of social support" (p. 10). This concept bears similarity to role set but differs in two important ways. First, it is defined by the giving and receiving of social support rather than by a person's position in a formal organization. Second, and perhaps more important, the convoy implies movement, whereas a role is more static.

The concept of the convoy was chosen for the development of the present instrument because it carries with it the notions of person–environment interaction and change over time, both important in the conceptualization of nursing. The convoy implies that support needs change with time and are dependent on the characteristics of the person and the environment. This is seen to be congruent with an instrument that measures social support in chronic illness as supplied by individuals who are most important to the recipient at that point in his or her life cycle. It is expected that the amount and kinds of support needed will vary with characteristics of the individual and characteristics of the illness but that patterns will emerge that will be useful to nurses who are assessing social support resources of clients and planning interventions to increase support when deficiencies are noted.

The model of stress, coping, and health is a combination of those used by Kahn and Quinn (1976) and Hogue (1977). The former focus on the social support convoy and the latter on the more specific steps of the stress-coping model.

In this model, personal and social resources are considered together as coping resources, both of which determine whether or not potentially threatening situations lead to responses supportive of health or illness. "Coping resources may influence whether or not situations are perceived as threatening to a given person; they may allow persons who perceive threat to deal creatively with the threat, and/or they may influence the impact of health changes on the individual" (Hogue, 1977, p. 66). Kahn (1979) sees the research utility of the convoy in the specification and measurement of properties of the convoy as a whole, as well as properties of the separate dyadic links between the focal person and each of the convoy members.

The theoretical definition used in the development of the SSCII is based on Barrera and Ainlay's (1983) review of the social support literature. Social support is defined as a diversity of natural helping behaviors of which individuals are recipients in social interactions: tangible aid (material aid and behavioral assistance), intimate interaction, guidance, feedback, and positive social interaction. This definition is congruent with the theoretical framework and was chosen because (1) it is based on a review of the extant social support literature, (2) it subsumes most other categories of support that have been deductively derived, and (3) it is compatible with Gottlieb's (1978) categories of natural helping behaviors, which were inductively derived.

The SSCII is used for support in relation to chronic illness, such as hypertension, diabetes, cardiac disease, and end stage renal disease. All of these diagnoses carry with them the necessity for long-term life-style adjustments, especially in the areas of activity, diet, and medication. As several authors have noted (Cohen & Syme, 1985; Dimond, 1985), it is important to examine the need for support longitudinally, an approach that is congruent with the theoretical framework of the convoy.

The concept of the convoy does not include the dimension of organized support. Kahn and Quinn (1976) define convoys as "natural helping groups" (p. 4). The items that were developed for the SSCII cover the broad range of supportive behaviors, many of which are found primarily in natural supportive relationships such as expressions of affection and spending time together in social interaction. Therefore, the questionnaire has less utility for assessing supportive functions of organized relationships.

The SSCII is designed in such a way that responses may be subjective or objective, in the sense that the items may be completed by either the recipient or the provider of the support in relation to the frequency with which the behaviors are supplied. Respondents may also be asked to indicate the quality of the support received by indicating their degree of satisfaction with each behavior, as indicated in the directions on the questionnaire at the end of this chapter.

PURPOSE OF THE MEASURE

The purpose of the instrument is to examine behaviors supplied by individuals in a specific situation: chronic illness. The decision to develop a specific measure has implications for decisions on a number of other dimensions of support.

For example, because of the specificity of the instrument, the unit of analysis will be the dyadic relationship or group rather than the network. The instrument is designed in such a way that the respondent may give information in relation to any individual or in relation to a specific group of individuals such as friends or fellow workers. As House and Kahn (1985) have suggested, subjects could nominate persons who are close or important to them. It would also be possible to examine support from various individuals or groups in relation to outcomes in order to determine the differential effect of the source of support.

PROCEDURES FOR DEVELOPMENT

The literature was reviewed to locate social support measures that focus on specific behaviors of supportive individuals rather than on the network or global measures of satisfaction with received support. Four scales were located that contained specific behaviors contributing to social support for individuals in a variety of situations: the Inventory of Socially Supportive Behaviors (ISSB) (Barrera & Ainlay, 1983), Social Support Items (SSI) (Lin, Dean, & Ensel, 1981), the Social Support Questionnaire (SSQ) (Sarason, Levine, Basham, & Sarason, 1983), and the Perceived Support for Friends/Family (PSS-Fr, PSS-Fa) (Procidano & Heller, 1983). Additionally, two instruments were located that were appropriate for health-related situations: the Support Behaviors Inventory (SBI) (Brown, 1986) and the Spouse Support Questionnaire (SSQ) (Hilbert, 1983). However, none of these instruments measures all aspects of social support in relation to chronic illness.

Forty-five items were developed for the SSCII based on the literature, previously developed questionnaires, and interviews with myocardial infarction (MI) patients (Hilbert, 1983). Sixty-four percent of the items are from the SSQ (Hilbert, 1983), which included items from the ISSB (Barrera & Ainlay, 1983).

A decision was made to measure perceived satisfaction with each of the supportive behaviors. The literature review indicated conflicting opinions about whether quality is a more significant dimension than quantity. However, previous research with MI patients indicated that satisfaction with support appeared to be more important than the number of times a behavior occurred (Hilbert, 1983).

ADMINISTRATION AND SCORING

The items were placed on a 6-point Likert scale ranging from "Dissatisfied" to "Very Satisfied." Using a paper-and-pencil format, subjects were instructed to "identify the one person who is most important to you at the present time. In the past month, how satisfied were you with the helping behaviors of that person toward you? Indicate your degree of satisfaction with each behavior listed by circling the number that applies. The number

1 indicates dissatisfaction. The number 6 indicates that you are very satisfied."

Scores for each of the 38 items are summed, with a possible range of 38 to 228. The higher the score, the greater the degree of satisfaction with the support supplied by the person named as most important to the subject. Time required for completing the questionnaire is 10 to 15 minutes. General support items were included for all categories of Barrera and Ainlay's (1983) social support. Specific items were included for guidance and feedback. Material aid and behavioral assistance were combined to form a Tangible Assistance subscale, based on the report of a factor analysis that showed those items loading together (Barrera & Ainlay, 1983) and in order to have each subscale contain at least four items. As shown in Figure 6.1, items 1 to 10 form the Intimate Interaction subscale; 11–17 and 30–36, the Guidance subscale; 18–20, 37, and 38, the Feedback subscale; 21–24, the Tangible Assistance subscale; and 25–29, the Positive Social Interaction subscale.

RELIABILITY AND VALIDITY ASSESSMENTS

Content validity was determined by two experts in the area of social support. These experts rated each of the 45 original items on relevancy to the purpose of the instrument on a 4-point scale. The 38 items with 100% agreement as very relevant or quite relevant were retained. The result was 29 general-support items and 9 chronic illness–specific items (see Figure 6.1).

SAMPLE

For the present study, chronic illness was defined as an altered health state that will not be cured by a simple surgical procedure or a short course of therapy (Miller, 1983). A sample size of 190 was recruited from a variety of sites, including diabetic education centers, blood pressure screenings, health fairs, hemiodialysis clinics, and cardiac rehabilitation centers. Delimitations included no concurrent acute illness and a diagnosis of at least one of the following: hypertension, diabetes, cardiac disease, or end stage renal disease. Informed consent was obtained.

A little more than half (54%) of the sample were females. Average age was 56 years; average education was 13 years. The majority of subjects were white (76%), with 19% black, 4% American Indian, and 1% Hispanic. Two thirds were married, and 14% were widowed. Forty-nine percent had diabetes; 35%, heart disease; 66%, hypertension; and 35%, end stage renal disease. This adds up to over 100% because many had more than one diagnosis. Average time since diagnosis was as follows: diabetes, 12 years; heart disease, 7 years; hypertension, 12 years; and end stage renal disease, 2.7 years. Fifty-eight percent of respondents named the spouse as the most supportive person, with daughter named in second place in 13% of responses.

Results

Distributions

The range for this sample was 74 to 228, with 36 subjects (19% of the sample) having the maximum score of 228. The mean was 195, and the standard deviation was 33.9.

Reliability

Reliability procedures were determined on the basis of the SSCII being a norm-referenced measure (Waltz, Strickland, & Lenz, 1984). Coefficient alpha for the total scale was .98. Reliability coefficients for the subscales ranged from .84 to .94, as shown in Table 6.1. The individual items demonstrated item-to-total correlations ranging from .56 to .87. All items met the criterion of .30 to .70 correlation with at least 50% of the total items (Kerlinger, 1986). Correlations between subscales ranged from .56 to .87.

Test–retest reliability was done for 26 subjects, using a 2-week interval. The Pearson correlation coefficient was .48. It should be noted that social support does change over time.

Factor Analysis

A principal-component factor analysis without iteration (Nie, Hull, Jenkins, Steinbrenner, & Bent, 1970) was done as an assessment of construct validity. There was a subject-to-item ratio of 5 to 1 for the factor analysis procedure. Inspection of the eigenvalues of the factors, the points of discontinuity of the percentage of explained variance, and distribution of the variables within the factors did not substantiate the five theorized factors. Using the criteria of including variables that loaded at .40 or higher

TABLE 6.1 Reliabilities and Intercorrelations of Support Subscales

	Intimate interaction	Guidance	Feedback	Tangible aid	Positive social interaction
Intimate interaction	[.95]	.80	.75	.56	.78
Guidance		[.95]	.87	.69	.70
Feedback			[.93]	.69	.81
Tangible aid				[.84]	.67
Positive social interaction					[.92]

Note. Numbers in brackets are internal consistency reliability coefficients.

FIGURE 6.1 Derivation and content mapping of items on the SSCII.

Content	Factors	General items	Factors	Specific items
Intimate interaction	I	[a] 1. Told me that I am OK just the way I am.		
	I	[a] 2. Comforted me by showing some physical affection.		
	I	[a] 3. Let me know that (s)he can be counted on if I need help.		
	I	[a] 4. Expressed interest and concern in my well-being		
	I	[a] 5. Told me that (s)he feels very close to me.		
	I	[c] 6. Was available to listen when I wanted to talk.		
	I	[d] 7. Enjoyed hearing about what I think.		
	I	[e] 8. Consoled me when I was upset.		
	I	[d] 9. Allowed me to come to him/her when I was feeling down.		
	I	[e]10. Accepted me totally, including my worst and best parts		
Guidance		[a]11. Made it clear what was expected of me.		
		[a]12. Gave me some information on how to do something.	II	[b]30. Shared information with me about recommendations that were made by the health team.
		[a]13. Gave me some information to help me understand a situation I was in.	II	31. Helped me to understand about my disease.
		[a]14. Told me who I should see for assistance.	II	[b]32. Told me whom I should see for assistance when I had problems with the health team recommendations.
		[a]15. Told me what to expect in a situation that was about to happen.	II	[b]33. Told me how useful the health team recommendations were in preventing complications.
		[a]16. Taught me how to do something.	II	[b]34. Taught me how to carry out the health team recommenda-

		[c]17. Talked with me about a problem in order to help me solve it.	II	35. Talked with me about problems I was having with the health team recommendations.
				[g]36. Encouraged me to take proper care of myself.
Feedback		[a]18. Checked back with me to see if I had followed the advice I was given.		[b]37. Checked back to see if I had carried out recommendations I consider important.
		[a]19. Helped me understand why I didn't do something well.		
		[a]20. Gave me feedback on how I was doing without saying it was good or bad.		[b]38. Commented favorably when (s)he noticed me doing something that the health team recommended.
Material Aid		[b]21. Contributed to my income or gave me money.		
		22. Gave me a gift.		
Behavioral assistance		[b]23. Did a task that is usually done by me.		
		24. Provided transportation for me.		
Positive social interaction		[a]25. Did some activity together to help me get my mind off of things.		
		[a]26. Talked with me about some interests of mine.		
	III	[a]27. Joked or kidded to try to cheer me up.		
	I	[d]28. Shared an interest.		
	III	[e]29. Could count on her/him to distract me from worries.		

[a]ISSB
[b]SSQ-Hilbert
[c]SSI
[d]PSS-Fr, PSS-Fa
[e]SSQ-Sarason et al.
[f]SSI
[g]Gottlieb

TABLE 6.2 Factor Analysis for SSCI

	Eigenvalue	% Variance	Cumulative %
Factor I	21.48	56.5	56.5
Factor II	3.23	8.5	65.0
Factor III	1.58	4.2	69.2

and also showed at least .15 difference from high loadings on other factors, three factors were identified. These factors are noted in Figure 6.1.

Factor I clearly included all of the items that were theorized to measure intimate interaction. One additional variable loaded on that factor: "shared an interest" (positive social interaction). Factor II included six of the seven items in the specific guidance subscale. Factor III included two of the five items from Positive Social Interaction. All of the Positive Social Interaction items also loaded at .40 or above on Factor I.

The drop in eigenvalues after Factor I, as shown in Table 6.2, indicated one main factor and two less important factors. Although this may have been an indication that social support in chronic illness is a unidimensional concept, it may also have been an artifact of the principal-component factor analysis, which searches for the most economical set of relationships that are expressed in the first factor. These results also may be the result of the sample size. Although the sample size was minimally acceptable given the number of items on the tool, Nunnally (1978) suggests a subject-to-item ratio of 10 to 1 for stable results when using factor analysis.

To further test the one-factor solution, a Rao canonical factor analysis was done (Nie et al., 1970). This procedure seeks a specified number of factors to account for the observed correlation matrix. The results confirmed the one main factor explanation in that the first factor accounted for 74.4% of the variance.

DISCUSSION AND CONCLUSIONS

The high mean for the total social support scale, as well as the fact that 19% of the subjects circled 6 for each item, indicates that, for the present sample, perceived social support was not normally distributed. The negative skew may result from the fact that subjects were asked to select the individual in their support system who was most helpful. One would expect that there would be greater satisfaction with that person than with others in the support system. If subjects had been asked to rate their satisfaction with the total support system, there might have been a more normal distribution of scores.

The high reliability for the total scale, the correlations among subscales, and the results of the factor analyses suggest that social support in chronic illness is a unidimensional concept. However, the factors that did emerge are consistent with three of the five categories of support that were theorized. Reports in the literature on unidimensionality versus multidimensionality of support are conflicting. Although Barrera and Ainlay (1983) reported four categories of supportive behavior based on their factor analysis of the ISSB, Stokes and Wilson (1984) found the ISSB to be a global measure of support. Brown (1986) reported a dominant construct of social support during pregnancy that organized at the broad level. In the study of MI patients, Hilbert (1983) found two clearly delineated categories of support that were similar to intimate interaction and directive guidance.

The variations in the findings may have been caused by the homogeneous versus heterogeneous nature of the samples. It may be that several dimensions of support emerge in clearly delimited samples experiencing similar stresses. For the present study it would appear that for those with chronic illness, emotional support and specific guidance are important factors in their perceptions of social support, with emotional support emerging as the primary factor.

The majority of subjects in the present sample were beyond the period of initial adjustment to the demands of their illness. For them, generalized emotional support would assume more importance than specific guidance. The specific guidance factor was second in importance and clearly less significant. The results of the factor analysis might have been different for those who were newly diagnosed. Those individuals would need more guidance in carrying out the specific demands of the regimens.

Further development of the instrument includes adding subjects to the data set to increase the number to 380, or 10 subjects per item. Eventually, a shortened version of the SSCII will be developed on the basis of factor analysis with the larger sample size.

Further validation studies include the experimental manipulation approach to construct validity, which uses the theoretical framework underlying the questionnaire's design to state hypotheses regarding the behavior of individuals with varying scores on the measure. The hypotheses are then tested, and inferences are made on the basis of the findings regarding whether or not the underlying rationale is adequate (Waltz et al., 1984). This study, now in the proposal stage, involves testing the hypothesis that MI patients with higher levels of social support will experience less emotional distress and more positive physical outcomes at 3 and 6 months posthospitalization.

REFERENCES

Antonucci, T. (1985). Social support: Theoretical advances, recent findings and pressing issues. In I. G. Sarason & B. R. Sarason (Eds.), *Social support: Theory, research and applications* (pp. 78–91). Dordrecht, Netherlands: Martinus Nijhoff.

Antonucci, T. C., & Depner, C. F. (1982). Social support and informal helping relationships. In T. A. Wells (Ed.), *Basic processes in helping relationships* (pp. 233–254). New York: Academic Press.

Barrera, M., & Ainlay, S. L. (1983). The structure of social support: A conceptual and empirical analysis. *Journal of Community Psychology, 11,* 133–143.

Brown, M. A. (1986). Social support during pregnancy: A unidimensional or multidimensional construct? *Nursing Research, 35,* 4–9.

Bruhn, J. G., & Phillips, B. V. (1984). Measuring social support: A synthesis of current approaches. *Journal of Behavioral Medicine, 7,* 151–169.

Caplan, G. (1974). *Support systems and community mental health.* New York: Behavioral Publications.

Caplan, R. D., Robinson, C. A. R. French, J. R. P., Jr., Caldwell, J. R., & Shinn, M. (1976). *Adhering to medical regimens: Pilot experiments in patient education and social support.* University of Michigan, Ann Arbor.

Cobb, S. (1976). Social support as a moderator of life stress. *Psychosomatic Medicine, 38,* 300–314.

Cohen, S., & Syme, S. L. (1985). Issues in the study and application of social support. In S. Cohen & S. L. Syme (Eds.), *Social support and health* (pp. 3–22). Orlando, FL: Academic Press.

Dimond, M. (1985). A review and critique of the concepts of social support. In R. A. O'Brien (Coordinator), *Social support health: New directions for theory development and research.* Symposium conducted at the University of Rochester (pp. 1–32), Rochester, NY.

Gottlieb, B. H. (1978). The development and application of a classification scheme of informal helping behaviors. *Canadian Journal of Behavioral Science, 10,* 105–115.

Gottlieb, B. H. (1983). *Social support strategies.* Beverly Hills, CA: Sage Publications.

Gottlieb, B. H. (1985). *Marshaling and augmenting social support for medical patients and their families,* In R. A. O'Brien (Coordinator), *Social support and health: New directions for theory development and research.* Symposium conducted at the University of Rochester (pp. 107–148), Rochester, NY.

Hilbert, G. A. (1983). *The relationship between spouse support and compliance of myocardial infarction patients.* Unpublished doctoral dissertation, University of Pennsylvania, Philadelphia.

Hogue, D. D. (1977). Support systems for health promotion. In J. E. Hall & B. R. Weaver (Eds.), *Distributive nursing practice: A systems approach for community health* (pp. 65–79). Philadelphia: J. B. Lippincott.

House, J. S. (1981). *Work, stress and social support.* Reading, MA.: Addison-Wesley.

House, J. S., & Kahn, R. L. (1985). Measures and concepts of social support. In S. Cohen & S. L. Syme (Eds.), *Social support and health* (pp. 83–100). Orlando, FL: Academic Press.

Kahn, R. L. (1979). Aging and social support. In M. W. Riley (Ed.), *Aging from birth to death: Interdisciplinary perspectives* (pp. 77–91). Boulder, CO: Westview.

Kahn, R. L., & Quinn, R. P. (1976). *Mental health, social support and metropolitan problems.* Unpublished manuscript, Institute for Social Research, University of Michigan, Ann Arbor.

Kerlinger, F. N., (1986). *Foundations of behavioral research* (3rd ed.). New York: Holt, Rinehart & Winston.

Lin, N., Dean, A., & Ensel, W. M. (1981). Social support scales: A methodological note. *Schizophrenia Bulletin, 7,* 73–89.

Miller, J. F. (1983). *Coping with chronic illness: Overcoming powerlessness.* Philadelphia: F. A. Davis.

Nie, N. H., Hull, C. H., Jenkins, J. G., Steinbrenner, K., & Bent, D. J. (1970). *Statistical package for the social sciences.* New York: McGraw-Hill.

Norbeck, J. S. (1981). Social support: A model for clinical research and application. *Advances in Nursing Science, 4,* 43–59.

Norbeck, J. S. (1985). Measurement of social support: Recent strategies and continuing issues. In R. A. O'Brien (Coordinator), *Social support and health: New directions for theory development and research.* Symposium conducted at the University of Rochester (pp. 73–106), Rochester, NY.

Nunnally, J. C. (1978). *Psychometric theory* (2nd ed.). New York: McGraw-Hill.

Procidano, M. E., & Heller, K. (1983). Measures of perceived social support from friends and family: Three validation studies. *American Journal of Community Psychology, 11,* 1–24.

Sarason, I. G., Levine, H. M., Basham, R. B., & Sarason, B. R. (1983). Assessing social support: The Social Support Questionnaire. *Journal of Personality and Social Psychology, 44,* 127–139.

Stokes, J., & Wilson, D. G. (1984). Inventory of socially supportive behaviors: Dimensionality, prediction, and gender differences. *American Journal of Community Psychology, 2,* 53–64.

Tilden, V. (1985a). Cost and conflict: The darker side of social support. In R. A. O'Brien (Coordinator). *Social support and health: New directions for theory development and research.* Symposium conducted at the University of Rochester (pp. 154–158), Rochester, NY.

Tilden, V. (1985b). Issues of conceptualization and measurement of social support in the construction of nursing theory. *Research in Nursing and Health, 8,* 199–206.

Waltz, C. F., Strickland, O. L., & Lenz, E. R. (1984). *Measurement in nursing research.* Philadelphia: F. A. Davis.

Weiss, R. (1974). The provisions of social relationships. In A. Rubin (Ed)., *Doing unto others* (pp. 17–26). Englewood Cliffs, NJ: Prentice-Hall.

Wilcox, B. L., & Vernberg, G. M. (1985). Conceptual and theoretical dilemmas facing social support. In I. G. Sarason & B. R. Sarason (Eds.), *Social support: Theory, research and applications* (pp. 3–20). Boston: Martinus Nijhoff.

Wortman, C. B., & Conway, T. L. (1985). The role of social support in adaptation and recovery from physical illness. In S. Cohen & S. L. Syme (Eds.), *Social support and health* (pp. 281–302). Orlando, Fl: Academic Press.

Wortman, C. B. & Lehman, D. R. (1985). Reactions to victims of life crises: Support attempts that fail. In I. G. Sarason & B. R. Sarason (Eds.), *Social support: Theory, research and applications* (pp. 463–389). Dordrecht, Netherlands: Martinus Nijhoff.

Directions

This section refers to the person whom you named as most important to you in terms of being helpful on a day-to-day basis. In the past month, how satisfied were you with the helping behaviors of that person toward you? Indicate your degree of satisfaction with each behavior listed below by circling the number that applies to you. The number 1 indicates dissatisfcation. The number 6 indicates that you are very satisfied.

HOW SATISFIED ARE YOU WITH THE AMOUNT THE PERSON YOU NAMED DOES THIS FOR YOU?

	Dissatisfied	Somewhat Dissatisfied	Partly Satisfied	Somewhat Satisfied	Satisfied	Very Satisfied
1. Told me that I am OK just the way I am	1	2	3	4	5	6
2. Comforted me by showing some physical affection	1	2	3	4	5	6
3. Let me know that (s)he can be counted on if I need help	1	2	3	4	5	6
4. Expressed interest and concern in my well-being	1	2	3	4	5	6
5. Told me that (s)he feels very close to me	1	2	3	4	5	6
6. Was available to listen when I wanted to talk	1	2	3	4	5	6
7. Enjoyed hearing about what I think	1	2	3	4	5	6
8. Consoled me when I was upset	1	2	3	4	5	6
9. Allowed me to come to him/her when I was feeling down	1	2	3	4	5	6
10. Accepted me totally, including my worst and best parts	1	2	3	4	5	6
11. Made it clear what was expected of me	1	2	3	4	5	6
12. Gave me some information on how to do something	1	2	3	4	5	6
13. Gave me some information to help me understand a situation I was in	1	2	3	4	5	6
14. Told me who I should see for assistance	1	2	3	4	5	6
15. Told me what to expect in a situation that was about to happen	1	2	3	4	5	6
16. Taught me how to do something	1	2	3	4	5	6
17. Talked with me about a problem in order to help solve it	1	2	3	4	5	6
18. Checked back with me to see if I had followed the advice I was given	1	2	3	4	5	6
19. Helped me understand why I didn't do something well	1	2	3	4	5	6
20. Gave me feedback on how I was doing without saying it was good or bad	1	2	3	4	5	6
21. Contributed to my income or gave me money	1	2	3	4	5	6
22. Gave me a gift	1	2	3	4	5	6
23. Did a task that is usually done by me	1	2	3	4	5	6

24. Provided transportation for me	1	2	3	4	5	6
25. Did some activity together to help me get my mind off of things	1	2	3	4	5	6
26. Talked with me about some interests of mine	1	2	3	4	5	6
27. Joked or kidded to try to cheer me up	1	2	3	4	5	6
28. Shared an interest	1	2	3	4	5	6
29. Could count on her/him to distract me from worries	1	2	3	4	5	6
30. Shared information with me about recommendations that were made by the health team	1	2	3	4	5	6
31. Helped me to understand about my disease	1	2	3	4	5	6
32. Told me whom I should see for assistance when I had problems with the health team recommendations	1	2	3	4	5	6
33. Told me how useful the health team recommendations were in preventing complications	1	2	3	4	5	6
34. Taught me how to carry out the health team recommendations	1	2	3	4	5	6
35. Talked with me about problems I was having with the health team recommendations	1	2	3	4	5	6
36. Encouraged me to take proper care of myself	1	2	3	4	5	6
37. Checked back to see if I had carried out recommendations I consider important	1	2	3	4	5	6
38. Commented favorably when (s)he noticed me doing something that the health team recommended	1	2	3	4	5	6

7

Measuring Parental Coping When a Child Is Chronically Ill

Debra P. Hymovich

This chapter discusses the Coping Scale of the Chronicity Impact and Coping Instrument: Parent Questionnaire (CICI:PQ), a measure of the coping of parents with a chronically ill child.

The purpose of this chapter is to describe the psychometric properties of the Coping Scale of the Chronicity Impact and Coping Instrument: Parent Questionnaire (CICI:PQ) (Hymovich, 1983, 1984). Included in the chapter is a review of relevant literature, tools, procedures, and issues related to measuring the concept of coping. These discussions are followed by a description of the psychometric properties of the CICI:PQ Coping Scale and the revised scale (Parent Perception Inventory: Coping).

REVIEW OF THE LITERATURE

Coping, Chronic Illness, and the Family

There are an increasing number of studies related to coping, chronic illness, and families. The majority of chronic illness studies deal with how adults with various illnesses cope with the problems they encounter. Studies related to how parents cope with a child's chronic illness are limited. Early studies of coping looked at individuals involved in acute crises such as severe burns (Cobb & Lindemann, 1943; Hamburg, Hamburg, & deGoza, 1953), grief (Lindemann, 1944), and surgery (Janis, 1958). Studies of parents were related to children with malignant diseases (Chodoff, Friedman, & Hamburg, 1964; Friedman, Chodoff, Mason, & Hamburg, 1963).

The author wishes to thank Dr. Carolyn Waltz, consultant on this project, Dr. Ruth McCorkle, and Dr. Barbara Munroe for their assistance in conducting the psychometric analysis. This study was partially supported by Grant No. T32 NR07036.

Most of the work focusing on family issues consists of poorly controlled studies of how nuclear family members are affected by the presence of a child who is chronically ill or how various family members influence the coping of the chronically ill child (Bradley & Burish, 1983). McCubbin (1979) noted that coping strategies used within the family, as well as family transactions with the community, have received little attention in either research or theory building. He views coping as an important dimension of family adaptation to stress. McCubbin and his colleagues have attempted to systematically assess coping behaviors of parents of children with several chronic illnesses. They used the Coping Health Inventory for Parents (CHIP), described later in this chapter. Coping includes the behavioral responses of family members as well as the responses of the family as a unit in an attempt to manage a stressful situation. Coping is defined as the "ability to acquire and use the resources needed for family adaptation" (Patterson & McCubbin, 1983, p. 30).

Conceptual Issues in the Assessment of Coping

The CICI:PQ Coping Scale measures coping strategies used by parents of a chronically ill child. Although there are nearly as many definitions of coping as there are authors writing about it, there are several definitions that appear consistently in the chronic illness literature (Lazarus & Launier, 1978; Pearlin & Schooler, 1978; Weisman, 1984; Weisman & Worden, 1976–1977). Regardless of the specific definition, coping basically refers to a purposeful and intentional self-regulatory process that reduces or prevents responses that normally occur under stress (Burish & Bradley, 1983).

The concept of coping is difficult to study because there is no accepted unifying theoretical position or definition and no uniform way of measuring it. In addition, there is no overall complete bibliography of coping studies (Singer, 1984). Investigators from many disciplines, including psychology, psychiatry, medicine, and nursing, are doing research related to the concept of coping, each from his or her own perspective.

Theoretical Issues

Coping may be conceptualized as either a disposition (personality trait or style), a process (Averill & Opton, 1968), or an outcome (Stewart, 1980). Another way of conceptualizing coping is to consider it in relation to the concept of stress, either as an endrocrinologic and physiologic process (Selye, 1976) or as an interactionist, cognitively oriented process (Folkman, Schaefer, & Lazarus, 1979).

Singer (1984) suggested that the two major views of stress and coping (neuroendocrine, interactionist) be incorporated into a single model with a three-part flow: "from (1) the stressor through (2) transmission channels to (3) the organism" (p. 2304). A coping process can attempt to modify the stressor itself, modify the evaluation and appraisal, or change the reactions of the organism (Pearlin & Schooler, 1978). The degree of success of a coping process will depend on what is to be accomplished. If the coping processes are successful, they would reduce the stress in very different ways, depending on the processes used.

Many investigators believe that coping should be conceptualized as a multidimensional behavior or phenomenon (Fleishman, 1984; Pearlin & Schooler, 1978). From this perspective, coping includes a number of types of behaviors, it functions at a number of levels, and it is accomplished by many different behaviors, cognitions, and perceptions. Various lists of coping strategies have been proposed (e.g., Pearlin & Schooler, 1978; Sidle, Adams, Moos, & Cady, 1969; Weisman, 1984; Weisman & Worden, 1976–1977). Mages and Mendelsohn (1979) reduce these lists to three broad categories: (1) techniques designed to minimize stress, (2) activities that attempt to deal with specific issues, and (3) activities that involve others. Techniques to deal with distress may involve efforts to avoid certain situations or feelings, to control events, and to detach oneself from potentially upsetting situations. Efforts to deal with specific issues may include seeking information, participating in decision making, or learning new skills to compensate for lost functions. Others with whom one may become involved include one's family and friends of self-help groups.

Folkman and Lazarus (1980) differentiate between problem-focused and emotion-focused coping. Problem-focused coping refers to actions taken to remove or alleviate the source of stress, whereas emotion-focused coping refers to attempts to reduce the psychological distress, that is, to make the person feel better.

Methodologic Issues in the Assessment of Coping

Barofsky (1981) noted that "the measurement of coping is critically dependent on its definition" (p. 60). Because there is no uniform way to measure coping, investigators have developed their own ways based on their theoretical orientation and definitions. Burish and Bradley (1983) summarize the unresolved issues regarding the assessment of coping within the chronic disease literature as follows:

1. Coping may be evaluated either as a relatively stable disposition or as a process.
2. The measurement of coping is confounded by the fact that acts of coping change in response to environmental demands over time.
3. Little is known about relationships among the various measures of coping (e.g., self-report, observer report, and physiological measures).
4. Judgments of coping effectiveness may vary with different domains (e.g., social versus vocational) or across different time periods (e.g.,

immediately after a myocardial infarction or during the rehabilitation period).

5. Coping is usually assessed in only one specific situation, and it may not be appropriate to generalize findings to other situations.

An important methodological issue to be addressed involves how coping behavior is determined to be effective of adaptive (Barofsky, 1981; Singer, 1984). This is, in part, a question of judging the intent or purpose of the behavior. It also requires making this judgment between different domains of the individual (physical, psychological, social), over different periods of time (short-term, long-term), and as a function of different situations (e.g., diagnosis, hospitalization). For example, in studies of adults, Hackett and Weisman (1964) found that denial was psychologically beneficial for patients with myocardial infarction at one stage of their illness but not for patients with terminal cancer. Determining the outcome of coping also means imposing a set of value judgments that may vary across individuals and cultures, making it likely that different outcomes will be attributed to the coping strategies.

Other issues related to the design of studies with chronically ill adults have to do with specifying the exact nature of the population to be studied, establishing reliable and valid patient diagnoses, failing to assess the efficacy of patients' coping strategies at different disease stages, and obtaining sufficiently large samples of subjects and an adequate control group (Burish & Bradley, 1983; Watson & Kendall, 1983). Although it may be possible to obtain sufficient subjects in a large medical center specializing in specific illnesses (e.g., diabetes, cystic fibrosis), the extent to which the findings can be generalized to other patient populations is unknown. Most studies have focused on maladaptive patterns of patient coping or the effectiveness of interventions designed to improve patient coping. There has been very little attention to predicting people who are likely to cope poorly or are most likely to benefit from professional or self-help interventions (Bradley & Burish, 1983). These issues and difficulties also apply to conducting studies with parents of chronically ill children.

Measurement of Coping

Self-reports and observer reports are used to measure coping, although the relationship between the two has not been studied extensively. Specific methodologies for measuring coping include in-depth interviews and observations of individuals in crisis, essay and sentence-completion techniques, and short-story and problem-situation techniques (Moos, 1974). Self-reports are especially useful for assessing subjective experiences (e.g., mood, pain perception, feelings). However, they pose problems when used to measure anything other than subjective experiences unless their validity can be determined by observable behaviors. Self-report instruments are inadequate as sole measures of outcome because many of them have psychometric deficiencies (Prokop & Bradley, 1981; Watson & Kendall, 1983).

Adequate reliability and validity of assessment measures are essential. Many chronic illness researchers have not fully considered or reported the reliability and validity of their instruments. A review of the literature by Watson and Kendall (1983) suggested that researchers often evaluated coping in a limited fashion by using only a single measure or by combining measures that may have little correlation with one another. It has frequently been reported that the various facets of coping are not highly correlated with one another. People are likely to use both problem-focused and emotion-focused coping strategies in relation to the same stressful event. Because both types of coping can be used in times of stress, it would be important to include both types in any instrument to be developed.

Coping instruments have been developed in a variety of disciplines, including medicine, psychology, and nursing. They have been developed for use in a variety of situations and with different patient populations. Tools have been developed to measure coping in adults who have hypertension, who are undergoing dialysis, and who are visiting an emergency room (Baldree, Murphy, & Powers, 1982; Jaloweic, & Powers, 1981, postsurgical patients (Ziemer, 1983), psychiatric patients (Fontanna, Marcus, Noel, & Rakusin, 1972), and nurses (Chiriboga, Jenkins, & Bailey, 1983; Jacobsen, 1983). There have been only a few instruments developed to measure the coping of parents of chronically ill children. Most of these instruments were reported after 1978, when the CICI:PQ development began.

CHIP

McCubbin and colleagues (1981) developed the Coping Health Inventory for Parents (CHIP). The items were developed from studies of family responses to stress, family stress theory, and theories of the individual psychology of coping. The CHIP is a self-report hand scoreable instrument containing 45 items. Responses are recorded in terms of how helpful each strategy is perceived to be. There are three levles of abstraction (coping behaviors, coping patterns, and coping strategies). Coping behaviors are specific items on the CHIP, coping patterns are based on factor analysis of the items, and coping strategies are the combination of patterns used by an individual. The reliabilities for the three factors, called coping patterns, range from .71 to .79. Validity assessments of the CHIP were made using correlations with the Family Environment Scale (Moos, 1976) and two indices of changes in the child's health. Another validity check involved the use of discriminant analysis between low-conflict and high-conflict families of children with cerebral palsy.

Parent Coping Scale

Another instrument to measure coping, the Parent Coping Scale, was developed by Damrosch, Lenz, and Perry (1985). The Parent Coping Scale contains 81 items with seven subscales. Internal consistency reliabilities of the subscales, using coefficient alpha, ranged from .68 to .91. This tool is new, and its psychometric properties have not been reported fully. Although it appears to have potential for use with parents of chronically ill children, it was not available in 1978 when the CICI:PQ was developed.

CICIP:PQ

The other instrument developed for parents of chronically ill children is the Chronicity Impact and Coping Instrument: Parent Questionnaire (CICI:PQ) developed by Hymovich in 1978 (Hymovich, 1981). The development and revision of this instrument is reported more fully in the following section.

CONCEPTUAL BASIS OF THE INSTRUMENT

The conceptual basis for the CICI:PQ was the evolving framework developed by Hymovich (1981, 1984). As the framework evolved, the coping instrument was modified to reflect the changes. The current framework states that coping strategies are parents' perceptions of what they do to manage problems faced in raising a chronically ill child. The conceptual definition of coping was that of Weisman and Worden (1976–1977): "what one does about a perceived problem in order to bring about relief, reward, quiescence, or equilibrium" (p. 3). These strategies are either problem-focused or emotion-focused (Folkman & Lazarus, 1980) and may or may not be effective in resolving the problem (stressor) (Hymovich, 1987).

PURPOSE OF THE INSTRUMENT

The Coping Scale of the CICI:PQ (Hymovich, 1981, 1983, 1984; Hymovich & Baker, 1985) was designed to measure how parents of chronically ill children cope with stressors related to their child's illness.

DEVELOPMENT OF THE INSTRUMENT

The CICI:PQ, developed in 1978, is a 167-item questionnaire with eight sections. Two of these sections include coping items. One set of items is related to coping strategies used by the person completing the instrument; the other set is related to that person's perceptions of spousal coping.

The CICI:PQ was developed in two phases. The *first phase* was designed to develop the categories for the tool, including the list of coping strategies (behavior). To elicit information about coping strategies, parents were asked to describe an incident that was stressful to them, what they did to manage the situation, and how effective their coping was in managing the situation. Content analysis of the tape-recorded interviews resulted in a coping category with seven subcategories of strategies: Seeking behaviors (to obtain information or resources), utilizing behaviors (to make use of information and resources), managing stressors (actions to manage child's physical needs and parents' emotional responses), modifying strategies (to alter conditions or situations affecting family functioning), anticipatory planning, educating others, and helping/supporting others.

The *second phase* of the study consisted of developing the CICI:PQ and pilot-testing the instrument. The initial tool contained 213 coping items taken from the categories and subcategories. Three pilot tests were conducted with parents of chronically ill children. The sample sizes ranged from 29 to 44 parents. After a fourth revision, the 167-item tool was published (Hymovich, 1983) so that it could be used by other nurse researchers. A large sample was required to test the psychometric properties of the instrument, and nurses using the instrument expressed a willingness to share their raw data with the researcher for this purpose.

ADMINISTRATION AND SCORING

A Likert-type format was used for the items comprising the Coping Scale. The Coping Scale consists of three subscales: COPECHLD (coping with problems and concerns related to the child's health), COPESPOU (coping when upset with spouse), and SPOUCOPE (parent's perception of how spouse copes when upset with parent completing instrument). The COPECHLD and COPESPOU items can be combined to produce a SELF-COPE scale. Each subscale contains the same 13 coping strategies. Parents are asked to indicate whether they used each coping strategy more, less, or about the same as under usual circumstances (see instrument at the end of this chapter). Scoring of each scale consists of summing the subject's score to obtain a composite score. Items that are checked as being used (more, less, the same) can be given a score of 1, and the items not used can be given a score of 0. The total number of coping strategies is then summed to give the total number of strategies used.

RELIABILITY AND VALIDITY ASSESSMENTS

Sample

The sample for the psychometric analysis of the CICI:PQ consisted of 497 parents of children with a wide range of chronic illnesses. These data were obtained from nurses throughout the United States and Canada who had used the CICI:PQ, agreed to share the raw data, and returned the data before July 1987. Because of missing data for 45 of the subjects, only 452 of the subjects were used for the analyses. The majority of the parents were white (86%), married (84%), and between 30 and 39 years of age (43%). Fifty-five percent of the sample had a 12th-grade education or lower, and 45% had at least some college education. Incomes ranged from under $10,000 per year (18%) to over $30,000 (35%). The remainder were evenly distributed between $11,000 and $30,000. Parents of children with cystic fibrosis represented approximately 40% of the sample; spina bifida, 19%; asthma, 16%; and other, 25%.

Reliability

Internal consistency reliability was obtained for the three early versions of the CICI:PQThese coefficients are listed in Table 7.1. After each pilot study, the questionnaire was modified to reduce redundancy, increase reliability, improve clarity, and decrease the time required for parents to complete it (Hymovich, 1984). Reliability coefficients for Version 4 of the CICI:PQ are listed in Table 7.1, Time 4.

Internal consistency of the scales (Cope with child, Cope with spouse, Spouse cope, Selfcope with child and spouse) for the sample of 452 parents was examined using Cronbach's (1951) alpha coefficient. Coefficients were determined separately for mothers and fathers and for mothers and fathers within the four disability categories. SPSSX (1986) was used to run this analysis. A coefficient alpha of .86 for mothers and .88 for fathers was obtained for the total Coping Scale. This supports homogeneity of the content of the scale. Homogeneity is further supported by substantial correlations between the subscales and the total scale score (range: .55 to .96 for mothers, .41 to .95 for fathers). (See Tables 7.2 and 7.3.) Means, standard deviations, and ranges of the Coping Scale are reported in Table 7.4. Internal consistency reliabilities of the scales for the three diagnostic groups ranged from .72 to .88 for the cystic fibrosis group, .68 to .84 for

TABLE 7.1 Reliability of the CICI:PQ Coping Scale for the First Four Revisions

Scale	Time	Subjects *(n)*	Items *(n)*	Reliability
COPING	1	29	213[a]	.84[b]
COPING	2	33	165[a]	.89[b]
COPING	3	44	42[a]	.93[b]
SELFCOPE	4	161	40[b]	.80[c]
SPOUCOPE	4	161	15[b]	.80[c]

[a]Many of the same coping items were repeated with different stems.
[b]*r* = Hoyt's coefficient.
[c]*r* = Cronbach's alpha.

TABLE 7.2 Intercorrelations for the CICI:PQ Coping Scale and Subscales for Mothers (n = 313)

	COPETOT	COPECHILD	COPESPOU	SELFCOPE	SPOUCOPE
COPETOT	—				
COPECHILD	.85	—			
COPESPOU	.90	.67	—		
SELFCOPE	.96	.92	.91	—	
SPOUCOPE	.87	.55	.69	.68	—

TABLE 7.3 Intercorrelations of the Coping CICI:PQ Scale and Subscale for Fathers (n = 139)

	COPETOT	COPECHILD	COPESPOU	SELFCOPE	SPOUCOPE
COPETOT	—				
COPECHILD	.79	—			
COPESPOU	.92	.65	—		
SELFCOPE	.95	.92	.92	—	
SPOUCOPE	.83	.41	.68	.61	—

the spina bifida group, and .62 to .82 for the asthma group. For overall reliability standards, a coefficient of .70 is sufficient for new scales (Nunnally, 1978). Some of the scales had reliability coefficients somewhat below this level for some of the diagnostic groups. When the groups were combined, the only scale with an alpha coefficient below .70 was COPECHLD (.68).

The item-to-total correlations generated by the internal consistency program were examined to see if there were items that correlated weakly ($r < .25$) with their respective scales. If an item correlated weakly, its relationships to other items and to the empirical factors were examined. The frequency with which the item was used and the evaluation of the item by raters was also considered. If several of the data sources indicated an item was weak, that item was considered for deletion. Two items, smoke (7) and pray (12), consistently had weak relationships. However, when a reliability analysis was run with the two items deleted, the alpha coefficients were comparable to those with the total scale. Therefore, these items were left in the scale for preliminary analyses.

Validity

Content Validity

To establish the content validity of the instrument, a two-stage process was used (Lynn, 1986). The development phase of the CICI:PQ involved

TABLE 7.4 Means, Standard Deviations, and Ranges of the CICI:PQ Coping Scale for Mothers and Fathers

Scale	Items	Mothers (n = 313)			Fathers (n = 139)			Theoretical
	N	Mean	SD	Range	Mean	SD	Range	range
COPETOT	39	84.0	17.2	42–121	84.2	17.9	40–124	39–156
SELFCOPE	26	56.2	11.8	27–52	56.4	12.5	27–85	26–104
COPECHILD	13	28.0	6.3	13–28	28.4	6.5	13–41	13–52
COPESPOU	13	28.6	6.5	12–27	27.9	7.4	13–44	13–52
SPOUCOPE	13	27.9	6.8	13–31	28.4	7.2	13–47	13–52

identifying the categories and subcategories that emerged from the parent interviews (dicussed above) and a review of the literature. Content validity was established in 1978 by submitting the CICI:PQ to a clinical psychologist, three nurses working with families of chronically ill children, and one nurse working with chronically ill adults. Each item of the CICI:PQ was screened to be certain that each category and subcategory was included in the instrument. Content validity was also evident because the items in the instrument came from parents' statements of their coping behaviors during the interview phase of the tool's development. Content validity of the fourth revision of the CICI:PQ was established by giving the tool to three professional nurses working with the parents of chronically ill children and two parents of chronically ill children. Lynn recommends a minimum of five experts to provide a sufficient level of control for chance agreement. The parents and professionals were given a list of the instrument's objectives and the coping items and asked to (1) assess the relevancy of the items to the objectives on a 4-point scale ("not relevant" to "relevant") and (2) judge whether the items accurately represent the range of content of coping behaviors. They were also asked to identify additional coping strategies that should be included in the instrument. In retrospect, although these nurses and parents were experts in caring for chronically ill children, they were not experts in the concept of coping. Therefore, the content validity index obtained is not appropriate for assessing the concept being measured by the instrument.

A secondary analysis of the original interview data and a recent literature review were conducted. The current version of the CICI:PQ no longer reflects all of the coping items in the interview data. Some of the items, particularly the problem-focused ones, were reworded as concerns or needs for help. Other coping items, such as "attending parents' meetings," are listed separately rather than incorporated into the scale. Some items that were originally problem-focused coping strategies were removed from the concern scale because they were redundant or were not used by at least 40% of the parents.

Construct Validity

Factor analysis is a useful technique in instrument development, and it was used to determine the construct validity of the coping scales. Aggregate measures are generally more reliable than individual variables (Watson & Kendall, 1983). Using SPSSX (1986), factor analysis was performed on the Coping Scale data for 452 parents. Separate analyses were run for mothers and fathers because the literature suggests that there may be gender differences in coping (Folkman & Lazarus, 1980) and to ensure that each family was represented only once in the analysis (for some families, two parents completed the instrument). Also, Nunnally (1978) indicates that a heterogeneous sample (sex, age, educational level) will influence the factors that result. Because the mother sample was larger (n = 313) than the father sample (n = 139), the initial factor analysis was limited to the mother sample. The father sample was used to determine the extent to which the resulting factor scales could be replicated. The four diagnostic categories (cystic fibrosis, spina bifida, asthma, other) were analyzed for homogeneity of variance. Since there were no significant differences in variance for either mothers or fathers, the diagnostic categories were combined for the analyses.

Because construction of the instrument involved reducing redundancy, resulting in low correlations among some of the items, Bartlett's test of sphericity was performed to determine the feasibility of doing the factor analysis. The results of the test indicated that an identity matrix was not present; that is, there was sufficient correlation among the items to proceed with the analysis. The number of variables that can be included in factor analysis is related to sample size. Most writers advise at least 5 (Comrey, 1978; Gorsuch, 1974) or 10 (Nunnally, 1978) subjects for each variable included in a factor analysis. Comrey (1978) recommends a minimum of 200 subjects for factor analysis and indicates that increasing the number of subjects improves the clarity of results. Because not all parents in the sample were married and could not respond to the entire coping scale, it was decided to look at each of its scales separately. The number of items in each of the three subscales analyzed was 13. The subscales were COPECHLD (cope with child), COPESPOU (cope with spouse), and SPOUCOPE (how spouse copes). There were 313 mothers (24 per item) and 139 fathers (10 per item).

The principal-components method was used for extracting factors to determine the minimum number of independent factors that would satisfactorily produce the correlations between variables. An eigenvalue of 1.00 or greater was used as a cutoff for determining the number of potentially interpretable factors in the data. For those factors that met the criteria for inclusion in the factor extraction step, a varimax (orthogonal) factor rotation was performed to maintain maximum independence of the factors. This method is usually desirable for instrument development where one is looking for independent subscales (Dixon, 1986; Kim & Mueller, 1978). The criterion for minimally acceptable factor loadings was a cutoff point of .30 (Cattell, 1978; Nunnally, 1978).

The initial varimax solution for mothers yielded four factors for the COPECHLD scale, five for the COPESPOU scale, and three for SPOUCOPE. For the fathers, the COPECHLD and COPESPOU scale yielded five factors each, and the SPOUCOPE scale yielded three factors. These findings suggest that coping is a multidimensional concept, especially in relation to the affective domain.

The four-factor solution was the most meaningful conceptually. The factors were named avoidance behaviors, seeking emotional support, problem solving and exercise, and tension-reducing activities. The most consistent factors across the three subscales for mothers and fathers were avoidance behaviors and tension-reducing activities. These findings are

TABLE 7.5 Four-Factor Solution of the CICI:PQ COPECHILD Scale for Mothers and Fathers

	Mothers[a]				Fathers[a]			
Coping strategy	1	2	3	4	1	2	3	4
Hide feelings	.75				.61			
Ignore/forget	.74				.70			
Busy self	.52		.42		.45		.51	
Get away	.51			.35	.60			
Take alcohol		.66						.68
Smoke		.62		–.41	.59			
Yell/slam doors		.61			.41	.33		
Take medicine		.54						.81
Cry			.74				.72	
Pray			.60				.72	
Exercise	.32			.69		.75	.30	
Ask for help			.38	.66			.72	
Talk with someone			.52	.55		.55	.40	
Eigenvalue	2.8	1.7	1.2	1.1	2.9	1.6	1.4	1.1
% Variance	21.7	13.4	9.4	8.6	22.6	12.1	10.7	8.3
Cum %	21.7	35.1	44.5	53.0	22.6	34.7	45.5	53.8
alpha	.62	.50	.36	.57				

[a]Factor loadings above .30.

consistent with those of Aldwin and colleagues (Aldwyn, Folkman, Schaefer, Coyne, & Lazarus, 1980), who used principal-components analysis with varimax rotation to empirically determine the coping strategies in Folkman and Lazarus's Ways of Coping Check List. Of the seven factors, one problem-focused and six emotion-focused coping factors were derived. The items and factor loadings for the mothers' and fathers' Coping with child (COPECHLD) scales are shown in Table 7.5. For mothers, the rotated four-factor matrix accounted for 53% of the total variance in the data for COPECHLD, 54% for COPESPOU, and 59% for SPOUCOPE. For fathers, the amount of explained variance was 54% for COPECHLD, 59% COPESPOU, and 58% SPOUCOPE. Items "busy self" and "yell/slam doors" displayed the weakest distinctions between factors.

Based on factor loadings and content, each of the 13 items was assigned to one category. In this initial factoring procedure, no items were discarded. If an item loaded on only one factor, it was designated as belonging to the category represented by that factor. If an item loaded on more than one factor, irrespective of the relative loadings, the classification was determined by the nature of the items in the other category.

Scores for each factor subscale were obtained by summing the ratings for all items within the scale. Coefficient alphas for each subscale (and for the total scale) were obtained. The alpha coefficients ranged from .36 to .71; all but one was over .50. Because the number of items in each factor was small and many of the coefficients were low, further analyses to compare data based on the subscales were not conducted.

Criterion Validity

As part of a study of parents of children with cystic fibrosis (Hymovich & Baker, 1985), data were collected from the professional staff about how well the parents were coping. Data were available for 43 mothers. These scores were correlated with the parent scores on the SELFCOPE (COPECHLD and COPESPOU) and SPOUCOPE scales to look at criterion-related validity. There was a significant correlation (r = 28, p = .04) for both scales using Pearson product-moment correlation coefficient.

DISCUSSION OF FINDINGS RELATED TO THE CICI:PQ COPING SCALE

Although results indicate general support for the preliminary validity and reliability of the Coping Scale of the CICI:PQ, the coping items do not reflect the multidimensionality of the coping concept. Reliability of the scales was adequate for preliminary analyses but needs to be increased. Some of the items were skewed, and variability on some of the items was limited. For example, smoking, medicine, and alcohol were used by only about 25% of the parents. Although these items have limited variability, they were retained because of their clinical significance in helping parents cope with their child's illness. Also, deleting them from the scale reduced its reliability. In addition, skewed items and reduced variability can artificially deflate the alpha coefficient (Waltz, Strickland, & Lenz, 1984). Before these items are deleted, they should be tested in a wide range of situations so that frequency of item response can be compared. Modifications can then be made in a manner that will minimize the danger of deleting items that appear to have no value in ine population or context but are, in fact valuable in another.

The Coping Scale of the CICI:PQ (COPECHLD, COPESPOU, SPOUCOPE) consists primarily of emotion-focused items. Only 2 of the 13 items are problem-focused. Emotion-focused coping has been found to be associated with studies of adults coping with physical illness and disabilities (Cohen & Lazarus, 1979; Lipowski, 1970; Moos, 1976). These studies show that much of the coping is directed toward managing feelings of anxiety, fear, and dread and toward restoring self-esteem and interpersonal relationships. It is possible that emotion-focused coping is more prevalent in parents of chronically ill children and that the parents and nurses reviewing the content validity of the CICI:PQ coping items responded to this prevalence. The instrument needs to be reviewed by experts in the area of coping rather than experts in the care of the chronically ill.

It was found that the format for the Coping Scale was difficult for parents to complete because they must first identify whether or not the strategy is used and then how they changed its use. It is questionable how parents actually responded to this item.

Further refinement of the coping portion of the CICI:PQ was needed and was undertaken. A new instrument, the Parent Perception Inventory: Coping (PPICOPE) was developed and is now ready for testing.

PARENT PERCEPTION INVENTORY: COPING (PPICOPE)

The process used for developing the PPICOPE was that suggested by Waltz, Strickland, and Lenz (1984). The steps included mapping the typologies of coping, specifying the variables (and their dimensions) to be measured, and identifying observable indicators for these variables. Because coping is a multidimensional concept, the PPICOPE was developed to incorporate as many of the dimensions as possible. Additional coping strategies for the PPICOPE came from a secondary review of the parent interviews, from the coping literature, and from suggestions made by those who reviewed and used the instrument as it was being developed.

The coping items of the CICI:PQ were retained and incorporated into the PPICOPE. The PPICOPE is a norm-referenced measurement tool to differentiate between the number, types, and effectiveness of coping strategies reported by parents of chronically ill children. It is a self-report instrument, based on the assumption that perceptions of coping are a subjective phenomenon and can be measured only by self-report. Only one situation, coping with child-related problems was retained for the revised scale. This was done to make the instrument more parsimonious because it was necessary to increase the number of items for the scale. The child situation was selected for this instrument because there is evidence that the presence of a chronically ill child affects the parenting role to a greater extent than the marital role (Kazak & Marvin, 1984). Responses to the scale were changed to provide two interval-level scales rather than one ordinal-level scale. Instead of asking whether the item was used more than, less then, or the same as before, the frequency of use is being assessed.

The number of items was increased from 13 to 29 to increase the scale reliability from .68 to .85. To estimate the test length, the formula suggested by Nunnally (1978) was used. The PPICOPE (see sample items in Hymovich's PPICOPE at the end of this chapter) has two separate scales: one to measure the degree to which each coping strategy is used (not at all, rarely, sometimes, often) and one to measure the degree of helpfulness of the strategies ("never helps" to "always helps"). For each item, the respondent is asked to indicate whether the coping strategy has been used within the past 3 months. The 3-month time referent provides a sufficient length of time for a problem to be present and yet is short enough that the respondent is likely to recall the event. Completion of the PPICOPE usually requires about 10 to 15 minutes. The scales are scored by summing the values of each response, giving two scores: a coping strategy score and an effectiveness score.

According to Lazarus (1975, 1977), the way a person appraises a situation has a strong effect on the coping strategies used. Therefore, an item is included to state the extent to which parents believe they have some control over the situation (problems related to child care). Other items have been included to obtain parent perceptions of their overall beliefs about how well they are coping (see "Hymovich's PPICOPE" at the end of this chapter).

A pilot test of the PPICOPE is currently underway with several groups of parents of chronically ill children. Coefficient alpha will be used to measure internal consistency reliability. Construct validity will be measured by using two groups of high and low scorers (upper and lower thirds) on the Coping Strategies and Helpfulness scales. Test–retest reliability, using the Pearson product-moment correlation coefficient, will be obtained by administering the tool at a 2-week interval. Factor analysis for construct validity, using principal components and orthogonal rotation, will also be performed.

SUMMARY AND CONCLUSIONS

This study has described the psychometric properties of the Coping Scale of the CICI:PQ. Four psychometric properties of the Coping Scale were studied: (1) internal consistency reliability of the scale, (2) content validity, (3) construct validity using factor analysis, and (4) criterion validity. Because a number of weaknesses were noted, a new instrument, the PPICOPE was constructed, using items from the CICI:PQ. A pilot test to determine the psychometric properties of the PPICOPE is in progress. This instrument is relevant to nursing practice. It has been suggested that how people cope with their illnesses may be as important as the medical care they receive in determining satisfactory outcomes (Stewart, 1980). If nurses can determine which coping responses facilitate parent adaptation to a child's chronic illness, and consequently improve the child's and family's quality of life, we may be able to help persons to plan coping strategies that will increase their chance of achieving this outcome.

In conclusion, a review of the psychometric properties of the CICI:PQ Coping Scale indicated the need for a number of revisions. These revisions resulted in a new instrument, the Parent Perception Inventory: Coping (PPICOPE). It is anticipated that this new instrument, that contains both problem-focused and emotion-focused items will be useful to nurses who are trying to help parents adapt to their child's chronic illness.

REFERENCES

Aldwin, C., Folkman, S., Schaefer, C., Coyne, J., & Lazarus, E. (1980, September). *Ways of coping checklist: A process measure.* Paper presented at the annual meeting of the American Psychological Association, Montreal.

Averill, J. R., & Opton, E. M., Jr. (1968). Psychophysiological assessment: Rationale and problems. In P. McReynolds (Ed.), *Advances in psychosocial assessment* (Vol. 1, pp. 265–268). Palo Alto, CA: Science and Behavior.

Baldree, K. S., Murphy, S. P., & Powers, M. J. (1982). Stress identification and coping patterns in patients on hemodialysis. *Nursing Research, 31,* 107–112.

Barofsky, I. (1981). Issues and approaches to the psychosocial assessment of the cancer patient. In K. Proktop & L. A. Bradley (Eds.), *Medical psychology: Contributions to behavioral medicine* (pp. 55–65). New York: Academic Press.

Bradley, L. A., & Burish, T. G. (1983). Coping with chronic disease: Current status and future direction. In T. G. Burish & L. A. Bradley (Eds.), *Coping with chronic disease* (pp. 475–482). New York: Academic Press.

Burish, T. G., & Bradley, L. A. (1983). Coping with chronic disease: Definitions and issues. In T. G. Burish & L. A. Bradley (Eds.), *Coping with chronic disease* (pp. 3–12). New York: Academic Press.

Cattell, B. (Ed.). (1978). *The scientific us of factor analysis in behavioral and life sciences.* New York: Plenum.

Chiriboga, D. S., Jenkins, G., & Bailey, J. (1983). Stress and coping among hospice nurses. *Nursing Research, 32,* 294–299.

Chodoff, P., Friedman, S. B., & Hamburg, D. A. (1964). Stress, defenses and coping behavior: Observations in children with malignant disease. *American Journal of Psychiatry, 120,* 743–749.

Cobb, S., & Lindemann, E. (1943). Coconut Grove burns: Neuropsychiatric observations. *Annals of Surgery, 117,* 814–824.

Cohen, R., & Lazarus, R. S. (1979). Coping with the stresses of illness. In G. C. Stone, F. Cohen, & N. E. Adler (Eds.), *Health psychology: A handbook* (pp. 217–254). Sand Francisco: Josey-Bass.

Comrey, A. L. (1978). Common methodological problems in factor analytic studies. *Journal of Consulting and Clinical Psychology, 46,* 648–659.

Damrosch, S. P., Lenz, E. R., & Perry, L. A. (1985). Use of parental advisors in the development of a parental coping scale. *Maternal-Child Nursing Journal, 14,* 103–109.

Dixon, J. (1986). Grouping techniques. In B. M. Munro, M. A. Visintainer, & E. B. Page (Eds.), *Statistical methods for health care research* (pp. 265–289). Philadelphia: J. J. Lippincott.

Fleishman, J. A. (1984). Personality patterns and coping patterns. *Journal of Health and Social Behavior, 25,* 229–244.

Folkman, S., & Lazarus, R. S. (1980). An analysis of coping in a middle-aged community sample. *Journal of Health and Social Behavior, 21,* 219–239.

Folkman, S., Schaefer, C., & Lazarus, R. S. (1979). Cognitive processes as mediators of stress and coping. In V. Hamilton & D. M. Warburton (Eds.), *Human stress and cognition: An information processing approach* (pp. 265–298). London: Wiley.

Fontanna, A. F., Marcus, J. L., Noel, B., & Rakusin, J. M. (1972). Prehospitalization coping styles of psychiatric patients: The goal-directedness of life events. *Journal of Nervous and Mental Diseases, 155,* 311–321.

Friedman, S. B., Chodoff, P., Mason, J. W., & Hamburg, D. A. (1963). Behavioral observations of parents anticipating the death of a child. *Pediatrics, 32,* 610–625.

Gorsuch, R. L. (1974). *Factor analysis.* Philadelphia: W. B. Saunders.

Hackett, T. P., & Weisman, A. D. (1964). Reactions to the imminence of death. In G. H. Grosser, H. Wechsler, & M. Greenblatt (Eds.), *The threat of impending death* (pp. 300–311). Cambridge, MA. M.I.T. Press.

Hamburg, D. A., Hamburg, B., & deGoza, S. (1953). Adaptive problems and mechanisms in severely burned patients. *Psychiatry, 16,* 1–20.

Hymovich, D. P. (1981). Assessing the impact of chronic childhood illness on the family and parent coping. *Image, 13,* 71–74.

Hymovich, D. P. (1983). The chronicity impact and coping instrument: Parent questionnaire. *Nursing Research, 32,* 275–281.

Hymovich, D. P. (1984). Development of the chronicity impact and coping instrument: Parent questionnaire (CICI:PQ). *Nursing Research, 33,* 218–222.

Hymovich, D. P. (1987). Assessing families of children with cystic fibrosis. In L. M. Wright & M. Leahey (Eds.), *Families and chronic illness* (pp. 133–146). Springhouse, PA: Springhouse.

Hymovich, D. P., & Baker, C. D. (1985). The needs, concerns and coping of parents of children with cystic fibrosis. *Family Relations, 34,* 91–97.

Jacobsen, S. F. (1983). Stress and coping strategies in neonatal intensive care unit nurses. *Research in Nursing and Health, 6,* 33–40.

Jaloweic, A., & Powers, M. J. (1981). Stress and coping in hypertensive and emergency room patients. *Nursing Research, 30*(1), 10–15.

Janis, I. L. (1958). *Psychological stress: Psychoanalytic and behavioral studies of surgical patients.* New York: Wiley.

Kazak, A., & Marvin, R. (1984). Differences, difficulties, and adaptation: Stress and social networks in families with a handicapped child. *Family Relations, 33,* 66–67.

Kim, J., & Mueller, C. W. (1978). *Factor analysis: Statistical methods and practical issues.* Beverly Hills, CA: Sage.

Lazarus, R. S. (1975). The self-regulation of emotion. In L. Levi (Ed.), *Emotions: Their parameters and measurement* (pp. 47–67). New York: Raven.

Lazarus, R. S. (1977). Cognitive and coping processes in emotion. In A. Monat & R. S. Lazarus (Eds.), *Stress and coping* (pp. 145–158). New York: Columbia University Press.

Lazarus, R. S., & Launier, R. (1978). Stress-related transactions between person and environment. In L. A. Pervin & M. Lewis (Eds.), *Perspectives in international psychology* (pp. 287–327). New York: Plenum.

Lindemann, E. (1944). Symptomatology and management of acute grief. *American Journal of Psychiatry, 101,* 141–148.

Lipowski, Z. J. (1970). Physical illness, the individual and the coping process. *Psychiatry in Medicine, 1,* 91–102.

Lynn, M. R. (1986). Determination and quantification of content validity. *Nursing Research, 35,* 382–385.

Mages, N. L., & Mendelsohn, G. A. (1979). Effects of cancer on patients' lives: A personological approach. In G. C. Stone, F. Cohen, & N. E. Adler (Eds.), *Health psychology: A handbook* (pp. 255–284). San Francisco: Jossey-Bass.

McCubbin, H. I. (1979). Integrating coping behavior in family stress theory. *Journal of Marriage and the Family, 41,* 237–244.

McCubbin, H. I., Patterson, J. M., Cauble, A. E., Comeau, J., Larsen, A. S., & SKinner, D. A. (1981). *Systematic assessment of family stress, resources, and coping: Tools for reseach, education and clinical investigation.* St. Paul, MN: University of Minnesota.

Moos, R. H. (1974). Psychological techniques in the assessment of adaptive behavior. In G. V. Coelho, D. A. Hamburg, & J. E. Adams (Eds.), *Coping and adaptation* (pp. 334–399). New York: Basic Books.

Moos, R. (1976). *Human adaptation: Coping with life crisis.* Washington, DC: Heath.

Nunnally, J. C. (1978). *Psychometric theory* (2nd. ed.). New York: McGraw-Hill.

Patterson, J. M., & McCubbin, H. I. (1983). Chronic illness: Family stress and coping. In C. R. Figley & H. I. McCubbin (Eds.), *Stress and the family: Vol. 2. Coping with catastrophe* (pp. 21–36). New York: Brunner/Mazel.

Pearlin, L. I., & Schooler, C. (1978). The structure of coping. *Journal of Health and Social Behavior, 19*(March), 2–21.

Prokop, C. K., & Bradley, L. A. (1981). Methodological issues in medical psychology and behavioral medicine research. In C. K. Prokop & L. A. Bradley (Eds.), *Medical psychology: Contributions to behavioral medicine* (pp. 485–496). New York: Academic Press.

Selye, H. L. (1976). *The stress of life* (rev. ed.). New York: McGraw-Hill.

Sidle, A., Adams, J., Moos, R., & Cady, P. (1969). Development of a coping scale. *Archives of General Psychiatry, 20,* 226–232.

Singer, J. E. (1984). Some issues in the study of coping. *Cancer, 53*(Suppl.), 2303–2315.

SPSSX users guide (2nd ed.). (1986). Chicago: SPSSX Marketing Department.

Stewart, A. L. (1980, October). *Coping with serious illness: A conceptual overview.* Santa Monica, CA: Rand Corporation.

Waltz, C. F., Strickland, O. L., & Lenz, E. R. (1984). *Measurement in nursing research.* Philadelphia: F. A. Davis.

Watson, D., & Kendall, P. C. (1983). Methodological issues in research on coping with chronic disease. In T. G. Burish & L. A. Bradley (Eds.), *Coping with chronic disease* (pp. 39–81). New York: Academic Press.

Weisman, A. D. (1984). *The coping capacity: On the nature of being moral.* New York: Human Sciences Press.

Weisman, A. D. & Worden, J. W. (1976–1977). The existential plight of cancer: Significance of the first 100 days. *International Journal of Psychiatry in Medicine, 7,* 1–15.

Ziemer, M. M. (1983). Effects of information on postsurgical coping. *Nursing Research, 32,* 282–287.

Coping Items from the CICI:PQ

1. Parents handle their concerns in many different ways. There are times when you may have more problems or concerns because of your child's condition. In what ways do you do things differently when these problems come up? (Please put an "X" in the appropriate column. Do not mark on the lines.)

COPING*	Does not apply (1)	Do less (2)	Do about the same (3)	Do more (4)
Cry				
Busy self with other things				
Talk with someone				
Ignore/try to forget				
Hide feelings				
Get away				
Smoke				
Yell/scream/slam doors, etc.				
Exercise				
Ask for help				
Take alcohol				
Pray				
Take medicine				

***Additional stems for same coping items**

2. People do many different things when they become upset with their spouse. Please indicate the ways in which you do things differently when you are upset with your spouse than when you are not upset (Please put an "X" in the appropriate box. Do not mark on the lines.)
3. In what ways does your spouse do things differently when upset with you than when not upset? (Please put an "X" in the appropriate box. DO Not mark on the lines.)

Hymovich's PPICOPE

Parents cope with their concerns in many different ways. There are times when you may have more problems or concerns because of your child's needs. The first column has a list of some ways people cope (manage their problems).

1. If you do not use a coping method in the list, circle the 0 in the first column.
2. The next 3 columns are choices about how often people do things to cope with (manage) problems related to their child's needs. Circle the number that shows *how often* you used the coping method *in the past 3 months* when you had a problem related to your child's needs.
3. The last four columns are choices about how helpful you find these ways of coping. Circle the number that reflects *how helpful* you find each of these ways of handling problems.
4. Leave the How Often and How Helpful sections blank if you do not use the coping method.

The format is as follows:

COPING	HOW OFTEN				HOW HELPFUL			
	(0) DO NOT DO THIS	(1) Very rarely	(2) Some-times	(3) Very often	(0) Never helps	(1) Some-times helps	(2) Almost always helps	(3) Always helps

Items added to the CICI:PQ

Look at options
Change my expectations
Ask questions
Use advice of others
Try to figure out what to do
Find help
Solve problem myself
Read about the problem
Wish problem would go away
Weigh choices
Get information
Try to change things

1. What have been your sources of information about your child's problems or needs? Check all that apply.

____ (1) clergy	____ (9) social worker
____ (2) doctor	____ (10) nutritionist
____ (3) friend	____ (11) therapist
____ (4) nurse	____ (12) library
____ (5) teacher	____ (13) newspapers/magazines
____ (6) relatives or spouse	____ (14) support group
____ (7) pharmacist	____ (15) community agency
____ (8) other parents	____ (16) other ______

2. How often have you *not known* what to do when you needed information or help?
   ____ (1) never ____ (2) sometimes ____ (3) often ____ (4) always
3. In general, how well do you believe you are coping with problems related to your child's needs?
   ____ (0) not well ____ (1) fairly well ____ (2) very well
4. In general, how well do you believe you are coping with your feelings and concerns about your child?
   ____ (0) not well ____ (1) fairly well ____ (2) very well
5. Would you like us to help you with any problems you are having?
   ____ (1) no ____ (2) not sure ____ (3) yes
6. How satisfied are you with the way you are able to cope with the stresses you have?

____ (1) very dissatisfied	____ (3) satisfied
____ (2) dissatisfied	____ (4) very satisfied

8

Assessment of Two Instruments That Measure Coping Strategies of Seriously Mentally Ill Young Adults

Joan Ramsey Wilk

This chapter discusses an assessment of the Jalowiec Coping scale and the Ways of Coping Checklist for their usefulness with mentally ill adults.

The lack of data about coping styles or strategies of mentally ill young adults is due in part to the lack of information about the appropriateness of use of available coping instruments with this particular population. Because of this, a pilot study was conducted with 15 mentally ill young adults living in the community to see how they identified coping strategies through use of the Jalowiec Coping Scale (Jalowiec, 1988) and the Ways of Coping Checklist (Lazarus & Folkman, 1988). A normal group of 15 young adults without reported mental or physical illness was used for comparison. In addition to testing coping styles, the similarities, differences, and appropriateness, of the Jalowiec Coping Scale (JCS) and the Ways of Coping (WOC) Checklist (Lazarus & Folkman, 1984) were assessed for use with people with serious mental illness.

Serious mental illness has traditionally been defined by diagnosis, duration of hospitalization, and impairment of role performance or daily living skills (Goldman, 1982). Until fairly recently, people with serious mental illness were institutionalized. Today, mentally ill young adults who are considered chronically or seriously ill do not fit the traditional criteria, nor do they follow the treatment pattern of prior years. Usually, they have

This research was partially supported by a grant from the Nurses' Foundation of Wisconsin.

had episodic and infrequent contact with the mental health care delivery system. Most spend little time in hospitals or other institutions (Pepper, Kirshner, & Ryglewicz, 1981). Their diagnoses include schizophrenia, affective disorders, and some personality disorders.

Functional disability, believed by some to be the basis for judgment of serious mental illness, appears to be a dominant theme for young adults with serious mental illness. Unlike older mentally ill persons, seriously mentally ill young adults report fewer physical disabilities but more psychiatric symptoms, behavior problems, and difficulty with daily living skills (Pepper & Ryglewicz, 1982). In particular, a problem associated with this population is their high vulnerability to stress and their deficiencies in coping skills. Not only do they experience stress with greater frequency, but they seem to have more severe reactions, which may lead to an increase in psychiatric symptoms (Zubin & Spring, 1977).

REVIEW OF RELATED LITERATURE

"Dealing with problems," "finding strategies to reduce stress," and "managing demands" are a few of the ways of coping that have been described. Reports of the measurement of coping strategies of people with serious mental illness focus primarily on relapse or rehospitalization as criteria for coping success or failure. Because seriously mentally ill young adults are sporadic users of the mental health care delivery system, these outcome measures may have questionable value. Coping or failure to cope may go unnoticed unless the client becomes involved with a crisis center or hospital emergency room.

An early controlled experimental approach to the measurement of coping in hospitalized and nonhospitalized chronically mentally ill adults was described by Stein, Test, and Marx (1975). They evaluated a treatment model designed to help mentally ill patients acquire necessary coping skills so that community adjustment would be enhanced. Coping of patients was measured by a symptomatology rating scale and a community adjustment form. Although patients in the community did well and learned coping skills, it is not clear what strategies they used, nor were the outcome measures related to specific strategies used by patients.

Leff (1976) examined relapse rates of patients in 21 families judged to meet the criteria for high expressed emotion and compared the relapse rates of patients from 16 families with low expressed emotion. There was a significant relationship between high expressed emotion and relapse (Fisher's exact test, $p = .007$), as was described in the findings of Brown, Birley, and Wing (1972) and replicated by Vaughn and Leff (1976). In describing the coping behaviors of the schizophrenic subjects in the study, Leff (1976) found a significant relationship between the patient's social withdrawal in families with high expressed emotion and reduced relapse rates, as long as patients were on drug therapy. Although coping as an outcome was not identified specifically in this study, the implication was that patients who were unable to cope were rehospitalized.

Much of the work published about seriously mentally ill young adults is descriptive, focusing on clinical and social characteristics and service utilization patterns. Schwartz and Goldfinger (1981) did a review of every third patient seen in the psychiatric emergency outpatient department of the San Francisco General Hospital for 3 months in 1980. In addition to descriptive data, they found deficiencies in patients' reality testing under stress, poor impulse control, and disturbances of affect.

Caton (1981) described the clinical and social functioning of 119 new chronic mentally ill patients entering treatment in New York City. The patients were tracked for 1 year to describe suicides, criminal activity, psychotic symptoms, use of mental health services, and social life. High levels of rehospitalization, poor treatment compliance, and increased symptomatology were indications of poor coping. Interviewers used the Global Assessment Scale and the Psychiatric Evaluation Form.

In a comprehensive review of the research on life events, stress, and coping in the course of schizophrenia, Lukoff, Snyder, Ventura, and Nuechterlein (1984) found that people with schizophenia tend to overevaluate the threat of a stressful life event, feel less capable of resolving situations because of low self-esteem, and rely on a limited number of coping responses. In addition, behavioral coping to alter the stressful condition was inadequate. This may mean stress is experienced more intensely and lasts longer for schizophrenic individuals than for those who are not schizophrenic. The authors concluded that coping responses are an "avenue that shows promise for exploration" (p. 265).

Brenner, Boker, Muller, Spichtig, and Wurgler (1987) studied coping responses of neurotic, schizophrenic, and "normal" subjects and indicated that because schizophrenic individuals incorporate a stressful event so intensely, they work even harder at coping with it. Rather than rationalize or withdraw to deal with stress, the schizophrenic subjects in this study concentrated very seriously on confronting the source of their stress, more so than the other two groups.

It appears from the review of the literature on coping and serious mental illness that there is much that remains to be discovered relative to coping strategies. In fact, with few exceptions, the strategies used by people with serious mental illness are seldom specifically addressed. In addition, coping instruments used with other populations to describe coping strategies need to be examined for appropriateness to subjects who have serious mental illness.

CONCEPTUAL BASIS OF THE MEASURES

Lazarus and Folkman (1984) define coping as "constantly changing cognitive and behavioral efforts to manage specific external and/or internal demands that are appraised as taxing or exceeding the resources of the person" (p. 141). They believe coping is influenced by personal factors (commitments, beliefs) and situational factors (novelty, predictability, uncertainty) that effect cognitive appraisal. Further, coping is described as a process, not a trait, that must be viewed as a dynamic, reciprocal, transactional relationship between the person and the environment.

According to Jalowiec and Powers (1981), coping styles are either general behaviors or situation-specific behaviors and are problem-oriented or affective-oriented. Problem-oriented methods are those that "primarily are aimed at solving a problem or handling a stressful situation" (Baldree, Murphy, & Powers, 1982, p. 108). Affective-oriented methods are those used to manage the emotions evoked by a stressful situation. Ideally, a balance between problem-oriented and affective-oriented coping strategies is desirable for optimal health (Jalowiec & Powers, 1981).

Schizophrenia is a serious mental illness in which cognitive processes are disturbed at times. A person with this illness may have difficulty with the appraisal of a stressful event and the cognitive and behavioral strategies needed to manage stress. Although coping with stress has been a frequent focus of research, there are few descriptions of the coping experience from the perspective of seriously mentally ill young adults. If they are unsuccessful in coping with a stressful event, their behavior may come to the attention of family members or caregivers. Little is known, though, about their attempts to manage stress or the ways in which they deal successfully with stress. In addition, reliability and validity of coping measurements used with this group need to be assessed.

PURPOSE OF INVESTIGATION

The purpose of studying coping strategies of people with serious mental illness was to learn about strategies they identified as enabling them to cope with stress and to assess the appropriateness of two coping instruments for use with this population. Specifically, the JCS (Jalowiec, 1988) and the WOC Checklist (Lazarus & Folkman, 1988) were administered to 15 subjects with serious mental illness and 15 subjects with no reported mental illness in order to provide more detailed information on the use of these instruments with a population that is particularly vulnerable to stress.

PREVIOUS INSTRUMENT DEVELOPMENT PROCEDURES

The Jalowiec Coping Scale

The JCS has been used to determine the frequency of use of problem-oriented and affective-oriented strategies by hypertensive versus emergency room patients (Jalowiec & Powers, 1981), as well as by dialysis patients (Baldree et al., 1982).

The research on stress and coping in hypertension and emergency room patients had as its purpose the comparison of stressful life events reported for the year prior to illness onset, identification of coping methods, and exploration of coping, stress, and health relationships (Jalowiec & Powers, 1981). Two different patient populations were used. Twenty-five newly diagnosed hypertensive patients were selected from a record review in a university medical clinic and compared to 25 emergency room patients seeking care for nonserious acute illness. Stress was measured using a Stressful Life Events Scale developed by Rahe (1975).

Forty coping behaviors were identified by Jalowiec from an extensive literature search for descriptive commonalities. Reliability was determined by test–retest, and a pilot study using 28 volunteers yielded reliability of .79 ($p < .001$) using Spearman's rank ordering. After piloting, a panel of 20 judges classified coping methods as problem-oriented or affective-oriented ways of coping. Overall agreement by the panel of judges was 85%. Survey data were gathered in face-to-face interviews, and t tests were used to test for differences between the two sample means. Findings indicated significant differences in stress identified and coping behaviors used by an acute and chronic population.

The purpose of the research on stress and coping in hemodialysis patients (Baldree et al., 1982) was to design and test an instrument to evaluate treatment-associated stress, to determine coping strategies, and to explore the relationship between the two. Although stress associated with dialysis treatment had been linked in past studies, coping had not.

A convenience sample of 35 hemodialysis patients was chosen from 160 patients in treatment. The scale developed in the previously described study was used to measure coping, and the tool used to examine stressors was developed for the study and based on a critical review of the literature. Means, standard deviations, and t tests were used to describe the findings. Stressors were ranked, and problem-oriented coping methods were found to be used more than affective-oriented methods ($t = 7.06$, $p < .001$).

Psychometric information for the JCS was further addressed, and more detail was given regarding the reliability and validity of the tool in a subsequent report (Jalowiec, Murphy, & Powers, 1984). Stability was first established by test–retest after 2 weeks. Reliability coefficients of .79 for total coping scores, .85 for problem-oriented scores, and .86 for affective scores were reported.

Internal consistency reliability of the JCS was assessed using Cronbach's alpha on data from 141 subjects. A coefficient alpha of .86 was obtained from hypertensive and emergency room patients, a general population, and dialysis patients. This indicated a high degree of homogeneity of the content of the scale. Correlations between subscale scores and total scale scores were reported by Jalowiec, Murphy, and Powers (1984). Scores ranged from .77 to .86 in two reported studies in which problem-oriented scores and affective scores were both correlated with the total coping scores.

Content validity, while not addressed in detail in the psychometric analysis of the JCS, was substantiated by the "systematic manner of tool development, by the large number of items used to tap the domain, and by the inclusion of diverse coping behaviors" (Jalowiec et al., 1984, p. 159). Construct validity was substantiated by factor analysis. Twelve of the 15 problem items loaded on Factor 1, identified as the problem-oriented factor. Inappropriately loading were three factors that could enhance problem resolution, according to the authors. Fourteen of the 25 affective items loaded significantly on Factor II, identified as the affective factor. This seemed to reflect problems associated with "the forced-choice nature of the earlier classification study" (Jalowiec et al., 1984, p. 159). Because nine items did not load significantly on either factor, the authors considered the need for at least one more factor, and they indicated that coping may be multidimensional rather than dichotomous. A four-factor solution was suggested: cognition, powerlessness, tension-modulating mechanisms, and other-directed coping methods. Cronbach's alpha was computed, and alpha coefficients were .86, .73, .75, and .55, respectively.

Jalowiec (1988) has continued to revise the JCS, and the most recent version contains 60 items in two parts so that subjects rate use *and* effectiveness of items, plus a 4-point rating scale from "never" (0) to "often" (3) for each part. Data from 22 investigators and 1,400 subjects have recently been analyzed. Three factors that demonstrate conceptual potential have been identified and labeled as confrontive, emotive, and palliative strategies. This information has recently been published (Jalowiec, 1988).

The Ways of Coping Checklist

The WOC Checklist (Lazarus & Folkman, 1984) was developed to measure self-reports of subjects on what they thought or did in relation to a specific stressful event. In the revised version of the scale (Lazarus & Folkman, 1988), respondents are asked to think about a stressful situation and respond to 66 items on a Likert-type 4-point scale. Responses range from not using a particular coping strategy (0) to "used a great deal" (3).

From pooled observations of interviews of 75 married couples once a month for 5 months, eight scales were produced as a result of factor analysis. The eight scales accounted for 46.2% of the variance. The scales and their alphas are as follows: confrontive (.70), distancing (.61), self-controlling (.70), seeking social support (.76), accepting responsibility (.66), escape–avoidance (.72), planful problem solving (.68), and positive reappraisal (.79) (Lazarus & Folkman, 1988).

The WOC Checklist and a supporting manual were published by Consulting Psychologists Press, Inc. (Palo Alto, California) in the summer of 1988. The JCS is available from the author through Loyola University of Chicago.

ADMINISTRATION AND SCORING OF INSTRUMENTS

The JCS and WOC Checklist were scored in their usual way. Each instrument has a 4-point rating scale. The JCS has two parts (Jalowiec, 1988). Part A addresses how often a particular strategy is used, and responses may range from "never used" (0) to "often used" (3). Part B is an effectiveness-rating scale, and responses may range from "not helpful" (0) to "very helpful" (3). Subjects are instructed to respond to each coping strategy listed by circling a number from 0 to 3 in Part A to indicate how often they used a particular coping strategy and to indicate in Part B how effective each strategy was. Scores are derived by adding all subjects' use ratings within a given coping style, for a use score, and all subjects' effectiveness ratings within a given coping style, for an effectiveness score. Ranges vary for each style depending on the number of items per style. The coping styles, possible range of scores for each style, and sample items from the JCS are as follows:

1. Confrontive (0–30): "Tried to find out more about the problem."
2. Evasive (0–39): "Put off facing up to the problem."
3. Optimistic (0–27): "Tried to think positively."
4. Fatalistic (0–12): "Prepared for the worst that could happen."
5. Emotive (0–15): "Got mad and let off steam."
6. Palliative (0–21): "Exercised or did some physical activity."
7. Supportant (0–15): "Depended on others to help you out."
8. Self-reliant (0–21): "Preferred to work things out ourself."

The WOC responses range from "not used" (0) to "used a great deal" (3). Fifty items comprise eight coping scales, and subjects were instructed to circle the response that best described the extent of use of each item. Scores for each of the eight scales are summated. Coping subscales, possible score ranges, and item examples are as follows (Lazarus & Folkman, 1988):[1]

1. Confrontive (0–18): "Tried to get the person responsible to change his or her mind."
2. Distancing (0–18): "Went along with fate; sometimes I just have bad luck."
3. Self-controlling (0–21): "Tried not to burn my bridges, but leave things open somewhat."
4. Seeking social support (0–18): "Talked to someone to find out more about the situation."
5. Accepting responsibility (0–12): "I apologized or did something to make up."
6. Escape–avoidance (0–24): "Slept more than usual."
7. Planful problem solving (0–18): "I knew what had to be done, so I doubled my efforts to make things work."
8. Positive reappraisal (0–21): "I was inspired to do something creative."

RELIABILITY AND VALIDITY ASSESSMENT

Fifteen young adults with schizophrenia who were clients of an outpatient clinic were subjects of this study. The young adults were selected from a list of eligible participants in an agency that delivered services to people with serious mental illness. Subjects were chosen who were between the ages of 18 and 35 and had a primary diagnosis of schizophrenia. A list of clients who met these criteria was prepared by the clinic coordinator, and clients who were not capable of providing informed consent were removed from the potential pool of subjects. Of the 35 clients who met the criteria, 8 indicated that participation in the study would be too stressful. Fifteen clients were chosen from the remaining 27.

Fifteen college students without chronic illness were used as a comparison group. Students between the ages of 18 and 35 were individually approached in the student union of a large metropolitan university and asked to voluntarily participate following a thorough explanation of the investigation. The study was reviewed by an institutional review board for the protection of human subjects, and written informed consent was obtained from all participants.

All subjects completed a demographic information form, the JCS, and the WOC Checklist. The subjects with schizophrenia completed the JCS and WOC a second time 3 weeks later so that stability of the instruments for use with a mentally ill population could be examined.

An additional measure, the Global Assessment Scale (GAS) (Endicott, Spitzer, Fleiss, & Cohen, 1976) was completed by the client subjects' caseworkers. The purpose of the GAS was to assess the overall functioning of the subjects with serious mental illness. The scale ranges are divided into 10 equal intervals from 1 (the sickest individual) to 100 (the healthiest). Most individuals in outpatient programs range between 31 and 70 (Endicott et al., 1976). Rating is based on examples of client behavior during the assessment period, and clinicians are advised to disregard diagnosis or prognosis.

Scores on the GAS ranged from 41 to 80, and the mean score for the group of 15 schizophrenic clients was 60. The GAS was completed twice, and scores were within 4 points of each other (except for one client who was rated higher by 8 points at the second rating). The clinic coordinator was asked to rate each client independently, and 87% of the ratings were in agreement with the caseworkers' ratings. The scores indicated clients were generally functioning well and had mild to moderate symptoms, such as flat affect, depressed mood, and self-doubt. It was important to assess their functioning so that one could have confidence in the use of two instruments that involve self-report.

Stability, internal consistency, and equivalence of these measurements with this particular population was addressed. The stability of both tools when used with the client subjects was examined by retesting the subjects with serious mental illness after 3 weeks. Pearson product-moment correlation coefficient was taken as the estimate of test–retest reliability. Correlational coefficients ranged from .22 (self-controlling) to .72 (distancing) on the WOC Checklist. Other coefficients were as follows: confrontive, .46; seek social support, .56; accept responsibility, .67; escape–avoidance, .55; planful problem solving, .54; and positive reappraisal, .50. All were significant at the $p < .05$ level except for the self-controlling coping strategy.

The JCS reliabilities ranged from .07 (palliative [effectiveness scale]) to .64 (self-reliant [use scale]). The higher use scores ($p < .05$) were confrontive (.58), optimistic (.45), fatalistic (.58), emotive (.60), and self-reliant (.64). Lower scores were evasive (.36), palliative (.09), and supportant (.14). The higher effectiveness scores ($p < .05$) were confrontive (.48), evasive (.48), optimistic (.53), and self-reliant (.48). Lower effectiveness scores, in addition to palliative (.07), were fatalistic (.19), emotive (.26), and supportant (.15).

The mean scores obtained on coping styles were subjected to t tests to see if there were significant differences between the first and second administration of the tools. The second administration of the JCS yielded significantly lower scores for *use* of self-reliant coping styles ($t = 2.45, p < .05$) and *effectiveness* of emotive coping styles ($t = 3.35, p < .01$). None of the scales on the WOC Checklist differed significantly with the second administration.

Internal consistency, the homogeneity of the subparts of the instruments, had been supported in previous testing with both tools. For this investigation, alpha coefficients were calculated as the estimate of reliability for subscales as well as for the total tool. Since both instruments contain subscales, alphas were determined for each set of homogeneous items (Waltz, Strickland, & Lenz, 1984).

Cronbach's coefficient alpha was computed on coping scale data to estimate the internal consistency reliability of the instruments. Alphas were tabulated for total scale content for the subjects with serious mental illness for the JCS Part A (use), Part B (effectiveness), and the WOC Checklist. Reliability coefficients for total coping scores were .91 for the JCS Part A (use), .93 for the JCS Part B (effectiveness), and .85 for the WOC Checklist. This indicates overall homogeneity of the content on the scales. The alphas for each subscale for both instruments appear in Table 8.1.

In previous studies of the JCS, both problem-oriented scores and affective scores were correlated with the total coping scores to further examine the correlations between subscale scores and total scale scores. The WOC questionnaire has been similarly analyzed. Both instruments were recently revised. In fact, Jalowiec has indicated that the two-factor problem and affective subscores may be refined to a three-factor model (Jalowiec, 1988).

Equivalence, to determine the consistency of the instruments to yield measurements of the same traits in the same subjects, was assessed. Each instrument was administered to each client subject in immediate succession and randomly alternated in the order of their administration. The Pearson

TABLE 8.1 Reliability Coefficients of the Ways of Coping Subscales and the Jalowiec Coping Scale Subscales for Mentally Ill Subjects (n = 15)

Ways of Coping subscales		Jalowiec Coping Scale subscales	Use	Effectiveness
Confrontive	.46	Confrontive	.73	.88
Distancing	.42	Evasive	.65	.71
Self-controlling	.33	Optimistic	.41	.93
Seeking social support	.59	Fatalistic	.58	.70
Accepting responsibility	.68	Emotive	.80	.59
Escape–avoidance	.64	Palliative	.85	.37
Planful problem solving	.64	Supportant	.75	.37
Positive reappraisal	.56	Self-reliant	.58	.52

r statistic was calculated to examine the relationship between the coping styles of the WOC Checklist and the JCS Part A (use). There were a number of significant relationships between scale styles (shown in Table 8.2). Relationships that were significant at the .001 level were planful problem solving (WOC) and confrontive (JCS), escape–avoidance (WOC) and fatalistic (JCS), seeking social support (WOC) and supportant (JCS), self-controlling (WOC) and self-reliant (JCS), and positive reappraisal (WOC) and self-reliant (JCS).

Validity, or the degree to which the instruments measure what they are intended to measure, was addressed by two master's-prepared psychiatric nurses who work with the seriously mentally ill. Both nurses had experience in outpatient clinics and had expertise in working with clients similar to the subjects who chose to participate in the study. They reviewed the objectives that guided the construction of test items and a separate list of items for each instrument. They were then asked to rate the items as to their representativeness of coping styles or strategies. Both judges rated all items on both instruments as relevant or very relevant, making the value of the content validity index 1.00.

Construct validity was assessed by using a contrasted-groups approach. Scores obtained from 15 subjects of a similar age, ethnic background, and marital status, who were not mentally ill, were compared to those of the mentally ill group. Results of t tests used to examine the differences between the means of the two groups indicated that there were some significant differences between scores of the subjects with serious mental illness and scores of the subjects with no mental illness. On the WOC Checklist, client subjects had significantly higher scores on the distancing subscale ($t = 3.71, p < .01$) and on the escape–avoidance subscale ($t = 2.65, p < .01$). Mean score differences on the JCS were apparent for two coping styles. Client subjects scored significantly higher on the fatalistic (Part

TABLE 8.2 Correlations between Ways of Coping Subscales and Jalowiec Coping Scale Subscales (Part A—Use) for Mentally Ill Subjects (n = 15)

	Con-frontive	Distancing	Self-controlling	Seeking social support	Accepting responsi-bility	Escape–avoidance	Planful problem solving	Positive reappraisal
Con-frontive	.170	.105	.288	.139	.502	–.061	.663*	.502
Evasive	.101	.410	.421	–.198	.244	.452	.026	.182
Optimistic	.059	.438	.287	.094	.286	.129	.395	.446
Fatalistic	.304	.499	.337	.313	.416	.609*	.020	.470
Emotive	.476	–.025	–.064	.362	.405	.166	.172	.095
Palliative	.229	.314	.050	.256	.365	.264	.311	.298
Supportant	.247	.124	.012	.549*	.522	.081	.289	.291
Self-reliant	.016	.403	.529*	–.005	.410	.203	.516	.553*

*p < .001.

A—use) subscale ($t = 3.00$, $p < .01$) and the evasive (Part B—effectiveness) subscale ($t = 2.19$, $p < .05$). On both scales, higher scores indicate greater use of a particular coping style or strategy.

DISCUSSION AND CONCLUSIONS

Appropriateness of the JCS and the WOC Checklist for use with a population with serious mental illness was assessed by this pilot study. By examining scale scores following two administrations, it appeared that, with the exception of the self-controlling subscale, the WOC Checklist subscales had greater stability over a 3-week period. The JCS, with moderate correlations, had two subscales that were particularly low: palliative and supportant. A further analysis of stability indicated that scores on the WOC Checklist did not change significantly on a t test following retest after 3 weeks. The second aministration of the JSC, however, did yield two significantly lower scale scores on a t test for self-reliant strategies (Part A—use) and for emotive strategies (Part B—effectiveness). Stability of all subscales would have to be reexamined with a larger population, and, in particular, subscales with questionable stability should be scrutinized.

Although total reliability coefficents for the two instruments were high, the subscale coefficients indicated a low to moderate degree of homogeneity of the subparts. On the WOC Checklist, alphas ranged from .33 (self-controlling) to .68 (accepting responsibility). The JCS subscale alphas were higher and ranged from .37 (palliative and supportant [effectiveness scale]) to .93 (optimistic [effectiveness scale]). Both scales yielded lower coefficients than reported by either Jalowiec et al. (1984) or Folkman, Lazarus, Dunkel-Schetter, DeLongis, & Gruen (1986). These results may be due to the small sample and the more homogeneous nature of the mentally ill subjects because alphas may be spuriously lowered by decreased variances (Waltz et al., 1984). Although the reliabilities of the coping subscales in this pilot study are generally in the low to moderate range, consideration must also be given to the fact that both instruments have been revised, and reevaluation with a larger population will be necessary following the recent publication of revisions.

Equivalence, the consistency of the two instruments in yielding measurements of the same traits in the same subjects, was evaluated by using two forms of coping instruments with the sample of people with serious mental illness. The significant correlation between the two sets of scores (WOC Checklist and JCS—Part A [use]) on a number of coping strategies indicated that both instruments measured many of the same attributes. Again, this aspect of reliability needs to be reexamined with a larger sample of mentally ill adults.

Content validity for both instruments was supported by descriptions of tool development and evaluation by a panel of experts. Construct validity, examined by use of a contrast group of students, was supported for the subscales of distancing and excape–avoidance (WOC Checklist) and fatalistic (use) and evasive (effectiveness) (JCS). These strategies, indicative of pessimism, powerlessness, and hopelessness, are consistent with the feelings of low self-esteem and perceived lack of capability to resolve situations identified in the literature on coping and schizophrenia (Lukoff et al., 1984). Distancing, escape–avoidance, and fatalistic and evasive coping strategies are also emotion-focused strategies, and it is of interest to note that significant differences between groups was in the realm of emotion-focused or affective-oriented coping strategies, which were used significantly more by subjects with serious mental illness.

Although this was a pilot study, results indicated that people with serious mental illness were able to identify the coping strategies they use and even to distinguish between use and effectiveness on instruments requiring self-report. In addition, a number of client subjects indicated to their caseworkers that they had new ideas about coping as a result of completing the instruments. They said this was particularly true of the JCS. Assessing and teaching coping strategies may be an appropriate way to increase the range of coping options available to people with mental illness. As nurses participate in this endeavor, outcomes might be measured by using one or both of these instruments before and after and intervention. More data are necessary to further support that these instruments are reliable and valid for the mentally ill adult population.

REFERENCES

Baldree, K., Murphy, S., & Powers, M. (1982). Stress identification and coping patterns in patients on hemodialysis. *Nursing Research, 31,* 107–112.

Brenner, H., Boker, W., Muller, J., Spichtig, L., & Wurgler, S. (1987). Autoprotective efforts of schizophenics, neurotics and controls. *Acta Psychiatrica Scandinavica, 75,* 405–414.

Brown, G., Birley, J., & Wing, J. (1972). Influence of family life on the course of schizophrenic disorders: A replication. *British Journal of Psychiatry, 121,* 241–258.

Caton, C. (1981). The new chronic patient and the system of community care. *Hospital and Community Psychiatry, 32,* 475–478.

Endicott, J., Spitzer, R., Fleiss, J., & Cohen, J. (1976). The global assessment scale: A procedure for measuring overall severity of psychiatric disturbance. *Archives of General Psychiatry, 33,* 766–771.

Folkman, S., Lazarus, R., Dunkel-Schetter, C., DeLongis, A., & Gruen, R. (1986). The dynamics of a stressful encounter: Cognitive appraisal, coping, and encounter outcomes. *Journal of Personality and Social Psychology, 50,* 992–1003.

Goldman, H. (1982). Mental illness and family burden: A public health perspective. *Hospital and Community Psychiatry, 33,* 557–560.

Jalowiec, A. (1988). Confirmatory factor analysis of the Jalowiec Coping Scale. In C. Waltz & O. Strickland (Ed.), *Measurement of nursing outcomes: Measuring client outcomes* (Vol. 1, pp. 287–308). New York: Springer Publishing Co.

Jalowiec, A., Murphy, S., & Powers, M. (1984). Psychometric assessment of the Jalowiec Coping Scale. *Nursing Research, 33,* 157–161.

Jalowiec, A., & Powers, M. (1981). Stress and coping in hypertensive and emergency room patients. *Nursing Research, 30,* 10–15.
Lazarus, R., & Folkman, S. (1984). *Stress, appraisal and coping.* New York: Springer Publishing Co.
Lazarus, R., & Folkman, S. (1988). *Ways of Coping Checklist.* Palo Alto, CA: Consulting Psychologists Press.
Leff, J. (1976). Schizophrenia and sensitivity to the family environment. *Schizophrenia Bulletin, 2,* 566–574.
Lukoff, D., Snyder, K., Ventura, J., & Nuechterlein, K. (1984). Life events, familial stress, and coping in the developmental course of schizophrenia. *Schizophrenia Bulletin, 10,* 258–292.
Pepper, B., Kirshner, M., & Ryglewicz, H. (1981). The young adult chronic patient: Overview of a population. *Hospital and Community Psychiatry, 32,* 463–469.
Pepper, B., & Ryglewicz, H. (Eds.). (1982). *The young adult chronic patient: New directions for mental health services.* San Francisco: Jossey-Bass.
Rahe, R. H. (1975). Epidemiological studies of life change and illness. *International Journal of Psychiatry in Medicine, 6,*(1–2), 133–146.
Schwartz, S., & Goldfinger, S. (1981). The new chronic patient: Clinical characteristics of an emerging subgroup. *Hospital and Community Psychiatry, 32,* 470–474.
Stein, L., Test, M., & Marx, A. (1975). Alternative to the hospital: A controlled study. *American Journal of Psychiatry, 132,* 517–521.
Vaughn, C., & Leff, J. (1976). Influence of family and social factors on the course of psychiatric illness: A comparison of schizophenic and depressed neurotic patients. *British Journal of Psychiatry, 129,* 125–137.
Waltz, C., Strickland, O., & Lenz, E. (1984). *Measurement in nursing research.* Philadelphia: F. A. Davis.
Zubin, J., & Spring, B. (1977). Vulnerability—a new view of schizophrenia. *Journal of Abnormal Psychology, 86,* 103–126.

PART III
Measures of Client Perceptions in Health and Illness

9
The Perlow Self-Esteem Scale

Michael Perlow

This chapter discusses the Perlow Self-Esteem Scale, a measure of one's self-esteem, which is designed to be feasible for use in nursing clinical settings.

Self-esteem is a construct that has generated a great deal of theoretical and research interest in the past two decades. Perhaps some of the interest has occurred because of the elusive nature of this construct. Certainly, the primary reason for the interest is the potential widespread applicability of a self-esteem construct both for research and for helping the human condition.

Although theoretical descriptions have been thought-provoking, progress in clarifying and measuring the construct has lagged. Two reasons have been offered for this methodological lag. First, development of self-esteem measures has produced instruments that are global in nature and lack a distinct theoretical link. Second, the attempts at validating these instruments do not meet standards deemed necessary for tool validation. O'Brien (1980) considered both a distinct theoretical link and methodologic rigor in validation to be necessary components of any self-esteem measure. Wylie (1974, 1979) also called for methodologic rigor and distinct theoretical links in determining the validity of any self-esteem measure.

Stanley Coopersmith (1981) developed his Self-Esteem Inventory (SEI) as such a measure of self-esteem. The SEI was constructed to measure self-esteem in four dimensions: general, social, work, and peer self-esteem. These dimensions, however, were different from the constructs, success, aspirations, values, and defenses that Coopersmith used to describe self-esteem. The discrepancy between the theoretical constructs and the dimensions of the tool prohibits construct validity of the SEI. Because Coopersmith's theory was considered to be potentially of value, Perlow (1987) developed the Perlow Self-Esteem Scale (PSES) employing the constructs from Coopersmith's theory.

REVIEW OF LITERATURE

The literature reviewed consists of material provided to describe the reliability and validity of the two instruments used in the study. Each of the instruments, the PSES and Zung's (1971) Self-Rating Anxiety Scale (SAS) will be considered separately. Previous reliability and validity estimates of the PSES are provided in this section. Development and scoring of the PSES are addressed later in the chapter. Development, scoring, and previous reliability and validity estimates will be given for the SAS.

Perlow Self-Esteem Scale

Perlow (1987) developed, tested, and then revised the PSES with a sample of 112 adults. Originally, the PSES was developed with three items from each of the four constructs—power, significance, virtue, and competence—that Coopersmith used to define success. Three items were developed for each of the remaining three constructs: values, aspirations, and defenses. These 21 items were confirmed as having content validity by a group of three individuals familiar with Coopersmith's theory. An alpha factor analysis with varimax rotation was performed on the items scores, with two factors, self-control and ethical self, as the best solution. Using the items defining each factor and eliminating one redundant item, the final PSES consisted of 17 items. Internal consistency–reliability of the PSES was .87. The 30-day stability coefficient was $r = .84$.

Construct validity estimates from known-group comparision of PSES scores were significantly different, $F(1, 110) = 9.42$, $p < .003$. The PSES was significantly correlated with Coopersmith's SEI, $r = .78$, and a semantic differential (SD) measure of self-esteem ($r = .65$) (Perlow, 1987).

Bryant (1988) employed the PSES to estimate validity for a newly developed tool designed to measure acceptance of self. Twenty-three individuals completed the prepilot study, and 18 completed the pilot study. During both of the data collection times the respondents completed the Acceptance of Self scale and the PSES to test for the hypothesized positive relationship between self-esteem and self-acceptance. The prepilot study correlation coefficients involving the PSES were $r = .21$ for Form I and $r = .45$ for Form II. Pilot study correlation coefficients involving the PSES were $r = .60$ for Form I and $r = .59$ for Form II. The Acceptance of Self tool functioned as hypothesized and supported concurrent validity of the PSES.

Zung's Self-Report Anxiety Scale

The SAS was developed to meet a need for measuring anxiety and to fulfill the criteria that the SAS would (1) reflect the symptoms of anxiety, (2) quantify anxiety, and (3) be short and simple to use (Zung, 1971, 1974, 1979, 1980). This tool was originally developed from interview responses made by an unspecified number of psychiatric patients who were being treated for anxiety. The patients' responses to the interview provided the final 20 items for the SAS (Zung, 1971). A copy of the SAS is provided at the end of this chapter.

Each of the items consists of a brief statement describing a symptom of anxiety. Respondents select along a 4-point Likert-type scale as to the frequency of the symptoms. Those items reflecting higher anxiety are scored 4 for "most of the time" to 1 for "none of the time." Those items reflecting lower anxiety are scored the reverse of the above. The item scores are summed to quantify anxiety, with the higher scores reflecting higher anxiety (Zung, 1971).

Zung (1971, 1974) tested the instruments on 225 psychiatric patients and 100 normal adults. The subjects completed the Anxiety Status Inventory (ASI), the SAS, and the Taylor Manifest Anxiety Scale (TMAS). Split-half correlation coefficient as a measure of internal consistency was $r = .71$ for the SAS. The correlation coefficient between the SAS and the ASI was $r = .74$, and the correlation coefficient between the SAS and TMAS was $r = .30$. Although statistics were not provided, the author claimed that scores on the SAS differentiated between a group of patients with a diagnosis of anxiety and a group with other psychiatric diagnoses. SAS scores also differentiated between anxious patients and the "normal" population. Although the results were impressive, inclusion of the statistics would have been helpful.

Further validating information for the SAS was provided by Zung (1979). Both the SAS and the Hamilton Anxiety Scale (HAS) were completed by 548 otherwise unidentified respondents. The reported correlation coefficient between the SAS and HAS was $r = .75$. Again, the provision of a greater description of the study would have been helpful.

Jegede (1977) examined the SAS with 206 normal and 142 psychiatric outpatients. Coefficient alpha was .69 for the normal subjects and .81 for the psychiatric outpatients. SAS scores differentiated between the two groups, $t\,(346) = 8.16$, $p < .001$. That SAS scores once again differentiated between groups chosen for anxiety supported SAS construct validity.

CONCEPTUAL FRAMEWORK

Conceptual Descriptions

Coopersmith's (1981) theory describing self-esteem has four constructs: success, values, aspirations, and defenses (four additional constructs—power, significance, virtue, and competence—are subsumed under success). Each of the concepts, as well as self-esteem, is described in the following paragraphs.

Success. Coopersmith (1981) selected success as one aspect of self-esteem from the writings of William James (1890). Success is one's perception of achievement in a situation and is internally defined. Although employing standards similar to those of all individuals, the perception of success is entirely personal and not dependent on any external criteria. Success is further described with four dimensions: power, significance, virtue, and competence. Power is one's ability to control behavior, both one's own and that of others. Significance is the acceptance and popularity given an individual by others. Virtue is adherence to a prescribed set of ethics, and competence is the individual's level of achievement. That is to say, a successful person is one who has considerable competence and power, has high standards, and is well accepted by others.

Values. As with success, the construct of values was taken from the work of William James (1890). Values are measures of the importance that an individual attaches to a situation. These values arise from social norms and are consistent within similar cultures. The social context of these values becomes so firmly entrenched that any personal values have a minimal effect (Coopersmith, 1981).

Aspirations. The third construct from William James (1890)is that of aspirations. Aspirations are the goals individuals establish for themselves. These goals arise from two sources: public and personal. Public goals are consistent throughout a culture, whereas personal goals vary with the individual (Coopersmith, 1981).

Defenses. Coopersmith (1981) included in his theory defenses from the work of H. S. Sullivan (1953). Defense is defined differently from the psychoanalytic use of the term. In this context defense refers to one's ability to resist devaluation of one's self-esteem (Coopersmith, 1981).

Self-esteem. Self-esteem is the perception of success weighted against values, measured against aspirations, and filtered through defenses (Coopersmith, 1981).

Theoretical Relationships

Coopersmith (1981) offered three stated relationships among the four concepts of success, values, aspirations, and defenses. The relationship statements are as follows:

1. As success increases, self-esteem increases.
2. As self-esteem increases, aspirations increase.
3. As self-esteem increases, defenses increase.

A fourth relationship statement may be inferred from the conceptual definition of success and the relationship between success and self-esteem. The inferred relationship is as follows: As the sum of power, significance, virtue, and competence increases, self-esteem increases.

PURPOSE OF THE MEASURE

The purpose of the PSES is to measure one's self-esteem in a clinically feasible manner based on Coopersmith's (1981) theory of self-esteem.

PROCEDURES FOR DEVELOPMENT

The PSES was developed in an attempt to do justice to and adequately test Coopersmith's (1981) theory (Perlow, 1987). Three items were developed from each of the four constructs—power, significance, virtue, and competence—that Coopersmith employed to describe success. Three items were developed for each of the remaining constructs—values, aspirations, and defenses. The initial PSES, therefore, consisted of 21 items, 3 drawn from each of Coopersmith's constructs.

The items are simple statements the respondents select as being either like or unlike themselves. The items were assumed to sample the domain of self-esteem because they were written closely following Coopersmith's (1981) constructs. Once developed, the items were submitted to a panel of individuals familiar with Coopersmith's theory. This panel concurred that the items reflected the essence of the theoretical constructs. Therefore, there is evidence for the content validity of the PSES based on the fact that items were developed to be congruent with the underlying theory and agreement by content specialists on the tool's validity.

Initial testing of the PSES revealed that four of the original items did not contribute to the measurement of self-esteem. The current version of the PSES, the one examined in this study, consisted of the remaining 17 items. A copy of the PSES appears at the end of this chapter.

ADMINISTRATION AND SCORING OF THE PSES

The respondents are instructed to indicate how each of the 17 statements is either like or unlike themselves. They are requested to choose their responses on the basis of their feelings and are further informed that there are no right or wrong answers.

The responses are recorded on a 5-point Likert-type scale. The divisions of the Likert-type scale range from 5 to 1 between the responses "like me" and "unlike me." Statements representing positive self-esteem are scored 5 points ("like me") to 1 point ("unlike me"). Statements representing negative self-esteem are reverse-scored. The reverse-scored items are 2, 5, 10, 13, and 15. The item values are then summed to provide a total score for each respondent. The higher the score, the higher the respondent's self-esteem. The potential score range is 17 to 85.

RELIABILITY AND VALIDITY ASSESSMENTS

The respondents for the study consisted of 98 individuals who completed both the PSES and the SAS. These respondents were approached about participating and were permitted to take the instruments to complete and return by mail. The respondents were free to refuse to participate in the study, and no information to identify them was collected.

The mean age of the sample was 27.93 years, with a standard deviation of 10.10 years. The average education of the group was 14.85 years, with a standard deviation of 1.77 years. Thirty-one percent of the respondents were married and 94% were female. None of the demographic variables accounted for more than 3% of the variance in PSES scores.

Reliability

Two approaches were employed to provide estimates of PSES reliability. First, Cronbach's alpha statistic was determined as an estimate of the internal consistency of the PSES. The alpha for the PSES was .81. Second, a Pearson product-moment correlation coefficient was obtained as a measure of the stability over time of the PSES. Sixty-six of the original 98 subjects completed a 30-day retest of the PSES. The retest coefficient was $r = .51$, which was statistically significant but low, based on reliability standards. However, this may be due to the prolonged interval between test and retest periods.

Internal consistency and stability were also obtained for the SAS. The alpha for the SAS was .70, and the 30-day retest was $r = .29$. The SAS retest coefficient was also statistically significant but low.

Validity

Because Sullivan (1953) and later Coopersmith (1981) both believed that there was a direct, inverse relationship between self-esteem and anxiety, two hypotheses were established to test PSES construct validity, as follows:

1. An inverse relationship exists between anxiety as measured by Zung's SAS and self-esteem as measured by the PSES.
2. Two groups defined by the top and bottom of SAS scores will have significantly different levels of self-esteem.

Hypothesis 1. To test the first hypothesis a Pearson product-moment correlation coefficient was obtained between PSES and SAS scores; it was significant at $r = -.38$. Because the correlation coefficient was a significant, inverse one, the first hypothesis and therefore PSES construct validity was supported.

Hypothesis 2. To test the second hypothesis the respondents were divided into two groups according to their SAS scores. The average SAS

TABLE 9.1 Summary of PSES Scores by Group

Group	*n*	*Mean*	*SD*
1 (SAS < 34)	49	71.53	6.23
2 (SAS > 35)	38	63.32	10.13

TABLE 9.2 Summary of One-way ANOVA Findings for PSES between High- and Low-Anxiety Groups

	df	*SS*	*MS*	*F*	*p*
Between groups	1	210.82	210.82	9.31	.003
Within groups	85	1925.11	22.65		
Total	86	2135.93			

score was 34.62. The group with lower anxiety was the group of respondents with an SAS score of less than 34; the higher-anxiety group had SAS scores greater than 35. The PSES scores for the two groups is shown in Table 9.1. The group with lower anxiety had higher self-esteem scores than did the higher-anxiety group. To test for significance a one-way analysis of variance was obtained on PSES scores between the high- and low-anxiety groups. The results of the one-way ANOVA are in Table 9.2. The two groups that were selected because of their high or low anxiety scores had significantly different levels of self-esteem. Because of the significant group differences, the second hypothesis, and therefore PSES construct validity, was supported.

RELIABILITY AND VALIDITY

This section of the chapter contains a discussion of the results of the reliability and validity assessments conducted for this study. First, the results of the reliability assessment for the PSES are discussed; then the validity results are provided.

Reliability

Reliability–Internal Consistency

To obtain an estimate of internal consistency, Cronbach's alpha statistic was calculated from the respondent's PSES scores. The internal consistency of the PSES was .81, similar to that obtained previously. The initial report of PSES internal consistency was .87 for 112 subjects (Perlow, 1987). The similarity of the two coefficients of internal consistency indicated that the PSES demonstrated adequate internal consistency.

Reliability–Stability

To obtain a measure of stability for the PSES, a 30-day test–retest correlation coefficient was obtained for 66 of the original 98 subjects. The test–retest reliability of the PSES was $r = .51$. The initial stability estimate for the PSES was $r = .84$. Although the smaller number of subjects could account for some decrease in the stability estimate and the coefficient was significant ($p < .02$), adequate stability of the PSES was not in evidence. It is recommended that the interval between test and retest be about 2 weeks. The 30-day retest interval used may have adversely affected the results.

Validity

Two hypotheses were established to provide estimates of the construct validity of the PSES. First, an inverse relationship was hypothesized between PSES and SAS scores. Second, the upper and lower halves of SAS scores were hypothesized to identify groups that differed in levels of self-esteem. Both hypotheses were supported.

The relationship between the PSES and SAS was the first such estimate attempted. Previous work involving the PSES revealed concurrent validity estimates with Coopersmith's (1981) SEI ($r = .78$) and a semantic differential designed to evaluate self-esteem ($r = .69$) (Perlow, 1987).

Known-group comparison as a strategy to measure construct validity also supported validity of the PSES. The original comparision of two groups known to differ in self-esteem indicated that the PSES did discriminate, F (1, 110) = 9.42, $p < .003$ (Perlow, 1987).

CONCLUSIONS

The PSES was an internally consistent measure of self-esteem that again demonstrated acceptable estimates of construct validity. Stability of the PSES was previously demonstrated (Perlow, 1987) yet was not strongly supported in the current study. The lack of stability may indicate that the PSES is a measure of state rather than trait self-esteem. Certainly, any such designation requires further study.

Although a new instrument, the PSES has maintained its claim to internal consistency as well as construct validity. The question of stability needs to be resolved. Once the difficulty of stability is resolved, an extensive factor analysis should be obtained to examine the underlying structure of the PSES.

The implications of a reliable and valid measure of self-esteem for nursing are readily evident. Self-esteem is directly related to the psychological well-being of the individual. Behaviors arising from interpersonal interactions are affected by self-esteem, and the effect of psychological constructs on the physical self is just beginning to be examined.

The value of a tool like the PSES, with few items, is especially significant. Because of its brevity and simplicity, use of the PSES in clinical settings would likely invoke less resistance from staff and greater acceptance from clients. The encouraging results and the obvious advantages of the PSES warrant further testing.

REFERENCES

Bryant, S. (1988, March). *Development of an instrument to measure acceptance of self.* Paper presented at the Measurement of Clinical and Educational Nursing Outcomes Conference, San Diego, CA.

Coopersmith, S. (1981). *The antecedents of self-esteem.* Palo Alto, CA: Consulting Psychologist Press.

James, W. (1890). *The principles of psychology* (Vol. 1). New York: Holt.

Jegede, R. O. (1977). Psychometric attributes of the self-rating anxiety scale. *Psychological Reports, 40,* 303–306.

O'Brien, E. J. (1980). The self-report inventory: Development and validation of a multi-dimensional measure of the self-concept and sources of self-esteem. *Dissertation Abstracts International, 41,* 3191B–3192B.

Perlow, M. (1987). *Coopersmith's adult form self-esteem inventory: A construct validation study.* Unpublished doctoral dissertation, Indiana University, Indianapolis.

Sullivan, H. S. (1953). *The interpersonal theory of psychiatry.* New York: Norton.

Wylie, R. (1974). *The self concept* (Vol. 1) (rev. ed.). Lincoln, NE: University of Nebraska Press.

Wylie, R. (1979). *The self concept* (Vol. 2). Lincoln, NE: University of Nebraska Press.

Zung, W. (1971). A rating instrument for anxiety disorders. *Psychosomatics, 12,* 371–379.

Zung, W. (1974). The measurement of affects: Depression and anxiety. In P. Pichot (Ed.), *Modern problems in pharmacopsychiatry* (Vol. 7, pp. 170–188). Paris, Basel: Karger.

Zung, W. (1979). Assessment of anxiety disorder: Qualitative and quantitative approaches. In W. E. Fann, I. Karacan, A. Pokorny, & R. Williams (Eds.), *Phenomenology and treatment of anxiety* (pp. 1–17). New York: Spectrum.

Zung, W. (1980). *How normal is anxiety?* Kalamazoo, MI: Upjohn.

PSES

		Like Me 5	Somewhat Like Me 4	Neither Like or Unlike Me 3	Somewhat Unlike Me 2	Unlike Me 1
I have high standards for my behavior.						
My life is out of control.	X					
I have realistic values.						
I have big plans.						
My values are not well defined.	X					
I have control of my life.						
People like me for what I am.						
I have stable values.						
I am virtuous.						
My standards are less than others' standards.	X					
People pay attention to me.						
I can control my anxiety.						
People do not always understand the real me.	X					
I am able to achieve what I desire.						
I can't get what I want.	X					
My aims are high.						
I am able to influence others.						

Those indicated "X" are reverse-scored.

The Self-Rating Anxiety Scale (SAS)

Name No.	Age Date	Sex: M F

		None or a little of the time	Some of the time	Good part of the time	Most or all of the time
	1. I feel more nervous and anxious than usual	1	2	3	4
	2. I feel afraid for no reason at all				
	3. I get upset easily or feel panicky				
	4. I feel like I'm falling apart and going to pieces				
X	5. I feel that everything is all right and nothing bad will happen				
	6. My arms and legs shake and tremble				
	7. I am bothered by headaches, neck and back pains				
	8. I feel weak and get tired easily				
X	9. I feel calm and can sit still easily				

	10. I can feel my heart beating fast				
	11. I am bothered by dizzy spells				
	12. I have fainting spells or feel like it				
X	13. I can breathe in and out easily				
	14. I get feelings of numbness and tingling in my fingers, toes				
	15. I am bothered by stomachaches or indigestion				
	16. I have to empty my bladder often				
X	17. My hands are usually dry and warm				
	18. My face gets hot and blushes				
X	19. I fall asleep easily and get a good night's rest				
	20. I have nightmares				

Those indicated "X" are reverse-scored.

10

The Role Inventory: A Tool to Measure Role Identity

Marci Catanzaro

This chapter discusses the Role Inventory, an instrument that measures one's role identity associated with the social positions of parent, partner, and worker.

As the prevalence of chronic disease continues to spiral, nurses increasingly will be concerned with treating the human responses of individuals and families living with long-term illness (American Nurses' Association, 1985). Cross-sectional and case studies have demonstrated that chronic illness affects many aspects of life, including social identity, physical mobility, family and friend relations, and work (Burish & Bradley, 1983; Catanzaro, 1982; Eisenberg, Sutkin, & Jansen, 1984; Hanks & Poplin, 1981; Strauss, 1984; Weinert, 1982; Wright, 1983). Notably absent from the literature were reports of longitudinal studies of adults living with progressive disease.

An integrated theoretical model is being tested in the longitudinal study of the effects of progressive neurologic disease during middle age. The outcome variables in this model are the individual's adjustment to the role transition in terms of identity and social participation. The qualitative data from this study have indicated that when chronically ill middle-aged adults are forced to make changes in the social positions of parent, partner, or worker because of increasing disability, the role identity associated with that social position changes.

REVIEW OF THE LITERATURE

A search of the social science literature and consultation with experts in the field of identity and symbolic interaction indicated that there were many

This project was supported in part by BRSG S07 RR05758, awarded by the Biomedical Research Support Grant Program, Division of Research Resources, National Institutes of Health. The author acknowledges Dr. Clarann Weinert, Montana State University, for her support and material assistance in mailing the Role Inventory to participants in the Northwest Family Health Study.

instruments to measure global identity, gender identity, and ethnic identity. Instruments were available to measure role function of parents and workers and role salience. However, no instruments were found to measure the specific role identity of parent, partner, or worker. The Role Inventory, developed to measure role identity, is a semantic-differential instrument designed to index the connotative meaning of the role identity associated with the status positions of parent, partner, and worker.

CONCEPTUAL BASIS OF THE MEASURE

Role identity, a subunit of the global concept of self, is "the character and the role that an individual devises for [herself or] himself as an occupant of a particular social position" (McCall & Simmons, 1978, p. 65). Role identities are reciprocal relationships that are dependent on recurrent interactions between the person and others. Role identity differs from role salience in that the latter concerns the perceived importance of a role rather than an evaluation of the character of the role. Role function pertains to the ability of an individual to carry out specific tasks associated with a role.

Mead (1934) suggested a relationship between self and role. The reality of self is phenomenological; to have a self is to view oneself from the standpoint of others with whom one interacts. Each of us has many selves, limited only by the number of others or categories of others who respond to us (James, 1910; Mead, 1934). In other words, self is the way in which we describe our relationships to others and is the result of our ability to evaluate our own behavior in terms of the response we believe the behavior would elicit in others (Stryker, 1964, 1980).

Identity is the subjective component of role. Identities are meanings we attribute to the self as an object in a social situation. These meanings of self become known and understood by us through interaction with others in situations in which others respond to us as performers in particular roles. The responses of others provide cues to appropriate role performance and, by implication, to a relevant identity for one who performs in suitable ways. The self is constituted from multiple and interrelated role identities.

PURPOSE OF THE MEASURE

The purpose of the Role Inventory is to measure role identity associated with the status positions of parent, worker, and partner. Role identity is the imaginative view that we devise for ourselves as occupants of a particular social positions. The measurement of role identity involves the measurement of the meaning that an individual attaches to the role.

PROCEDURES FOR DEVELOPMENT

Because no instruments were identified to measure role identity, the measurement literature was reviewed. Use of the semantic-differential format is generally accepted as the most appropriate way of measuring meaning, including the meaning of role identity (Burke, 1980; Burke & Tully, 1977; Friedman & Gladden, 1969; Osgood, Suci, & Tannenbaum, 1957).

Item Generation

Qualitative data obtained from 50 dyads, consisting of an individual living with progressive neurologic disease and his or her partner, were used to identify descriptors of role identity associated with the social positions of parent, partner, and worker. These descriptors served as the foundation for item construction of a norm-referenced semantic-differential instrument to index the connotative meaning of parent, partner, and worker. Adjectives used by the respondents were listed and duplicates eliminated.

The list of 140 adjectives was submitted to a panel of five parents, five workers, and five partners, who were asked to judge (a) whether the adjectives could be used to describe their role in each of the positions and (b) whether the content domain of the constructs had been adequately sampled. Two content experts in identity and identity measurement also evaluated the appropriateness of the adjectives. The 17 judges were asked to evaluate the adjectives as "highly useful," "somewhat useful," or "not useful" to describe their roles. Judges also were asked to list other adjectives that would be useful in describing a parent, partner, or worker. No new adjectives were added. The 19 adjectives that were ranked "highly useful" by all 17 panel members formed the basis of a semantic-differential scale. Bipolar adjectives were selected for each remaining word using the "Semantic Atlas for American English" (Snider & Osgood, 1969). The same list of bipolar adjectives was used to evaluate each of the three status positions. The directions at the top of each page were changed to reflect the concepts of parent, worker, or spouse/partner.

ADMINISTRATION AND SCORING

The scale is self-administered. Respondents are directed to place an "X" on the 5-point line between each pair of bipolar adjectives in the position that best describes themselves as parent [worker, spouse/partner]. The same list of adjectives is used for each concept (see instrument at the end of this chapter).

Each concept is scored by converting the line between the bipolar adjectives to a numerical score, with the high values assigned to the positive adjective. The same list of adjectives was used for each concept. Ratings were summed over all scales (adjectives) in each factor (concept). Scale scores (adjectives) are calculated by assigning numbers to the 5-point line between each pair of bipolar adjectives, with 1 assigned to the negative adjective and 5 to the positive adjective. Total concept scores are obtained by summing the weight of the responses across all adjective pairs. Possible concept scores range from 19 to 95 for each concept, with high scores indicating a positive image of self in the role and low scores indicating a negative image of self. Scores for the concepts of worker, parent, and spouse/partner are calculated separately because each part of the Role Inventory is designed to be used independently of the others.

RELIABILITY AND VALIDITY ASSESSMENTS

Sample and Selection

With the approval of the Human Subjects Review Committee, the Role Inventory and demographic questions were mailed to 200 families randomly selected from a pool of 600 families participating in the Northwest Family Health Study, a national survey of families living with multiple sclerosis. These families initially were recruited through newsletters published by the National Multiple Sclerosis Society.

Usable questionnaires were returned by 194 families, representing a 97% response rate. There were 232 (60.6%) women and 153 (39.4%) men in the sample, including 77 single parents (missing data = 3). The mean age of respondents was 42.5 years (SD = 7.5) with a range of 27 to 70 years (n = 382). Ninety-seven percent (n = 370) of the respondents were Caucasian, with Afro-Americans, Hispanics, Asian Americans, and Native Americans making up the remaining 5%. The respondents were generally well educated. Nearly one half (n = 173) had at least one college degree, including four with doctorates, 41 with master's degrees, 82 with bachelor's degrees, and 50 with associate degrees. Fourteen (3.7%) had not completed high school. Men and women with multiple sclerosis and their spouses completed the survey. The greatest percentage of respondents were ill women and their husbands (see Table 10.1). Six single men and 71 single women participated.

TABLE 10.1 Distribution of Wives and Husbands (n = 310)

Value Label	Frequency	%Valid
Ill wife	119	30.67
Well husband	104	26.80
Ill husband	45	11.60
Well wife	42	10.82

Procedures

The questionnaire booklets were developed according to the guidelines suggested by Dillman (1978). The booklets were mailed and included an addressed, stamped envelope for return of the questionnaires. In addition to the Role Inventory these families completed a battery of questionnaires on individual and family characteristics, disease characteristics, stress, social support, individual functioning, and family functioning. These data will be used to study the relationships between the Role Inventory and other variables that are believed to influence changes in role identity. Reminders to return the questionnaire packet were not sent because of the very high response rate at the end of 3 weeks. Thank you letters were sent to all respondents.

The demographic data and responses to the Role Inventory were coded, entered on a microcomputer, and analyzed with the CRUNCH statistical package. Psychometric evaluation of the instrument included Cronbach's alpha and coefficient theta for internal consistency, item-to-total-scale correlations to determine whether each item met the underlying model of the summated scale, and factor analysis to determine dimensionality.

Reliability

Internal consistency was estimated with Cronbach's alpha, utilizing a covariance matrix, and with coefficient theta derived from the factor analysis. Listwise deletion of missing values was used; an observation with any missing data among the items being intercorrelated was deleted from all correlations.

Partner/Spouse

The concept-of-partner/spouse questionnaire was completed by 307 individuals living with partners at the time of the study. Single parents and widowed and separated individuals were excluded from this portion of the analysis. Seventy-six percent (n = 239) of the sample had been married more than 10 years, and 9% (n = 29) had been married less than 5 years. There were no differences on total concept scores between groups married less than 1 year, 1–4 years, 5–10 years, or more than 10 years.

The mean adjective scale score for spouse was 3.98 (SD = .33; median = 4; mode = 4). Total concept scores ranged from 40 to 95, with a scale mean of 70.99 (SD = 20.2). Internal consistency, estimated with Cronbach's alpha and utilizing a covariance matrix, was .91. The theta coefficient was .87. Interitem correlations ranged from .056 to .665, with an average interitem correlation of .358. Item-to-scale correlations ranged from r = .37 to r = .69.

TABLE 10.2 Current or Usual Occupation (n = 356)

Category	Frequency	%
Professional	84	23.6
Manager	36	10.1
Sales	17	4.8
Clerical	84	23.6
Craft	5	1.4
Operative	20	5.6
Service	45	12.6
Laborer	24	6.7
Farm	9	2.5
No occupation	32	9.0

Worker

The concept-of-worker questionnaire was completed by 372 individuals. These data included single parents as well as those respondents who were living with spouses. The Hollingshead (1965) Social Status Index was used to categorize occupations (see Table 10.2). Full-time employment was held by 176 (47.3%) respondents, and 43 (11.6%) were employed part-time. The remaining 153 (41.1%) were retired or currently unemployed.

The mean adjective scale score for worker was 4.11 (SD = .39; median = 5; mode = 4). Cronbach's alpha was .90, and theta was .86. Total concept scores ranged from 46 to 95, with a scale mean of 74.62 (SD = 18.2). Interitem correlations ranged from .002 to .662, with an average interitem correlation of .336. Item-to-scale correlations ranged from r = .391 to r = .693.

Parent

Parent status was claimed by 325 respondents. The mean number of children was 2.3, with a standard deviation of 1.02. The ages of children ranged from 1 year to 46 years.

The individual scale scores had a mean of 3.91 (SD = .42; median = 4; mode = 4). Total concept scores ranged from 42 to 95 (mean = 62.98; SD = 28.06). Cronbach's alpha internal consistency reliability was established for the concept of parent at .91. Coefficient theta was .85. Interitem correlations ranged from –.133 to .706, with an average interitem correlation of .305. Item-to-scale correlations ranged from r = .254 to r = .634.

Validity

The content validity of the adjectives emanates from the manner in which the list of adjectives was derived. One hundred individuals were asked, during face-to-face interviews, to describe themselves as parents, as partners, and as workers. All 140 unique adjectives that were used in response to this open-ended question were listed and submitted to a panel of 17 judges. Only the 19 adjectives that were ranked by all 17 judges as "highly useful" to describe a parent, a partner, and a worker were retained.

Construct validity was assessed using exploratory factor analysis. Principal-components factor analysis with orthogonal varimax rotation was done with the CRUNCH statistical software. Only those participants were retained who had responded to all 19 adjective pairs for the concept being analyzed. A three-factor solution was achieved for each of the concepts of partner, worker, and parent that is consistent with the conceptual framework for the Role Inventory and with other authors' work with semantic differential measurement techniques (Osgood, 1962; Osgood, et al., 1957, Snider & Osgood, 1969). The evaluative factor is characterized by the scales "good–bad," "kind–cruel," and "fair–unfair." The potency factor is characterized by scales like "strong–weak," "brave–cowardly," and "rugged–delicate." The final factor, activity, which is independent of both evaluation and potency is characterized by scales like "calm–agitated," "active–passive," and "relaxed–tense."

With the concept of partner, the "good–bad" scale contributed 40.54% of the variance and had an eigenvalue of 7.7033. The four adjective pairs "good–bad," "deep–shallow," "fresh–stale," and "sacred–profane" loaded on two factors, and "beautiful–ugly" loaded equally on all three components (see Table 10.3).

The adjective pair "good–bad" explained 37.54% of the variance for

TABLE 10.3 Varimax Rotated Component Loadings for Partner/Spouse

	Evaluative factor	Potency Factor	Activity factor
Nice	.756		
Fair	.724		
Kind	.712		
Honest	.694		
Pleasant	.659		
Clean	.652		
Sacred	.511		
Strong		.772	
Rugged		.721	
Active		.721	
Brave		.626	
Valuable		.544	
Relaxed			.763
Calm			.754
Happy			.700
Deep	.464	.432	
Fresh	.439	.553	
Good	.429		.482
Beautiful	.310	.303	.352

TABLE 10.4 Varimax Rotated Component Loadings for Worker

	Evaluative factor	Potency Factor	Activity factor
Kind	.757		
Nice	.720		
Honest	.684		
Pleasant	.646		
Fair	.630		
Clean	.546		
Strong		.757	
Rugged		.732	
Active		.715	
Brave		.661	
Fresh		.618	
Valuable		.591	
Relaxed			.829
Calm			.773
Happy			.536
Good	.451	.523	
Deep	.411	.515	
Beautiful	.340	.412	
Sacred	.425		.407

the concept of worker and had an eigenvalue of 7.1322. The adjectives "good–bad", "beautiful–ugly," "deep–shallow," and "sacred–profane" loaded on two factors (see Table 10.4).

The adjective pairs "good–bad" explained 35.16% of the variance (83.4%) for the concept of parent. "Good–bad" had an eigenvalue of 6.6800. The adjective pairs "brave–coward" and "fresh–stale" loaded on two components, and the pairs "good–bad," "beautiful–ugly," and "valuable–worthless" loaded on three components (see Table 10.5).

DISCUSSION AND CONCLUSIONS

The Role Inventory can be completed by individuals living in the community. The variation in total scores among the concepts of worker, parent, and partner indicate that the respondents do not place the same connotative meaning on each of these status positions.

A review of individual profiles (the pattern of responses across all scales within each concept) revealed that one single parent and one married parent consistently marked the negative end of the line between the bipolar adjectives for each of the three concepts. Including those two outliers, the median and modal scale response for each word was 4, except for "relaxed–tense," which had a median scale response of 3 and "clean–dirty" and "honest–dishonest," which had median scale responses of 5. Alterations in role identity have been studied over a 3-year period in a

TABLE 10.5 Varimax Rotated Component Loadings for Parent

	Evaluative factor	Potency Factor	Activity factor
Nice	.756		
Kind	.721		
Fair	.714		
Pleasant	.647		
Honest	.627		
Deep	.612		
Sacred	.552		
Clean	.505		
Rugged		.763	
Strong		.698	
Brave		.596	
Active		.582	
Relaxed			.835
Calm			.826
Happy			.667
Fresh	.470	.456	
Good	.389	.295	.410
Beautiful	.344	.281	.242
Valuable	.410	.377	.438

longitudinal study of families living with progressive neurologic disease. Qualitative data have indicated that individuals who experience a role transition associated with the status positions of partner, worker, and parent describe themselves differently when asked to describe themselves as a parent (or worker, partner/spouse) after they have experienced a change in that status position. It is unknown at this time whether the current version of the Role Inventory will show these changes over time.

Alpha reliability coefficients were .90, .91, and .91 for worker, spouse, and parent, respectively. A reliability of .90 is the minimum that should be tolerated in applied settings where important decisions are to be made about intervention with families living with long-term illness (Nunnally, 1978). The alpha coefficient of worker could be raised slightly by deleting the adjective pair "rugged–delicate," but deletion of this adjective pair has virtually no effect on the alpha coefficient of parent or partner. This word pair is one of four adjective pairs that loads consistently on the potency factor.

Factor analysis supported the theoretical constructs of evaluation, potency, and activity. However, the adjective pairs "good–bad" and "beautiful–ugly" loaded on at least two of the three factors. This finding varies from those of other investigators who have used semantic differential in which the word pair "good–bad" had high loadings on the evaluative factor (Osgood et al., 1957; Snider & Osgood, 1969).

The stability of the construct role identity has not been established. As a subunit of the global concept of self, role identity would be expected to be a stable state; however, data from individuals living with long-term illnesses have indicated that role identity does change with changes in status. Normative data for individuals experiencing role transitions not associated with long-term illness have not been obtained.

Further testing of the tool will be done to assess whether the instrument can be used to assess change over time in role identity in the areas of working, living with a partner, and parenting that occur as a result of role transitions. For example, qualitative data have indicated that parents who become less able to participate in activities because of increasing physical disability described themselves as parents more negatively than they did 3 years prior to the role transition. Those who experienced difficulty carrying out role functions as workers because of symptoms of long-term illness described themselves more positively as workers following a change to work that was within their physical capacity. The Role Inventory will be useful for assessing nursing intervention designed to prevent the development of a negative role identity following major role transitions in the lives of chronically ill and other middle-aged adults.

REFERENCE

American Nurses' Association, Cabinet on Nursing Research. (1985). *Directions for nursing research: Toward the twenty-first century.* Kansas City, MO: Author.

Burish, T. G., & Bradley, L. A. (Eds.). (1983). *Coping with chronic disease: Research and application.* San Francisco: Academic Press.

Burke, P. J. (1980). The self: Measurement requirements from an interactionist perspective. *Social Psychology Quarterly, 43,* 18–29.

Burke, P. J., & Tully, J. C. (1977). The measurement of role identity. *Social Forces, 55,* 881–897.

Catanzaro, M. (1982). *Shamefully different: A personal meaning of urinary bladder dysfunction* (Doctoral dissertation, Union for Experimenting Colleges and Universities, 1980). *Dissertation Abstracts International, 42,* 4166A (University Microfilm No. DEO 82-04984).

Dillman, D. A. (1978). *Mail and telephone surveys: The total design method.* New York: Wiley.

Eisenberg, M. G., Sutkin, L. C., & Jansen, M. A. (Eds.). (1984). *Chronic illness and disability through the life span.* New York: Springer Publishing Co.

Friedman, C. J., & Gladden, J. W. (1969). Objective measurement of social role via the semantic differential. In J. G. Snider & C. E. Osgood (Eds.), *Semantic differential technique: A sourcebook* (pp. 484–492). Chicago: Aldine.

Hanks, M., & Poplin, D. E. (1981). The sociology of physical disability: A review of literature and some conceptual perspectives. *Deviant Behavior, 2,* 309–328.

Hollingshead, A. B. (1965). *Four factor index of social status.* Unpublished manuscript, Yale University, Department of Sociology, New Haven, CT.

James, W. (1910). *Psychology: The briefer course.* New York: Holt.

McCall, G. J., & Simmons, J. L. (1978). *Identities and interactions.* New York: Free Press.

Mead, G. H. (1934). *Mind, self, and society.* Chicago: University of Chicago.

Nunnally, J. (1978). *Psychometric theory* (2nd ed.). New York: McGraw-Hill.

Osgood, C. E. (1962). Studies on the generality of affective meaning systems. *American Psychologist, 17,* 10–28.

Osgood, C. E., Suci, G. J., & Tannenbaum, P. H. (1957). *The measurement of meaning.* Chicago: University of Illinois Press.

Snider, J. G., & Osgood, C. E. (1969). *Semantic differential technique: A sourcebook.* Chicago: Aldine.

Strauss, A. S. (1984). *Chronic illness and quality of life.* St. Louis: C. V. Mosby.

Stryker, S. (1964). The interactional and situational approaches. In H. T. Christensen (Ed.), *Handbook of marriage and the family* (pp. 125–170). Chicago: Rand McNally.

Stryker, S. (1980). *Symbolic interactionism.* Menlow Park, CA: Benjamin/Cummings.

Weinert, C. (1982). Long-term illness, social support, and family functioning (Dissertation, University of Washington, Seattle, 1981). *Dissertation Abstracts International, 42,* DA8212647A.

Wright, B. A. (1983). *Physical disability: A psychosocial approach* (2nd ed.). New York: Harper & Row.

Role Inventory

In this section we would like you to describe yourself as a parent, worker, and partner. For each of these roles there is a list of nineteen word pairs that are opposites. For *each* pair of words, please place an "X" on the line in the position that best describes you. For example, if you believed that you are an absolutely fair parent all of the time you would mark the item:

FAIR: __X__ : _____ : _____ : _____ : _____ :UNFAIR

On the other hand, if you are an unfair parent sometimes you would mark the item:

FAIR: _____ : _____ : _____ : __X__ : _____ :UNFAIR

Now use the list of words to describe yourself as a PARENT. If you have never been a parent check here _____ and go to the next page.

PARENT

GOOD: _____ : _____ : _____ : _____ : _____ :BAD
BEAUTIFUL: _____ : _____ : _____ : _____ : _____ :UGLY
STRONG: _____ : _____ : _____ : _____ : _____ :WEAK
CLEAN: _____ : _____ : _____ : _____ : _____ :DIRTY
CALM: _____ : _____ : _____ : _____ : _____ :AGITATED
VALUABLE: _____ : _____ : _____ : _____ : _____ :WORTHLESS
KIND: _____ : _____ : _____ : _____ : _____ :CRUEL
DEEP: _____ : _____ : _____ : _____ : _____ :SHALLOW
PLEASANT: _____ : _____ : _____ : _____ : _____ :UNPLEASANT
HAPPY: _____ : _____ : _____ : _____ : _____ :SAD
SACRED: _____ : _____ : _____ : _____ : _____ :PROFANE
RELAXED: _____ : _____ : _____ : _____ : _____ :TENSE
BRAVE: _____ : _____ : _____ : _____ : _____ :COWARDLY
NICE: _____ : _____ : _____ : _____ : _____ :AWFUL
HONEST: _____ : _____ : _____ : _____ : _____ :DISHONEST
ACTIVE: _____ : _____ : _____ : _____ : _____ :PASSIVE
FRESH: _____ : _____ : _____ : _____ : _____ :STALE
FAST: _____ : _____ : _____ : _____ : _____ :SLOW
RUGGED: _____ : _____ : _____ : _____ : _____ :DELICATE

Note to Users of Instrument: The same list of bipolar adjectives is used to evaluate the status positions of partner and worker. Directions at the beginning of each list of adjectives should reflect the concept measured (i.e., parent, spouse/partner, or worker). The author holds the copyright on the Role Inventory. Permission for use may be obtained from Marci Catanzaro, Ph.D., University of Washington, Physiological Nursing SM-28, Seattle, WA 98195.

11
A Measure of Power As Knowing Participation in Change

Elizabeth Ann Manhart Barrett

This chapter discusses the Power As Knowing Participation in Change Tool, a measure of one's perceived power.

Rogers's (1970, 1986) "science of unitary human beings" postulates that humans can knowingly participate in change. Barrett's (1983, 1986) power theory proposed that power is the way humans knowingly participate in creating their reality by actualizing some potentials for unitary change rather than others. Power was defined as the capacity to participate knowingly in the nature of change characterizing the continuous patterning of the human and environmental fields as manifested by awareness, choices, freedom to act intentionally, and involvement in creating changes (Barrett, 1983, 1986). The methodological focus of Barrett's research concerned development of an instrument to measure the theoretical power construct.

REVIEW OF RELATED LITERATURE

Power

Beginning with the Greeks, philosophers have essentially defined power as "being" (Bergson, 1907/1944; May, 1972; Nietzsche, 1883–1888/1968; Tillich, 1960). Further roots can be traced to the writings of Western European scholars such as Machiavelli (1518/1952) and Hobbes (1651/1950).

Conceptions of social power have focused primarily on process or outcome (Pollard & Mitchell, 1972). Field theories (Cartwright, 1959;

French & Raven, 1959; Lewin, 1951) and exchange theories (Blau, 1964; Emerson, 1962; Thibaut & Kelley, 1959) are process theories. Social and political decision-making theories (Dahl, 1957; Etzioni, 1968; Harsanyi, 1962; March, 1955; McClusky, 1976; Weber, 1927/1947) are outcome theories.

Family theorists have viewed power developmentally and functionally as a system property (Haley, 1976; Madanes, 1981). Connections between sex and power have been a persistent theme (Adler, 1933/1964; Hobbes, 1651/1950; Millett, 1971; Nietzsche, 1883–1888/1968).

Over the past 35 years power motivation theory and research have constituted the major empirical exploration of power in psychology (McClelland, 1975; Veroff & Veroff, 1971; Winter, 1973). Several instruments have been developed to measure power motivation (Good & Good, 1972; Uleman, 1966; Veroff, 1975; Winter, 1973).

The underpinnings of numerous theoretical explorations of power as a capacity of the individual can be traced to Nietzsche's (1883–1888/1968) philosophy. Adler (1933/1964), Frankl (1966), Maslow (1968), and Carl Rogers (1977) ascribed to Nietzsche's idea of will to power as self-actualization. May (1972) viewed power as a human birthright and defined power as "the ability to cause or prevent change" (p. 99).

Although representing a different theoretical base, the concept of participation in quantum physics is consistent with the concept of knowing participation in nursing science. Quantum mechanics "leads to the possibility that our reality is what we choose to make it" (Zukav, 1979, p. 54).

Humans have an active relationship with their environment: awareness plays a role in making choices (Ford & Urban, 1963). The perception of freedom is a universal subjective experience (Knight, 1946) whereby all human beings believe they have some measure of freedom in their choices and decisions (Dubos, 1972). Freedom of will is opposed to determinism (Frankl, 1969). Intentionality contrasts with Descartes's dichotomy of mind and body (May, 1969).

Knowing participation in change is the major axiom in this power theory. Humans are not bystanders; rather, they are participants in experience (Bugental, 1965). Change is the central theme throughout the power literature.

CONCEPTUAL FRAMEWORK

Rogers (1986) maintains that nursing's phenomenon of concern is people and their world. According to the science of unitary human beings, people and their world are four-dimensional energy fields; this means reality is a nonlinear domain without spatial or temporal attributes. More than and different from the sum of their parts, unitary humans are irreducible wholes. Pattern defines the uniqueness of each human and environmental field. Pattern is continuously changing in an acausal reality of openness (Barrett, 1986; Rogers, 1986). Rogers's (1970, 1986) building blocks of energy fields, openness, pattern, and four dimensionality along with the homeodynamic principles of resonancy, integrality, and "helicy" guided the derivation of the power theory.

Power, like energy, can neither be directly observed nor measured. However, the pattern manifestations that characterize power can be operationalized. These field manifestations of power are awareness, choices, freedom to act intentionally, and involvement in creating changes. The knowing participation of power is being aware of what one is choosing to do, feeling free to do it, and doing it intentionally. Awareness and freedom to act intentionally guide participation in choices and involvement in creating changes (Barrett, 1986).

Feeling free to act as one wishes is crucial to having power because it impacts on the types of choices one makes. The theory suggests that to have power is to be involved in creating changes. To involve oneself in creating changes requires feeling free to act intentionally. The degree to which one feels free is related to the kinds of choices one makes and the potency of those choices. This entire process involves awareness. It is the interrelationship of the concepts of awareness, choices, freedom to act intentionally, and involvement in creating changes that constitutes power. Power, a continuous theme in the flow of life experiences, dynamically describes the way humans interact with their environment to actualize some potentials for unitary change rather than others and thereby share in the creation of their human and environmental reality.

PURPOSE OF MEASURE

The purpose of the instrument development was to use the semantic differential technique to measure the meaning of operational indicators of power defined as knowing participation in change.

The semantic differential technique was chosen because it is a methodologically sound approach for measuring the meaning that certain concepts have for certain people at certain times. The model has been shown to be reliable and valid, and it lends itself to statistical techniques for validation purposes (Heise, 1969; Osgood, Suci, & Tannenbaum, 1957). It is an uncomplicated approach that requires a short amount of time to complete. Osgood, Suci, and Tannenbaum (1957) defined the measurement of meaning of a concept by rating the concept against a group of bipolar adjective scales. There are usually seven alternatives on the bipolar-adjective semantic space for responding to a concept. The direction and distance of responses on the set of scales used to measure the concept define the quality and intensity of meaning of the conept for that person (Heise, 1969).

PROCEDURES FOR DEVELOPMENT

Procedures for development consisted of three phases of instrument development: judges' studies, a pilot study, and a validation study. Each phase will be discussed sequentially.

Judges' Studies

Nursing faculty who were considered knowledgeable concerning Rogers's science of unitary human beings served as judges in two studies. A different tool was developed for each of the judges' studies. In the first study five judges were each given a brief written description of a theoretical rationale for the beginning power theory and were asked to check from a list of words or phrases those that were consistent with the given description of power. Those words or phrases represented concepts from the power domain; they were human field behaviors that characterized power. This procedure assisted in the selection of the concepts used to operationalize power. Next, using a 7-point semantic differential approach, judges rated how well 43 bipolar adjective pairs described power according to the theoretical rationale and the science of unitary human beings.

In the second judges' study (n = 4), a description of the theoretical rationale was followed by instructions to rate, using Likert scaling technique, four concepts that characterized power ("awareness," "choices," "freedom to act intentionally," and "involvement in creating changes"). Each concept was further specified by three contexts considered to be indices of the human ("myself") and environmental ("family," and "occupation [work and/or school]") fields. Thus, there were 12 concept-context combinations.

Finally, judges were instructed to use semantic differential technique and make judgments concerning how well each of 38 bipolar adjective pairs described power as characterized by the concepts–contexts previously identified. They were informed that the purpose of such judgments was to discriminate between scales so that the instrument would contain scales that further specified power in a way that was meaningful and consistent with the theoretical rationale and Rogers's science of unitary human beings. The 12 concepts–contexts received a mean rating of 5.0 or above (7-point scale) and therefore were all retained. The 38 adjective scales used to rate the concept of "power" received mean ratings of 4.0 to 6.75. A high score indicated that the juges consistently considered a scale to be relevant. Twenty-four scales were selected for the pilot instrument, including nine reference scales (Jakobovits, 1966; Osgood et al., 1957) that previously had loaded, three per factor, on the factors of Evaluation (E), Potency (P), and Activity (A) (Heise, 1969).

In summary, semantic differential technique was used to construct a power measure comprised of four concepts, three contexts, and 24 scales. The concepts were different field behaviors that characterized power. A different scale, selected from the pool of 24 scales, appeared twice on the list of scales for each of the 12 concept–context combinations. These 12 scales constituted retest reliability items. The word "power" did not appear on the tool.

This measure was pilot-tested. Based on the findings from the analysis of the pilot data, the instrument was revised. The revised version was used in the validation study and consisted of four concept–context combinations plus an additional scale that constituted a retest reliability item.

Sample

A national volunteer sample that was diverse in terms of age, gender, marital status, city size, and geographical residence and that represented various occupations and educational backgrounds was secured. Different subjects participated in a pilot study (n = 267; response rate = 53%) and a validation study (n = 625; response rate = 61%). Subjects were solicited by mail or in person through three routes: (1) computer-generated mailing lists of national professional organizations; (2) membership directories of national professional organizations; (3) various occupational groups accessible to the investigator or colleagues.

Materials

Subjects were given or mailed a packet of materials and asked to return it within 2 weeks. In a cover letter they were asked to read the directions carefully, mark a response for every item, and answer as honestly as possible. They were advised that scores were confidential and would be processed by a code number and that only the results of group data would be reported. It should be noted that the word "power" did not appear on the instrument, nor was it mentioned in any of the accompanying materials. The power instrument contained instructions to check the space on the 7-point semantic differential scale that best reflected the meaning that the concept had for them. Subjects were asked to make one check mark for each bipolar set of words.

Pilot Study

Pilot analysis

The data were analyzed using the SPSS statistical package (Nie, Hull, Jenkins, Steinbrenner, & Bent, 1975). Responses for each subject (n = 267) on the concept–context scale combinations (4 concepts × 3 contexts × 24 scales = 288 variables) were strung out in a single matrix and factor-analyzed using principal components with varimax rotation (Maguire, 1973; Mayerberg & Bean, 1978). Three factors with eigenvalues greater than 1.0 emerged. The first factor accounted for 42% of the variance; the second and third factors accounted for an additional 9% of the variance. Simple structure was not obtained (Thurstone, 1947). This suggested that although the factors were statistically orthogonal, they described several related aspects of one construct rather than comprising relatively distinct dimensions of power.

A subsequent oblique solution did not increase the clarity of the factors sufficiently to compensate for the loss of statistical orthogonality. Thus, varimax rotation of principal factors was used in the factor analyses.

The three factors with eigenvalues greater than 1.0 did not fit the typical semantic differential model of E, P, and A factors. When the instrument was constructed, three reference scales for each of the usual semantic differential factors of E, P, and A were included (Heise, 1969; Jakobovits, 1966; Osgood et al., 1957). Contrary to expectations, these scores did not serve as marker scales by loading on three different factors. Rather, each factor consisted of a composit of EPA scales. Additionally, when the nine reference scales were factored separately, only one factor emerged.

When scales do not have their usual alignment on the EPA structure, this phenomenon is called concept-scale interaction. It may indicate methodological artifacts such as homogeneous concept selection or response set or true concept-scale interaction, whereby scales are either irrelevant or their meaning depends on the environment provided by the concept (Heise, 1969).

The next group of factor analyses was designed to determine if subjects differentiated among indices of the human field ("myself") and environmental field ("family," "occupation") when the concepts of "awareness," "choices," "freedom to act intentionally" and "involvement in creating changes" were held constant. The three contexts were listed across the four concepts to determine if subjects responded differently to the concepts in terms of "myself," "family," and "occupation." Conversely, a further group of factor analyses was computed to examine whether or not subjects made differentiations among the four concepts when the contexts were held constant. Respectively, two-factor and three-factor solutions presented the most interpretable picture of these groups of factor-analyzed data. However, regardless of the way the data were arranged, similar factor structures seemed to indicate a consistency of latent traits underlying the scales regardless of the particular strung-out matrices.

To more precisely determine whether or not contexts or concepts differentiated scale responses, congruence coefficients were computed from the two factor solutions. Coefficients of congruence indicate the degree of similarity or stability among factor structures (Merrifield, 1974).

In the case of the contexts, subjects did *not* substantially differentiate among indices of the human and environmental fields. Congruence coefficients ranged from .86 to .98. This offered beginning support for Rogers's (1970) proposition that whereas the human and environmental fields are by definition different, they are integral with one another. Contexts representing indices of the human and environmental field were initially employed in this instrument in order to empirically validate whether or not power generalized across contexts.

Similarly, in the case of the concepts, subjects did not substantially differentiate among the field behaviors that characterize power. Congruence coefficients ranged from .72 to .98.

Congruence indicated that power is a single dimension in terms of both contexts ("myself," "family," "occupation") and concepts ("awareness," "choices," "freedom to act intentionally," "involvement in creating changes"). The related aspects describe power as a unitary phenomenon that does not break down into separate parts.

Next, factor score means were examined in order to select from the pool of 12 concept–context combinations those that most distinctively measured the most highly discriminating aspects of the underlying dimension of power. These means ranged from –.31 ("involvement in creating changes in relations with family") to .17("awareness in relation to occupation").

Revised instrument

The revised version of the instrument was named the Power As Knowing Participation in Change Tool, Version I (PKPCT, VI) and consisted of four concept–context combinations. They were "awareness in relation to occupation," "choices in relation to myself," "freedom to act intentionally in relations with family," and "involvement in creating changes in relations with family."

To allow for further validation of congruence of the human and environmental fields, two additional concepts–contexts were included. Thus, "involvement in creating changes" was examined in relation to "myself" and "occupation" as well as "family."

Scales that loaded simultaneously on more than one factor or that did not load on any factor were eliminated in the revised instrument because they did not help to define the factors. To control for response set, a table of random numbers was used to select the varying order in which the 12 scales used to rate the four concept–context combinations appeared. Also, the polarity of the scales was reversed randomly throughout the instrument. A different scale, selected from the pool of 12 scales, appeared twice on the list of scales for each of the concept–context combinations. These scales constituted retest reliability items.

The pilot version of the instrument was tested for reliability and validity. The results will be reported following the discussion of the validation study.

Validation Study

Validation analysis

Data were collection from the sample of 625 women and men and were analyzed. After reordering the scales to correspond to the order of the first

TABLE 11.1 Factor Loadings and Commonalities of Scales on Four Power Concept–Context Combinations (n = 624)

Scale	Factor 1	Commonality
Superficial–profound	.59	.35
Avoiding–seeking	.70	.50
Worthless–valuable	.63	.40
Unintentional–intentional	.61	.37
Timid–assertive	.62	.39
Following–leading	.56	.31
Chaotic–orderly	.56	.32
Shrinking–expanding	.60	.36
Unpleasant–pleasant	.60	.36
Uninformed–informed	.62	.38
Constrained–free	.59	.35
Unimportant–important	.66	.43

concept–context combination on the PKPCT, VI, responses on these combinations (6 concepts–contexts × 12 scales = 72 variables) were arranged in a single data matrix (Maguire, 1973; Mayerberg & Bean, 1978). One factor with an eigenvalue greater than 1.0 emerged.

Next, the data were analyzed by subsets. The first subset was used to further test the instrument (PKPCT, VI). The second subset was used to test for congruence of the human and environmental fields. Discussion of the analyses of the first and second subset, respectively, follows.

The four concepts ("awareness," "choices," "freedom to act intentionally," and "involvement in creating changes"), along with the associated contexts that had demonstrated in the pilot study greater ability to measure discriminating aspects of the concepts, were factor-analyzed. When data were arranged in a single matrix, one factor with an eigenvalue greater than 1.0 emerged and accounted for 43% of the variance. Varimax rotation of principal components revealed that all scales loaded on this factor (.56–.70). Table 11.1 presents the factor loadings and commonalities.

The factor was named Unitary Power. Unitary reflects the synergistic composite of concepts–contexts–scales; Power reflects knowing participation in change. Unitary Power has a valuable, intentional, important, pleasant, and orderly quality; the strength is profound, informed, assertive, and expanding and is accompanied by activity that is leading, free, and seeking.

The factor score means revealed the same rank order as had occurred in the pilot study. Means ranged from –.25 to .22.

Next, the second subset of data was analyzed to test for congruence. Each set of scales was factor-analyzed to determine if subjects differentiated among indices of the human ("myself") and environmental fields ("family," "occupation") when the concept of "involvement in creating changes" was held constant. Similar factor structures seemed to indicate consistency regardless of context.

To more precisely determine the degree of similarity among factor structures, congruence coefficients were computed (Merrifield, 1974). Findings similar to the results of the pilot study were replicated. Subjects did not substantially differentiate among indices of the human and environmental fields; rather, power generalized across concepts. Congruence coefficients were .99 in each instance.

The means for the power semantic differential scales when four concepts–contexts were merged were negatively skewed. Although the scores ranged from 1 to 7, the means for the scales ranged from 5.06 to 6.07. Standard deviations for the scales ranged from 1.00 to 1.35. It appeared that the tool has an inherent bias toward the high-frequency descriptors. This is possibly due to response set or lack of scales that precisely discriminate the variance on the constructs being measured. Alternatively, the sample may have been biased in the direction of higher power. Given the sources of the sample, this is a logical and highly likely explanation.

Power as Knowing Participation in Change Test, Version II

Congruence coefficients of .99 in the final study provided evidence that power generalized across contexts. Subjects did not respond to a concept in a substantively different manner when the concept was considered in relation to self, family, and occupation. Therefore, a second form of the instrument was proposed. This tool, the Power As Knowing Participation in Change Test, Version II (PKPCT, VII) is identical to the PKPCT, VI, except that the scales measure the four power concepts ("awareness," "choices," "freedom to act intentionally," and "involvement in creating changes") *without* the contextual modifiers ("myself," "family," and "occupation").

ADMINISTRATION AND SCORING

Administration

The power instrument contains instructions to check the space on the 7-point semantic differential scale that best reflects the meaning that the concept has for the subject. Subjects are asked to make one check for each bipolar set of words.

Administration of the PKPCT, VI, or PKPCT, VII, does not require a face-to-face data collection procedure. However, this approach is preferred because it allows for standardizing test conditions.

Scoring

Two types of scoring are appropriate for the PKPCT, VI, and PKPCT, VII. Factor scores allow for greater measurement precision than summation scores and therefore are recommended when variable measurement is for the purpose of hypothesis testing. However, scale scores can be summed for each of the power concepts. With summation scores the range is 12–84 for each power concept and 48–336 for the total score. Lower scores indicate lower power; higher scores indicate higher power. An example of scoring the PKPCT, VII, using the summation method, follows samples from the instrument at the end of this chapter. Although reversed randomly throughout the instrument, the adjectives indicating higher power are profound, seeking, valuable, intentional, assertive, leading, orderly, expanding, pleasant, informed, free, important. One segment of the instrument is presented in the Scoring Guide. Note that the numbers are for the purpose of illustrating the scoring procedure; numbers do not appear on the actual instrument. Use of the tool requires permission from the author.

RELIABILITY AND VALIDITY ASSESSMENTS

Demographic Characteristics

Demographic characteristics of both samples (pilot study, $n = 267$; validation study, $n = 625$.) were similar and will be reported for the sample in the validation study that followed the pilot study. Fifty-five percent of the subjects were women and 45% were men. Ages ranged from 21 to 60; the median age was 35. Sixty-five percent were married. The median educational level was the bachelor's degree. Ninety-four percent were born in the United States, and 99% specified English as the language they best read, wrote, and spoke. Fifty-one percent of the subjects lived in rural communities (less than 70,000 population), and 49% lived in urban areas (greater than 70,000 population). Geographically, each of the 50 states and Washington, DC were represented. Twelve occupational groups as well as a miscellaneous occupational category were represented.

In this beginning attempt to develop an instrument with national norms, the representativeness of the sample met the criteria for diversity in some respects. However, subjects were more highly educated than the U.S. norm. Furthermore, the occupational groups did not represent a cross-section of categories; the professions were overrepresented and skilled and unskilled occupations were underrepresented. One-way analyses of variance revealed no statistically significant differences between gender and power or between education and power. There were some significant relationships between age and power and between occupation and power. However, in both instances correlations were low ($r < .22$).

Pilot Study

Reliability

The reliability of the pilot version of the instrument is reported as the variance of the factor scores obtained for the first factor when all data were merged into a single factor analysis (Kim & Mueller, 1978). These variances were .55 for "awareness in relation to occupation," .58 for "choices in relation to myself," .74 for "freedom to act intentionally in relations with family," and .93 for "involvement in creating changes in relations with family." Reliabilities for the additional concept–context combinations used to further validate integrality of the human and environmental fields were .77 for "involvement in creating changes in relation to myself," and .99 for "involvement in creating changes in relation to occupation." The coefficients of stability for the retest reliability items ranged from .57 to .90.

Validity

Factor loadings were an indication of the construct validity of the scales (Nunnally, 1978). The loadings for the scales selected for the revised instrument, the PKPCT, VI, ranged from .49 to .78.

Validation Study

Reliability

Variances of the factor scores obtained for the first factor when data from the four concepts–contexts were merged into a single factor analysis constituted reliabilities (Kim & Mueller, 1978). These variances were .63 for "awareness in relation to occupation," .75 for "choices in relation to myself," .95 for "freedom to act intentionally in relations with family," and .99 for "involvement in creating changes in relations with family."

The last scale for each of the concept–context combinations was a retest item. The coefficients of stability for these four retest items ranged from .70 to .78.

Validity

The factor loadings for the four concepts–contexts are validity coefficients and indicated construct validity of the scales (Nunnally, 1978). The range was from .56 to .70. Tables 11.2 and 11.3 present a summary of the reliability and validity estimates.

DISCUSSION AND CONCLUSIONS

Discussion

This research presented a beginning theoretical-empirical alternative for measuring power according to Rogers's science of unitary human beings. A beginning instrument designed to measure theoretically proposed behaviors that characterize power was developed, tested, and revised. Judges' studies, a pilot study (n = 267), and a validation study (n = 625) were conducted. The instrument used semantic differential technique and op-

TABLE 11.2 Reliability of Power As Knowing Participation in Change Tool Based on Variance of Factor Scores and Item Retest Reliability

	Pilot study (n = 267)	Validation study (n = 625)
Variance of factor scores		
Awareness in relation to occupation	.55	.63
Choices in relation to myself	.58	.75
Freedom to act intentionally in relations with family	.77	.95
Involvement in creating changes in relation to myself	.77	—
Involvement in creating changes in relations with family	.93	.99
Involvement in creating changes in relation to occupation	.99	—
Correlation coefficients for retest items		
Awareness in relation to occupation	.64	.78
Choices in relation to myself	.68	.73
Freedom to act intentionally	.90	.76
Involvement in creating changes in relation to myself	.60	—
Involvement in creating changes in relations with my family	.69	.70
Involvement in creating changes in relation to occupation	.75	—

erationalized concepts from the power theory derived by Barrett (1983, 1986) from Rogers's conceptual model.

Power was defined as the capacity to participate knowingly in the nature of change characterizing the continuous patterning of the human and environmental fields as manifested by awareness, choices, freedom to act intentionally, and involvement in creating changes. Knowing participation is being aware of what one is choosing to do, feeling free to do it, and doing it intentionally. Awareness and freedom to act intentionally guide participation in choices. Power is the way humans knowingly participate in actualizing some potentials for unitary change rather than others (Barrett, 1983, 1986).

The volunteer national samples of 267 (pilot study) and 625 (validation study) adult women and men represented educationally and occupationally diverse groups. The pilot version of the instrument was revised and used in the validation study (PKPCT, VI). Reliability (.63–.99) and validity as indicated by factor loadings (.56–.70) were acceptable for a beginning measurement instrument. Factor analyses of the power concepts reflected related aspects of one dimension even though evaluation, potency, and activity scales were included in the instrument. Varying factor score means indicated that the salience of the power concepts differed. The loading of all of the scores on one factor, accounting for 43% of the

TABLE 11.3 Summary of Construct Validity of the Power As Knowing Participation in Change Tool Based on Factor Analysis

	Pilot study (*n* = 267)		Validation study (*n* = 625)
	Factor		
	1	2	1
Superficial–profound	.56	—	.59
Shrinking–expanding	.63	—	.60
Following–leading	.51	—	.56
Worthless–valuable	.72	—	.63
Slow–fast	.39	.39	—
Uninformed–informed	.57	—	.62
Rigid–flexible	.33	.28	—
Unintentional–intentional	.52	—	.61
Cautious–risk-taking	.15	—	—
Giving in or giving up–perservering	.41	.31	—
Rounded–angular	–.25	–.35	—
Apathetic–enthusiastic	.52	.51	—
Delicate–rugged	—	.08	—
Unpersuasive–persuasive	.41	.44	—
Indecisive–decisive	.42	.41	—
Chaotic–orderly	—	.49	.56
Timid–assertive	—	.51	.62
Unpleasant–pleasant	—	.78	.60
Avoiding–seeking	—	.63	.70
Powerless–powerful	.48	.51	—
Unimportant–important	.61	—	.66
Seldom–often	.47	.38	—
Static–dynamic	.50	.41	—
Constrained–free	—	.51	.59

variance, is unclear. It may be due to concept-scale interaction, specifically, homogeneous concept selection and/or response set (Heise, 1969).

Congruence coefficients of .99 in the validation study provided evidence that power generalized across contexts. Subjects did not repond to a concept in a substantively different manner when the concept was considered in relation to self, family, and occupation. Thus, a second version of the power instrument was proposed. Specifically, the PKPCT, VII, uses semantic differential technique to measure the four concepts with a set of 12 bipolar adjective scales and one retest scale. It is identical to the PKPCT, VI, except that the concepts of "awareness," "choices," "freedom to act intentionally," and "involvement in creating changes" are not modified by the contexts of "myself," "family," and "occupation."

Trangenstein (1988) tested the PKPCT, VII, with 326 registered nurses and reported the following estimates of reliability using Cronbach's alpha: "awareness," .86; "choices," .88; "freedom to act intentionally," .89;

"involvement in creating changes," .92; and total power (four concepts considered together), .96.

Conclusions

1. One factor, composed of evaluation, potency, and activity scales, emerged from the data. Factor score means for the four power concepts indicated that the salience of the constructs differed.
2. Congruence of the human and environmental fields was demonstrated by similarity of factor structures and suggested that power generalized across indices of the human and environmental fields. This supported Rogers's proposition that the two fields are integral with one another.
3. Age, gender, and education were not important predictors of power.
4. Reliability and construct validity of the PKPCT, VI, were supported.

Recommendations

Further theoretically based methodological development of both versions of the Power As Knowing Participation in Change Tool is indicated. Specific recommendations are proposed.

1. Replicate the validation study with careful attention to selecting a sample that is representative of the diversity of adults who reside in the United States. The relationship of age, gender, education, and occupation to power needs to be examined more critically (Barrett, 1986). A replication study using the PKPCT, VI, and the PKPCT, VII, with a randomly selected national sample is currently in progress (Barrett, 1987).

2. Face-to-face data collection rather than sending materials through the mail or distributing them for later completion would allow for standardizing testing conditions. This would assure clarity of directions and perhaps a decrease in response set through encouragement of careful discrimination of the scales according to the particular concepts being rated. The high means reflected the possibility of a lack of precise discrimination and/or social desirability (Barrett, 1986).

3. Consideration needs to be given to using other measurement approaches such as Likert scaling techniques, multidimensional scaling, and the visual analogue method as means of measuring the power concepts (Barrett, 1986).

In summary, this methodological research concerned development of an instrument to measure power as knowing participation in change from the perspective of Rogers's science of unitary human beings. Power is essential for effective nursing practice (Gorman & Clark, 1986) from the perspective of enhancing the capacity of both the nurse and the client to participate knowingly in change.

Rogers's scientific legacy to nursing sparks exciting possibilities for expanding knowledge of human change. Development of the power theory and instrument provides a means for further exploring the capacity of humans to participate in the creation of their own reality.

REFERENCES

Adler, A. (1964). *Social interest: A challenge to mankind.* New York: Capricorn Books. (Original work published 1933)

Barrett, E. A. M. (1983). *An empirical investigation of Martha E. Rogers' principle of helicy: The relationship of human field motion and power* (Doctoral dissertation, New York University. (University Microfilms No. 84-06, 278).

Barrett, E. A. M. (1986). Investigation of the principle of helicy: The relationship of human field motion and power. In V. Malinski (Ed.), *Explorations on Martha Rogers' science of unitary human beings* (pp. 173–184). Norwalk, CT: Appleton-Century-Crofts.

Barrett, E. A. M. (1987). *Human field motion and power: A replication and extension.* Unpublished manuscript.

Bergson, H. (1944). *Creative evolution* (A. Mitchell, Ed. and Trans.). New York: Modern Library. (Original work published 1907)

Blau, P. M. (1964). *Exchange and power in social life.* New York: Wiley & Sons.

Bugental, J. F. T. (1965). *The search for authenticity.* New York: Holt, Rinehart and Winston.

Cartwright, D. (1959). A field theoretical conception of power. In D. Cartwright (Ed.), *Studies in social power.* Ann Arbor, MI: Institute for Social Research.

Dahl, R. A. (1957). The concept of power. *Behavioral Science, 2,* 201–218.

Dubos, R. (1972). *A God within.* New York: Charles Scribner's Sons.

Emerson, R. M. (1962). Power-dependence relations. *American Sociological Review, 27,* 31–40.

Etzioni, A. (1968). *The active society.* New York: Free Press.

Ford, D. H., & Urban, H. B. (1963). *Systems of psychotherapy.* New York: Wiley & Sons.

Frankl, V. E. (1966). Self-transcendence as a human phenomenon. *Journal of Humanistic Psychology, 6,* 97–106.

Frankl, V. E. (1969). *The will to meaning.* New York: New American Library.

French, J. R. P., Jr., & Raven, B. (1959). The bases of social power. In D. Cartwright (Ed.), *Studies in social power* (pp. 150–167). Ann Arbor, MI: Institute for Social Research.

Good, L. R., & Good, K. C. (1972). An objective measure of the motive to attain social power. *Psychological Reports, 30,* 247–251.

Gorman, S., & Clark, N. (1986). Power and effective nursing practice. *Nursing Outlook, 34*(3), 129–134.

Haley, J. (1976). *Problem-solving therapy: New strategies for effective family therapy.* San Francisco: Jossey-Bass.

Harsanyi, J. C. (1962). Measurement of social power in n-person reciprocal power situations. *Behavioral Science, 7,* 81–91.

Heise, D. R. (1969). Some methodological issues in semantic differential research. *Psychological Bulletin, 72,* 406–422.

Hobbes, T. (1950). *Leviathan.* New York: E. P. Dutton. (Original work published 1651.)

Jakobovits, L. A. (1966). Comparative psycholinguistics in the study of cultures. *International Journal of Psychology, 1,* 15–37.

Kim, J., & Mueller, C. W. (1978). Factor analysis: Statistical methods and practical issues. In J. L. Sullivan (Ed.), *Quantitative applications in the social sciences* (pp. 7–87). (Series No. 07-0 14). Beverly Hills, CA: Sage.

Knight, R. P. (1946). Determinism, "freedom," and psychotherapy. *Psychiatry, 9,* 251–262.

Lewin, K. (1951). *Field theory in social science: Selected theoretical papers* (D. Cartwright, Ed.). New York: Harper & Brothers.

Machiavelli, N. (1952). *The prince* (L. Ricci & E. R. P. Vincent. Trans.). New York: New American Library. (Original work published 1518.)

Madanes, C. (1981). *Strategic family therapy.* San Francisco: Jossey-Bass.

Maguire, T. O. (1973). Semantic differential methodology for the structuring of attitudes. *American Education Research Journal, 10,* 295–306.

March, J. G. (1955). An introduction to the theory and measurement of influence. *American Political Science Review, 49,* 431–451.

Maslow, A. H. (1968). *Toward a psychology of being* (2nd ed.). New York: Van Nostrand.

May, R. (1969). *Love and will.* New York: Dell.

May, R. (1972). *Power and innocence.* New York: Dell.

Mayerberg, C. K., & Bean, A. G. (1978). Two types of factors in the analysis of semantic differential attitude data. *Applied Psychological Measurement, 2,* 469–480.

McClelland, D. C. (1975). *Power: The inner experience.* New York: Irvington.

McClusky, J. E. (1976). Beyond the carrot and the stick: Liberation and power without control. In W. G. Bennis, K. D. Benne, R. Chin, & K. E. Corey (Eds.), *The planning of change* (3rd ed.) (pp. 382–403). New York: Holt, Rinehart, & Winston.

Merrifield, P. R. (1974). Factor analysis in educational research. In F. N. Kerlinger & J. B. Carroll (Eds.), *Review of research in education* (Vol. 1, pp. 393–434). Itasca, IL.: Peacock.

Millett, K. (1971). *Sexual politics.* New York: Avon Books.

Nie, N. H., Hull, C. H., Jenkins, J. G., Steinbrenner, K., & Bent, D. H. (1975). *SPSS: Statistical package for the social sciences* (2nd ed.). New York: McGraw-Hill.

Nietzsche, F. (1968). *The will to power* (W. Kaufmann, Ed. and Trans., & R. J. Hollingdale, Trans.). New York: Random House. (Original work 1883–1888.)

Nunnally, J. C. (1978). *Psychometric theory* (2nd ed.). New York: McGraw-Hill.

Osgood, C. E., Suci, C. J., & Tannenbaum, P. H. (1957). *The measurement of meaning.* Chicago: University of Illinois Press.

Pollard, W. E., & Mitchell, T. R. (1972). Decision theory analysis of social power. *Psychological Bulletin, 78,* 433–446.

Rogers, C. (1977). *Carl Rogers on personal power.* New York: Delacorte Press.

Rogers, M. E. (1970). *An introduction to the theoretical basis of nursing.* Philadelphia: F. A. Davis.

Rogers, M. E. (1986). Science of unitary human beings. In V. Malinski (Ed.), *Explorations on Martha E. Rogers' science of unitary human beings.* Norwalk, CT: Appleton-Century-Crofts.

Thibaut, I. W., & Kelley, H. H. (1959). *The social psychology of groups.* New York: Wiley & Sons.

Thurstone, L. L. (1947). *Multiple-factor analysis.* Chicago: University of Chigago Press.

Tillich, P. (1960). *Love, power and justice: Ontological analyses and ethical applications.* New York: Oxford University press.

Trangenstein, P. A. (1988). *Relationships of power and job diversity to job satisfaction and job involvement.* Unpublished doctoral dissertation, New York University, New York.

Uleman, J. (1966). *A new TAT measure of the need for power.* Unpublished doctoral dissertation, Harvard University, Cambridge, MA.
Veroff, J. (1975). Development and validation of a projective measure of power motivation. *Journal of Abnormal and Social Psychology, 54,* 1–8.
Veroff, J., & Veroff, J. B. (1971). Theoretical notes on power motivation. *Merrill-Palmer Quarterly, 17,* 59–69.
Weber, M. (1947). *The theory of social and economic organization* (T. Parsons, Ed., and A. M. Henderson & T. Parsons, Trans.). New York: Free Press. (Original work published 1927.)
Winter, D. G. (1973). *The power motive.* New York: Free Press.
Zukav, G. (1979). *The dancing wu-li masters.* New York: Morrow.

Barrett PKPCT, VI

Today ___ Mo ___ Day 19 ___ ID Number ___|___|___ Birthday ___ Mo ___ Day 19 ___
Sex M ___ F ___

Check the spaces below that best reflect your feelings about your AWARENESS as it relates to your occupation. Make one check for each bipolar set of words.

In relation to my OCCUPATION (work and/or school):

MY AWARENESS IS

profound	___	___	___	___	___	___	___	superficial
avoiding	___	___	___	___	___	___	___	seeking
valuable	___	___	___	___	___	___	___	worthless
unintentional	___	___	___	___	___	___	___	intentional
timid	___	___	___	___	___	___	___	assertive
leading	___	___	___	___	___	___	___	following
chaotic	___	___	___	___	___	___	___	orderly
expanding	___	___	___	___	___	___	___	shrinking
pleasant	___	___	___	___	___	___	___	unpleasant
uninformed	___	___	___	___	___	___	___	informed
free	___	___	___	___	___	___	___	constrained
unimportant	___	___	___	___	___	___	___	important
unpleasant	___	___	___	___	___	___	___	pleasant

Check the spaces below that best reflect your feelings about your CHOICES as they relate to yourself. Make one check for each bipolar set of words.

In relation to MYSELF:

MY CHOICES ARE

shrinking	___	___	___	___	___	___	___	expanding
seeking	___	___	___	___	___	___	___	avoiding
assertive	___	___	___	___	___	___	___	timid
important	___	___	___	___	___	___	___	unimportant
orderly	___	___	___	___	___	___	___	chaotic
intentional	___	___	___	___	___	___	___	unintentional
unpleasant	___	___	___	___	___	___	___	pleasant
constrained	___	___	___	___	___	___	___	free
worthless	___	___	___	___	___	___	___	valuable
following	___	___	___	___	___	___	___	leading
superficial	___	___	___	___	___	___	___	profound
informed	___	___	___	___	___	___	___	uninformed
timid	___	___	___	___	___	___	___	assertive

Barrett PKPCT, VI, Part 2

ID Number ___|___|___

Check the spaces below that best reflect your feelings about your FREEDOM TO ACT INTENTIONALLY as it relates to your family. Make one check for each bipolar set of words.

In relations with my FAMILY:

MY FREEDOM TO ACT INTENTIONALLY IS

timid ___|___|___|___|___|___|___ assertive
uninformed ___|___|___|___|___|___|___ informed
leading ___|___|___|___|___|___|___ following
profound ___|___|___|___|___|___|___ superficial
expanding ___|___|___|___|___|___|___ shrinking
unimportant ___|___|___|___|___|___|___ important
valuable ___|___|___|___|___|___|___ worthless
chaotic ___|___|___|___|___|___|___ orderly
avoiding ___|___|___|___|___|___|___ seeking
free ___|___|___|___|___|___|___ constrained
unintentional ___|___|___|___|___|___|___ intentional
pleasant ___|___|___|___|___|___|___ unpleasant
orderly ___|___|___|___|___|___|___ chaotic

Check the spaces below that best reflect your feelings about the INVOLVEMENT IN CREATING CHANGE as it relates to your family. Make one check for each bipolar set of words.

In relations with FAMILY:

MY INVOLVEMENT IN CREATING CHANGE IS

unintentional ___|___|___|___|___|___|___ intentional
expanding ___|___|___|___|___|___|___ shrinking
profound ___|___|___|___|___|___|___ superficial
chaotic ___|___|___|___|___|___|___ orderly
free ___|___|___|___|___|___|___ constrained
valuable ___|___|___|___|___|___|___ worthless
uninformed ___|___|___|___|___|___|___ informed
avoiding ___|___|___|___|___|___|___ seeking
leading ___|___|___|___|___|___|___ following
unimportant ___|___|___|___|___|___|___ important
timid ___|___|___|___|___|___|___ assertive
pleasant ___|___|___|___|___|___|___ unpleasant
superficial ___|___|___|___|___|___|___ profound

THANK YOU

Barrett PKPCT, VII

Today ___ Mo ___ Day 19 ___ ID Number ___ ___ ___ Birthday ___ Mo ___ Day 19 ___
Sex M ___ F ___

Check the spaces below that best reflect your feelings about your AWARENESS. Make one check for each bipolar set of words.

MY AWARENESS IS

profound								superficial
avoiding								seeking
valuable								worthless
unintentional								intentional
timid								assertive
leading								following
chaotic								orderly
expanding								shrinking
pleasant								unpleasant
uninformed								informed
free								constrained
unimportant								important
unpleasant								pleasant

Check the spaces below that best reflect your feelings about your CHOICES. Make one check for each bipolar set of words.

MY CHOICES ARE

shrinking								expanding
seeking								avoiding
assertive								timid
important								unimportant
orderly								chaotic
intentional								unintentional
unpleasant								pleasant
constrained								free
worthless								valuable
following								leading
superficial								profound
informed								uninformed
timid								assertive

Barrett PKPCT, VII, Part 2

ID Number ___|___|___

Check the spaces below that best reflect your feelings about your FREEDOM TO ACT INTENTIONALLY. Make one check for each bipolar set of words.

MY FREEDOM TO ACT INTENTIONALLY IS

timid ___|___|___|___|___|___|___ assertive
uninformed ___|___|___|___|___|___|___ informed
leading ___|___|___|___|___|___|___ following
profound ___|___|___|___|___|___|___ superficial
expanding ___|___|___|___|___|___|___ shrinking
unimportant ___|___|___|___|___|___|___ important
valuable ___|___|___|___|___|___|___ worthless
chaotic ___|___|___|___|___|___|___ orderly
avoiding ___|___|___|___|___|___|___ seeking
free ___|___|___|___|___|___|___ constrained
unintentional ___|___|___|___|___|___|___ intentional
pleasant ___|___|___|___|___|___|___ unpleasant
orderly ___|___|___|___|___|___|___ chaotic

Check the spaces below that best reflect your feelings about the INVOLVEMENT IN CREATING CHANGE. Make one check for each bipolar set of words.

MY INVOLVEMENT IN CREATING CHANGE IS

unintentional ___|___|___|___|___|___|___ intentional
expanding ___|___|___|___|___|___|___ shrinking
profound ___|___|___|___|___|___|___ superficial
chaotic ___|___|___|___|___|___|___ orderly
free ___|___|___|___|___|___|___ constrained
valuable ___|___|___|___|___|___|___ worthless
uninformed ___|___|___|___|___|___|___ informed
avoiding ___|___|___|___|___|___|___ seeking
leading ___|___|___|___|___|___|___ following
unimportant ___|___|___|___|___|___|___ important
timid ___|___|___|___|___|___|___ assertive
pleasant ___|___|___|___|___|___|___ unpleasant
superficial ___|___|___|___|___|___|___ profound

THANK YOU

Scoring Guide for Power As Knowing Participation in Change Test

MY INVOLVEMENT IN CREATING CHANGES IS

unintentional	1	2	3	4	5	6	7	intentional
expanding	7	6	5	4	3	2	1	shrinking
profound	7	6	5	4	3	2	1	superficial
chaotic	1	2	3	4	5	6	7	orderly
free	7	6	5	4	3	2	1	constrained
valuable	7	6	5	4	3	2	1	worthless
uninformed	1	2	3	4	5	6	7	informed
avoiding	1	2	3	4	5	6	7	seeking
leading	7	6	5	4	3	2	1	following
unimportant	1	2	3	4	5	6	7	important
timid	1	2	3	4	5	6	7	assertive
pleasant	7	6	5	4	3	2	1	unpleasant
superficial (retest)	1	2	3	4	5	6	7	profound

Sum ____

12
Perception of Empathy Inventory

Kathleen Wheeler

This chapter discusses the Perception of Empathy Inventory, a measure of the patient's perception of the nurse's empathy.

Although empathy has long been recognized as a cardinal characteristic of any helping relationship, the systematic analysis of the theoretical and measurement features of this concept as it relates to the nurse–patient relationship has not been undertaken.

Empathy is a complex variable. It has been described as an ability, an experience, a skill, a tool, a means of communication, a mode of perceiving, a process, a response, and a means of understanding. Empathy as a process is seen as hierarchical in nature. That is, first the nurse must perceive the patient's feelings, then communicate this perception to the patient; finally, the patient must perceive understanding from the nurse. It is this last step that researchers suggest is the most conceptually valid measure of empathy (Gagan, 1983; LaMonica, 1979; Stetler, 1977). The focus of measurement for this tool is this end stage in the process of empathy, the patient's perception of the nurse's empathy.

REVIEW OF THE LITERATURE

Historically, empathy has always been recognized as an essential component of the nurse–patient relationship (Johnson & Martin, 1958; Nightingale, 1946). In an effort to clarify the nature of empathy, exploratory studies have measured the degree of empathy in nurses. Conflicting results have been found. Several studies report that nurses are low in empathic ability (Kalisch, 1971a; LaMonica, Garew, Winder, Bernazza Haase, &

The author gratefully acknowledges consultation with Dr. Godfrey T. Barrett-Lennard and Dr. Geraldine Padilla. This research was supported by PSC-CUNY Research Grant No. 6-67405.

Blanchard, 1976), while others report that nurses are average or above for helping professionals (Forsyth, 1979; Kunst-Wilson, Carpenter, Poser, Verker, & Kushner, 1981; Rogers, 1986). MacDonald (1977), using Hogan's Self Report Empathy Scale, found that male nurses rated higher in empathy than female nurses. Some researchers have observed nurses in an actual clinical situation. Davitz and Davitz (1980) studied empathic nurses in a pilot study of nurses. Two cardinal characteristics of highly empathic nurses emerged: (1) high self-esteem and (2) high value on caring for others. Hardin and Halaris (1983) looked at nonverbal behavior of high- and low-empathy nurses. The only significant finding was that high-empathy nurses had less leg movement during interaction with clients than did low-empathy nurses. Mansfield (1973) used videotapes to identify empathic behavior of a psychiatric nurse with six schizophrenic clients.

Empathic understanding implies a sense that one's feelings are cared about and that there is genuine concern about one's welfare. Empathy confirms the patient's sense of self and validates his or her worth. This confirmation of self, Jourard (1968) says, is having one's feelings, and thus one's existence, acknowledged by another. Drew (1986) asked patients themselves what caregiver behaviors they experienced as confirming themselves as persons. Through an interview schedule, critical attributes of confirmation emerged. Those theoretically consistent with empathy and those descriptive of subjective feelings of self-confirmation are included as critical attributes for the development of the tool for this project.

Most of the research in nursing has measured empathy as an outcome variable in education studies. These studies have measured nurses' or students' empathy after a workshop or educational experience designed to enhance empathy. Kalisch (1971a) found that students who were given an intensive empathy training course achieved significantly higher levels of both actual and perceived empathic ability than did control students. Kunst-Wilson and colleagues (1981) examined whether students exhibited greater levels of empathy at higher educational levels, using Kagan's Affective Sensitivity Scale. Results showed that educational level was a significant predictor of empathic ability even when controlling for the effects of age and nursing experience. LaMonica and colleagues (1976) measured empathy as an outcome variable in their study of the effects of a staff development program on empathy in 39 staff nurses. Using Carkhuff's (1969) tool, they found that the experimental group raised their empathy levels but that these levels were still reported as quite low for a helping relationship. Mynatt (1985) measured empathy in relation to teachers selected as role models, type of nursing program, work experience, differences between family and student empathy levels. Layton (1979b) measured empathy as an outcome variable after giving students four different experimental treatments designed to enhance empathy. She found that only junior nursing students had increased their empathy, not senior students. Rogers (1986), using LaMonica's Empathy Construct Rating Scale (ECRS), found that educational progression was not associated with significant increases in empathy. These studies demonstrate that empathy is a skill that can be learned and can be increased as an ability or trait; however, it appears that nursing education has not adequately included teaching empathy as part of the curriculum.

The idea of utilizing empathy as a therapeutic tool is emerging in the nursing literature. The underlying premise in utilizing empathy as a tool is that if empathy affects the client's feeling and self-worth, then empathy can be used to effect overt and measurable changes in the nurse–patient relationship (LaMonica, 1985). The idea of using empathy as a therapeutic tool coincides with recent psychoanalytic literature (Kohut, 1982).

Consistent with this idea, researchers are looking at nurses' empathy and selected client behaviors or client outcomes. Northouse (1979) explored interpersonal trust and empathy in nurse–patient relationships. He found a strong negative correlation between specific trust and empathy. Welch-McCaffrey (1984) and Tyner (1985) link the concept of empathy to anxiety in that they believe the more anxious the nurse is, the less capable of empathy she is.

Williams (1979) found that empathy did affect client outcomes. She measured self-concept in institutionalized elderly clients before and after they were given group therapy by nurses who measured high and low on the Accurate Empathy Scale. She found that 47% of the subjects who were in the group run by the nurse low on empathy showed a decrease in positive self-concept, whereas 68.4% who attended the group run by the highly empathic nurse increased their positive self-concept. They conclude that if nurses can empathize with their clients' feelings, positive outcomes will occur. Drew's (1986) phenomenological study of caregiver behaviors concurs and suggests that validating the patient as a person does affect recovery/healing. Patients reported that they felt more "relaxed, confident and stronger" when cared for by a caregiver who confirmed them as persons. Thus, it would be expected that the patient feeling more relaxed after care by an empathic nurse would also be less anxious.

A recent study compared hypertensive patients with diabetic patients and perceived clinician empathy (Dawson, 1985). Interesting results were obtained in that hypertensive patients perceived clinicians as least empathic and thus had difficulty in discussing their responses to health care. This study is important because it demonstrates the importance of the client's perception. Even if a nurse measures high on empathic ability, it is the client's perception that determines responsiveness or receptiveness to that quality.

Recent literature has emphasized the client's view of empathy. Hardin and Halaris (1983) state that empathy is a dynamic process by which the empathizer steps (metaphorically) into the other's shoes and the empathee feels understood. Empathy involves the current feelings of the patient as well as the accurate perception of these feelings by the nurse. Watson (1979) further delineates the nature of empathy from the client's perspective. She says the nurse experiences the other person's private world and this implies an understanding and acceptance of others that is nonjudgmental. Empathy connects people to each other and includes both verbal and nonverbal responses.

Tools That Measure Empathy

Most of the research on empathy in nursing has utilized tools from psychology to measure this concept (see Table 12.1). Some of these instruments measure the subject's attitudes or values by presenting either a situation or excerpt to which the individual responds (Hogan, 1969); other measures are based on a judge's evaluation of the subject's empathic performance from a real or simulated interview (Carkhuff, 1969; Truax & Carkhuff, 1967); still others measure the evaluation of empathy from the client's perspective (Barrett-Lennard, 1962).

The most widely used tool to measure empathy in nursing is the Barrett-Lennard Relationship Inventory (BLRI) (Barrett-Lennard, 1962). This instrument consists of five subscales that measure clients' perception of their therapist's empathic understanding, level of regard, unconditionality of regard, congruence, and willingness to be known. The empathy subscale from this tool, which measures empathy from the client's point of view, has frequently been employed to measure empathy in nursing. The basic assumption is that clients are most directly affected by what they themselves experience.

Although the BLRI has been employed extensively in nursing research, several problems have been identified in the literature. Gagan (1983) used the BLRI to explore the relationship between fear of death and empathic ability in nurse subjects. She states that because the tool was originally developed to evaluate the relationships between a therapist and client, it is not always applicable to the nurse–patient relationship. Components of the therapist–client relationship differ in that exploration and confrontation are typically used, whereas the nurse–patient relationship is usually seen as more supportive and nurturing. Also, nursing is more action-oriented; that is, nurses actually care for patients in a "hands-on" way. This component is not addressed in the BLRI empathy subscale.

Another difference between the therapist–client and nurse–patient relationship is the setting where the interaction occurs. Comments by patients about specific questions indicated that not all of the items are relevant to the nurse–patient setting. Gagan (1983) identifies problem questions such as "She/he appreciates what my experiences feel like to me" and "Her/his own attitudes toward some of the things I say, or do, stops her/him from really understanding me." Layton (1979b) also identified difficulty in the use of the BLRI with simulated patients. Two of the 16 items in the empathy subscale were deleted because of inconsistent interpretation by the patient.

A further problem identified is that of assuming that all respondents can operate at a level of mental abstraction needed to respond to some of

TABLE 12.1 Summary of tools used in nursing empathy studies

Instrument	Description of tool	Administration and scoring	Reliability	Validity	Positive points	Negative points
Psychology tools						
Barrett-Lennard Relationship Inventory Empathy Subscale (BLRI) (tool developed by Barrett-Lennard, 1962) (Dawson, 1985; Forsyth, 1979; Gagan, 1983: Hardin & Halaris, 1983; Kalisch, 1971b; Layton, 1979a; Stetler, 1977)	Empathy subscale from this tool measures the evaluation of empathy from the client's perspective. 16 statements describe either an empathic or nonempathic therapist from a phenomenological reference. Measures empathy in the therapist-client relationship.	Subjects are asked to rate their therapist or nurse on a 6-point scale for each of the 16 items; objectively scored by summing response values across items.	Internal reliability $r = .84$ test–retest $r = .83$	Factor analysis = high interitem-correlation. Content validity with expert judges. Predictive validity, i.e., clinician empathy r with client improvement.	Consistent with a fulfillment/ phenomenological frame of reference. Measures empathy from the client's perspective. Ease of administration.	Not appropriate for use with simulated clients. Some items have been identified as not relevant in the nurse–patient relationship.
Carkhuff Empathy Scale. (tool developed by Carkhuff, 1969) (LaMonica, et. al, 1976; Layton, 1979a)	Situational self-report of 16 paragraphs that suggest feelings and content often revealed within a counseling situation.	Original scale had a 9-point scale later modified because it was difficult to discriminate between the different levels.	$r = .84$ interrater correlation coefficient.	No convergent validity with ECRS.	High reliability between independent judges and ability to make discriminations among different degrees of empathy.	Measures the subject's cognitive appreciation of empathy rather than demonstrated ability.

TABLE 12.1 *Continued*

Instrument	Description of tool	Administration and scoring	Reliability	Validity	Positive points	Negative points
	or Simulated audiotape of an interview.	Five-point scale by which empathy is judged by raters (1 = low empathy, 5 = high empathy).	Test–retest $r = .43$ for $p < .01$ after 3 weeks. Interrater $r = .97$	Convergent validity Empathy Test II & BLRI.		Expensive and time-consuming especially if videotapes are used. Raters should be trained and rules for rating and special cases discussed.
Hobart and Fahlberg sociology tool. (tool developed by Hobart & Fahlberg, 1965) (Northouse, 1979)	40 forced-choice agree–disagree statements about job-related nursing issues.	E = no. of correct predictions a nurse makes of a target nurse's dissimilar responses divided by the total number of statements on which the nurse and target have dissimilar responses.	Must be determined for each use.	Predictive validity: $r = -.51$ between specific trust and E.	Sorts out projection and likeness-bias from empathy score; says empathy represents the ability to see the uniqueness and differences in others, emphasis is on the perceptual accuracy dimension of the empathic process.	Not related to client perception or outcome.

Hogan's Self-Report Empathy Scale (ES) (tool developed by Hogan, 1969) (Forsyth, 1979; MacDonald, 1977)	39 "true/false" items on empathy descriptors; 64 questions used in MacDonald's (1977) study.	Self-administered; high scores indicate the individual is likable, warm, and at ease in interpersonal relationships; low scores indicate the individual is aloof, disaffected, and disposed to alienate people.	r = .80 for original scale based on Spearman-Brown formula.	Q-sort by experts = .71. Original scale validity = .62.	Measures the empathic personality.	Does not measure the ability to discriminate or communicate empathy.
Kagan's Affective Sensitivity Scale (ASS) (tool developed by Danish & Kagan, 1971) (Kunst-Wilson et al, 1981)	Series of videotaped interactions; after viewing each vignette, observers receive multiple-choice questions that ask the best description of how the individual in the scene was feeling.	The correct answer is based on self-reports by the interactors; the overall empathy score is determined by adding the number of "correct responses."	Cronbach's alpha = .75; test–retest r = .63	Predictive validity: r = .22 between education level and E; r = .45 for self-report E and E on ASS.	Measures empathy as an ability; assesses empathy from a cognitive–perceptual/behavioral frame.	Restricts the time frame in which subjects have to respond.

TABLE 12.1 *Continued*

Instrument	Description of tool	Administration and scoring	Reliability	Validity	Positive points	Negative points
Truax Accurate Empathy Scale (AE) (tool developed by Truax & Corkhuff, 1967) Mansfield, 1973; Mynatt, 1985; Williams, 1979)	Videotape of actual nurse–client interactions are rated on a 9-point scale from stage 1 (complete lack of empathy) to stage 9 (high empathy).	Scoring based on trained judges' subjective opinions about the empathic qualities of the interview segment.	Interrater reliability developed for each study.	Construct validity lacking. Predictive validity for client outcome.	Measures the discrimination and communication of empathy. Assesses the client's experience of being understood.	Judges must be trained, which is time-consuming. Also need equipment to videotape actual nurse–patient interactions, which is both costly and time-consuming. Not found to be related significantly to client perception.
Nursing tools						
LaMonica Empathy Profile (LaMonica, 1986)	30 statements with a forced-choice format that describes behavioral responses that the individual selects as the one he/she would most likely use.	Self-administered; the total no. of answers in each of the 5 empathy modes are tabulated and then graphed in relation to others so that a profile for each mode is ascertained. The % is based on comparison with scores of others.	None available at present.	None available at present.	Ease of administration. Provides a profile for the helper that may be useful to pinpoint problem areas to increase the use of empathy as a skill.	Questionable validity for use as client-centered tool.

Empathy Construct Rating Scale (LaMonica, 1981) (Rogers, 1986) Unpublished tool.	84 items that describe the way a person may feel or act toward someone. Includes a self-report and a client rating.	Self-administered; each statement is rated on a 6-point Likert scale (+3 to –3; extremely like to extremely unlike). Scored by reversing the scaling of negative items and adding all items.	Reliability alternate forms (form A = .97; form B = .98) Split-half (form A = .89; form B = .96)	Content validity: judges and students. Construct: used factor analysis and multitrait–multimethod with 8 empathy instruments as comparison. Discriminant validity: self and client = .20; self and peer = .10; client and peer = 0. Convergent validity = 0.	Good reliability. Validity OK for construct as a trait or skill from the nurse's perspective.	84 items too lengthy and time-consuming for patient response. Questionable validity for use as client-centered tool.
Empathy Interaction Skills Schedule (Clay, 1984)	Videotape recording of nurse–patient interaction; then subject rates the interaction according to 5 categories of empathic behavior.	Each behavior is coded or scored, with the evaluation of the coding up to the assessor.	r = .96–.98 interrater; r = .91–.86 intrarater.	Content validity; criterion-related validity r = .87; r = .96 between nurse's empathy rating and nurse teachers coding of interaction in the clinical area.	Useful as a teaching tool in the classroom and also as an assessment tool in nurse–patient interactions. Measures empathy as a skill.	Evaluation of the interaction somewhat arbitrary, categories of behavior difficult to interpret. Need videotape equipment, which can be costly and inconvenient.

TABLE 12.1 *Continued*

Instrument	Description of tool	Administration and scoring	Reliability	Validity	Positive points	Negative points
Empathy Test Form I & II (Layton, 1979b)	2 forms, each with 3 parts. Part 1 is 12 t/f statements; Parts 2 and 3 are 12 2-choice forced-choice statements about empathy situations.	Self-administered; to score, tabulate no. of correct responses.	KR#20 r = .34 for Form I and r = .27 for Form II.	Content validity: faculty; construct: r = .46 Form II and the Carkhuff Scale; no r for Form I.	Ease of administration and scoring; alternate form available, measures empathy as an ability or skill.	Self-report not a good indicator of client outcome.
Nurse-Patient Empathic Functioning Scale (Kalisch, 1973)	Excerpts describing an interaction between helper and helped.	Each excerpt is rated on a 5-point scale (0 = no empathy, through 4 = high empathy).	None.	None.	Ease of administration.	Projection bias may occur if subjects perceive object persons in form as like themselves.
The Empathy Inventory (Brucklik, et al., 1967)	Self-administered 8 forms of sentence completion with a stem and forced-choice response.	Faculty who pick the same response as the students are rated as empathic.	None.	None.	Developed to measure empathy of faculty for student.	Not useful to measure empathy in nurse–patient relationship.

the questions. Patients in hospitals may be more heterogeneous and less sophisticated than those seeking psychological counseling. Thus, it must be easily understood by the general population.

The problem of response bias has been raised. Forsyth (1979) found that 98% of patients see their nurses as highly empathic using the BLRI, whereas the Hogan Empathy Scale given to these nurses found only 50% of them to be high in empathy. Thus, it was posited that all patients may perceive their nurses as empathic whether they really are or not. However, it may be the sampling procedure that produced the bias in that the nurses who were being studied referred their patients as subjects. Thus, they may have referred only those who they felt would rate them high on such a scale. A random sample of a nurse's patients might yield more representative data. The problems raised by the BLRI and its use in nursing were addressed, and the tool developed for this project is based on the empathy subscale of the BLRI.

Nursing Empathy Tools

The two most sophisticated instruments developed by nurse researchers are those of Layton (1979a) and LaMonica (1981, 1986). Although LaMonica says the ECRS was developed to measure empathy by three methods of measurement—self, peer, and client—it is not clear how this is accomplished. The same 84 items are used for both self- and client ratings for the nurse. Questions are raised as to how valid the client ratings are because the same items are used to measure two different points of the empathic process. Measuring empathy as a skill or ability that an individual possesses is the first phase of this process, but it does not tap the end phase of this process: how the client perceives or receives the nurse's empathy. Rogers's (1986) results confirm this in that she found no significant effects using the ECRS on client-rated empathy for different nursing programs but did report significant differences in self-rated empathy. Normative data has been reported for the ECRS; however, the tools used to establish construct validity for the ECRS were those measuring similar constructs from the empathizer's perspective rather than the client's. Bias is introduced in establishing normative data for this tool in that the nurses themselves selected patients who rated them on the tool. Thus, the subjects may only be responding as they feel their nurse would like them to respond. The ECRS was never published, but this tool evolved into the LaMonica Empathy Profile, which has been published. This is a 30-statement forced-choice questionnaire that describes behavioral responses the individuals feel they would most likely use (LaMonica, 1986). However, normative data is not available at this time.

Layton's (1979a) Empathy Test is a self-administered three-part, forced-choice test that reports moderate reliability and validity. It measures empathy as a trait or ability. Clay's (1984) Empathy Interaction Skills Schedule consists of videotapes and a skill checklist with categories of behavior listed. This tool was developed to help nurse educators teach students empathy skills. Good validity and reliability are reported. Two other tools that are early efforts at empathy instrument development are The Empathy Inventory (Brunckklik, Thurston, & Feldhusen, 1967) and Kalisch's (1973) Nurse–Patient Empathy Functioning Scale. Several other nursing studies devised methods of analyzing verbal and/or nonverbal responses during interactions with either simulated or real patient encounters (Mansfield, 1973; Stetler, 1977).

The different methods of assessing empathy reflect the complexity of this concept. Confusion exists in terms of the theoretical basis of the various measures. For example, most of the nursing literature on empathy is based on Carl Rogers's (1975) fulfillment/phenomenological frame of reference. This model is concerned with the internal experiences of the individual. Within this model, empathy involves entering "the private perceptual world of the other" (p. 4). Thus, it is the client's subjective experience that is important in defining the empathic process. However, the existing tools in nursing do not measure empathy from the client's perspective but from the nurse's perspective as an ability or trait.

CONCEPTUAL BASIS FOR THIS TOOL

Empathy is defined as a process of understanding whereby the nurse enters the patient's perceptual world, the patient perceives this understanding, and confirmation of self occurs as part of this process. The subconcept of confirmation is to have one's existence acknowledged by another. It is the end stage of this process of understanding, the client's perception of the nurse's empathy, that is the focus of measurement for the proposed instrument.

The conceptual basis for this tool is Carl Rogers's, (1975) fulfillment/ phenomenological frame of reference. From Rogers's frame, the individual is seen as having innate potential and being in lifelong pursuit of fulfilling it.

PURPOSE AND OBJECTIVE

The purpose of the Perception of Empathy Inventory (PEI) is to measure the patient's perception of the nurse's empathy. The objective for this tool is for the patient respondents to rate the level of empathy they perceive in their nurses given a set of descriptive, subjective phenomena characteristic of empathy.

DEVELOPMENT OF THE TOOL

Eight items from the BLRI empathy subscale were used in this tool. Questions on the BLRI that had been pinpointed as problematic in the nursing literature were deleted. After a review of the nursing literature, a list of critical attributes of empathy with confirmation was prepared. Several additional items were then deleted. Only items thought to be representative of the nurse–patient relationship on the BLRI (items 1, 2, 4, 7, 10, 12, 14, and 16) were included. Further items were then prepared, based on the list of critical attributes. A total of 38 items was developed. Five of these 38 items were deleted after content and face validity procedures, leaving a total of 33. (See sample items from the PEI at the end of this chapter.)

ADMINISTRATION AND SCORING

The Likert scale used on the BLRI is a 1–6 scale with three grades of yes responses and three grades of no responses. This was changed to a 1–4 scale with two grades of yes (very true and moderately true) and two grades of no (somewhat true and not at all true). This was done out of concern that acutely ill patients in the hospital may find it easier to choose the most appropriate answer with a simpler rating scale. This type of rating reflects how certain the patient feels about an item being either true or false. Concern is with the subject's feelings about the nurse.

Two subscales were identified with questions 1, 5, 6, 8, 10, 12, 14, 16, 18, 20, 22, 24, 26, 28, and 31 in the overall empathy scale and questions 2, 4, 9, 13, 17, 21, 25, 29, and 32 in the confirmation subscale. Negative items included items 3, 7, 11, 15, 19, 23, 27, 30, and 33. Positive and negative items were arranged in random fashion, avoiding sequences that might result in a response set. Also, items from the overall empathy scale and confirmation subscale were separated. To score, theoretically negative items are reversed so that the higher the score, the more empathic the nurse. Thus, the possible range of scores is 33 to 132, with a score of 33 representing a patient perceiving a nurse as totally unempathic and a score of 132 representing a patient perceiving the nurse as totally empathic.

RELIABILITY AND VALIDITY ASSESSMENTS

The sample consisted of 81 volunteer subjects hospitalized in one of four primary care medical units where 20 full-time registered nurses are employed. Thirty-nine subjects were male, and 41 were female; ages ranged from 27 to 87 years. The subjects were limited to those who could read English.

Several measures were taken to avoid the response-bias issues that have plagued empathy research in the past. The patients chosen represented a convenience sample and were chosen by a researcher or research assistant who did not work in the unit. The subjects were chosen on the basis of their feeling well enough to fill out the form. All AIDS patients were excluded in an effort to control for extraneous emotional factors that might bias the nurse–patient relationship. Approximately 60 physicians' patients were contacted. Thus, the nurses themselves did not select which patients would rate them, and in most cases the nurses were unaware that their patients had participated in the study.

To further control for response bias, the patients were contacted at the end of their nurses' 8-hour shift by the researcher or the research assistant. They were given a letter explaining the study and stressing the confidential nature of their answers and the importance of their answering as honestly as possible. Subjects were assured that their answers would not be seen by their nurses' employers and that all data would be coded, further ensuring anonymity. Both nurses and patients were assigned numbers. The patient was then asked to sign the consent form and fill out the PEI while the research assistant waited outside the room. The patient then sealed the PEI in an envelope provided.

In order to demonstrate the *reliability* of the PEI, Cronbach's alpha was found to be .94 for the entire 33-item scale. In addition item-to-total correlations were calculated for each item. The range of item-to-total correlations was .21 to .83. Items 6, 11, 19, 28, 30, and 33 all fell below .30. These items with weaker correlations will be dropped in the revised tool. No items were found to have negative item-to-total correlations, and the standardized item alpha was .94.

To determine *content validity* for the PEI the index of content validity (CVI) was employed. Two nurse raters were given a list of the critical attributes, information about the purpose of the test, and the items. The nurse raters were both university professors in nursing education, and each had a specialty in psychiatric nursing. They were therefore considered experts in empathy. Each was asked to independently rate the relevance of each item to the attribute, using a 4-point scale: (1) not relevant, (2) somewhat relevant, (3) quite relevant, and (4) very relevant. The CVI was the proportion of items given a rating of quite/very relevant by both raters. Three of the 38 items were rated as not or somewhat relevant, so they were dropped from the tool, leaving the CVI 35/35 or 1.00.

Face validity was determined by giving four patients the tool to inspect. Two further items were deleted before there was agreement that the instrument did measure empathy and confirmation.

One hypothesis was tested as a measure of *construct validity*. It was hypothesized that there would be a positive relationship between the patient's rating of nurse empathy and patient state anxiety. Since one of the effects of empathy is relaxation, it was expected that a decrease in anxiety would indicate that the patient was cared for by a nurse who was perceived as empathic. For a limited sample of 22 of the 81 patients, preshift and postshift anxiety measures were obtained, using the Spielberger State Anxiety Inventory (Spielberger, 1983).

The Spielberger State Anxiety Inventory is a 20-item questionnaire assessing current feelings of apprehension, tension, nervousness, and worry. Cronbach alpha coefficients consistently measure above .90, and validity has been established with factor analysis identifying state anxiety-absent and anxiety-present factors for both sexes. This tool has been used more extensively in research than any other anxiety measure.

To assess the construct validity of the PEI, the total empathy scores were correlated with a change in pre- and postshift patient anxiety levels. A significant relationship was found between total empathy scores assigned to the nurse and reduction in patient anxiety ($r = .52$, $p = .008$). Those patients who saw their nurses as relatively more empathic tended to show a greater reduction in anxiety over the shift; those who saw their nurses as relatively less empathic were more likely to show an increase in anxiety. Thus, there was a positive relationship between the patient's rating of nurse empathy and the reduction in patient state anxiety over an 8-hour shift. The confirmation of this hypothesis demonstrates construct validity in terms of anxiety reduction for the PEI.

Pearson correlation coefficients were also calculated for several demographic variables and the PEI. The total scores on the 33-item scale were not significantly related to marital status, sex of the patient, days hospitalized, days the nurse had cared for the patient, unit the data was collected in, collection of data by research assistant, or whether the nurse was the patient's primary nurse. Empathy scores assigned to the nurse were unrelated to or independent of any of the above variables assessed. This indicates that the measurement of the patient's perception of the nurse's empathy is not mediated by any of the above background variables.

Age was the only significant demographic variable that correlated with change in preshift and postshift anxiety scores. Older patients were more likely to be anxious at the end of the shift; younger patients were more likely to be less anxious ($r = .42$, $p = .039$).

DISCUSSION AND CONCLUSIONS

This study was a beginning effort to establish reliability and validity data for the PEI. It appears that the PEI has excellent reliability. However, it is particularly important to calculate further reliability estimates whenever this tool is used in order to determine that response-bias issues have been addressed for that particular sample.

Several procedures that supported the face and construct validity of the PEI were carried out. Future validity studies will investigate PEI rating and other patient psychological and behavioral variables.

Investigating empathy from the patient's perspective has vast implications for practice. The impact of the caring, empathic nurse on client outcomes has not been examined. Empathy is relevant for all areas where nurses interact with patients but especially for hospital settings. It is the nurse who is intensely and intimately involved with patients on a one-to-one basis. Literature from other disciplines document the importance of caring human relationships to well-being (Kohut, 1982; Lynch, 1977). In therapist–client relationships, the level of empathy, derived from the client's experience of the therapist is strongly linked to outcome (Gurman, 1977; Kurtz & Gurman, 1972). Nursing provides a fertile area to explore the impact of empathy.

REFERENCES

Barrett-Lennard, G. T. (1962). Dimensions of therapist response as causal factors in therapist change. *Psychological Monographs, 76,* (43, Whole No. 562).

Brunckklik, H., Thurston, J. R., & Feldhusen, J. (1967). The Empathy Inventory. *Nursing Outlook, 15,* 42–45.

Carkhuff, R. R. (1969). *Helping and human relationships: A primer for lay and professional helpers.* New York: Holt, Rinehart and Winston.

Clay, M. (1984). Development of an empathic interaction skills schedule in a nursing context. *Journal of Advanced Nursing, 9,* 343–350.

Danish, S. J., & Kagan, N. (1971). Measurement of affective sensitivity: Toward a valid measure of interpersonal perception. *Journal of Counseling Psychology, 18,* 51–54.

Davitz, L. L., & Davitz, J. R. (1980). *Nurses' response to patient's suffering.* New York: Springer Publishing Co.

Dawson, C. (1985). Hypertension, perceived clinician empathy and patient self-disclosure. *Research in Nursing and Health, 8,* 191–198.

Drew, N. (1986). Exclusion and confirmation: A phenomenology of patients' experiences with caregivers. *Image, 18,* 39–43.

Forsyth, G. C. (1979). Exploration of empathy in nurse–client interaction. *Advances in Nursing Science, 1*(2), 53–61.

Gagan, J. S. (1983). Methodological notes on empathy. *Advances in Nursing Science, 5,* 65–72.

Gurman, A. S. (1977). The patient's perception of the therapeutic relationship. In A. S. Gurman & A. M. Razin (Eds.), *Effective psychotherapy: A handbook of research.* New York: Pergamon.

Hardin, S. B. & Halaris, A. L. (1983). Non-verbal communication of patients and high and low empathy nurses. *Journal of Psychosocial and Mental Health Services, 2,* 14–20.

Hobart, C. W., & Fahlberg, N. (1965). The measurement of empathy. *American Journal of Sociology, 70,* 595–603.

Hogan, R. (1969). Development of an empathy scale. *Journal of Consulting and Clinical Psychology, 33,* 307–316.

Johnson, M. M., & Martin, H. W. (1958). A sociological analysis of the nurse's role. *American Journal of Nursing, 58,* 373–377.

Jourard, S. (1968). *Disclosing man to himself.* New York: Van Nostrand.

Kalisch, B. J. (1971a). An experiment in the development of empathy in nursing students. *Nursing Research, 20,* 202–211.

Kalisch, B. J. (1971b). Strategies for developing nurse empathy. *Nursing Outlook, 19,* 714–718.

Kalisch, B. J. (1973). What is empathy? *American Journal of Nursing, 75,* 1548–1553.

Kohut, H. (1982). Introspection, empathy, and the semicircle of mental health. *International Journal of Psychoanalysis, 63,* 395–407.

Kunst-Wilson, W., Carpenter, L., Poser, A., Verker, I., & Kushner, K. (1981). Empathic perceptions of nursing students' self-reported and actual ability. *Research in Nursing and Health, 4,* 283–293.

Kurtz, R. R., & Gurman, D. L. (1972). Different approaches to the measurement of therapist empathy and their relationship to therapy outcomes. *Journal of Consulting and Clinical Psychology, 37,* 106–115.

LaMonica, E. L. (1979). Empathy in nursing practice. *Issues in Mental Health Nursing, 2,* 1–13.
LaMonica, E. L. (1981). Construct validity of an empathy instrument. *Research in Nursing and Health, 4,* 389–400.
LaMonica, E. L. (1985). *The humanistic nursing process.* Belmont, CA: Wadsworth Health Sciences Division.
LaMonica, E. L. (1986). *LaMonica Empathy Profile.* Tuxedo, NY: Xicom.
LaMonica, E. L., Garew, D. K., Winder, A., Bernazza Haase, A. M., Blanchard, K. (1976). Empathy training as the major thrust of a staff development program. *Nursing Research, 25,* 447–451.
Layton, J. M. (1979a). Empathy test-forms I and II. In M. J. Ward & M. Fetler (Ed.), *Instruments for Use in Nursing Education,* Denver, CO: Wiche.
Layton, J. M. (1979b). The use of modeling to teach empathy to nursing students. *Research in Nursing and Health, 2,* 163–176.
Lynch, J. J. (1977). *The broken heart: The medical consequences of loneliness.* New York: Basic Books.
MacDonald, M. R. (1977). How do men and women students rate in empathy? *American Journal of Nursing, 77,* 998.
Mansfield, E. (1973). Empathy: Concept and identified psychiatric nursing behaviors. *Nursing Research, 22,* 525–530.
Mynatt, S. (1985). Empathy in faculty and students in different types of nursing preparation programs. *Western Journal of Nursing Research, 7,* 333–348.
Nightingale, F. (1946). *Notes on nursing: What it is and what it is not.* New York: Appleton-Century. (Facsimile of 1859 edition)
Northhouse, P. (1979). Interpersonal trust and empathy in nurse-patient relationships. *Nursing Research, 28,* 365–368.
Rogers, C. (1975). Empathic: An unappreciated way of being. *The Counseling Psychologist, 5,* 2–9.
Rogers, I. A. (1986). The effects of undergraduate nursing education on empathy. *Western Journal of Nursing Research, 8,* 329–342.
Spielberger, C. D. (1983). *Manual for the State-Trait Anxiety Inventory.* Palo Alto, CA: Consulting Psychologists Press.
Stetler, C. B. (1977). Relationship of perceived empathy to nurses' communication. *Nursing Research, 26,* 432–438
Truax, C., & Carkhuff, R. (1967). *Toward effective counseling and psychotherapy.* Chicago: Aldine.
Tyner, R. (1985). Effects of empathic care for dying patients and their families. *Nursing Clinics of North America, 20,* 393–401.
Watson, J. (1979). *The philosophy and science of caring.* Boston: Little, Brown.
Welch-McCaffrey, D. (1984). Promoting the empathic development of nursing students in the care of the patient with cancer. *Journal of Nursing Education, 23,* 73–76.
Williams, C. L. (1979). Empathic communication and its effect on client outcome. *Issues in Mental Health Nursing, 2*(1), 15–26.

PERCEPTION OF EMPATHY INVENTORY

[The PEI is still in the development phase. The following are sample items.]

Below are listed many different ways that you might feel about your nurse ________.
Please circle the number beside each statement that best describes how you feel about the truth of that statement.

1. I feel it is not at all true.
2. I feel it is somewhat true.
3. I feel it is moderately true.
4. I feel it is very true.

NOT AT ALL TRUE
SOMEWHAT TRUE
MODERATELY TRUE
VERY TRUE

1. She/he tries to see things through my eyes	1	2	3	4
2. She/he cares about me and is genuinely concerned about my welfare	1	2	3	4
3. She/he does not acknowledge my feelings	1	2	3	4
4. I feel comforted just being with her/him	1	2	3	4
5. When I do not say what I mean at all clearly, she/he still understands me	1	2	3	4
6. She/he can be fully aware of my pain and not be overwhelmed or distressed by it	1	2	3	4
7. I feel she/he is too busy to really listen to me	1	2	3	4
8. She/he accepts me as I am	1	2	3	4
9. She/he instills hope in me	1	2	3	4
10. She/he nearly always knows exactly what I mean	1	2	3	4

Please contact Dr. K. Wheeler for more information: 500A East 87th Street, New York, New York 10128

13
A Measure of Clients' Perceptions about Intrusions of Territory and Personal Space by Nurses

Patricia L. Lane

This chapter discusses the Territorial Intrusion—Personal Space Scale, a measure of the client's perceptions regarding intrusions of territory or personal space.

Nonverbal communication is an important part of the nurse–client relationship, which includes the nurse's presence in the client's room (territory) and close proximity to the client (personal space). The concepts of territory and personal space relate to the category of proxemics (the human structuring and perception of space), which pertains to the area of environmental control. In studying nursing theory, "person," "nursing," "society," and "environment" are the four concepts that are commonly defined and examined. Of these four, little attention has been given to developing the concept of environment (Flaskerud & Halloran, 1980) despite its pervasive effect on the person, on nursing, and on society.

Many studies have dealt with the concepts of territory and personal space, but a limited number address these concepts within the health care setting. Territory and personal space have important implications for nurse–client interactions because the use of space is an integral part of each encounter (Tyler, 1982).

Although authors report that the space of clients is being invaded (King, 1981; Roberts, 1973; Selye, 1956; Tate, 1980), there has been minimal documentation of clients' feelings in response to nurses being in their proximity. Meisenhelder (1982) stated that "the client's reaction to intrusion of his personal space in the health-care setting has yet to be scientifically documented" (p. 19). Kerr (1982) presented similar implications for research based on an overview of theory and research related to space used in hospitals.

Hayduk (1978) emphasized that a subject's experience of crowding, intrusion, or inadequate space is of concern rather than the actual physical dimensions of some available space. He attributed the dearth of studies dealing with this area to a lack of methodological tools and research strategies for investigating subjective experiences. He concluded that more work is needed on the consideration of the subjective experience of personal space and the specification of the intrusion-discomfort function.

For these reasons, The Territorial Intrusion—Personal Space Scale (the TIPS Scale) (see instrument at the end of this chapter) has been developed to measure clients' subjective perceptions in response to intrusions of their territory and personal space. Because it is common for clients to feel depersonalized in the hospital setting, it can be helpful to determine their perceptions in response to nursing care. With this feedback from clients, nurses may be able to adapt their nursing care to enhance the client's identity and sense of environmental control and to decrease feelings of depersonalization.

REVIEW OF RELATED LITERATURE

Concepts of Territory and Personal Space

"Territory" refers to a place or geographic area having definite boundaries that are relatively stationary, nonfluctuating, and observable by others (Sommer, 1959, 1969). When people enter the hospital, they are no longer in their usual territory; therefore, they will require territory in the form of their hospital rooms. The areas that clients claim, however, are part of the "nursing" unit; usually, the nurses working in that unit are very familiar with the clients' assigned areas and may claim these areas as their own as well (Minckley, 1968).

In order to provide care, nurses frequently enter this territory and work within the client's personal space. Personal space is usually much smaller than territory (Pastalan, 1970) and has been defined as a 4-foot "bubble" immediately surrounding the individual (Hall, 1966). Personal space is carried around by the individual with the person's body as the center (Sommer, 1959, 1969); it is not directly observable by others and can vary in shape and size (Strube & Werner, 1982).

Most nursing procedures represent a direct intrusion into the personal space of clients (Roberts, 1973), with nurses deciding how close to come to clients and/or how much physical contact to use during communication with them. Individuals who are unable to avoid intrusions may experience discomfort and anxiety (Insel & Lindgren, 1978) or acute embarrassment (Garfinckel, 1964), none of which is conducive to their well-being. On the other hand, because touch is a crucial aspect of most human relationships

(Knapp, 1978), individuals may want nurses to be in their rooms within close proximity and to touch them.

Territorial and personal space behaviors serve as mechanisms to control one's degree of interaction with others, to attain the desired level of privacy (Altman, 1975). In many situations, defense of personal space is so entangled with defense of an immediate territory that one sees them as part of a single process: the defense of privacy. Thus, privacy is a unifying concept under which both territory and personal space are critical elements.

Analysis of Existing Tools

The following four methods are used to study territory and personal space: behavioral, simulated or projective, physiological, and pen-and-paper methods.

Behavioral Methods

Behavioral, or "real life," methods involve subjects' responding by actually distancing themselves from others in some manner in either a controlled (laboratory) or natural (field) setting. These methods are primarily face-valid.

In a controlled setting, subjects may be aware of the measurement, such as with the stop-distance procedure. With this procedure, the experimenter approaches the subject and the subject tells the approacher to stop when moving any closer would cause the subject discomfort; the distance between them is then measured (Argyle & Dean, 1965; Dosey & Meisels, 1969; Louis, 1978; Pedersen, 1973). The stop-distance technique yields high test–retest reliabilities of $r = .93$ (Pedersen, 1973) but suffers from artificiality and possible reactivity. In a natural setting, subjects may be unaware that their personal space is being measured (Becker & Mayo, 1971; Edney & Jordan-Edney, 1974; Ellsworth, Carlsmith, & Henson, 1972; Felipe & Sommer, 1966; Nesbitt & Stevens, 1974; Scherer, 1974; Sommer, 1959). These measures suffer from confounding due to uncontrolled variables.

Simulated Methods

A simulated (or projective) method is the most popular strategy for studying personal space. This method involves the subject's manipulating a representation of self and/or responding to a situation verbally as to one's perceived behavior in the situation. Examples of simulation include the placement of figures or live actresses (Geden & Begeman, 1981; Kuethe, 1962; Little, 1965), dolls (Baxter & Deanovich, 1970), magnets (Gottheil, Corey, & Paredes, 1968), photos (DeWever, 1977; Smith, 1954), and slides (Day, 1973). The main problem with most of these measures is that they are dependent on the subjects' cognitive abilities. Subjects must be able to imagine a physical setting in which they view themselves from a distance and to ascribe characteristics to the other person in the situation as well.

Physiological Methods

Several phsyiological methods have been used to measure the effect of intrusion on personal space by proximity or touch, with mixed results. Examples include the galvanic skin response (McAulay, 1977; Felipe & Sommer, 1966; McBride, King, & James, 1965), arousal effects of closeness on urination (Middlemist, Knowles, & Matter, 1976), and vital signs such as heart rate, respiratory rate, and blood pressure (Knable, 1981; McCorkle, 1974). These physiological methods seem to be rather indirect measures of the psychological dimension of intrusions.

Pen-and-Paper Methods

A number of pen-and-paper methods exist that produce nominal, ordinal, or ratio level data. The following three instruments pertain to nominal level data: (a) the Gough Adjectival Checklist (Gough & Heilbrun, 1965) was used to rate the actual amount of dysphoria a subject experienced (Baxter & Deanovich, 1970); (b) the Comfort When Touched Inventory, a 28-item instrument, was used to measure perceived comfort or discomfort when touched (DeWever, 1977); and (c) the Nonverbal Behavior Worksheet (McCorkle, 1979), an observational checklist, was used to assess nonverbal communication in response to the nurse's being at various distances from the client (McCorkle, 1974).

The Anxiety Due to Territory and Personal Space Intrusion Questionnaire (Allekian, 1973), a Likert-type scale producing ordinal level data, is the prototype for measuring client perceptions in response to space intrusions. According to the reviewers of the instrument (Allekian, 1979), responses related to anger and embarrassment were incongruent with the overall concept of anxiety. They also cited certain concept statements as complex sentences, which made it difficult to determine the part of the sentence to which the clients were responding. Although no psychometric data concerning reliability and validity were given in reports of this study, this tool has been used in other studies without having been substantiated by psychometric data (Johnson, 1979; Punongbayan, 1981).

A magnitude-estimation procedure has also been used in conjunction with items adapted from those designed by Allekian (1972) to provide a direct method of obtaining ratio-scaled data in relation to territorial and personal space intrusions (Donahue, 1980). The training session to understand and practice the technique, in addition to time to respond to a series of stimuli, was approximately 1½ to 2 hours long.

Subjects in the Donahue study (1980) were asked to estimate the amount of sensation produced from a stimulus by drawing a line in relation to a given standard, thereby providing a measure of the intensity of their response. The more traditional method is to ask for a verbal response to an item by assigning a number that reflects the intensity of the reaction in relation to a given standard, as was done in Hinshaw and Schepp's (1983) study. Although ratio level data is obtained by this method, time-consuming interviews may be an imposition on hospitalized adult clients, so this method may not be as useful in an acute-care setting.

In summary, there were several pen-and-paper methods in use to collect data concerning intrusions of space in nursing situations. None of them, though, had a wide selection of response adjectives at an ordinal or higher level that could be obtained during a short period of data collection.

CONCEPTUAL BASIS OF THE TIPS SCALE

The conceptual basis for the TIPS Scale relates to the key concepts of personal space, territory, intrusion, and perception. Personal space is theoretically defined as an extension of the body to include the area immediately around the individual in which the majority of interactions take place (Little, 1965) and is operationally defined as a 4-foot "bubble" immediately surrounding the individual (Hall, 1966).

It is assumed that individuals are surrounded by personal space that can be intruded upon. Intrusion of personal space was operationally defined as the nurse being within 4 feet of the client, with or without instrumental or affective touch. The Personal Space subscale of the TIPS Scale consists of eight sentences (or concept statements) in its final version.

Territory is theoretically defined as the object or area belonging to its owner (Bakker & Bakker-Rabdau, 1973) and is operationally defined in this study as the assigned hospital room and its contents, including the client's personal belongings. Intrusion of territory is defined as the nurse being in the client's room at a distance of 4 feet or more from the client, with our without touch of the client's room possessions or personal belongings. The Territory subscale consists of seven sentences (or concept statements) in its final version.

Perception is theoretically defined as the unique interpretation of selected stimuli from the environment that each individual makes by way of the senses. This interpretation is based on the assumption that each individual has antecedent conditions (such as heredity, learning, past experiences, current needs, and future goals) of which the individual may or may not be aware, and it leads to the labeling of one's response to another individual's behavior as either a positive or negative emotion (King, 1981; Patterson, 1976; Peplau, 1952).

Perception is operationally defined as response choices on 7-point semantic differential scales (Snider & Osgood, 1969) on the TIPS Scale. It is assumed that clients are able to accurately report their perceptions regarding descriptions of situations involving intrusions of their space. The adjective pairs for the territory subscale are "Disagreeable–Agreeable," "Bad–Good," "Annoyed–Pleased," and "Disrespectful–Respectful," for the

Personal Space subscale they are "Nervous–Calm," "Uncomfortable–Comfortable," "Annoyed–Pleased," and "Tense–Relaxed."

The Perceptual Model of the Interpersonal Relationship Between the Nurse and the Client was developed as the conceptual framework by the investigator, based on the work of Argyle & Dean (1965), King (1981), and Peplau (1952). The nurse and client are viewed as both having antecedent conditions that affect how they interpret what they take in through their senses. Based on these conditions, the client may interpret the nurse's nonverbal behavior (in terms of intrusions of territory and/or personal space) as perceptions that are either positive emotions (such as feeling comfortable, agreeable, relaxed, pleased) or negative emotions (such as feeling uncomfortable, disagreeable, tense, annoyed).

The behavior, then, of one individual who intrudes into another's territory or personal space is consciously and/or unconsciously assessed by the other on the basis of antecedent conditions. Assessment leads to perception through interpretation as a positive or negative emotion. The perceptions and actions of each individual affect those of the other.

Concerning the interpersonal relationship between the nurse and the client, the nurse is responsible for assessing the client's positive and negative reactions to intrusions of the client's territory and personal space and for being aware of both verbal and nonverbal behavioral responses during their interactions. The nurse can then use appropriate nonverbal behavior with the client to enhance their interpersonal relationship.

PURPOSE OF THE TIPS SCALE

The overall purpose for developing the TIPS Scale is to provide a psychometrically sound tool to determine client perceptions in response to space intrusions. By using a standard tool, perceptions of clients can also be compared across groups and settings.

PROCEDURES FOR DEVELOPMENT

The TIPS Scale (Lane, 1986) was developed from the earlier work of Allekian (1972), as well as from substantial literature review and the definition and analysis of concepts. The Anxiety Due to Territory and Personal Space Intrusion Questionnaire (Allekian, 1972) was developed as part of a master's thesis and is the prototype for measuring client perceptions in response to space intrusions. The questionnaire consisted of two separate parts: Part I, territorial intrusions, and Part II, personal space intrusions. The items on Allekian's tool were based on an analysis of factors that constituted intrusions. The situations designated were reviewed for corroboration by persons who had previously been hospitalized. The following Likert-type scale responses were based on an analysis of terminology used in describing the emotion of anxiety: "pleased," "agreeable," "indifferent," "annoyed," and "very annoyed" for the Territorial subscale, and "pleased," "agreeable," "indifferent," "uneasy," and "embarrassed" for the Personal Space subscale. The questionnaire was tested on a sample population of 14 patients from two different general hospitals. On the basis of information obtained and suggestions made, the Anxiety Due to Territory and Personal Space Intrusion Questionnaire was modified by refining the situations described and changing the format.

Although Allekian's (1972) questionnaire has been used in other studies, it has not been substantiated with psychometric data concerning reliability and validity. Reviewers of this instrument (Allekian, 1979) also cited a number of problems that needed correction. During two pilot studies and two actual research studies, the current investigator extensively revised the concept statements and response scales of Allekian's tool.

Preliminary Work

Preliminary work consisted of two phases that were conducted in the process of developing the original version of the TIPS Scale. A questionnaire construction plan was written for each stage of tool development delineating the items representing the content area.

An exploratory study was conducted to examine factors viewed by 10 hospitalized adult surgical clients as intrusions of either their territory or personal space. A tool named the Territory and Personal Space Questionnaire (TSPQ), a 32-item instrument, was adapted from Allekian's (1973) Likert-type response questionnaire in the following ways: (a) "nurse" was the only health care provider included in the statements, (b) new items were added based on the investigator's experience in working with surgical clients, and (c) items were randomly arranged to reduce response bias, so they were no longer grouped into two separate subscales.

The decision was later made to revise the format of the responses because there was a limited number of feeling responses on the TSPQ scale. The response scale was changed to a 7-point semantic differential scale, with 16 bipolar adjective pairs under each statement (Snider & Osgood, 1969). These adjective pairs were based on a review of literature on responses to intrusions and on feedback from clients during preliminary work.

Concept statements on the TSPQ that referred to more than one nurse were omitted, several similar concept statements were changed, and four new concept statements were added. The instrument was renamed the Nursing Care Questionnaire (NCQ). It contained 23 concept statements and had the following directions: "What do you think this sentence means to hospitalized adult medical-surgical clients?" Twenty-two female registered nurses who were doctoral students completed the NCQ, which was then altered on the basis of data analysis and the nurses' feedback.

Concept statements that lacked variability in responses, that did not differentiate between territory and personal space for either the TSPQ or NCQ, or that were intrusions through the air, were omitted. Therefore, the original TIPS Scale had 105 items. It consisted of 15 concept statements (6 representing territory and 9 representing personal space) and seven adjective pairs that loaded highest on the evaluative dimension. These were retained because they showed more variance or were considered to be important for inclusion.

Minor changes in the TIPS Scale were made to change its readability from a seventh-grade level to a fourth-grade level. This revision involved using shorter sentences and words with fewer syllables; it was calculated using the Fry Readability Graph (Fry, 1968).

Research Studies

A dissertation study was conducted (Lane, 1986) in which the TIPS Scale was administered to 80 adults, ages 20 to 65 years, from one private hospital, who had had surgery and who were returning for postop visits in outpatient department. Based on data from the dissertation study, response scales were reduced from seven to five adjective pairs on each subscale according to which adjective pairs received more variable responses. There were 17 concept statements and 5 response scales for a total of 85 items on the revised version of the TIPS Scale.

As part of the University of Maryland Measurement Project, a follow-up study was conducted with the revised version of the TIPS Scale. Based on data analysis from this follow-up study, a sample page was later added to the directions to show that each of the five response scales should have a circle on them. (Clients, especially those who were age 60 years and over, occasionally circled a number on only one line per page.) The two new concept statements that had been added to the Personal Space subscale, in which the nurse stands at the bedside while the client is either sitting up or lying down, were deleted because responses indicated variance of less than 1.25 and their inclusions had lowered the Cronbach's alpha for the Personal Space subscale from .8741 to .8699. Thus, there remained eight personal space statements, seven territorial statements, and their five response scales, for a total of 75 items. The decision was also made to separate the subscales and place the Personal Space subscale before the Territorial subscale because there is a possibility that the territorial statements may bias subjects' responses toward the personal space statements.

ADMINISTRATION AND SCORING

Administration

Each concept statement with its corresponding adjective pairs was typed on a separate half-page so that the subject would be responding to only one statement at a time. The TIPS Scale is in a booklet, 5½ inches by 8½ inches, consisting of 24 half-pages, with one vertical staple near the upper left edge and one near the lower left edge. "The TIPS Scale" is used as the title because the acronym is probably less reactive than inclusion of the word "intrusion" in the full title. Color-coding of the questionnaires that were administered to different groups allowed for quick differentiation of questionnaires among groups.

It is helpful, but not mandatory, for the investigator to discuss with subjects the directions that pertain to semantic differential technique and review a sample concept statement and response scale, asking the subject to make a choice from 1 to 7 on the response scale and to circle that number. Otherwise, the subject will be self-directed in completing the questionnaire.

Scoring

The final revised version of the TIPS Scale consists of 15 sentences, with five adjective pairs comprising the response scales under each sentence. These adjective pairs are assigned a score of 1 to 7, with 7 being the most favorable response or most positive emotion and 1 being the least favorable response or most negative emotion. The midpoint, 4, is considered to be neutral or indicating that the concept statement has no meaning to the subject.

Those adjectives listed last in the following pairs will be considered the more favorable adjectives, representing more positive emotions: "Disagreeable–Agreeable," "Annoyed–Pleased," "Uncomfortable–Comfortable," "Nervous–Calm," "Tense–Relaxed," "Disrespectful–Respectful," and "Bad–Good." The first five of the above adjective pairs belong in the response scales for the Personal Space subscale; the first three and the last two of the above pairs belong in the response scales for the Territory subscale.

Subjects indicate their responses to each concept statement by circling a number on a 7-point scale between each set of adjective pairs. The polarity of the adjective pairs was randomly reversed to reduce the possibility of response bias, so those pairs will require recoding in order to be scored correctly. Items to be recoded are 6, 8, 9, 11, 13, 17, 19, 20, 22, 24, 25, 27, 31, 32, 34, 35, 38, 39, 43, 44, 46, 47, 52, 53, 54, 56, 57, 60, 61, 62, 63, 64, 68, 70, 72, and 73.

A summative score can be obtained by adding the five individual response scores together under each concept statement. This summation will result in one score for each of the concept statements. The scores for concept statements in each subscale can be added together, with one score per subscale. Items 1–35 relate to the Personal Scale subscale, and items 36–75 relate to the Territorial subscale. The two subscale scores can be added together for a total TIPS Scale score. (See the TIPS Scale at the end of this chapter.)

In the two main studies that have been conducted by the investigator utilizing the TIPS Scale, response means tended to range from scores of 2 (moderately negative) to 4 (neutral) for the Territory subscale and from 4 (neutral) to 6 (moderately positive) for the Personal Space subscale.

RELIABILITY AND VALIDITY ASSESSMENTS

During the follow-up study, the revised version of the TIPS Scale was administered to a purposive sample of 180 hospitalized surgical clients, ages 20 to 80 years, from three private hospitals. Those who consented to be in the study were asked to take the questionnaire home, complete it, and mail it to the investigator. The sample included surgical clients who had been hospitalized for at least 48 hours; where U.S.-born; had no physical, psychiatric, or neurologic handicaps; were able to read and write English; did not have cancer; and had the allowable number of hospital admissions (four to eight). There was a 70% return rate.

Data analysis consisted of descriptive statistics and reliability and validity measures. The *Statistical Package for the Social Sciences* (SPSS) (Nie, Hull, Jenkins, Steinbrenner, & Bent, 1975) was the computer package used for data analyses on the original version of the TIPS Scale, and SPSS-X (Nie, 1983) was used for data analysis of the revised version.

Item Analysis

Descriptive statistics, including the mean, median, mode, standard deviation, variance, and range, were calculated for subjects' responses. In studies involving the measurement of variations of attributes among people, attributes that vary considerably should be measured (Nunnally, 1978). For this reason, the investigator selected the following criteria for determining variability: Concept statements and response items with a standard deviation *(SD)* of at least 1, variance (Var.) of 1.25, and range (R.) of 4. On the original version, all items met these specified criteria levels; however, on the revised version, the two added concept statements (in which the nurse stands near the client's bed while the client is either lying down or sitting up) did not. Therefore, these two sentences were deleted from the revised version of the TIPS Scale.

Reliability

Internal Consistency

Coefficient alpha (Cronbach's alpha), as the basic formula for determining internal consistency, should be applied to all new measurement methods and should be obtained prior to other estimates of reliability (Nunnally, 1978). Therefore, Cronbach's alpha was computed to measure the consistency of performance of subjects across the items on the TIPS Scale.

The overall Cronbach's alpha remained at an acceptable level of .85 even when the questionnaire was shortened. Results were consistently

TABLE 13.1 Cronbach's Alpha Results for Two Versions of the TIPS Scale[a]

Subscale or scale	Original version[b] (80 Clients)	Revised version[c] (180 Clients)
Territory	.83 (42 items)	.72 (35 items)
Personal Space	.89 (56 items)	.87 (40 items)
TIPS	.85 (98 items)	.85 (75 items)

[a]Without concept statements that were deleted during data analysis.
[b]14 concept statements, 7 response scales.
[c]15 concept statements, 5 response scales.

higher for the Personal Space subscale than for the Territory subscale (see Table 13.1)

On the original version of the tool, the concept statement "The nurse gives you a shot in your buttocks" was later deleted from this analysis and from the TIPS Scale because its inclusion slightly lowered the Personal Space subscale alpha from .890 to .878, and it also consistently factored alone during factor analysis. On the revised version, two added concept statements were deleted because they did not cluster with the other personal space statements during factor analysis.

Stability

Stability of the questionnaire over time or test–retest reliabilty was obtained after a second completion of the TIPS Scale. The scores for the first and second aministration were correlated for each group by computing a Pearson's correlation coefficient (see Table 13.2). In the testing of both the original and revised versions of the TIPS Scale, retest questionnaires were mailed to randomly selected clients 2 weeks after their first questionnaires were returned. The test-retest reliability coefficients for the revised tool indicated that the overall TIPS Scale and subscales were stable at a satisfactory level above .70 (Polit & Hungler, 1983) (see Table 13.2)

TABLE 13.2 Test–Retest Reliability for Two Versions of the TIPS Scale

Subscale	Original version 30 Clients	Revised version 27 Clients
Territory	.639*	.826**
Personal Space	.865*	.764**
Total TIPS Scale	.747*	.772**

*p = .000.
** p = .0001.

Validity

Content Validity

Content validity for the concept statements was established by using the following method: Operational definitions of territory and personal space were written on two separate cards, followed by cards with one concept statement written on each card. Sixteen nurses matched each concept statement with the operational definition with which they thought it most closely corresponded; a third option of "undecided" could also have been selected. It was predetermined that when placement results for each concept statement showed that 12 of the 16 responses (75%) corresponded with the operational definition cited by the instrument developer, the statement would be included in the questionnaire without requiring revision.

Additional preliminary work was done to determine if concept statements and response items on the questionnaire represented situations and feelings that clients actually experienced during hospitalization. Eleven persons, ages 25 to 64 years, who had been hospitalized within the past year were asked for feedback about their having had the nurse in their hospital rooms and/or close to them. Minor changes were made based on their comments and suggestions concerning the questionnaire.

This portion of preliminary work provided further corroboration with clients who had been previously hospitalized, and it helped to validate the concept statements and response scales as realistic ones. The client responses were also insightful in illuminating the basis for their perceptions.

Construct Validity

Construct validity refers to the extent to which a given scale measures a theoretical construct(s). Factor analysis is the statistical procedure utilizied to identify clusters of related variables (Polit & Hungler, 1983). Factor loadings express the correlations between the individual variables (or concept statements); factor loadings above .30 or .40 reveal which concept statements "belong" to which factor (Polit & Hungler, 1983).

Because the bipolar adjective scales in the TIPS Scale loaded highest in the evaluative dimension, a summative score was obtained by adding the individual scale scores together under each concept statement (i.e., each concept statement was summed across the bipolar adjectives associated with that concept). This resulted in one score for each of the concept statements. Each concept statement represented one variable after the scores for adjective pairs were summed.

There were approximately 5 subjects per variable included in testing the original version of the TIPS Scale and 10 subjects per variable in testing the revised version. Because "The nurse gives you a shot in your buttocks" on the original TIPS Scale consistently factored alone in all analyses, the decision was made to remove it prior to further analysis. The same decision was later made for two concept statements on the revised tool (the nurse stands at the bedside while the client is either sitting up or lying down).

On the original version, there were side loadings on several territory concept statements, although these loadings were heavier on the Territory scale. However, in testing the revised version, these side loadings for the Territory subscale did not occur. This is probably due to the higher subject-to-item ratio, which results in more stable factors.

On the revised version, one concept statement that was designed for the Territory subscale did not load on either the Territory or Personal Space subscale. This sentence was related to opening and closing the window shades; it had been altered from the original version. Because it had loaded on the Territory subscale prior to its alteration, it will appear as it was originally written when used in the future (see Table 13.3).

Factor 1 represented the eight concept statements from the Personal Space subscale loadings, and Factor 2 represented the six concept statements (six of the seven statements on the revised version) from the Territory subscale for clients (see underlined factor loadings in Table 13.3). See Figures 13.1 and 13.2 for factor analysis plots showing two clusters.

Instrument Related to Outcome Variable

The Trust subscale of The Patient Satisfaction Instrument (P.S.I.) (Hinshaw & Atwood, 1982) is an 11-item Likert-type summated rating scale that measures patients' perceptions of satisfaction with the communication aspects of the nurse–patient interaction. The purpose of its inclusion was for construct validity assessment via hypothesis testing. Theoretically, there should be a relationship between the variable of perception of intrusion and the variable of perception of patient satisfaction.

During five studies, the Cronbach's alpha for internal consistency of the Trust subscale ranged from .82 to .98 (Hinshaw & Atwood, 1982), which meets the criterion level of .80 or above for mature psychosocial scales (Nunnally, 1978). Validity estimates, obtained by convergent and divergent strategy and predictive modeling (Nunnally, 1978), were strong for the Trust subscale of the P.S.I. (Hinshaw & Atwood, 1982).

Pearson correlation results for 179 subjects revealed a reliability coefficient of $r = .37$ ($p = .0001$) between the Personal Space and Trust subscales, $r = .19$ ($p = .01$) between the Territory and Trust subscales, and $r = .35$ ($p = .0001$) between the overall TIPS Scale and Trust subscale. These results indicate a moderate correlation between the Personal Space and Trust subscales but a weak correlation between the Territory and Trust subscales. Personal space intrusions, which involve entering an area close to the client, logically seem to be more associated with trust between the nurse and client than with territorial intrusions, which occur at a distance of 4 feet or more from the client.

TABLE 13.3 Varimax Rotated Factor Matrices for Two Versions of the TIPS Scale

Concept Statement	80 Clients (original version)		180 Clients (revised version)	
	Factor 1[a]	Factor 2[b]	Factor 1	Factor 2
1. Holds hand/ talk health	*.82*	–.26	*.78*	.15
2. Hand on arm	*.82*	–.28	*.79*	.18
3. Sits on bed	*.77*	–.03	*.63*	.27
4. Physical exam	*.51*	–.32	*.56*	.05
5. Sits close on bed	*.75*	–.15	*.75*	.24
6. Arm around shoulder	*.72*	–.18	*.80*	.35
7. Backrub	*.49*	–.24	*.61*	–.04
8. Holds hand/ treatment	*.57*	–.40	*.74*	–.08
9. Enters without knocking	.38	*.43*	.21	*.45*
10. Sits across room	.31	*.44*	.22	*.66*
11. Looks in closet (revised version only)	—	—	.05	*.67*
12. Stands in doorway	.34	*.75*	–.01	*.81*
13. Opens/closes window shade	.33	*.76*	.42	.27
14. Removes chair	.43	*.67*	–.02	*.59*
15. Leaves door open	.28	*.43*	.30	*.54*

[a]Factor 1 = Personal Space
[b]Factor 2 = Territory
Figures that are in italic represent higher factor loading.

Demographic Variables and Scores on The TIPS Scale

Analysis of variance (ANOVA) results in both studies testing the TIPS Scale revealed that there was a significant difference between male and female clients on the Personal Space subscale; males had consistently higher mean scores (more positive perceptions) than did females (F value 9.38, df 79, $p = .003$; F value 5.88, df 178, $p = .016$). When age differences were examined in the last study, there was also a significant difference in AN-

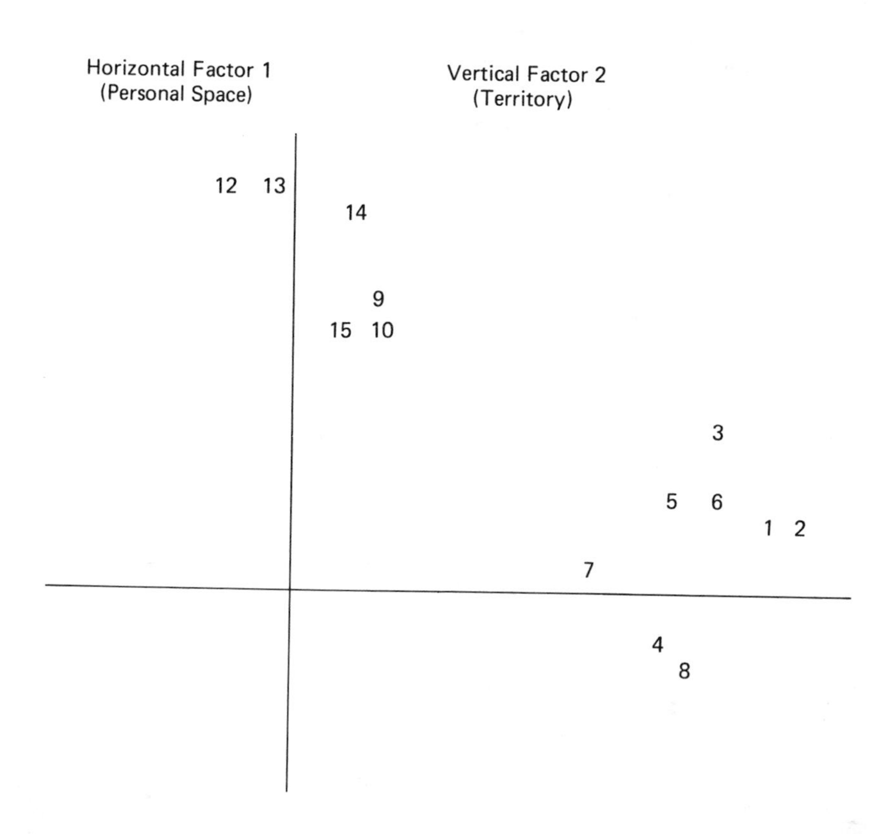

FIGURE 13.1 Factor analysis plot for 80 clients on original tool (varimax). 1 = holds hand/talk health; 2 = hand on arm; 3 = sits on bed; 4 = physical exam; 5 = sits close on bed; 6 = arm around shoulder; 7 = backrub; 8 = holds hand/treatment; 9 = enters without knocking; 10 = sits across room; 11 = looks in closet; 12 = stands in doorway; 13 = opens/closes window shade; 14 = removes chair; 15 = leaves door open.

OVA results on the Personal Space subscale (F value 4.33, *df,* 178, p = .015); the 60–79-year-old age group consistently had higher mean scores than did either the 20–39 or 40–59-year-old age groups (using Duncan's Multiple Range Test post hoc).

Because males and older adults in Western society are two groups that are viewed as having tactile hunger (Montagu, 1978), their responses on the TIPS Scale may reflect their more positive feelings in response to closeness and touch from the nurse. Thus, the TIPS Scale was sensitive to difference between groups during its testing.

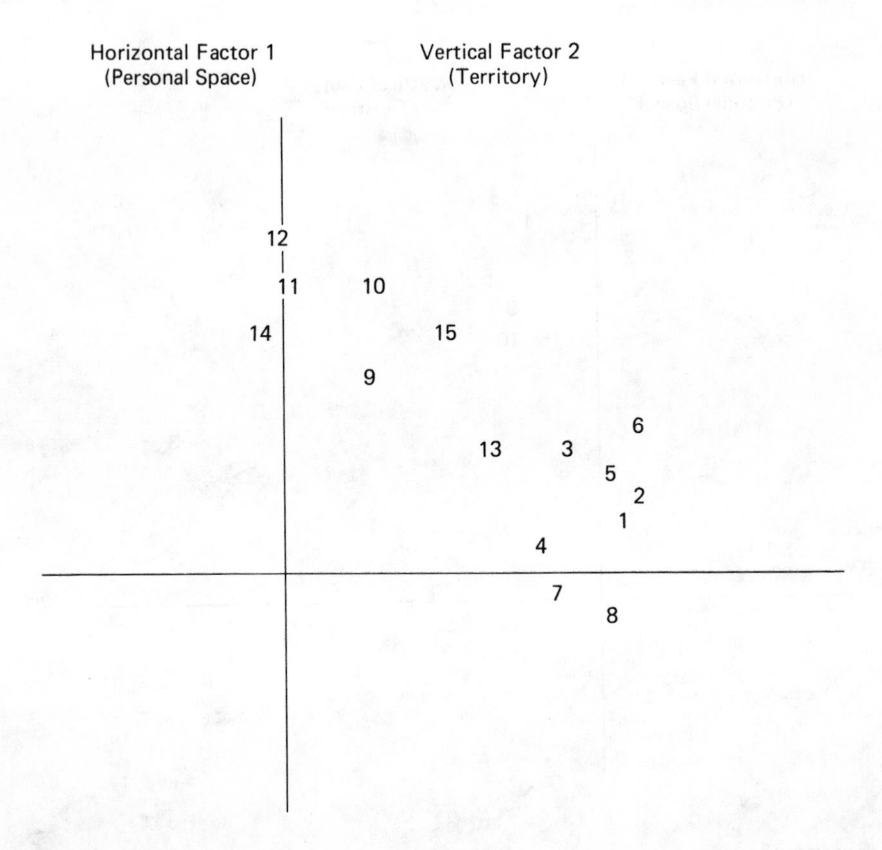

FIGURE 13.2 Factor analysis plot for 180 clients on revised tool (varimax). 1 = holds hand/talk health; 2 = hand on arm; 3 = sits on bed; 4 = physical exam; 5 = sits close on bed; 6 = arm around shoulder; 7 = backrub; 8 = holds hand/treatment; 9 = enters without knocking; 10 = sits across room; 11 = looks in closet; 12 = stands in doorway; 13 = opens/closes window shade; 14 = removes chair; 15 = leaves door open.

DISCUSSION AND CONCLUSIONS

The TIPS Scale has been systematically developed and tested. In terms of reliability, its internal consistency of $r = .85$ is acceptable. Test–retest reliability was also at an acceptable level, though results seemed to fluctuate across the two studies. Regarding construct validity, the two designed subscales were reflected in two separate factors during factor analysis (varimax rotation).

The TIPS Scale reflects a number of nurse–client interactions in the acute-care setting and can be adapted to other settings. The 7-point semantic differential scale allows for discrimination of degrees of various feelings.

Suggestions for Future Development and Testing

The TIPS Scale has already been tested and revised twice. It is recommended that the final version of the TIPS Scale (see instrument at the end of this chapter) be used as presented, except for adapting it to different settings. Reporting future research findings and psychometric data to the current investigator will make it possible to compare results across studies and settings.

Because the TIPS Scale has been administered to clients with a minimum of a high school education, a pilot study needs to be done prior to its administration to a less educated group of clients to determine their ability to understand the questionnaire. When administering the tool to an elderly client, explaining the directions is especially important because this age group of clients may have less experience with completing questionnaires.

Implications for Use of the TIPS Scale

The TIPS Scale has been used to compare perceptions about intrusions between clients and nurses (Lane, 1986) and to determine gender and age differences related to clients' perceptions of intrusions (Lane, 1988). Implications for the use of the TIPS Scale in the future include the following:

1. To compare responses to intrusions of the following groups of clients: (a) age groups of elderly adult clients who are young-old (55 to 75 years) and old-old (75 years and older) because there seem to be differences in their needs for closeness and touch; (b) chronically ill and acutely ill adult clients because the type of illness may affect their perceptions; (c) mildly ill and seriously ill adult clients because there are indications that seriously ill clients may need more touch than mildly ill clients (Day, 1973; McCorkle, 1974); (d) clients in a team nursing unit and those in a primary care nursing unit because the nurse–client relationship varies in these two types of units and may affect client perceptions; (e) clients from different ethnic groups.
2. To study responses to intrusions of clients in the following settings to better determine their needs related to territory and personal space: (a) community settings, where the clients' territory is seen as belonging to the client and the nurse may be seen as an intruder; (b) psychiatric settings (with clients who are reality-oriented); these clients need to know they are cared for yet may be even more likely to misinterpret touch than other types of clients; (c) pediatric settings (children age 10 years through adolescence) because developmental changes may affect these clients' perceptions of territory and personal space.
3. To compare male and female clients' perceptions of male registered nurses (RNs) because the number of males in nursing has increased and they may be perceived differently from female RNs.

Conclusions

The topic area of territory and personal space has only recently been applied to nursing, and there is still much to learn. Tool development to determine clients' perceptions can serve as a means to further application of proxemics research to nursing. Building on the current level of primarily descriptive research, nursing can establish a scientific basis for altering nursing behaviors to better meet clients' needs regarding their space.

REFERENCES

Allekian, C. I. (1972). *Intrusion of territory and personal space as an anxiety producing factor for hospitalized patients.* Unpublished master's thesis, De Paul University, Chicago.

Allekian, C. I. (1973). Intrusions of territory and personal space. *Nursing Research, 22,* 236–241.

Allekian, C. I. (1979). Anxiety Due to Territory and Personal Space Intrusion Questionnaire. In *Instruments for measuring nursing practice and other health care variables* (Vol. 1, pp. 100–105). (DHEW Publication No. HRA 78-53). Hyattsville, MD: U.S. Department of Health, Education and Welfare.

Altman, I. (1975). *The environment and social behavior.* Monterey, CA: Brooks/Cole.

Argyle, M., & Dean, J. (1965). Eye-contact, distance, and affiliation. *Sociometry, 28,* 289–304.

Bakker, C. B., & Bakker-Rabdau, M. K. (1973). *No trespassing! Explorations in human territory.* San Francisco: Chandler & Sharp.

Baxter, J. C., & Deanovich, B. F. (1970). Anxiety arousing effects of inappropriate crowding. *Journal of Consulting and Clinical Psychology, 35,* 174–178.

Becker, F. D., & Mayo, C. (1971). Delineating personal distance and territoriality. *Environment and Behavior, 3,* 375–381.

Day, F. A. (1973). The patient's perception of touch. In E. H. Anderson, B. S. Bergersen, M. Duffey, M. Lohr, & M. H. Rose (Eds.), *Current concepts in clinical nursing* (Vol. 4, pp. 266–275). St. Louis: C. V. Mosby.

DeWever, M. K. (1977). Nursing home patients' perception of nurses' affective touching. *The Journal of Psychology, 96,* 163–171.

Donahue, D. (1980). *Invasion of territorial and personal space as perceived by the surgical patient.* Unpublished master's thesis, University of Arizona, Tucson.

Dosey, M. A., & Meisels, M. (1969). Personal space and self-protection. *Journal of Personality and Social Psychology, 11,* 93–97.

Edney, J. J., & Jordan-Edney, N. L. (1974). Territorial spacing on a beach. *Sociometry, 37,* 92–104.

Ellsworth, P. C., Carlsmith, J. M., & Henson, A. (1972). The stare as a stimulus to flight in human subjects: A series of field experiments. *Journal of Personality and Social Psychology, 21,* 302–311.

Felipe, N. J., & Sommer, R. (1966). Invasions of personal space. *Social Problems, 14,* 206–214.

Flaskerud, J. H., & Halloran, E. J. (1980). Areas of agreement in nursing theory development. *Advances in Nursing Science, 2,* 1–7.

Fry, A. (1968). A readability formula that saves time. *Journal of Reading, 11,* 513–516.

Garfinckel, H. (1964). Studies of the routine grounds of everyday activities. *Social Problems, 11,* 225–250.

Geden, E. A., & Begeman, A. V. (1981). Personal space preferences of hospitalized adults. *Research in Nursing and Health, 4,* 237–241.

Gottheil, E., Corey, J., & Paredes, A. (1968). Psychological and physical dimensions of personal space. *Journal of Psychology, 69,* 7–9.

Gough, H. G., & Heilbrun, A. B. (1965). *The adjective checklist.* Palo Alto, CA: Consulting Psychologists.

Hall, E. T. (1966). *The hidden dimension.* Garden City, NY: Doubleday.

Hayduk, L. A. (1978). Personal space: An evaluative and orienting overview. *Psychological Bulletin, 85,* 117–134.

Hinshaw, A. S., & Atwood, J. (1982). A patient satisfaction instrument: Precision by replication. *Nursing Research, 31*(3), 170–175, 191.

Hinshaw, A. S., & Schepp, K. (1983, May). *Territorial intrusion and client outcomes: The use of magnitude estimation.* Paper presented at 16th annual Communicating Nursing Research Conference, Western Society of Research in Nursing, Portland, OR.

Insel, P. M., & Lindgren, H. C. (1978). *Too close for comfort: The psychology of crowding.* Englewood Cliffs, NJ: Prentice-Hall.

Johnson, F. L. P. (1979). Response to territorial intrusion by nursing home residents. *Advances in Nursing Science, 1,* 21–34.

Kerr, J. A. C. (1982). An overview of theory and research related to space use in hospitals. *Western Journal of Nursing Research, 4,* 395–405.

King, I. M. (1981). *A theory for nursing: Systems, concepts, process.* New York: John Wiley.

Knable, J. (1981). Handholding: One means of transcending barriers of communication. *Heart and Lung, 10,* 1106–1110.

Knapp, M. L. (1978). *Nonverbal communication in human interaction* (2nd ed.). Dallas, TX: Holt, Rinehart and Winston.

Kuethe, J. (1962). Social schemas. *Journal of Abnormal and Social Psychology, 64,* 31–36.

Lane, P. L. (1986). Development and testing of a semantic differential tool to measure and compare perceptions about intrusions of territory and personal space in the hospital between adult surgical clients and female registered nurses (Doctoral dissertation, The University of Texas). *Dissertation Abstracts International, 47–10,* 87-00223.

Lane, P. L. (1988, March). *Development of a semantic differential questionnaire to measure adult surgical clients' perceptions about intrusions of territory and personal space in the hospital.* Paper presented at The Measurement of Clinical and Educational Nursing Outcomes, Sand Diego, CA.

Little, K. B. (1965). Personal space. *Journal of Experimental Social Psychology, 1,* 237–247.

Louis, M. (1978). *Influence of sex, type of approach, and angle of approach on personal space boundary of elderly persons living in retirement housing.* Unpublished doctoral dissertation, The University of Texas, Austin.

McAulay, L. S. (1977). *The relationship between visual impairment and personal space with electrodermal response as indication of intrusion.* Unpublished doctoral dissertation, The University of Texas, Austin.

McBride, G., King, M. G., & James, J. W. (1965). Social proximity effects on galvanic skin responses in adult humans. *Journal of Psychology, 61,* 153–157.

McCorkle, R. (1974). Effects of touch on seriously ill patients. *Nursing Research, 23,* 125–131.

McCorkle, R. (1979). Nonverbal behavior worksheet. In *Instruments for measuring nursing practice and other health care variables* (Vol. 2, pp. 498–505). (DHEW Publication No. HRA 78-53). Hyattsville, MD: U.S. Department of Health, Education and Welfare.

Meisenhelder, J. B. (1982). Boundaries of personal space. *Image, 14,* 16–19.
Middlemist, R. D., Knowles, E. S., & Matter, C. F. (1976). Personal space invasions in the lavatory: Suggestive evidence for arousal. *Journal of Personality and Social Psychology, 33,* 541–546.
Minckley, B. B. (1968). Space and place in patient care. *American Journal of Nursing, 68,* 510–516.
Montagu, A. (1978). *Touching: The human significance of the skin* (2nd ed.). New York: Harper & Row.
Nesbitt, P. D., & Stevens, G. (1974). Personal space and stimulus intensity at a southern California amusement park. *Sociometry, 37,* 105–115.
Nie, N. H. (1983). *SPSSX: Statistical package for the social sciences* X. New York: McGraw-Hill.
Nie, N. H., Hull, C. H., Jenkins, J. G., Steinbrenner, K., & Bent, D. H. (1975). *SPSS: Statistical package for the social sciences* (2nd ed.). New York: McGraw-Hill.
Nunnally, J. C. (1978). *Psychometric theory.* New York: McGraw-Hill.
Pastalan, L. (1970). Spatial behavior: An overview. In L. A. Pastalan & D. H. Carson (Eds.), *Spatial Behavior of Older People* (pp. 111–125). Ann Arbor, MI: University of Michigan.
Patterson, M. L. (1976). An arousal model of interpersonal intimacy. *Psychological Review, 83,* 235–245.
Pedersen, D. M. (1973). Relationships among self, other, and consensual personal space. *Perceptual and Motor Skills, 36,* 732–734.
Peplau, H. E. (1952). *Interpersonal relations in nursing.* New York: G. P. Putnam's Sons.
Polit, D. F., & Hungler, B. P. (1983). *Nursing research: Principles and methods* (2nd ed.). Philadelphia: J. B. Lippincott.
Punongbayan, L. S. M. (1981). *Perceived intrusions into territorial and personal space as anxiety-producing factors to hospitalized patients: Implications to nursing.* Unpublished master's thesis, Concordia College, Manila, Philippines.
Roberts, S. L. (1973). Territoriality: Space and the aged patient in intensive care units. In I. M. Burnside (Ed.), *Psychosocial nursing care of the aged* (pp. 72–83). St. Louis: McGraw-Hill.
Scherer, S. E. (1974). Proxemic behavior of primary school children as a function of their socioeconomic class and subculture. *Journal of Personality and Social Psychology, 29,* 800–805.
Selye, H. (1956). *The stress of life.* New York: McGraw-Hill.
Smith, G. H. (1954). Personality scores and personal distance effect. *Journal of Social Psychology, 39,* 57–62.
Snider, J. G., & Osgood, C. E. (Eds.). (1969). *Semantic differential technique.* Chicago: Aldine.
Sommer, R. (1959). Studies in personal space. *Sociometry, 22,* 247–260.
Sommer, R. (1969). *Personal space: The behavioral basis of design.* Englewood Cliffs, NJ: Prentice-Hall.
Strube, M. J., & Werner, C. (1982). Interpersonal distance and personal space: A conceptual and methodological note. *Journal of Nonverbal Behavior, 6,* 163–170.
Tate, J. W. (1980). The need for personal space in institutions for the elderly. *Journal of Gerontological Nursing, 6,* 439–447.
Tyler, L. W. (1982). Increasing spatial awareness in undergraduate nursing students: A viable concept. *Journal of Nursing Education, 21,* 12–16.

THE TIPS SCALE

This part of the study is being conducted to learn more about nurse–patient communication in the hospital. The purpose of this questionnaire is to find out how you feel about your nurses' behavior this last time you were a patient in the hospital.

The "NURSE" in each sentence is a Female Registered Nurse (R.N.).

DIRECTIONS:

1. Each page has a sentence. There is a word at each end of each line under the sentence. Numbers 1, 2 and 3 relate to the word on the left of that line. Number 4 relates to neutral (or no meaning). Numbers 5, 6, and 7 relate to the word on the right of that line. Use the words above the numbers as a guide.
2. First, read each sentence and the 5 lines below it. Think how you feel about it. Then, circle the number of EACH line that best describes your feelings.
3. Be sure there is a circle on EACH line (5 circles/page).
4. Work at a fairly high speed. Do not worry or puzzle over the sentences. Give your first impression, your instant "feelings" about the sentences.
5. Sometimes you may think you have seen the same sentence before. This will not be the case, so try to avoid looking back at the pages you have completed. Please do not try to remember how you circled other lines earlier in the form.

MAKE A SEPARATE JUDGMENT FOR EACH LINE.

FOR EXAMPLE: Which number describes how you feel about this sentence? Circle one number on this SAMPLE line under the sentence:

THE NURSE STANDS NEAR YOUR BED WHILE YOU TALK TO HER.

	very	mod-erately	slightly	no meaning/ neutral	slightly	mod-erately	very	
Calm	1----------	2----------	3----------	4----------	5----------	6----------	7	Nervous

If you feel very calm, circle 1. If you feel moderately calm, circle 2. If you feel slightly calm, circle 3.

If you do NOT feel either calm or nervous, or if you feel that the sentence and the line(s) below it have no meaning to you, circle 4. If you are completely unable to decide which number to circle, circle 4.

If you feel slightly nervous, circle 5. If you feel moderately nervous, circle 6. If you feel very nervous, circle 7.

THIS SAMPLE SHOWS YOU WHAT A COMPLETED PAGE MIGHT LOOK LIKE:

very	mod-erately	slightly	no meaning/ neutral	slightly	mod-erately	very
1----------	2----------	3----------	4----------	5----------	6----------	7

THE NURSE STANDS NEAR YOUR BED WHILE YOU TALK TO HER.

(moderately nervous)
Nervous 1----2----3----4----5----6----7 Calm
(neutral)
Uncomfortable 1----2----3----4----5----6----7 Comfortable
(very pleased)
Pleased 1----2----3----4----5----6----7 Annoyed
(moderately agreeable)
Disagreeable 1----2----3----4----5----6----7 Agreeable
(slightly tense)
Relaxed 1----2----3----4----5----6----7 Tense

(Note how one number is circled on each line).

very	moderately	slightly	no meaning/ neutral	slightly	moderately	very
1	2	3	4	5	6	7

1. THE NURSE HOLDS YOUR HAND WHILE YOU TALK ABOUT YOUR HEALTH PROBLEM.

Tense 1----2----3----4----5----6----7 Relaxed
Annoyed 1----2----3----4----5----6----7 Pleased
Disagreeable 1----2----3----4----5----6----7 Agreeable
Nervous 1----2----3----4----5----6----7 Calm
Uncomfortable 1----2----3----4----5----6----7 Comfortable

very	moderately	slightly	no meaning/ neutral	slightly	moderately	very
1	2	3	4	5	6	7

2. THE NURSE PLACES A HAND ON YOUR ARM WHILE YOU TALK ABOUT YOUR HEALTH PROBLEM.

Agreeable 1----2----3----4----5----6----7 Disagreeable
Tense 1----2----3----4----5----6----7 Relaxed
Pleased 1----2----3----4----5----6----7 Annoyed
Comfortable 1----2----3----4----5----6----7 Uncomfortable
Nervous 1----2----3----4----5----6----7 Calm

very	moderately	slightly	no meaning/ neutral	slightly	moderately	very
1	2	3	4	5	6	7

3. THE NURSE SITS ON YOUR BED WHILE YOU ARE IN IT.

Agreeable 1----2----3----4----5----6----7 Disagreeable
Annoyed 1----2----3----4----5----6----7 Pleased
Calm 1----2----3----4----5----6----7 Nervous
Tense 1----2----3----4----5----6----7 Relaxed
Uncomfortable 1----2----3----4----5----6----7 Comfortable

very	moderately	slightly	no meaning/ neutral	slightly	moderately	very
1	2	3	4	5	6	7

4. AFTER ASKING YOU SOME QUESTIONS, THE NURSE EXAMINES YOU BY FEELING AND LISTENING TO PARTS OF YOUR BODY.

Tense 1----2----3----4----5----6----7 Relaxed
Pleased 1----2----3----4----5----6----7 Annoyed
Nervous 1----2----3----4----5----6----7 Calm
Agreeable 1----2----3----4----5----6----7 Disagreeable
Comfortable 1----2----3----4----5----6----7 Uncomfortable

very	moderately	slightly	no meaning/ neutral	slightly	moderately	very
1	2	3	4	5	6	7

5. THE NURSE SITS CLOSE TO YOU ON YOUR BED WHILE YOU SIT AND TALK ABOUT YOUR HEALTH PROBLEM.

Nervous 1----2----3----4----5----6----7 Calm
Agreeable 1----2----3----4----5----6----7 Disagreeable
Uncomfortable 1----2----3----4----5----6----7 Comfortable
Pleased 1----2----3----4----5----6----7 Annoyed
Relaxed 1----2----3----4----5----6----7 Tense

very	moderately	slightly	no meaning/ neutral	slightly	moderately	very
1	2	3	4	5	6	7

6. THE NURSE PUTS AN ARM AROUND YOUR SHOULDERS WHILE YOU TALK ABOUT YOUR HEALTH PROBLEM.

Disagreeable 1----2----3----4----5----6----7 Agreeable
Pleased 1----2----3----4----5----6----7 Annoyed
Uncomfortable 1----2----3----4----5----6----7 Comfortable
Tense 1----2----3----4----5----6----7 Relaxed
Nervous 1----2----3----4----5----6----7 Calm

very	moderately	slightly	no meaning/ neutral	slightly	moderately	very
1	2	3	4	5	6	7

7. THE NURSE GIVES YOU A BACKRUB.

Comfortable	1----2----3----4----5----6----7	Uncomfortable
Relaxed	1----2----3----4----5----6----7	Tense
Annoyed	1----2----3----4----5----6----7	Pleased
Agreeable	1----2----3----4----5----6----7	Disagreeable
Calm	1----2----3----4----5----6----7	Nervous

very	mod-erately	slightly	no meaning/ neutral	slightly	mod-erately	very
1	2	3	4	5	6	7

8. THE NURSE HOLDS YOUR HAND WHILE YOU RECEIVE A TREATMENT PROCEDURE.

Nervous	1----2----3----4----5----6----7	Calm
Tense	1----2----3----4----5----6----7	Relaxed
Comfortable	1----2----3----4----5----6----7	Uncomfortable
Pleased	1----2----3----4----5----6----7	Annoyed
Disagreeable	1----2----3----4----5----6----7	Agreeable

very	mod-erately	slightly	no meaning/ neutral	slightly	mod-erately	very
1	2	3	4	5	6	7

9. THE NURSE ENTERS YOUR ROOM WITHOUT KNOCKING ON THE DOOR.

Disrespectful	1----2----3----4----5----6----7	Respectful
Uncomfortable	1----2----3----4----5----6----7	Comfortable
Good	1----2----3----4----5----6----7	Bad
Agreeable	1----2----3----4----5----6----7	Disagreeable
Annoyed	1----2----3----4----5----6----7	Pleased

very	mod-erately	slightly	no meaning/ neutral	slightly	mod-erately	very
1	2	3	4	5	6	7

10. THE NURSE SITS ACROSS THE ROOM FROM YOU WHILE YOU TALK ABOUT YOUR HEALTH PROBLEM.

Good	1----2----3----4----5----6----7	Bad
Respectful	1----2----3----4----5----6----7	Disrespectful
Disagreeable	1----2----3----4----5----6----7	Agreeable
Uncomfortable	1----2----3----4----5----6----7	Comfortable
Annoyed	1----2----3----4----5----6----7	Pleased

very	mod-erately	slightly	no meaning/ neutral	slightly	mod-erately	very
1	2	3	4	5	6	7

11. WHILE YOU ARE LYING IN BED, THE NURSE LOOKS FOR SOMETHING IN YOUR CLOSET.

Disrespectful 1----2----3----4----5----6----7 Respectful
Pleased 1----2----3----4----5----6----7 Annoyed
Good 1----2----3----4----5----6----7 Bad
Agreeable 1----2----3----4----5----6----7 Disagreeable
Uncomfortable 1----2----3----4----5----6----7 Comfortable

very	moderately	slightly	no meaning/ neutral	slightly	moderately	very
1	2	3	4	5	6	7

12. THE NURSE STANDS INSIDE YOUR DOORWAY WHILE YOU TALK ABOUT YOUR HEALTH PROBLEM.

Good 1----2----3----4----5----6----7 Bad
Agreeable 1----2----3----4----5----6----7 Disagreeable
Annoyed 1----2----3----4----5----6----7 Pleased
Disrespectful 1----2----3----4----5----6----7 Respectful
Comfortable 1----2----3----4----5----6----7 Uncomfortable

very	moderately	slightly	no meaning/ neutral	slightly	moderately	very
1	2	3	4	5	6	7

13. THE NURSE OPENS OR CLOSES YOUR WINDOW SHADES (OR CURTAINS) WITHOUT ASKING HOW YOU WANT THEM.

Pleased 1----2----3----4----5----6----7 Annoyed
Agreeable 1----2----3----4----5----6----7 Disagreeable
Good 1----2----3----4----5----6----7 Bad
Comfortable 1----2----3----4----5----6----7 Uncomfortable
Disrespectful 1----2----3----4----5----6----7 Respectful

very	moderately	slightly	no meaning/ neutral	slightly	moderately	very
1	2	3	4	5	6	7

14. THE NURSE REMOVES A CHAIR FROM YOUR ROOM.

Bad 1----2----3----4----5----6----7 Good
Disagreeable 1----2----3----4----5----6----7 Agreeable
Comfortable 1----2----3----4----5----6----7 Uncomfortable
Annoyed 1----2----3----4----5----6----7 Pleased
Respectful 1----2----3----4----5----6----7 Disrespectful

very	moderately	slightly	no meaning/ neutral	slightly	moderately	very
1	2	3	4	5	6	7

15. THE NURSE LEAVES YOUR DOOR OPEN WHEN GOING OUT OF YOUR ROOM.

Annoyed	1----2----3----4----5----6----7 Pleased
Comfortable	1----2----3----4----5----6----7 Uncomfortable
Agreeable	1----2----3----4----5----6----7 Disagreeable
Bad	1----2----3----4----5----6----7 Good
Disrespectful	1----2----3----4----5----6----7 Respectful

Please go back and check that you have 5 circles on each page (1 circle per line).

BACKGROUND INFORMATION

In items A through N, circle the number that applies to you:

A. Circle the number that matches your sex:
   1. Female   2. Male

B. Circle the number that matches your age:
   1. 20–39 years old
   2. 40–59 years old
   3. 60–79 years old

C. Circle the number that matches your race:
   1. White
   2. Black
   3. Hispanic
   4. Oriental
   5. Other ______

D. Circle the number that matches your marital status:
   1. Never married
   2. Married
   3. Separated
   4. Divorced
   5. Widowed

E. What is the HIGHEST level of education the head of your household has achieved?
   1. Graduate professional training
   2. Standard college or university graduation
   3. Partial college training
   4. High school graduation
   5. Partial high school
   6. Junior high school
   7. Less than seven years of school

F. How many people usually live in the same household with you?
   1. None
   2. One
   3. Two to three
   4. Four or more

G. How many times have you been a patient in a hospital?
   1. 1–2
   2. 3–4
   3. 5–6
   4. 7–8

H. During this last stay in the hospital, what type of room(s) have you been in?
   1. Private
   2. Semi-private
   3. Both private and semi-private

I. Was a family member and/or close friend with you during this stay in the hospital?
   1. Yes   2. No

J. Who was the MOST comforting to you during this last stay in the hospital?
   1. family member(s)
   2. friend(s)
   3. nurses(s)
   4. Doctor(s)
   5. Other________________
K. How serious was your health during this stay in the hospital?
   1. not at all serious
   2. slightly serious
   3. moderately serious
   4. very serious
L. Write in the OCCUPATION of the head of your household. Write a one-sentence job description. ________________
M. NOTE:
   If the head of your household is not working, write in the PREVIOUS main source of earned income. Write a one-sentence job description. ________________
N. Would you have responded differently if the nurse had been a MALE R.N.?
   1. yes
   2. no
   3. undecided
   Please explain your answer:
   ____

Please write any comments/suggestions about the questionnaire on this page.
Thank you for your time & energy!

PART IV
Assessing Client Behaviors and Responses

14

The Krantz Health Opinion Survey: A Measurement Model

Sarah S. Strauss and Kathleen J. Sawin

This chapter discusses the Krantz Health Opinion Survey, an instrument that measures one's preferences for information and control over one's health care.

The concepts of preferences for information and desires for control in health care situations have received increasing attention in the nursing research literature (Ferington, 1986; Johnson, Christman, & Stitt, 1985; Lenz, 1984; Padilla et al., 1981). Findings from some studies suggest that people may differ in their desire to be informed and to exercise control in health care situations (Auerbach, Martelli, & Mercuri, 1983; Krantz, Baum, & Wideman, 1980). Furthermore, numerous researchers (Burger, 1984; Krantz et al., 1980; Rodin, 1985) have surmised that individuals tend to fare better in health care situations where treatment is congruent with expectations and coping style. The Krantz Health Opinion Survey (KHOS) (Krantz et al., 1980), developed to tap attitudes toward desire for active involvement in health care situations, is being increasingly used to measure control preferences. Therefore, it is important to ascertain its psychometric properties in different groups of patients.

REVIEW OF LITERATURE

There is an extensive research literature reporting results of informational, cognitive, and behavioral coping interventions for managing human responses to aversive medical procedures and surgery, much of it based on the work of Johnson and colleagues (Johnson, Fuller, Endress, & Rice, 1978; Johnson & Leventhal, 1974). Although pertinent to the concepts of information and behavior control preference, a review of this body of work

This project was supported by Sigma Theta Tau, National, and the National Center for Nursing Research, Grant No. 1R23NR01304-1A1.

is beyond the scope of this chapter. The literature on information and behavior control preferences will be briefly reviewed, followed by a selective review of alternative measurement instruments.

Information and Behavior Control Preferences

Krantz et al. (1980) and Auerbach et al. (1983) have suggested that despite commitment by caregivers to encourage patients to become active, informed participants in seeking and using health care services, some individuals may benefit more than others from being informed. Johnson (1984) surmised that interventions instructing patients to use specific coping strategies might effectively diminish patients' sense of control.

Several studies have used information and/or control preferences as individual difference variables. Auerbach et al. (1983) studied the effects of specific (similar to procedure information in nursing studies) versus general information on patient adjustment for high and low information preference in 40 general surgery patients. Information preference was measured using the KHOS. After seeing one of two information videotapes, patients' behaviors during the dental procedures were scored on tenseness, uncooperative responses, and verbal admission of pain. Patients with high information preferences demonstrated significantly better adjustment.

Padilla and associates (1981) studied 50 patients undergoing nasogastric tube insertion. Control preference was measured by asking patients to respond to a forced-choice question relative to their desire to "help" with what happened during the procedure or leave the entire procedure to the "professionals in charge." They then received an information intervention. Results indicated that the procedure with sensory information and coping behavior was the most effective for reducing intubation distress for patients preferring no control. These findings suggest that individuals who prefer control may experience greater distress and anxiety during the procedure.

More recently, Johnson and associates (1985) studied the effects of personal control in hysterectomy patients (N = 168) by evaluating the long- and short-term effects of interventions that provided varying amounts of control. The interventions included no instruction, cognitive coping instruction (focusing on positive aspects of the experience and diverting attention from negative aspects), and behavioral coping instruction (getting in and out of bed). The group receiving the cognitive strategy had a better physical recovery during hospitalization but a longer length of stay; the behavioral coping group took less pain medication. These investigators questioned the cognitive coping strategy as a viable intervention since only 17% of the patients reported using this technique.

Other Measures of Information and Control Preferences

Reflecting the interest in development and testing of measures for control over health care processes, Smith, Wallston, Wallston, Forsberg, and King

(1984) conducted a series of three known-group studies to obtain further information among three self-report control measures. The three health-related situations for which the instruments were administered were preparation for childbirth, choice of a place to die, and signing a living will. The three measures of desire for control over health care processes were the KHOS (Krantz et al., 1980), the Burger and Cooper (1979) Desire for Control Scale (DCS), a generalized measure, and the Desire for Control of Health Care (Smith et al., 1984), an investigator-developed measure that incorporated situation-specific wording of items (e.g., "a patient in this clinic"). Their findings indicated that the KHOS Information subscale was the best discriminator for childbirth preparation and a place to die. The generalized DCS and the situation-specific instrument designed by the investigators provided inconsistent discrimination between groups.

The DCS was developed in the same time frame as the KHOS. The tool contains items related to personal, interpersonal, and social desire for control in general statements. In a series of studies Burger and his colleagues first proposed a general desire for control scale (Burger & Cooper, 1979) and then used the tool in laboratory settings to predict depression (Burger, 1984), achievement-related behaviors (Burger, 1985), gambling (Burger & Schnerring, 1982), and learned helplessness (Burger & Arkin, 1980). In general, individuals with a high desire for control were more likely to have increased suicidal thoughts and increased gambling behavior. They were also highly motivated to perform on challenging tasks and were more persistent in their efforts to complete a difficult task. They had higher expectations for their performances and yet were able to set their expectancies in a more realistic manner. This scale, however, was not predictive of desire for control in the only clinical study reviewed (Smith et al., 1984).

Another tool measuring desire for control, the control want subscale of the Fundamental Interpersonal Relations Orientation Behavior Scale (FIRO-B) (Lake, Miles, & Earle, 1973) was used by Ferington (1986) in her study of spinal cord–injured men. She found that in persons with high desire for control, congruence between preference and perceived control was related to low levels of depression, and congruence between both expected/perceived and preferred/perceived control was associated with low levels of anxiety, as well as depression. For persons with low preference for control, no significant relationships were found with dependent variables. However, Sawin (1987) identified that the use of the FIRO-B subscale was questionable because of two factors: (1) only items in the interpersonal dimension are included, and (2) there is a reported sex bias for women (Ryan, 1977). The sample for the current study was predominantly female.

Development of the KHOS represented an attempt to increase the specificity of the expectancy measurement. Because the KHOS measures health care expectations, it is more specific than general instruments such as the DCS (Burger & Cooper, 1979) and locus of control scales often used in health care research. It is less specific, however, than the situation-based tools developed by Smith et al. (1984), which measured expectancy in a certain health care setting (e.g., labor and delivery). In this project involving individuals anticipating a surgical intervention, the KHOS was used to measure preference for information and general health care expectations.

CONCEPTUAL BASIS

Concepts of coping and decision making were selected as the conceptual linkages between information preference and behavior control preference in health care situations involving risk, specifically surgical intervention. In this study ideas from both models will be used to conceptualize information and behavior preferences. Several investigators have attempted to link stress and control theory. Lazarus and colleagues (Lazarus & Folkman, 1984; Lazarus & Launier, 1978) identified information seeking as a mode of coping. Problem-focused coping, characterized by cognitive and behavioral problem-solving strategies, involves direct action in management of stressful transactions between the individual and the environment. Emotion-focused coping strategies regulate the emotions generated by the stressful transaction. Information seeking is considered by Lenz (1984) to be a subconcept of decision making. Cox (1967) identified information seeking as a strategy used by consumers to reduce the amount at stake and/or increase subjective certainty around decision making. Logically, individuals who seek information as a means to reduce risk and increase certainty would be likely to exhibit a preference for information in order to make choices and hence exert control within a situation. Furthermore, increased participation and choice often lead to an increase in perceived control that can, at least in theory, enhance feelings of self-reliance, thus decreasing stress (Krantz et al., 1980).

Lazarus and Launier (1978) suggest that input from the environment is filtered through a human system with relatively stable characteristics or preferred patterns for responding to specific events. Hence, individuals may, over time, develop preferred patterns for responding to situations and eliciting information and controlling outcomes.

Therefore, for this study information preference was defined as preferred individual patterns in using active cognitive strategies—specifically, information seeking—to reduce risk and/or increase certainty. Specific behaviors include desire to ask questions and be informed in health care situations. Behavior control preference was defined as preferred patterns for degree of desired involvement and self-initiated action, relative to health decision making. In this project these concepts were operationalized by the information and behavior control subscales of the KHOS (see Table 14.1).

TABLE 14.1 Conceptual and Operational Definitions of Information and Behavior Control Preference

Concept	Conceptual Definition	Operational Definition
Information preference	Preferred individual patterns in using cognitive strategies—specifically, information seeking—to reduce risk and/or increase certainty. Specific behaviors include desire to ask questions and be informed in health care situations.	First subscale (Information) of KHOS
Control preference	Preferred patterns for degree of desired involvement and self-initiated action, relative to health decision making.	Second subscale (Behavior Control) of KHOS

PURPOSES/OBJECTIVES OF THE MEASURE

The concepts of information and control preference were measured by Krantz et al. (1980), who developed an instrument for patient preferences based on two of the most common types of psychological intervention in health care: providing information and encouraging active involvement. The KHOS (see instrument at the end of this chapter) is a first step toward identifying information and behavior control preferences as concepts separate from coping and locus of control.

PROCEDURES FOR DEVELOPMENT

The KHOS as a total scale measures individual differences relative to preferences for involvement in health care situations (Krantz et al. 1980). The total score yields a composite index reflecting attitudes toward involvement in treatment of minor medical conditions. Items do not refer to severe or traumatic illness. Increased scores reflect attitudes related to desiring to be informed and actively involved and self-directed in health decision making. The KHOS consists of two scales: (1) behavioral involvement (9 items), which measures attitudes toward self-treatment and behavioral involvement in medical care; and (2) information (7 items), which measures desire to ask questions and wanting to be informed on medical decisions.

Initial Study

Reliability was established on 200 undergraduate students (100 men and 100 women). Discriminant validity was established with three other measures: Health Locus of Control and the Minnesota Multiphasic Personality Inventory (MMPI) Hypochondriacs and Repression-Sensitization scales. Predictive and construct validity were established with three groups: (1) students enrolled in a self help course (n = 12), (2) dormitory residents (n = 56), and (3) students visiting the college infirmary for minor illness (n = 81). Students enrolled in the self-help course scored significantly higher on the total scale and the subscales than did the dormitory residents, suggesting some construct validity. Students visiting the infirmary were offered a choice of medication during a visit. In addition, the frequency of questions during the visit were documented, as were the frequency of visits.

Results of the initial studies conducted by Krantz, Baum, and Wideman (1980) establishing reliability and validity of the KHOS can be summarized as follows:

1. The tool has good internal consistency and test–retest reliability in an ambulatory student population with minor illness. Information scale test–retest reliability is marginal; the 7-week time period, however, was long. Most measurement sources (Waltz, Strickland, & Lenz, 1984) recommend a 2-week test–retest period.
2. The behavior and information subscales are relatively independent of each other.
3. The relationship between the KHOS and the Health Locus of Control (Wallston, Wallston, Kaplan, & Maides, 1976) is weak in college student outpatients. Auerbach and associates (1983) verified this weak to negligible relationship using the KHOS and the Rotter Internal-External Scale (Rotter, 1966) in lower socioeconomic status dental outpatients.
4. Frequency of infirmary visits and Behavior scale scores were negatively correlated with a linear trend, suggesting that higher behavior control scores were inversely related to frequency of infirmary visits. Behavior control scores were also related to choices in medication.
5. Increased Information scale scores were weakly related to number of questions asked but not to choice of medications. Behavior control scores, however, were not related to inquisitiveness.
6. Validity coefficients with the MMPI Hypochondriacs scale (Hathaway & McKinley, 1982) suggested that the total KHOS scale and the subscales are measuring different concepts.
7. Social desirability is not a factor in responding to the KHOS.

ADMINISTRATION AND SCORING

The KHOS uses a binary, yes/no response format. A total score of 16, with subscale scores of 7 on the information subscale and 9 on the behavior control subscale, is possible. High scores indicate strong preferences for information and/or behavioral control in health care situations. Information subscale items are 1, 3, 4, 8, 10, 15, and 16. Behavior control subscale items are 2, 5, 6, 7, 9, 11, 12, 13, and 14. Negatively worded items are reverse-scored (items 1, 3, 5, 6, 9, 10, 11, 12, 13, and 15).

RELIABILITY AND VALIDITY ASSESSMENTS: CURRENT STUDY

The current study sought to ascertain the psychometric properties of the KHOS with hospitalized subjects undergoing a procedure, elective surgery, frequently appraised as threatening and potentially harmful. In order to describe psychometric properties of the KHOS it was administered to hospital elective surgery patients, preoperatively and postoperatively. Traditional psychometric procedures and confirmatory factor analysis were performed on the data. A measurement model for the KHOS using LISREL was developed.

Description of the Sample

A total sample of 113 patients was selected for inclusion in the study over a 3-year period from 1984 to 1987. Participants who gave informed consent and who met the following criteria were considered eligible for the study: (1) 18 to 70 years of age; (2) undergoing elective surgery under general anesthesia; (3) admission the day prior to surgery; (4) capable of completing paper-and-pencil questionnaires in English with minimal assistance; (5) without serious visual, hearing, learning, or mental impairments; (6) no extensive education or work experience in the health care field.

Participants were drawn from two surgical units at an 1,100-bed health science center. The design for this study was a one group pre/postmeasurement design (O X O). Data were collected preoperatively (O) and 3 to 5 days postoperatively (O). X, or the intervening event, was surgery. The KHOS was administered as part of a larger project exploring relationships between risk-reduction strategies, preference for information and behavior control in health care situations, emotional factors, perception of the recovery process, situational factors (e.g., type of surgery), and sociodemographic factors.

The sample was composed primarily of women (24 men, 89 women). Types of surgery included hernia (n = 7), cholecystectomies (n = 11), vaginal and abdominal hysterectomies (n = 45), bladder repairs (n = 7), gastric bypass (n = 40), and other (n = 3). The sample was approximately evenly split between black and white subjects. The mean age of the sample was 39.2 years (*SD* = 10.9). Mean education was 11.7 years (*SD* = 3.1).

The mean for the total score on the preoperative KHOS was 6.47 (*SD* = 3.37). The information subscale mean score was 3.88 (*SD* = 2.18). The behavior control subscale had a low mean (2.58), given that the highest possible score was 9 (*SD* = 2.11).

Traditional Psychometric Analysis

Reliability Procedures

Internal consistency measures were derived for the KHOS total scale and Information and Behavior Control subscales. Since the response format is binary, the KR-20 was used. The KHOS and subscales showed good to fair internal consistency both preoperatively and postoperatively. The preoperative information scale had a KR-20 coefficient of .75; the behavior subscale, a coefficient of .68; and the total scale, a coefficient of .74. Postoperative KR-20 coefficients were slightly higher. For the total scale, the coefficient was .75. The postoperative Information and Behavior Control subscale coefficients were .78 and .70, respectively. Stability, or test–retest reliability, was initially assessed by computing a Pearson correlation coefficient between the preoperative and postoperative measurements. For the total KHOS, the correlation was .80. The Information and Behavior Control subscales had correlations of .81 and .75 between the preoperative and postoperative measurements. A more in-depth discussion of stability of the measures can be found in the discussion of the measurement model.

Item correlations were computed only on the preoperative data. For the Information Subscale, item correlations ranged from a high of .57 (Items 10 and 15) to .39 (Item 16). On the Behavior Control subscale, Items 2 and 14 had correlations of only .20; other items ranged from .31 (Item 12) to .54 (Item 9).

Validity

Construct validity for the KHOS was assessed by performing a principal-components factor analysis, followed by a confirmatory factor analysis on the preoperative data. Results of the factor analysis, using a two-factor solution with an orthogonal rotation, essentially supported the two-factor structure proposed by Krantz et al. (1980) (see Table 14.2). Items 2 and 14 (Behavior Control subscale) were only weakly loaded on the factor labeled Behavior. Item 14 also loaded weakly on the Information factor. Item 3, an Information subscale item, loaded more strongly (.52) on the Behavior Control subscale. Item 8, a behavior item loaded strongly (.74) on the Information subscale. Item 16, an information item loaded almost equally on both scales.

The Analytic Model

The confirmatory factor analysis performed on the preoperative KHOS data was the first step in the development of the measurement model. LISREL VI was used to perform the confirmatory factor analysis; the equation for the development of a measurement model for X, or the independent variable, was used (Joreskog & Sorbom, 1984). A second step in the analysis was the determination of the stability of the theoretical constructs via structural equation models. That is, the stability of the

TABLE 14.2 Principal-Components Factor Analysis, KHOS Rotated Factor Pattern (Preoperative Measurement)

Item	Original Scale	Factor 1 (Behavior)	Factor 2 (Information)
1	I	.13	.65
2	B	.23	–.10
3	I	.52	.40
4	I	–.11	.68
5	B	.63	–.04
6	B	.65	–.08
7	B	.56	–.05
8	B	–.08	.74
9	B	.69	.09
10	I	.49	.56
11	B	.54	.13
12	B	.47	.06
13	B	.53	.08
14	B	.29	.34
15	I	.09	.74
16	I	.39	.35

constructs information and behavior control preference were examined across the operative period. Although these steps permit the preoperative and the postoperative measures of information and control preference to be used as theoretical building blocks, statistics derived from these models are based on the assumption of large samples. Therefore, findings using these models with small sample sizes (less than 100) should be interpreted cautiously. The sample size in this project, 113, is clearly a limitation. Data generated by each step will be presented.

Confirmatory Factor Analysis

Confirmatory factor analysis is used to confirm theoretical constructs in which indicators of the underlying construct are estimated to eliminate errors of measurement (Long, 1983a). In this study, two constructs are of major theoretical interest, preference for being informed in a health care situation, measured by the KHOS information subscale, and desire for behavioral control, measured by the KHOS behavior control subscale. The indicators to be estimated were the individual items for each subscale.

Logically, measures of the variables of theoretical interest (xi) are imperfect; the errors of measurement (delta) represent unique factors (Long, 1983a). In Figure 14.1, the X values represent each item on the KHOS Information and Behavior Control subscales. Each item is treated as an independent indicator of information and control preference, respectively. The directional arrows (not causal) represent factor loadings (lambda), which indicate (1) whether the item is reflective of the underlying

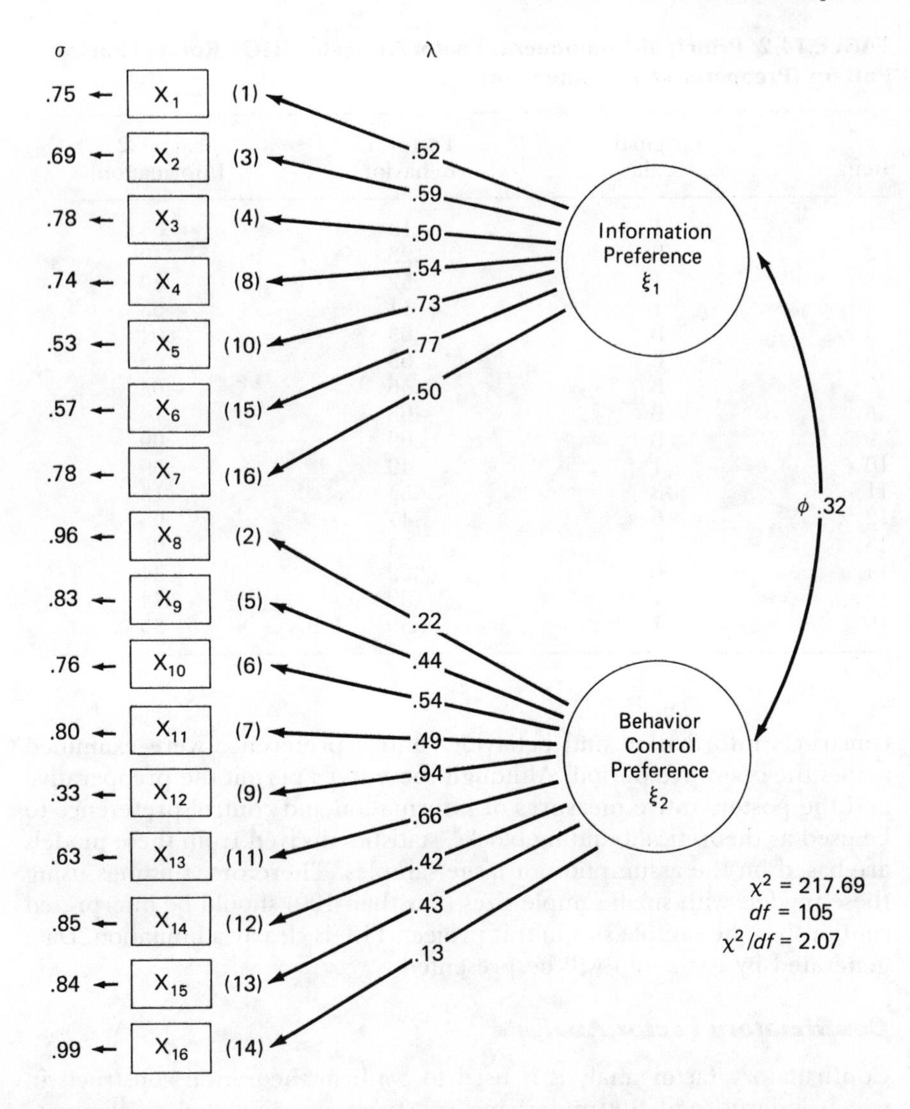

FIGURE 14.1. Confirmatory factor model, KHOS preoperative information and behavior control preference, original scale. ξ (xi) = constructs, information and behavior control preference; X_{1-7} = KHOS Information subscale items; X_{8-16} = KHOS Behavior scale items; $\delta\, X_{1-16}$ (delta) = error for each item; λ (lambda) = LISREL factor loadings; ϕ (phi) = relationship between constructs. *Note:* Numbers in () are item numbers (see Table 14.2).

concepts it proports to measure, information and control preference, and (2) whether the error terms are related. If error terms are low and the factor loadings are high, the indicator would be viewed as valid; that is, the constructs of information and control preference are accurately measured by the items on the KHOS.

Figure 14.1 depicts the results of the measurement model for information and behavior control preference for this sample as originally proposed by Krantz et al. (1980). The chi-square value derived from the maximum likelihood solution was 217.69. In confirmatory factor analysis, the chi-square test is used to conclude that the model does not fit the data (Loehlin, 1987). A high chi square is indicative of a poor fit of data with the proposed model. Exactly how high is high? Loehlin cites Joreskog as suggesting a ratio of chi square to degrees of freedom in exploratory model fitting (Loehlin, 1987). For the "original" model presented in Figure 14.1, the goodness of fit using Joreskog's chi square/degrees of freedom indicates a 2.07 ration of chi square to degrees of freedom. Loehlin states that the dividing line for determining the "best" fit of the data to the theoretical model is about 2.

Although the chi square for the original model is close to the dividing line, the LISREL factor loadings for Items 2 and 14, both Behavior Control subscale items are relatively weak (.22 and .13, respectively). Error (delta) related to measurement for these items is also high; .96 for Item 2 and .99 for Item 14. For example, examination of the modification indices of the lambda matrix indicated that Item 3 had a high modification index on the behavior factor. The modification indices provide a figure for each parameter or path in the model, which gives the number of points that the chi-square value would be lowered if that parameter was freed for estimation. This meant that when Item 3 was freed to load on the behavior factor, the overall chi square would be decreased.

Overall, LISREL factor loadings are higher and error terms are lower for the Information subscale than for the Behavior Control subscale in this initial model. Relatively high error terms for several of the items on the Behavior Control subscale is also indicative of the existence of a large degree of measurement error. Examination of the modification indices for the lambda (factor loadings) and the theta delta (TD) matrix (correlations between measurement error) supported freeing several paths.

Continued exploratory model fitting yielded the model found in Figure 14.2. Items 2, 14, and 16 were eliminated in this model. Correlated measurement error was freed for estimation between Items 9 and 1 (TD 10,1), 9 and 8 (TD 10,4), and 11 and 7 (TD 11,9). The chi square was 60.68 for the model in Figure 14.2. Joreskog's goodness-of-fit criteria, chi square/degrees of freedom, was 1.06. In this model Phi, however, was negligible (–.08). Therefore, when weak items were eliminated and measurement error in several other items was accounted for, the information and behavior control constructs were not related. This finding is in agreement

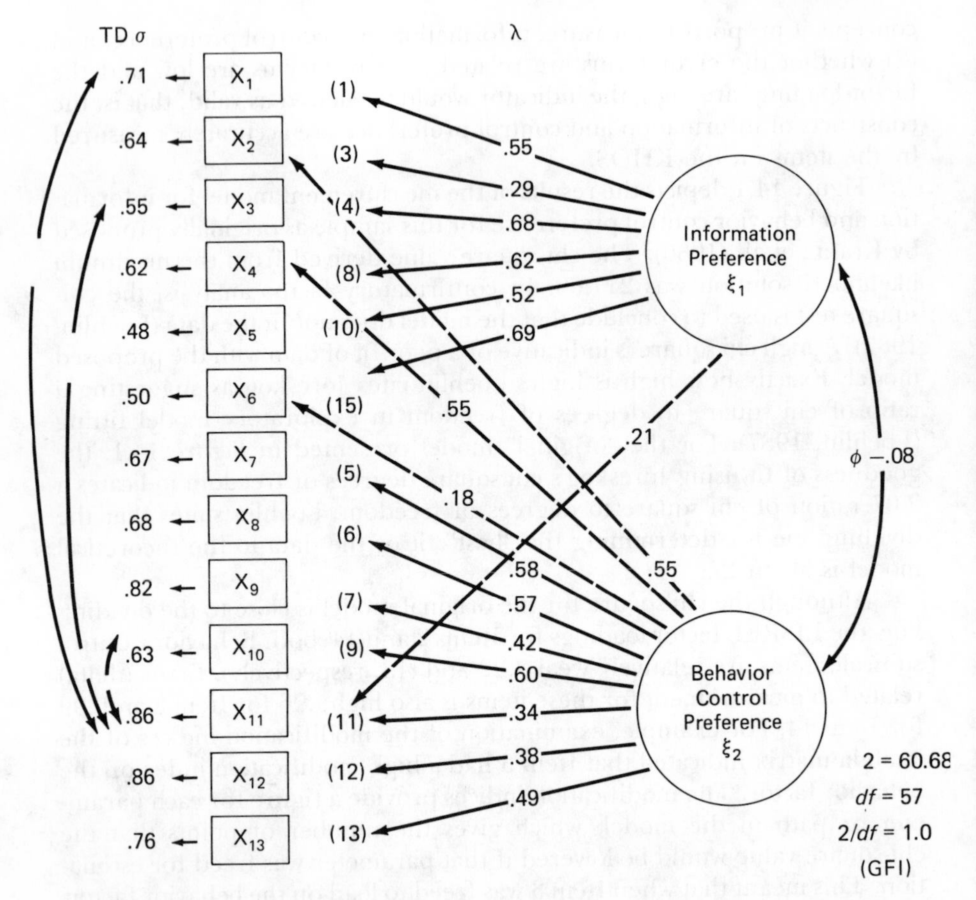

FIGURE 14.2. Confirmatory factor model, KHOS with error correlated and items 2, 14, and 16 deleted. ξ (xi) = constructs, information and behavior control preference; X_{1-5} = KHOS Information subscale items; X_{6-13} = KHOS Behavior control subscale items; $\delta\ X_{1-13}$ = (delta) = error for each item; λ (lambda) = LISREL factor loadings; ϕ (phi) = relationships between constructs; TD (theta delta) = correlated measurement error between X indicators. *Note:* Numbers in () are item numbers (see Table 14.2); *t* values for all reported coefficients, except phi, significant at $p < .05$.

with the conclusion of Krantz et al. (1980) in the study describing the development of the KHOS.

Since the constructs were not related, the final model (Figure 14.3) freed only items loading highest on one factor and fixed (set at 0) the loading on the other factor. Items 2, 14, and 16 were eliminated. Error measurement was freed only within indicators for that construct; that is,

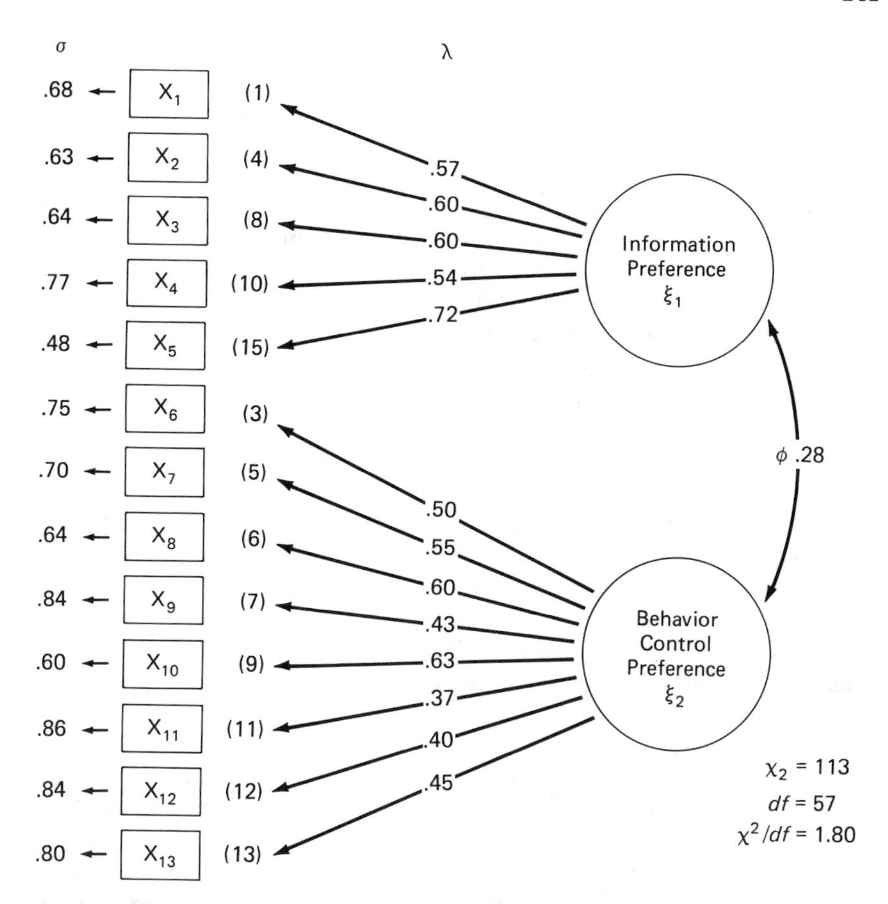

FIGURE 14.3. Confirmatory factor model for KHOS with independent constructs and items 2, 14, and 16 deleted. ξ (xi) = constructs, information and behavior control preference; X_{1-5} = KHOS Information subscale items; X_{6-13} = KHOS Behavior Control subscale items; δ X_{1-13} (delta) = error for each item; λ (lambda) = LISREL factor loadings; ϕ (phi) = relationships between constructs. *Note:* Numbers in () are items numbers (see Table 14.2); t values for all reported coefficients are significant at $p <$ .05.

error measurement was freed for estimation only for correlations within the designated items for each subscale. Only TD 11,9 was freed.

Structural Equation Models

The relationship of the constructs information and behavior control preferences were examined from the preoperative to the postoperative measurements, using a recursive covariance structural equation model.

The LISREL VI program was used for this analysis. The development of these models represented an attempt to ascertain stability of the measurement of the constructs over time. Because the relationship between behavior control preference and information preference was negligible in the final confirmatory factor model described previously (Figure 14.3), the constructs and their indicators (subscale items) were analyzed separately. Items 2, 14, and 16 were eliminated in this step of the analysis. The measurement model for this step of the analysis is identical to the one presented in Figure 14.3, where the indicators of the constructs information and behavior control preference are denoted by X and the constructs by xi. The notation for the structural equation models use Y to denote indicators and eta to denote constructs (see Figures 14.4 and 14.5.)

The structural equation for identifying a model, or fitting the data to a model, and estimating parameters depends on the forms of beta and psi (Long, 1983b). The model used for beta was the case where the first construct, preoperative measurement of information preference, affected the second construct, postoperative information preference (Figure 14.4); that is, there was only unidirectional causality. The same model was used for behavior control preferences (Figure 14.5). The diagonal form of psi was imposed; all errors in the equations were assumed to be uncorrelated or zero.

The Y indicators (KHOS subscale items) that had the highest LISREL factor loadings (lambda, LY) on the confirmatory factor analysis were fixed at 1.00; that is, Item 15 was fixed at 1.00 on the Information subscale, and Item 9 was fixed on the Behavior Control subscale. In both models, factor loadings for the constructs were assumed to be equal. For example, the factor loading for (LY 1,1) Item 1, preoperative, was equated to item 1, postoperative (LY 2,2). Note that the numbers in parentheses in Figures 14.4 and 14.5 are the KHOS item numbers (Table 14.1)

Results of the covariance structural analysis for the information subscale suggest stability of the model from the preoperative to the postoperative measurement. The preoperative information subscale accounted for 98% of the variance in the postoperative information subscale. Beta (B 2,1), the relationship between the constructs information preference from Time 1 (preoperative) to Time 2 (postoperative) was .996 (see Figure 14.4). Individuals who expressed a preference for information, preoperatively, essentially maintained, this preference, postoperatively, and the converse. Finally, preoperative error measurement for Y indicators (epsilon) ranged from a high of .76 for Y_4 (Item 4) to .51 for Item 15 (Y_5). Note that postoperative error for Y indicators varies slightly from the preoperative error measurement.

The fit of the specified model with the data was very good. The chi-square test for the final model was 33.76, with 35 degrees of freedom. Joreskog's goodness of fit index was .96. Based on modification indices,

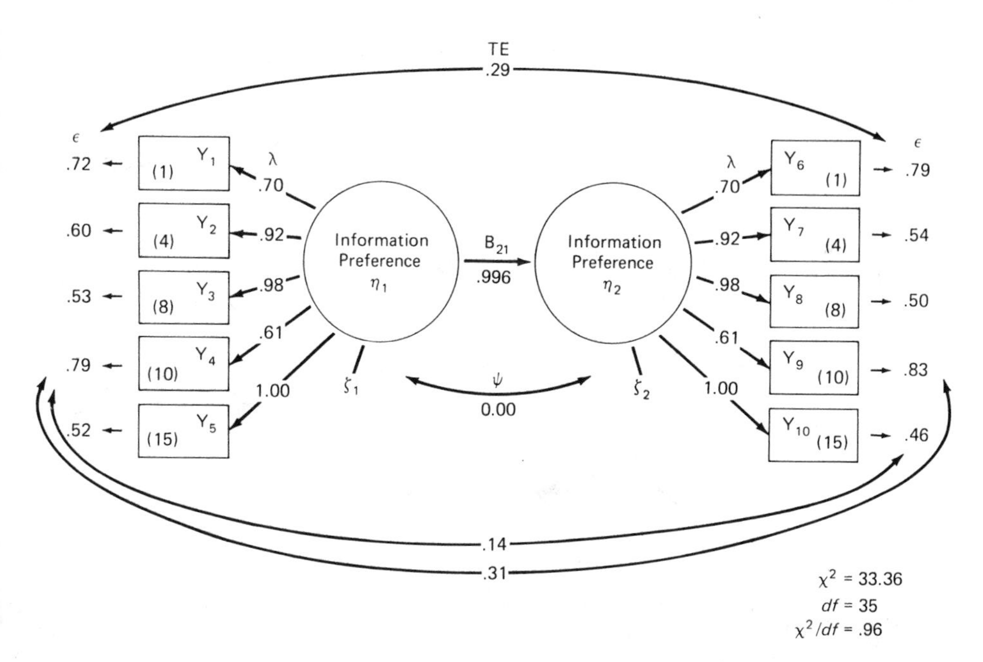

FIGURE 14.4. Structural equation model, information subscales, preoperative (O_1) to postoperative (O_2) measurements. ζ (zeta) = error associated with measurement of constructs; ψ (psi) = relationship between ζ_1 and ζ_2; η = constructs, information and behavior control preference; ϵ (epsilon) = measurement error of Y indicators (KHOS Information subscale items); λ = LISREL factor loadings preoperative Information subscale; LISREL factor loadings postoperative Information subscale; B_{21} = relationship between η_1 and η_2 (information and behavior control preference); TE (theta epsilon) = correlated measurement error between Y indicators. *Note:* Numbers in () are item numbers (see Table 14.2); t values for all reported coefficients, except psi, significant at $p < .05$.

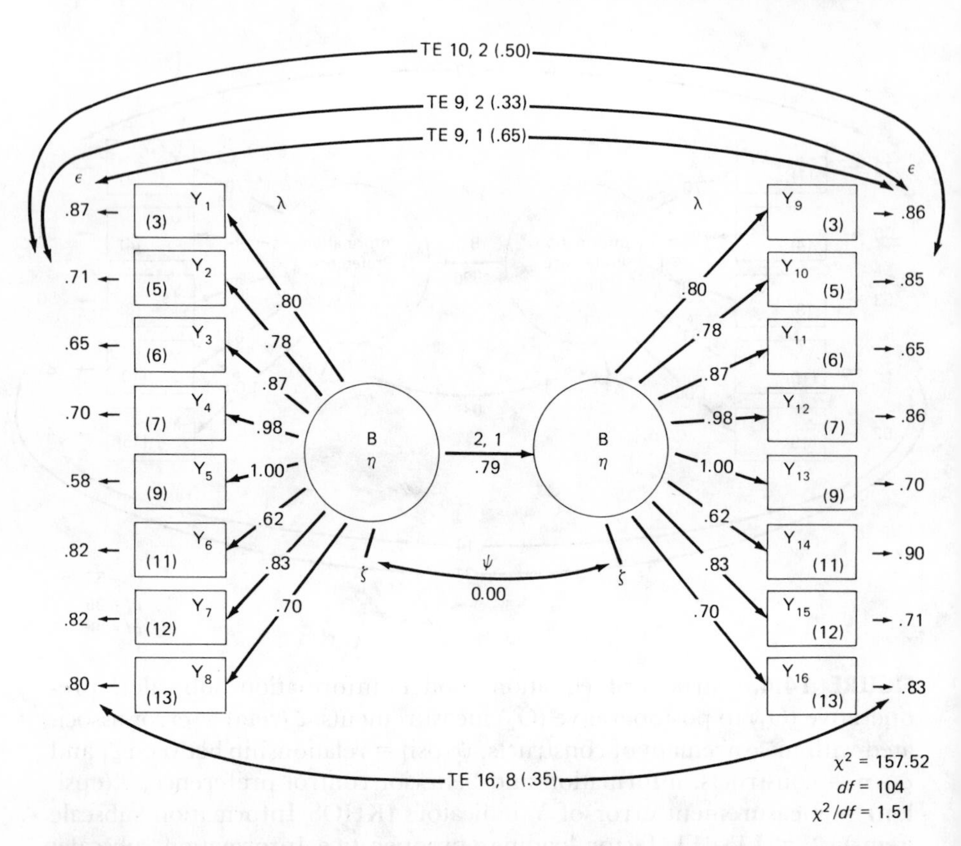

FIGURE 14.5. Structural equation model, behavior control subscales, preoperative (O_1) to postoperative (O_2) measurements. ζ (zeta) = error associated with measurement of constructs; ψ (psi) = relationship between ζ_1 and ζ_2; η (eta) = constructs, information and behavior control preference; ϵ (epsilon) = measurement error of Y indicators (KHOS Information subscale items); λ preoperative behavior control subscale items, postoperative behavior control subscale items; B_{21} = relationship between η_1 and η_2 (information and behavior control preference); TE (theta epsilon) = correlated measurement error between Y indicators. *Note:* Numbers in () are item numbers (see Table 14.2); t value for all coefficients, except psi, significant at $p < .05$.

three additional paths were freed to permit estimation of correlated error between items, thereby increasing the fit of the model (see Figure 14.4).

For the construct behavior control preference, 82% of the variance in the postoperative measurement was accounted for by the preoperative measurement. The beta between preoperative and postoperative measurements was .79. The chi square for the best-fitting model was 157.51, with 104 degrees of freedom. Joreskog's goodness-of-fit index was 1.51, suggesting a good fit of the data to the model. It should be noted that error associated with the Y indicators for the Behavior Control subscale is generally higher than for the Information subscale. Based on analysis of modification indices, several paths were freed so that measurement error could be estimated between several items (see Figure 14.5).

These data suggest that the information preference construct as measured by five items from the information subscale of the KHOS may be slightly more stable across a potentially threatening health care situation, elective surgery, than the construct behavior control preference, measured by 8 items (see Table 14.3). Both constructs, however, can be considered as stable during hospitalization for elective surgery.

DISCUSSION AND CONCLUSION

The following conclusions can be drawn from the preceding presentation of the data. First, the total KHOS scale and subscales (Information and Behavior Control) demonstrated fair to good internal consistency and good stability. Second, the structure of the original KHOS subscales with minor modification was supported by traditional psychometric analysis and the measurement model. Third, the use of confirmatory factor analysis permitted sharpening the measurement precision of the KHOS. Development of measurement models using LISREL provides a more powerful tool for preparing data for relationship analysis. Third, the simultaneous use of the measurement model and structural equations model yielded a more accurate picture of the relationships at Time 1 (preoperatively) and Time 2 (postoperatively). Finally, as other variables are introduced into the structural equations analysis, their true relationships with the constructs of interest can be more fully explored.

Information-seeking behavior and how information is used in making health decisions is an important area of study for nurses who view information sharing and teaching as significant to their role. A further benefit of precise measurement is clarification of the concepts. For example, the behavior control preference subscale may actually measure belief about self-care that may be distinct from desire for control. This study refined the constructs information preference and behavior control preference and supported their stability over time in a specific health care situation.

TABLE 14.3 Resulting Subscales of the KHOS in Measurement Model

Subscale	Item no.	Statement
Information	1	I usually don't ask the doctor or nurse many questions about what they're doing during a medical exam.
	3	I'd rather have doctors and nurses make the decisions about what's best than for them to give me a whole lot of choices.
	4	Instead of waiting for them to tell me, I usually ask the doctor or nurse immediately after an exam about my health.
	8	I usually ask the doctor or nurse lots of questions about the procedures during a medical exam.
	10	It is better to trust the doctor or nurse in charge of a medical procedure than to question what they are doing.
	15	I usually wait for the doctor or nurse to tell me the results of a medical exam rather than asking them immediately.
Behavior control preference	5	It is better to rely on the judgments of doctors (who are the experts) than to rely on "common sense" in taking care of your own body.
	6	Clinics and hospitals are good places to go for help since it's better for medical experts to take responsibility for health care.
	7	Learning how to cure some of your own illnesses without contacting a physician is a good idea.
	9	It's almost always better to seek professional help than to try to treat yourself.
	11	Learning how to cure some of your illness without contacting a physician may create more harm than good.
	12	Recovery is usually quicker under the care of a doctor or nurse than when patients take care of themselves.
	13	If it costs the same, I'd rather a doctor or nurse give me treatments than do the same treatments myself.

Further research is needed to identify the influence of these constructs on health behavior. If information-seeking preferences and behavior control preferences are shown to have a positive influence on health behavior, interventions aimed at supporting preferences will need to be developed.

REFERENCES

Auerbach, S. M., Martelli, M. F., & Mercuri, L. G. (1983). Anxiety, information, interpersonal impact, and adjustment to a stressful health care situation. *Journal of Personality and Social Psychology, 44,* 1284–1296.

Burger, J. M. (1984). Desire for control, locus of control and proneness to depression. *Journal of Personality, 52,* 71–79.

Burger, M. J. (1985). Desire for control and achievement-related behaviors. *Journal of Personality and Social Psychology, 48,* 1520–1533.

Burger, J. M., & Arkin, R. M. (1980). Prediction, control, and learned helplessness. *Journal of Personality and Social Psychology, 38,* 482–491.

Burger, J. M., & Cooper, H. M. (1979). The desirability of control. *Motivation and Emotion, 3,* 381–393.

Burger, J. M., & Schnerring, D. A. (1982). The effects of desire for control and extrinsic rewards on the illusion of control and gambling. *Motivation and Emotion, 6,* 329–335.

Cox, D. F. (1967). Risk-handling in consumer behavior—an intensive study of two cases. In D. F. Cox (Ed.), *Risk taking and information handling in consumer behavior* (pp. 34–82). Boston: Harvard University Press.

Ferington, F. E. (1986). Personal control and coping effectiveness in spinal cord injured persons. *Research in Nursing and Health, 9,* 257–265.

Hathaway, S. R., & Mckinley, J. C. (1982). *Minnesota Multiphasic Personality Inventory.* Minneapolis, MN: University of Minnesota Press, distributed by NCS Interpretive Scoring Systems.

Johnson, J. E. (1984). Coping with elective surgery. In H. Werley & J. Fitzpatrick (Eds.), *Annual Review of Nursing Research, 2,* 107–132.

Johnson, J. E., Christman, N. J., & Stitt, C. (1985). Personal control interventions: Short- and long-term effects on surgical patients. *Research in Nursing and Health, 8,* 131–145.

Johnson, J. E., Fuller, S. S., Endress, M. P., & Rice, V. H. (1978). Altering patients' responses to surgery: An extension and replication. *Research in Nursing and Health, 1,* 111–121.

Johnson, J. E., & Leventhal, H. (1974). Effects of accurate expectations and behavioral instructions on reactions during a noxious medical exam. *Journal of Personality and Social Psychology, 29,* 710–718.

Joreskog, K. G., & Sorbom, D. (1984). *LISREL VI: Short manual.* Moresville, IN: Scientific Software.

Krantz, D. S., Baum, A., & Wideman, M. (1980). Assessment of preferences for self-treatment and information in health care. *Journal of Personality and Social Psychology, 39,* 977–990.

Lake, D., Miles, M., & Earle, R. (1973). *Measuring human behavior.* New York: Teachers College Press.

Lazarus, R. S., & Folkman, S. (1984). *Stress, appraisal, and coping.* New York: Springer Publishing Company.

Lazarus, R. S., & Launier, R. (1978). Stress-related transactions between person and environment. In L. A. Pervin & M. Lewis (Eds.), *Perspective in interactional psychology* (pp. 287–327). New York: Plenum Press.

Lenz, E. R. (1984). Information seeking: A component of client decisions and health behavior. *Advances in Nursing Science, 6,* 59–72.

Loehlin, J. C. (1987). *Latent variable models: An introduction to factor, path, and structural analysis.* Hillsdale, NJ: Erlbaum.

Long, J. S. (1983a). *Confirmatory factor analysis.* Beverly Hills, CA: Sage.

Long, J. S. (1983b). *Covariance structure models: An introduction to LISREL.* Beverly Hills, CA: Sage.

Padilla, G. V., Grant, M. M., Rains, B. L., Hansen, B., Bergstrom, N., Wong, H. L., & Hanson, R. (1981). Distress reduction and the effects of preparatory teaching films and patient control. *Research in Nursing and Health, 4,* 375–387.

Rodin, J. (1985). *The application of social psychology.* In G. Lindzey & E. Aronson (Eds.), *The Handbook of Social Psychology* (Vol 2, pp. 805–881). New York: Random House.

Rotter, J. (1966). Generalized expectancies for internal versus external control of reinforcement. *Psychological Monographs, 80*(1), 1–28.

Ryan, L. R. (1977). *Clinical interpretation of the FIRO-B.* Palo Alto, CA: Consulting Psychologists Press.

Sawin, K. J. (1987). *The impact of the health belief model, desire for control, perceived control, and modifying variables on young women's contraceptive use.* Unpublished doctoral dissertation, Indiana University, Indianapolis.

Smith, R. A., Wallston, B. S., Wallston, K. A., Forsborg, P. R., and King, J. E. (1984). Measuring desire for control in health care processes. *Journal of Personality and Social Psychology, 47,* 415–426.

Wallston, B. S., Wallston, K. A., Kaplan, G. D., & Maides, S. A. (1976). Developmental validation of the Health Locus of Control (HLC) Scale. *Journal of Consulting and Clinical Psychology, 44,* 580–585.

Waltz, C. F., Strickland, O. L., & Lenz, E. R. (1984). *Measurement in Nursing Research,* Philadelphia: F. A. Davis.

Krantz Health Opinion Survey

	yes	no
1. I usually don't ask the doctor or nurse many questions about what they're doing during a medical exam.	( )	( )
2. Except for serious illness, it's generally better to take care of your *own* health than to seek professional help.	( )	( )
3. I'd rather have doctors and nurses make the decisions about what's best than for them to give me a whole lot of choices.	( )	( )
4. Instead of waiting for them to tell me, I usually ask the doctor or nurse immediately after an exam about my health.	( )	( )
5. It is better to rely on the judgments of doctors (who are the experts) than to rely on "common sense" in taking care of your own body.	( )	( )
6. Clinics and hospitals are good places to go for help since it's better for medical experts to take responsibility for health care.	( )	( )
7. Learning how to cure some of your own illnesses without contacting a physician is a good idea.	( )	( )
8. I usually ask the doctor or nurse lots of questions about the procedures during a medical exam.	( )	( )
9. It's almost always better to seek professional help than to try to treat yourself.	( )	( )
10. It is better to trust the doctor or nurse in charge of a medical procedure than to question what they are doing.	( )	( )
11. Learning how to cure some of your illness without contacting a physician may create more harm than good.	( )	( )
12. Recovery is usually quicker under the care of a doctor or nurse than when patients take care of *themselves.*	( )	( )
13. If it costs the same, I'd rather a doctor or nurse give me treatments than to do the same treatments myself.	( )	( )
14. It is better to rely less on physicians and more on your own common sense when it comes to caring for your body.	( )	( )
15. I usually wait for the doctor or nurse to tell me the results of a medical exam rather than asking them immediately.	( )	( )
16. I'd rather be given many choices about what's best for my health than to have the doctor make the decisions for me.	( )	( )

15
Behavioral Measurement of Distress during Painful Medical Procedures

Nancy Wells

This chapter discusses the Distress Checklist, an observational measure of distress during painful medical procedures in adults.

Distress is often used as an outcome variable in research in nursing. The construct has been defined and operationalized in many ways, depending on the theoretical orientation of the author. The purpose of this study was to develop a behavioral observation scale to measure distress during painful medical procedures, such as first-trimester uncomplicated abortion.

Review of Related Literature

Distress is used across many disciplines to describe an emotional state of negative quality. Bradburn (1969), from a social psychological perspective, defined distress as negative affect related to "difficulties in living." This focuses on emotional states arising from internal and environmental stress (Dohrenwend & Dohrenwend, 1974). The perception of an event as stressful (i.e., a threat) in the health sciences involves primarily threat of physical harm, including discomfort, pain, and loss of life. Psychological distress and physical pain are conceptualized as two independent dimensions of suffering by many authors (Davitz & Davitz, 1981; Johnson & Rice, 1974; Oberst, 1978). The focus of this instrument is the measurement of pain-related distress.

Beecher (1959) suggested a relationship between pain sensation and psychological reaction. The reactive component was unpleasant and did

This study was supported by Public Health Service National Research Service Award No. F31-NU05928. The assistance of Mary Derby, B.S., Geraldine Padilla, Ph.D., and the staff of Preterm Reproductive Health Clinic is acknowledged.

not vary directly (i.e., 1 : 1) with nociception. Emotions such as fear, anxiety, and terror were included as common psychological reactions (Beecher, 1959). In research on pain in wounded soldiers Beecher (1956) discovered that meaning or interpretation of pain modified the reactive component. This model proposed a stimulus–response relationship, modified by cognition.

Melzack and Wall (1982) criticized the use of a stimulus–response model of pain. Rather, the gate-control theory (Melzack & Wall, 1965, 1982) proposed three interdependent dimensions of pain: the sensory-discriminative, motivational-affective, and cognitive-evaluative. Properties of the motivational-affective dimension include aversive or unpleasant experiences that motivate behavior and concomitant autonomic arousal. The cognitive-evaluative dimension includes such psychological variables as meaning, perception of control, and anxiety (Melzack & Casey, 1968). If distress is conceptualized as negative affect involving cognition, then both of these dimensions of pain would be congruent with distress. Pain as a multidimensional construct encompasses distress but need not be present for distress to occur.

Johnson (Johnson, 1972, 1973; Johnson & Rice, 1974) built her definition of distress on Beecher's model of pain, emphasizing the unpleasant quality of the emotional state. Leventhal and Johnson (1983) explicitly delineated the behaviors associated with emotional response (including distress) as subjective report of emotional state, expressive reaction, postural changes indicative of tension, and psychophysiologic reactions. Three parameters of emotion are included: subjective, behavioral, and physiological.

Behavioral measures of emotion include one or more of the following categories: facial expression, posture, vocalization, and verbalization (Groen, 1975; Klinger, 1982). Observational instruments have been developed to measure distress in adults for a variety of health examinations. These instruments may be considered context-specific despite the number of behaviors observed across all situations.

Three tools were developed to observe distress in adults undergoing cardiac catheterization. Finesilver (1978) described a 5-point scale with five separate behaviors: motor, speech patterns, and interaction with environment. Rice, Caldwell, Butler, and Robinson (1986) modified Finesilver's tool, again using a 5-point scale, for six behaviors. This is the only scale to report internal consistency (alpha = .62), which indicates somewhat homgeneous items in this scale. Kendall and associates (1979) conceptualized their scale as adjustment rather than distress. The majority of these items reflect interaction with the environment, with only one measuring anxiety/tension.

Kaplan, Atkins, and Lenhard (1982) measured two categories of distress independently: motor and verbal behavior. This scale may tap the cognitive dimension of distress by including one verbal category of self-attributed distress. An example of this behavior is "I can't take this anymore," which suggests the inability to cope with the examination (sigmoidoscopy).

Fuller, Endress, and Johnson (1978) developed an observation checklist to measure distress during pelvic examination. Ten behaviors were operationally defined and scored as present or absent during the examination. Interrater reliability was adequate; no internal consistency data were reported. Construct validity was supported by significant changes in the predicted direction following a cognitive intervention. Because of the similarity in pelvic exam and abortion, this instrument provided the bases for the distress scale constructed.

CONCEPTUAL BASIS OF THE MEASURE

Distress was approached within a framework of emotional meaning, as developed by Davitz (1969). Four dimensions of emotion were defined, with a positive pole and two negative poles describing distinct negative emotional patterns. The four dimensions include activation (level of energy and arousal), unpleasantness, relatedness to the environment (approach–avoidance), and competence (a sense of how well one is adapting to the environment) (Davitz, 1969). The dimensions of activation and unpleasantness reflect internal, feeling states, whereas relatedness and competence reflect interaction with the environment. The essential characteristics of distress include the perception of threat, giving rise to a transitory negative emotional state that is described as unpleasant. This emotional state may be modified by cognition (i.e., incompetence, inadequacy, competence). The primary function of distress is to communicate the feeling of unpleasantness to self and others (Tomkins, 1984).

PURPOSE OF THE MEASURE

The Distress Checklist was developed to measure behavioral indicators of distress during a painful and anxiety-producing procedure, such as first-trimester uncomplicated abortion. This instrument taps the four dimensions of negative emotion proposed by Davitz (1969)—hyperactivation, tension, moving against, and inadequacy—and the four categories of emotional behavior: facial expression, posture, vocalization, and verbalization.

PROCEDURES FOR DEVELOPMENT

The behaviors selected were drawn from previous research. Twelve items were derived from the literature and direct observation of women during abortion. For example, behaviors reflecting tension included tension around eyes and mouth and expression reflecting pain and anxiety. Vocalization was limited to grunts, groans, and sighs, whereas verbalization

TABLE 15.1 Behaviors Sampled by Dimensions of Emotion and Parameters of Measurement

Behavior Observed	Parameter of Measurement	Dimension of Emotion
Tension—eyes (1)[a]	Facial expression	Tension
Tension—mouth (1)	Facial expression	Tension
Lack of eye contact (6)	Facial expression	Moving against
Restlessness (2,3)	Posture	Hyperactivation
Flinch (1,5)	Posture	Hyperactivation
Fists clenched (1)	Posture	Moving against
Resistance to position (1)	Posture	Moving against
Audible expression (1)	Vocalization	Tension
Pain expression (1,4)	Vocalization	Tension
Crying (6)	Vocalization	Tension
Verbal anxiety (1,4,5)	Verbalization	Tension
Requests termination (3,5)	Verbalization	Moving against
Lack of coping ability (3)	Verbalization	Inadequacy
Requests emotional support (5)	Verbalization	Inadequacy

[a]Source of behavior: (1) Fuller et al., 1978; (2) Rice et al., 1986; (3) Kaplan et al., 1982; (4) LeBaron & Zeltzer, 1984; (5) Katz et al., 1980; (6) Content experts.

was spoken words. Following content validity determination, two items were added (crying and lack of eye contact). For clarity, the behaviors were grouped according to the four parameters of emotional measurement, with a minimum of two behaviors per category (Table 15.1).

ADMINISTRATION AND SCORING

The instrument was used to observe patients during abortion procedures. It was designed as a checklist, with behaviors noted as present or absent during the procedure and summed for a total behavioral distress score. Although scoring of the actual behavior was criterion-related, the sum of behaviors exhibited placed the subject on a continuum (i.e., norm-referenced). Thus, higher scores reflect greater behavioral distress. This type of scoring was selected because of the increased probability of obtaining adequate interrater reliability. Because the procedure is short (5 to 7 minutes), the occurrence of the behavior during the procedure was used rather than time sampling. The time of observation for first-trimester abortion was defined as the introduction of the speculum into the vagina by the physician to the removal of the speculum.

RELIABILITY AND VALIDITY ASSESSMENTS

Reliability and validity of the Distress Checklist were determined on a sample of 36 women undergoing first-trimester abortion. Interrater reliability and internal consistency are appropriate for behavioral observation measures. Because of the transitory nature of distress, stability was not assessed. Following content validation by eight health care professionals, construct validity was tested. A correlational design was used to determine concurrent and discriminant validity. Concurrent validity was examined by the correlation among distress measures from three response modes: behavioral, subjective, and physiological. To discriminate behavioral distress from related concepts of pain and anxiety, the state anxiety scale of the State-Trait Anxiety Inventory (STAI) (Spielberger, Gorush, Lushene, Vagg, & Jacobs, 1983) and the McGill Pain Questionnaire (MPQ) (Melzack, 1975) were administered. Construct validity also was tested using the contrasted-groups approach. Patients have a choice of anesthesia, including local cervical block and intravenous (IV) sedation with diazepam (Valium®) and fentanyl (Sublimaze®). It was hypothesized that subjects undergoing abortion with local anesthesia would experience more distress as measured on the Distress Checklist than subjects undergoing abortion with IV sedation.

Procedure

Following consent to participate, the subject completed the 20-item state anxiety scale from the STAI (Spielberger et al., 1983). A baseline pulse was then obtained. These measures were collected 30 to 90 minutes prior to the abortion procedure. During the procedure, the subject's behaviors were rated by an observer using the Distress Checklist. Upon completion of the procedure, the subject completed the sensory and distress visual analogue scales (VASs), and an independent observer who was unaware of the content of the Distress Checklist completed a distress VAS. Once the subject was admitted to the recovery room, the MPQ was administered using an interview format (Melzack, 1975, 1983).

Sample

Subjects were recruited from a private abortion clinic. Patients who met the following criteria were approached for inclusion in this study: (1) age between 18 and 40 years; (2) undergoing first-trimester abortion with local anethesia or IV sedation, (3) English speaking, and (4) free from psychological disorders. A convenience sample of 39 women who were willing to participate was obtained. Of these subjects, data from five women undergoing abortion with local anesthesia were used to determine interrater reliability. Of the remaining 34 subjects, 31 women with complete data comprise the sample for reliability and validity testing.

Sample Characteristics

The mean age of the sample was 26 years ($SD = 6.2$), with women ranging from 18 to 39 years. Of the women who indicated a religious affiliation (*n*

= 14), the majority were Catholic. Forty-five percent of the women had some college education. More than half the sample had had at least one previous abortion (n = 17, 54.8%) and/or child (n = 16, 51.5%). The number of women with no previous pregnancies was small (n = 8). Gestational age of the fetus ranged from 4 to 13.5 weeks (M = 8.19, SD = 2.13).

McGill Pain Questionnaire

The MPQ was used to measure intensity of pain, using the Pain Rating Index (PRI) total score and the Present Pain Intensity (PPI). The PRI also may be divided into three subscales tapping sensory, affective, and evaluative dimensions of pain. Internal consistency of the PRI total was adequate in this sample (alpha = .84), whereas internal consistency of the subscales did not approach an acceptable level of mature instruments. Because of the questionable validity of the MPQ subscales (Turk, Rudy, & Salovey, 1985), the PRI total score was used as a measure of pain intensity. The mean PRI in this sample was 24.10, with a range from 6 to 51 (Table 15.2). The number of words chosen ranged from 4 to 20 (of a possible 20), with a mean of 9.90. The mean PPI, which is a graphic rating scale with approximately equal intervals between descriptors (Melzack, 1975), was 2.26 in this sample. These values indicate that first-trimester abortion is a moderately painful procedure for a majority of women.

State Anxiety

State anxiety was measured with the A-state of the State-Trait Anxiety Inventory (STAI), Form Y-1 (Spielberger et al., 1983). The A-state is composed of 20 items rated on a 4-point scale. Possible range on the A-state is 20 to 80. Mean internal consistency of the A-state across different age and gender groups is .93; similar internal consistency was found in the present study (alpha = .91). Stability is low, as expected in a measure of a dynamic state (Spielberger et al., 1983). Validity of the A-state was supported by the predicted decline from pre- to postsurgery (e.g., Auerbach, 1973; Spielberger, Auerbach, Wadsworth, Dunn, & Taulbee, 1973). Scores

TABLE 15.2 Means and Standard Deviations of Dependent Measures (n = 31)

Variable	Mean	*SD*	Range
State anxiety (STAI)	44.65	11.32	23–69
PRI total (pain intensity)	24.10	13.06	6–51
PPI (present pain intensity)	2.26	1.13	1–5
Pulse time 1	82.20	10.19	56–100
Pulse time 2	85.16	12.78	56–104
Pulse difference	3.00	7.94	−16–20
Pain sensation (VAS in millimeters)	53.48	28.00	0–100
Distress (VAS in millimeters)	45.74	27.58	1–98
Observer-rated distress (VAS)	33.40	25.11	1–90

on state anxiety in this sample ranged from 23 to 69, with a mean of 44.65 (Table 15.2). This is higher than the normative mean of women in nonanxious settings, indicating an elevation in state anxiety in women 30 to 90 minutes prior to abortion.

Heart Rate

The mean heart rate upon initial interview (Time 1) and immediately preabortion (Time 2) are presented in Table 15.2. The large amount of variance in this measure reflects the wide range of differences obtained and suggests this variable is unstable in this sample. In analyses, preabortion heart rate, controlling for baseline heart rate, was used as the dependent measure.

Self-report of Pain Sensation and Distress

Pain sensation and distress were obtained on two visual analogue scales. The value in millimeters was obtained by measuring from the left, zero, position to the subject's mark. The mean pain sensation was 53.48 (SD = 28.0), with a range from 0 to 100. Distress was slightly lower, with a mean of 45.74 (SD = 27.58) and a range from 1 to 98 (Table 15.2). The variability of both subjective measures is large.

Observer-rated Distress

An independent observer, who was unaware of the specific items on the Distress Checklist, rated the subject's distress on a VAS. Mean observer-rated distress was 33.40 (SD = 25.11), with a range from 1 to 90 (Table 15.2). Again, variability of this measure is large.

Interrater Reliability

Five subjects were observed by the investigator and a trained research assistant. Interrater agreement on behaviors exhibited by women undergoing abortion with local anesthesia reached 100% on the Distress Checklist for the final two subjects. Mean interrater correlation was $r = .90$, with only two items correlated less than 1.00. Thus, interrater reliability was supported.

Internal Consistency

Internal consistency was determined by interitem correlations and the KR-20. Several items had no variance over the 31 subjects and were deleted from the analysis. These items included restlessness, verbal anxiety, and lack of coping. The KR-20 for the remaining 11 items was .60. Lack of eye contact was negatively correlated with most of the other distress behaviors.

TABLE 15.3 Item-to-Total Correlations and Discrimination Indices of Retained Items (n = 31)

Parameter	Observed Behavior	Item–total r	Discrimination index
Facial expression	Tension around eyes	.49	.70*
	Tension around mouth	.60	.85*
Posture	Flinch	.44	.50*
	Fists clenched	.49	.72*
Vocalization	Audible expiration	.28	.40*
	Pain expression	.41	.82*
Verbalization	Requests termination	.26	.10 (NS)

*$p < .05$.

Three additional items had low item-to-total correlations (knees pulled together, crying, and requests for emotional support); these items were deleted from the analysis. The remaining seven items were adequately intercorrelated, providing a KR-20 of .71. Item-to-total correlations ranged from .26 to .60. The discrimination index of all items retained in the Distress Checklist except one were significant (Table 15.3).

These items appear to be tapping a relatively homogeneous concept—labeled behavioral distress—during first-trimester abortion. The items adequately sample three of the four parameters of emotion; verbalization has only one behavior remaining. The summed score of the seven items of the Distress Checklist were used in subsequent analyses. The revised Distress Checklist with operational definitions is presented at the end of this chapter.

Relationship of Demographic Data

Scores on the Distress Checklist ranged from 0 to 6, with a mean of 2.48 (SD = 1.86). Although the range is reduced by the decrease in items from 14 to 7, the variability of scores remains adequate. No association was found between behavioral distress and age (r = –.08, *NS*), number of previous abortions (r = .17, NS), number of previous childbirths (r = .20, NS), nor gestational age of the fetus (r = .19, NS). No differences were found for women with no previous pregnancies and those with previous experience (χ^2 (2) = 0.0, p = 1.00). Thus, behavioral distress as measured by the Distress Checklist appears to be unaffected by selected demographic variables.

Concurrent Validity

Concurrent validity is supported by the degree of association among the distress measures. Behavioral distress was significantly and positively correlated with self-reported distress and observer-rated distress using Pearson

TABLE 15.4 Correlation among Distress Measures (n = 31)

	1	2	3	4	5
1 Behavioral distress (Distress Checklist)	—	.35*	.74**	–.26	.40**
2 Self-reported distress (VAS)		—	.51**	–0.04	.61**
3 Observer-rated distress (VAS)			—	–.08	.49**
4 Heart rate at Time 2[a]				—	–.10
5 Pain–distress (PPI)					—

[a]Controlling for heart rate at Time 1.
*$p < .05$.
**$p < .01$.

correlation procedures. The PPI, which Melzack (1975) suggests is influenced by the emotional dimension of pain, was also significantly correlated with behavioral distress (Table 15.4)

The magnitude of correlations between self-report and observational measures of distress are moderate, explaining 12% to 16% of variance. The observer-rated correlation is stronger, and accounts for 55% of the variance in the Distress Checklist score. This suggests a communicative function of behavioral distress as measured by the Distress Checklist. Heart rate at Time 2, controlling for Time 1, was not related to any of the observed or subjective distress measures.

Construct Validity

Measures of state anxiety and pain intensity were used to determine whether behavioral distress is adequately differentiated from these concepts. Behavioral distress was significantly and positively correlated with self-report of pain sensation on the VAS. This correlation was stronger than the correlation between behavioral and self-reported distress. The correlation between self-reported sensation and distress was r = .66, suggesting a degree of overlap in these two measures. This may be related to the method of measurement or an inadequate explanation of the difference between these concepts to the subject. Behavioral distress was not related to state anxiety or pain intensity measured by the PRI total (Table 15.5). These findings support the notion that behavioral distress is distinct from state anxiety and pain intensity. The intercorrelation between VAS measures of sensation and distress requires further investigation.

Construct Validity Assessment through Contrasted-Groups Approach

The final method of determining construct validity was the contrasted-groups approach. It was hypothesized that women undergoing abortion

TABLE 15.5 Correlation among Behavioral Distress, Pain Intensity, and State Anxiety (n = 31)

	1	2	3	4
1 Behavioral distress (Distress Checklist)	—	.42**	.21	–.04
2 Pain sensation (VAS)		—	.67**	.24
3 Pain intensity (PRI)			—	.11
4 State anxiety (STAI)				—

**$p < .01$.

with local anesthesia would exhibit more behavioral distress than women undergoing abortion with IV sedation. The groups did not differ on demographic variables (age, gestational age of fetus, number of previous abortions and childbirths, educational level) nor potential intervening variables (length of time of procedure, length of time in recovery room). The women did not differ on initial state anxiety (t (29) = –0.27, p = .79). As hypothesized, women undergoing abortion with local anesthesia scored significantly higher on the Distress Checklist than women receiving IV sedation (t (29) = 2.99, p = .006).

There also was a significant difference in observer-rated distress on the VAS in the hypothesized direction (t (28) = 2.42, p = .02). The observers, however, were aware of the type of anesthesia administered, which may have biased their ratings of distress. Analysis of covariance, with heart rate at Time 1 as the covariate, yielded no significant differences on heart rate (Time 2) by type of anesthesia (F (1,27) = .16, p = .69). No significant differences were found for subjective report of distress on the VAS or pain–distress on the PPI (Table 15.6). Differences in group means were, however, in the expected direction. No significant differences were found for pain sensation on the VAS or pain intensity on the PRI. Thus, construct validity of the Distress Checklist is supported by the mean differences found by type of anesthesia.

Previous Experience

Previous experience may influence response to aversive events. As women who had previous abortions and children were included in this sample, data were analyzed to determine the effect of previous experience on distress. Women who had previous abortions (t (29) = –3.02, p = .005) and previous pregnancies (t (29) = –2.96, p = .006) were older than women who had not had these experiences. However, no significant differences were found on the pain intensity, distress, or anxiety measures between these groups. There were no significant differences on any variables between women who had and had not had children. Mean behavioral distress was greater for women who had previous abortions and children than women who had not, which suggests previous experience may have a sensitizing rather than distress-reducing effect in this setting.

TABLE 15.6 Mean Differences on Distress and Pain Intensity Measures by Type of Anesthesia ($n = 31$)

Measure	Type of Anesthesia	Mean	*SD*	*t*	*p*
Behavioral distress (Distress Checklist)	Local	3.40	1.60	2.99	.006**
	IV sedation	1.63	1.71		
Self-reported distress (VAS)	Local	53.53	29.54	1.56	.13
	IV sedation	38.44	24.28		
Observer-rated distress (VAS)	Local	43.67	27.93	2.42	.024*
	IV sedation	23.13	17.33		
Pain-distress (PPI)	Local	2.47	1.19	1.00	.326
	IV sedation	2.06	1.06		
Self-reported pain sensation (VAS)	Local	59.47	26.22	1.16	.256
	IV sedation	47.88	29.28		
Pain intensity (PRI total)	Local	24.60	12.65	0.20	.839
	IV sedation	23.63	13.83		

*$p < .05$.
**$p < .01$.

Discriminant Analysis

Discriminant analysis was used to determine the contribution of the subjective measures of distress and pain intensity, age, and previous experience with either abortion or childbirth in predicting behavioral distress. Because of the small sample size, behavioral distress was dichotomized by median split, yielding 21 subjects with low distress and 10 with high distress. The seven variables entered into the analysis (Table 15.7) explained a significant proportion of variance in behavioral distress (χ^2 (7) = 15.66, p = .028). The standardized discriminant coefficients revealed pain–distress (PPI) was the strongest predictor of behavioral distress, followed by state anxiety, pain sensation (VAS), pain intensity (PRI), and distress (VAS). Age and previous experience, which add to the predictive capacity of this set of variables, explain a smaller proportion of variance in behavioral distress. The deletion of age and previous experience reduce the explained variance from 46% to 41%. This set of seven variables accurately classified 87.10% of cases, which is considerably higher than would be expected by chance (58%).

DISCUSSION AND CONCLUSIONS

The Distress Checklist was tested on a sample of 31 women undergoing first-trimester uncomplicated abortion. The revised, seven-item Distress Checklist demonstrated adequate internal consistency for a newly developed instrument. Several aspects of construct validity were supported;

TABLE 15.7 Standardized Canonical Discriminant Function Coefficients (*n* = 31)

Variable	Coefficient	Correlation with Function
Pain–distress (PPI)	1.43	–0.67
State anxiety (STAI)	0.87	0.18
Pain sensation (VAS)	0.62	–0.36
Pain intensity (PRI)	0.56	–0.40
Distress (VAS)	0.37	–0.32
Age	0.29	–0.05
Previous experience	0.27	0.07

however, the deletion of half of the original items suggests inconsistency between conceptual and empirical definitions.

The revisions in the Distress Checklist significantly alter the content of the instrument. This suggests the conceptual development is inconsistent with the obtained empirical data based on observation. The majority of items retained (five of the seven) tapped the tension class of hedonic tone, thus sampling only the hyperactive (i.e., anxiety-related) dimension of emotion, which is more amenable to observation. However, the lack of correlation between behavioral distress and preabortion state anxiety suggests these are two distinct phenomena; the distinction may be related to response mode (i.e., behavioral observation and self-report) or the presence of pain. Retrospective reports of anxiety during the procedure might have resulted in a correlation with observed distress, however. Thus, the Distress Checklist may tap the hyperactive dimension of emotional response directly related to pain, whereas state anxiety a measured in this study is more generally related to the entire situation. The influence of state anxiety on behavioral distress, however, was demonstrated in discriminant analysis. Despite low association between these two measures, state anxiety was a predictor of behavioral distress. Consistent with the literature on acute pain, anxiety was a major intervening variable in this sample.

Relatedness to the environment, another dimension of emotion used in the conceptual framework, contains two items. In this respect the Distress Checklist reflects the communicative function of behavioral distress. This interpretation is supported by the large percentage of variance of the Distress Checklist explained by observer-rated distress ($r = .55$). Studies on distress in children also found a strong correlation between behavioral and observer-rated distress (Jay & Elliott, 1984; Jay, Ozolins, & Elliott, 1983; Katz, Kellerman, & Siegel, 1980, 1981; LeBaron & Zeltzer, 1984). Observer-rated distress has not been reported in samples of adults.

The conceptual-empirical inconsistencies of the Distress Checklist suggest it is tapping a specific type of distress: pain-related distress. Pain-related distress, in this sample, is distinct from but influenced by state anxiety. The strong correlation between observer ratings and behavioral distress indicates the communicative function of this concept.

The items retained on the Distress Checklist reflect increased muscle tension and vocalization related to pain. The items not retained reflect, in general, higher levels of distress. One item, lack of eye contact, was negatively correlated with the total scale score, indicating lower levels of distress associated with this behavior. Lack of eye contact was conceptualized as reflective of withdrawal or moving away and may represent a response that presents fewer observable distress behaviors. Lack of eye contact also may be conceived of as a means of coping with pain.

Restlessness, verbal anxiety, and lack of coping had no variance in this sample. Restlessness during abortion increases the risk of complications—for example, perforation of the uterus—and thus is controlled by the medical assistant. The women investigated verbalized anxiety prior to the procedure, but none verbalized anxiety during the procedure. This may occur because attention is focused, during the procedure, on the sensations and/or experience of pain rather than the emotional responses.

Lack of coping and requests for emotional support are both pleas for help—exhibiting these behaviors may have contradicted the woman's view of herself as an adult in control of the situation. Knees pulled together was deleted because of low item-to-total correlation and poor discrimination. This behavior typically occurs early in the procedure, prior to the insertion of the speculum. It may be a valid indicator of distress if the observation period is expanded to include the pelvic examination prior to the insertion of the speculum.

Crying, the final item deleted, was a poor discriminator of distress in this setting. It is possible that this was not considered a socially acceptable response by subjects and therefore was not exhibited. This behavior also may be more indicative of emotional distress than pain-related distress and therefore correlated poorly with the remaining pain-related distress behaviors.

The correlations among distress measures from behavioral, subjective, and physiological response modes is lower than desirable. However, this moderate association among measures of emotion has been frequently reported in the literature and may reflect variability in response mode (Miller, 1979) and/or adaptation to stressors (Lazarus, Averill, & Opton, 1970). Subjective distress as measured by the VAS accounts for 12% of the variance in behavioral distress. The PPI, which is conceptualized as a measure of pain–distress, accounts for 16% of the variance. Again, this may reflect the specific nature of the Distress Checklist in tapping pain-related distress. Heart rate was not associated with any distress measures. Research with patients undergoing short diagnostic and surgical procedures have found significant differences in heart rate following intervention (Fuller et al., 1978; Johnson, Morrissey, & Leventhal, 1973) and significantly correlated with behavioral distress (Jay & Elliott, 1984). In the present study the method of measurement or statistical treatment of the variable may have led to different results.

Discriminant validity of the Distress Checklist was supported by the lack of significant correlation between behavioral distress, pain intensity

(PRI), and state anxiety. Consistent with the hypothesized relationship between anxiety and acute pain (Chapman, 1978), preabortion anxiety was a significant predictor of distress during abortion. As well, the PRI contributed to the predictive ability of the set of variables used in discriminant analysis. The low correlation found between subjective distress as measured by the VAS and state anxiety ($r = .17, p = .19$) differs from findings in postoperative samples (Fortin, 1983; Taenzer, 1983). These differences may be related to the samples used, the proximity of induced pain to VAS rating, or the difficulty of the subjects in separating distress from pain sensation.

The high degree of association between subjective pain sensation and distress indicates an overlap in concepts. The correlation found in the present study ($r = .66$) falls between those found by Taenzer (1983) ($r = .88$) and Fortin (1983) ($r = .55$) in postoperative samples. If behavioral distress is conceptualized as pain-related, then an overlap in measures would be expected. Another source of association may be the method of administration. Both sensory and distress VASs were presented together, with the pain sensation rating preceding distress.

Construct validity was supported by the significantly higher behavioral distress scores found in women receiving local anesthesia when compared to IV sedation. This difference was found for both the original 14-item and revised 7-item scales. Although the lack of significant differences between groups on subjective distress weakens the construct validity of this measure, the differences were in the expected direction. This suggests a larger sample size may produce significant differences for subjective distress. Response bias may be a source of significant differences in observer-rated distress as observers were aware of the type of anethesia received.

To summarize, the Distress Checklist was tested in a sample of 31 women undergoing first-trimester uncomplicated abortion. Interrater reliability was assessed prior to validity testing and reached 100% over five subjects. Internal consistency of a revised seven-item scale was adequate but led to the reconceptualization of behavioral distress as a measure of pain-related distress. Construct validity was supported by distinction found between distress, pain intensity, and state anxiety. Construct validity also was supported by the significantly higher behavioral distress scores of women undergoing abortion with local anesthesia as compared to IV sedation. In conclusion, the Distress Checklist has demonstrated adequate preliminary reliability and validity. This instrument shows promise as a valid observational meaure of distress during medical procedures such as abortion. Further testing in different populations may produce a useful observational outcome measure in nursing research.

REFERENCES

Auerbach, S. M. (1973). Trait-state anxiety and adjustment to surgery. *Journal of Consulting and Clinical Psychology, 40,* 264–271.

Beecher, H. K. (1956). Relationship of significance of wound to pain experienced. *Journal of the American Medical Association, 161,* 1609–1613.
Beecher, H. K. (1959). *Measurement of subjective responses.* New York: Oxford University Press.
Bradburn, N. (1969). *The structure of psychological well-being.* Chicago: Aldine.
Chapman, C. R. (1978). Pain: The perception of noxious events. In R. Sternbach (Ed.), *The psychology of pain* (pp. 169–202). New York: Raven Press.
Davitz, J. R. (1969). *The language of emotion.* New York: Academic.
Davitz, J. R., & Davitz, L. L. (1981). *Inferences of patients' pain and psychological distress.* New York: Springer Publishing Co.
Dohrenwend, B. S., & Dohrenwend, B. P (Eds.). (1974). *Stressful life events: Their nature and effects.* New York: Wiley.
Finesilver, C. (1978). Preparation of adult patients for cardiac catheterization and coronary cineangiography. *International Journal of Nursing Studies, 15,* 211–221.
Fortin, J. (1983). *An investigation of the effects of a selected coping intervention on pain and anxiety in adult surgical patients.* Unpublished dissertation. Boston University, Boston.
Fuller, S. S., Endress, M. P., & Johnson, J. E. (1978). The effects of cognitive and behavioral control on coping with an aversive health examination. *Journal of Human Stress, 4*(4), 18–25.
Groen, J. J. (1975). The measurement of emotion and arousal in the clinical psychological laboratory and in medical practice. In L. Levi (Ed.), *Emotions: Their parameters and measurement* (pp. 727–746). New York: Raven Press.
Jay, S. M., & Elliott, C. (1984). Behavioral observation scales for measuring children's distress: The effects of increased methodological rigor. *Journal of Consulting and Clinical Psychology, 52,* 1106–1107.
Jay, S. M., Ozolins, M., & Elliott, C. H. (1983). Assessment of children's distress during painful medical procedures. *Health Psychology, 2,* 133–147.
Johnson, J. E. (1972). Effects of structuring patients' expectations on their reactions to threatening events. *Nursing Research, 21,* 499–504.
Johnson, J. E. (1973). Effects of accurate expectations about sensory and distress components of pain. *Journal of Personality and Social Psychology, 27,* 261–275.
Johnson, J. E., Morrissey, J. F., & Leventhal, H. (1973). Psychological preparation for an endoscopic examination. *Gastrointestinal Endoscopy, 19,* 180–182.
Johnson, J. E., & Rice, V. H. (1974). Sensory and distress components of pain: Implications for the study of clinical pain. *Nursing Research, 23,* 203–209.
Kaplan, R. M., Atkins, C. J., & Lenhard, L. (1982). Coping with a stressful sigmoidoscopy: Evaluation of cognitive and relaxation preparations. *Journal of Behavioral Medicine, 5,* 67–82.
Katz, E. R., Kellerman, J., & Siegel, S. E. (1980). Behavioral distress in children with cancer undergoing medical procedures: Developmental considerations. *Journal of Consulting and Clinical Psychology, 48,* 356–365.
Katz, E. R., Kellerman, J., & Siegel, S. E. (1981). Anxiety as an affective focus in the clinical study of acute behavioral distress: A reply to Shacham and Daut. *Journal of Consulting and Clinical Psychology, 49,* 470–471.
Kendall, P. C., Williams, L., Pechauk, T. F., Graham, L. E., Shisslack, C., & Herzoff, N. (1979). Cognitive-behavioral and patient education interventions in cardiac catheterization procedures: The Palo Alto Medical Psychology Project. *Journal of Consulting and Clinical Psychology, 47,* 49–58.
Klinger, E. (1982). On the self-management of mood, affect, and attention. In P. Karoly & F. H. Kanfer (Eds.), *Self-management and behavior change: From theory to practice* (pp. 129–164). New York: Pergamon.
Lazarus, R. S., Averill, J. R., & Opton, E. M. (1970). Towards a cognitive theory of emotion. In M. B. Arnold (Ed.), *Feelings and emotions* (pp. 207–232). New York: Academic.

LeBaron, S., & Zeltzer, L. (1984). Assessment of acute pain and anxiety in children and adolescents by self-reports, observer reports, and a behavioral checklist. *Journal of Consulting and Clinical Psychology, 52,* 729–738.
Leventhal, H., & Johnson, J. E. (1983). Laboratory and field experimentation: Development of a theory of self-regulation. In P. Wooldridge, M. Schmitt, J. Skipper, & R. Lenoard (Eds.), *Behavioral science and nursing theory* (pp. 189–262). St. Louis: C. V. Mosby.
Melzack, R. (1975). The McGill Pain Questionnaire: Major properties and scoring methods. *Pain, 1,* 277–299.
Melzack, R. (1983). The McGill Pain Questionnaire. In R. Melzack (Ed.), *Pain measurement and assessment* (pp. 41–48). New York: Raven Press.
Melzack, R., & Casey, K. (1968). Sensory, motivational, and central control determinants of pain: A new conceptual model. In D. Kenshalo (Ed.), *The skin senses* (pp. 423–443). Springfield, IL: Charles C. Thomas.
Melzack, R., & Wall, P. D. (1965). Pain mechanisms: A new theory. *Science, 150,* 971–978.
Melzack, R., & Wall, P. D. (1982). *The challenge of pain.* New York: Penguin.
Miller, S. M. (1979). Controllability and human stress: Method, evidence, and theory. *Behavior Research and Therapy, 17,* 287–304.
Oberst, M. T. (1978). Nurses' inferences of suffering: The effects of nurse-patient interaction and verbalization of distress. In M. J. Nelson (Ed.), *Clinical perspective in nursing research* (pp. 38–60). New York: Teachers College Press.
Rice, V. H., Caldwell, M., Butler, S., & Robinson, J. (1986). Relaxation training and response to cardiac catheterization. *Nursing Research, 35,* 39–43.
Spielberger, C. D., Auerbach, S. M., Wadsworth, A. P., Dunn, T. M., & Taulbee, E. S. (1973). Emotional reactions to surgery. *Journal of Consulting and Clinical Psychology, 40,* 33–38.
Spielberger, C. D., Gorush, R. L., Lushene, R. E., Vagg, P. R., & Jacobs, G. A. (1983). *STAI Manual for the State-Trait Anxiety Inventory (Form Y).* Palo Alto, CA: Consulting Psychologists Press.
Taenzer, P. (1983). Postoperative pain: Relationship among measures of pain, mood, and narcotic requirement. In R. Melzack (Ed.), *Pain measurement and assessment* (pp. 111–118). New York: Raven Press.
Tomkins, S. S. (1984). Affect theory. In K. R. Scherer & P. Ekman (Eds.), *Approaches to emotion* (pp. 163–195). Hillsdale, NJ: Erlbaum.
Turk, D. C., Rudy, T. E., & Salovey, P. (1985). The McGill Pain Questionnaire: Confirming the factor structure and examining appropriate uses. *Pain, 21,* 385–397.

Distress Checklist

Start ________ Finish ________
Pulse ________

tension around eyes ________
tension around mouth ________
flinch (sudden jerk) ________
fists clenched/clutching ________
audible expiration (sigh, grunt) ________
pain expression (oh, ouch, groan) ________
requests termination ________

Total/7 ________

COMMENTS:

Operational Definitions

Tension around eyes: eyes squeezed closed, flutter or wrinkle in eyelids.
Tension around mouth: tightened lips, chin puckered *or* jaw clenched.
Flinch: brief, sudden jerk of torso.
Fists clenched/clutching: fists tight, may have white knuckles, *or* clutching gown, table, or other's hand.
Audible expiration: audible expiration of sound; sigh, grunt.
Pain expression: vocal expression of pain; oh, ouch, groan.
Requests termination: states "stop," "I can't take this."

Administration and Scoring

Time of observation: Observation begins as the procedure begins. Time is recorded, and the subject is observed for the occurrence of the 7 behaviors until the procedure ends. Finish time is recorded. Each behavior can only be scored once.
Scoring: Each behavior is equally weighted, and scored as absent (0) of present (1). The total distress score is the sum, ranging from 0 (no distress) to 7 (extreme distress).

16
The Touch Instrument

Alicia Hucksstadt

This chapter discusses the Touch Instrument, a measure of the responses of the recipient of touch.

In health care interactions touch is a frequent intervention that is used for a variety of reasons. Although frequently used, touch involves considerable risk because it may be misinterpreted by either the practitioner or the patient. Touch is considered to be a means of communicating caring, support, and empathy; establishing rapport; and a mechanism for giving physical care. Unfortunately, the effect of the touch is often not known. The purpose for the development of the Touch Instrument was to provide nursing researchers with an instrument that includes an assessment of the touch given, specific physiological and psychological responses, and the recipient's perceived effects of the touch.

REVIEW OF RELATED LITERATURE

Touch is a vital sensory system that begins very early in the development of human beings and many other animals. Montagu (1986) reports that touch is the earliest sensory system to become functional in humans, other mammals, and bird species studied so far. The human embryo, as young as 8 weeks, can respond to tactile stimulation because the underlying neurological system is the first to myelinate (Thayer, 1982).

It also appears that touch by self and others is essential in the life and well-being of animals. Lack of contact through licking by mothers or self-licking has resulted in the death of the animal. It is interesting to note that the self-licking of many mammals probably has more to do with keeping its bodily systems functional than with keeping itself clean (Monta-

This study was partially funded by The Wichita State University, Department of Nursing. The assistance of expert panel members, Ruth McCorkle, RN, PhD, Karen Stolte, RN, PhD, and Sandra Weiss, RN, PhD, as well as the assistance of Bonnie Krenning, RN, BSN; Mary Koehn, RN, BSN; and Maurice Tinterow, MD, PhD, is acknowledged.

gu, 1986). The constant stimulation and pressure of the amniotic fluid and uterine contractions of labor in humans provide massive stimulations of the fetal skin that is important in the fetal development and life (Thayer, 1982). These stimulations seem to serve the function of licking in other animals (Montagu, 1986).

The importance of touch has been demonstrated in many reports of tactile stimulation/deprivation of animals and infants (Harlow, 1958; Kulka, Frye, & Goldstein, 1960; Montagu, 1986). More recently, studies have been able to document the benefits of maternal stimulation on premature infants (White-Traut, 1983). It is also beginning to be recognized that the biological need for touch continues throughout life and does not seem to decrease with aging but seems to increase (Montagu, 1986). Thronbury and Mistretta (1981) have found that elderly individuals have higher touch thresholds than younger adults, which may also indicate a greater need for increased tactile stimulation. The individual's desire for touch does not diminish, but his or her ability to distinguish touch is less than in younger people.

Cutaneous stimulation is important not only to physical and psychological development but also to social development. In primates tactile sensation is a complex source of communication. Biting, sexual presenting, grooming, hand stroking, and other forms of touch are important tactile signals in primate societies (Montagu, 1986). In humans touch has many meanings. Like most animals, humans tend to react pleasurably when their skin is stimulated. Henley and LaFrance (1984) state that "people report liking to be touched and touch seems more intimately associated with comfort and care than it does with aggression and assault" (p. 359). But because "touching another's body generates an immediate demand for a response, as well as a special intimacy or threat unique among communicative behaviors, touch is probably the most carefully guarded and monitored of all social behaviors" (Thayer, 1982, p. 266). For some individuals the need to touch and be touched may be observed with animals. Brickel (1979) found that elderly patients in a hospital-based geriatric population who had cat mascots frequently held, hugged, and stroked the cats. Staff of the unit in which the cats had been kept for 2 years reported the mascots stimulated patients' responsiveness, enhanced the treatment milieu, served as a form of reality therapy, and gave the patients pleasure.

In health care settings touching between humans is a common occurrence. There is a considerable amount of literature related to touch in health professions but a lack of well-controlled scientific studies examining the effect of touch on either the patient or the health practitioner. Still, numerous nursing authors have cited the importance of touch in nursing care (Burnside, 1973; DeThomaso, 1971; Goodykoontz, 1979, 1980; Henderson & Nite, 1978; Hollinger, 1980; Johnson, 1965; Preston, 1973; Tobiason, 1981; Ujhely, 1979). Barnett (1972) examined the theoretical construct of touch in nursing, which resulted in five broad categories relating touch to communication. Nursing textbooks often refer to touch as a means of communicating with patients. Parkinson (1986) stated that touch communicates caring and can be used to "gain and keep a person's attention; communicate caring when words seem inappropriate; communicate support and caring in a crisis situation" (p. 90) and other ways of communication. Other health professionals such as occupational therapists (Huss, 1977; Posthuma, 1985) and physiotherapists (Mason, 1985) have also emphasized the importance of touch to their practice.

A number of descriptive and experimental studies have been conducted in an attempt to identify the outcome of touch by nurses and other health care professionals. Studies have indicated changes in patient perceptions of health care providers and themselves (Belcore, 1981; Gioiella & Bevil, 1985), amount of self-care disclosure (Jourard & Friedman, 1970), physiological changes (Jay, 1982), pain levels (Hallstrom, 1968; West, 1981), anxiety levels (Heidt, 1981), responsiveness (Langland & Panicucci, 1982), and many others. But the findings of many of the above studies are conflicting. One possible reason has been suggested by other authors, many outside nursing and health care, who have cautioned that touch has differing meanings and is influenced by one's culture (Barnett, 1972; Watson & Graves, 1966; Willis & Reeves, 1976), age and gender (Goldberg & Lewis, 1969, Kagan, 1971; Noller, 1978), relationship with the toucher (Henley, 1977), body parts involved, setting, and other circumstances surrounding the event (Anderton & Heckel, 1985; Fisher, Rytting, & Heslin, 1976; Gergen, Gergen, & Barton, 1973; Kleinke, 1977). It has also been demonstrated that touch itself is very difficult to identify because it possesses many variables, such as duration, intensity, action, temperature, location, and others (Thayer, 1982; Weiss, 1979).

It is not surprising that a number of methodological problems have plagued many of the existing studies related to touch. Inability to control the above variables, small sample sizes, and unavailability of reliable and valid measuring instruments have contributed to inconsistent and perhaps invalid findings in some of the studies. An examination of existing instruments related to touch revealed a paucity for assessing touch and its effects in nurse–patient interactions. A number of instruments focused on the assessment of touch using college students as subjects in a variety of nonclinical settings. Two instruments that were used to assess various aspects of clinical touch include an observational schedule (Porter, Redfern, Wilson-Barnett, & May, 1986), and the Touch Assessment Tool, which included location, amount and intensity of touch (Copstead, 1980). The Body-Contact Questionnaire, which identified 18 regions on the human body (Jourard & Rubin, 1968), has been incorporated within several instruments. Other instruments were used in studies measuring a variety of physiological and psychological effects related to touch, such as discrimination ability (Nolan, 1985); thresholds (Thornbury & Mistretta, 1981); tactile defensiveness in children (Royeen, 1986); skin temperature, skin conduction, and electromyographic (EMG) level (Randolph, 1984); laboratory blood levels (Jay, 1982); intensity and duration of infant crying (Hallstrom,

1968); self-appraisal (Copstead, 1980); self-esteem (Silverman, Pressman, & Bartel, 1973); anxiety (Bell, 1984; Bramble, 1985; Heidt, 1981; Hubble, Noble, & Robinson, 1981; Quinn, 1984); self-disclosure (Jourard & Friedman, 1970; Hubble et al., 1981); depression (Bell, 1984); attitudes toward physicians (Belcore, 1981); and perceived effects on labor patients (Stolte, 1976). Many of the instruments reported in the literature were developed for a specific study purpose unrelated to patient care, and few reported information related to instrument development (e.g. validity and reliability information).

Some attempt has been made to categorize touch in health professions. Watson (1975) identified two types of touching by personnel (nurse, nurse's aide, orderly) in a geriatric nursing home. Instrumental touch was identified as the intentional physical contact occurring when another task is being performed, and expressive touch was identified as the touch that does not require a task component and is spontaneous and affective (e.g., comforting a patient). Watson found that instrumental touch occurred twice as often as expressive touch and was dependent on the role of the personnel. Expressive touching occurred more with higher staff (i.e., registered nurses). Another author (Thayer, 1982) suggested that this finding might be viewed in consideration of Henley's (1977) work, which has indicated that touching is frequently an indicator of the toucher's status and power (usually a man or superior). This higher status may give the toucher freedom to touch another person that may be at times abused. It is not known how the subjects in Watson's study perceived the touch.

Pratt and Mason (1984) also examined the categories of touch when they requested 76 health professional and lay respondents to categorize the intentions of practitioners in 28 specified examples of touching within health care. Ten categories were given by the authors, and subjects rated each of the specified examples of touching. Categories included communicative, diagnostic, incidental, personal care, assisting, accidental, guiding, pleasure giving, instrumental, and pleasure receiving. The rating scale ranged from 1 (not at all) to 5 (very much). In 7 of the 10 categories, the majority of subjects perceived the situations as revealing clear intentions by the practitioner. The practitioner's use of incidental, instrumental, and pleasure receiving were not clearly perceived. Respondents also indicated the need for two additional categories: one for implying control or restraint and the other for conveying concern or reassurance. The authors believed that the category of communicative would cover the concern or reassurance but suggested that further studies consider the examples of information conveyed to patients by means of touch, such as concern or lack of concern, confidence, competence, consideration, caring attitude, empathy, understanding, authority, status, assurance, reassurance, attention offered, attention required, orientation to outer world, anger, and love.

Weiss (1979) discussed the conceptual framework of touch in nursing research and practice. Using neurologic and sociopsychologic theory and research, Weiss described the six major tactile symbols in the language of touch: (1) duration—temporal length of touch; (2) location—area of the body contacted, includes threshold, extent, and centripetality; (3) action—rate of approach to a body surface with the attendant amount of physical energy exerted in the onset of the touch; (4) intensity—extent of indentation applied to the body surface by the pressure of the touch; (5) frequency—amount of touching; and (6) sensation—reaction to the touch. The significance of these symbols lies in their power to affect an individual's perception ability for sensory discrimination of his or her body, the pleasure/pain balance of the body, and self-cathexis, specifically for approval or liking of one's body.

The most recent studies found in the health professions relating to touch were in dissertations. El-Kafass (1983) conducted a descriptive study using nonparticipant observation that recorded the nurses' use of expressive touch or those touch behaviors used for reasons other than procedural. Four critical-care units (two medical intensive care units, or MICUs, and two surgical intensive care units, or SICUs) within a private general hospital and 60 critical-care patients and nurses assigned to their care were used. Observations occurred for 1 hour for each patient and indicated that 70% of the nurses touched their patients a total of 175 times during the 60 hours of observation, and 30% of the nurses did not touch their patients except for procedural reasons. Findings revealed

1. A significant relationship existed between the nurses' expressive touch and the different parts of the subject's body. The patient's arm, particularly the hand, was the body part most frequently touched by the nurse.
2. No significant difference was found in the frequency of expressive touch by the nurse with patients in MICU or SICU. A positive correlation was found between the amount of equipment in a patient's room and the amount of expressive touch by the nurse.
3. No relationship was found between the nurse's expressive touch and whether the time of observation was day, evening, or night.
4. The subject's age, sex, and race were not found to influence the nurses' use of expressive touch; but the more serious the patient's condition, the more frequently the nurses used expressive touch.
5. White nurses more frequently used expressive touch than did black nurses, and the nurse's age did not make a difference.
6. A pat and laying on of hands were the most frequent kinds of touch used by the nurses.
7. Eight major categories were identified for the expressive touch by nurses: to provide reassurance, to explain a procedure, to provide instruction, for physical protection, to orient the patient, to provide assistance, to communicate emotions and caring, and to provide comfort. It was found that nurses more frequently used expressive touch for reassuring the patient or for explaining procedures.

8. The responses of the patients to the expressive touch by nurses were primarily positive.

One recommendation by the researcher indicated the need for further studies to determine how patients and nurses perceive and interpret touch.

Clement's (1983) dissertation also examined the use of touch by nurses with patients in an intensive care unit. Thirty-two nurses were observed while giving care to 75 individual patients who were willing to participate in this descriptive study. A data collection instrument was designed by this author using Weiss's (1979) six major tactile symbols, described earlier in this chapter, and the division of the body guidelines described by Nguyen, Heslin, and Nguyen (1975). Clement found there was no significant difference in the frequency, location, duration, and purpose of touch by the nurses according to the age or sex of the patient, but there was a significant difference according to the diagnosis of the patient. Orthopedic and lethargic patients were more likely to be touched, and cardiac and neurological patients were less likely to be touched than any other groups studied.

Two dissertations were conducted within nursing homes. A 1984 dissertation by Bell reported the effects of supportive touch on depression and anxiety among 53 elderly female nursing home residents. The findings of this study revealed significant differences in self-reported depression and dysphoria when compared to a control group, but these differences were not significant on ratings or on levels of activity. Pepler's (1984) study focused on the level of congruence in messages communicated to nursing home residents by nurse aides through their touch and nontouch behaviors. Findings indicated that when the touch involved grooming, was more intense, or if the resident moved with discomfort, the congruence was significantly higher. The congruence was positively correlated with the aide's years of schooling but negatively correlated with communication skills in her training. Congruence was also lower when the aide had known the resident a longer time and when the aide was talking to someone else. Contrary to theory, congruence and mutual understanding were not correlated. The author suggested that long-standing relationships and validity in interpretive schemes were possible contributory factors and may explain the incongruency with the theory. Residents, aides, and the nurse judges rated the majority of the touches as associative and dominant, but the interactants viewed the same touch as both dominant and submissive. Aides and residents agreed that touches usually sent positive messages; but there was a low level of agreement about the dominance and submission, illustrating a need for further study in this area.

The most recent dissertation obtained was by Bramble (1985). This researcher investigated the effect of one touch modality on state anxiety during a hospital admission procedure. This experimental study included

50 subjects who were admitted through the admissions office of a large general hospital. The subjects were randomly assigned to experimental group (received the stationary touch) or the control group (no touch). No significant difference was found in the state anxiety, systolic blood pressure, or pulse between the experimental and control groups. Bramble indicated that these findings were inconsistent with prior findings and that the experiment may have been affected by comments that were made by the nursing staff to the subjects, for example, "Have they attacked you yet?" It was recognized that this comment may have increased the anxiety level of some subjects. Another variable may have been the sex of the research assistant. The majority of the subjects were female, and the data were collected by a male. In addition, the independent variable was given only once. After further analysis the touch group demonstrated a greater number of subjects with a decrease in their anxiety scores and a smaller number of subjects with increased anxiety scores than in the control group. Bramble indicated that a better-controlled study with repeated exposure to touch might yield different results.

In summary, the review of literature has revealed the numerous variables relating to touch and the difficulty in measuring touch and its effects. Prior studies have provided background for the development of the Touch Instrument that is intended for use in patient care interactions.

CONCEPTUAL BASIS OF THE MEASURE

Touch is conceptually defined as a sensory system that provides physiological, psychological, and social effects for the toucher and the recipient. Its initiation and interpretation are determined by numerous factors, such as the toucher's and recipient's age, gender, self-esteem, culture; relationship between individuals involved; reciprocity; body parts involved; setting and circumstances; and the type, quality, duration, intensity, temperature, and location of the touch. In nursing, touch is primarily viewed as a communicative technique (often called expressive or supportive touch) or as a means of assessing, monitoring, and providing physical care (often called procedural, technical, or instrumental touch). Weiss (1986) reported that nurses need to be conscious of their touch given to patients. Although studies have demonstrated the positive effects of touch by health providers, some touch may produce negative physiological and psychological effects in patients such as increased nervous system arousal. Weiss indicated an assessment of the tactile environment, including the nurse's own determination of the purpose of the touch and the patient's tactile response disposition, are important considerations of patient care. The therapeutic nature of the touch will be dependent on the congruency between the nurse and the patient within the tactile environment.

PURPOSE AND OBJECTIVES OF THE MEASURE

The purpose of the Touch Instrument is to assess the specific characteristics of the touch, the toucher, and the recipient (Part I); to measure the physiological and psychological changes occurring during and after the recipient is touched (Part II); and to measure the perceived effects by the recipient of the touch (Part III).

The objectives of the measure are as follows:

1. To obtain pertinent demographic information on the toucher and the recipient of the touch.
2. To assess the type and other characteristics of the touch given to the recipient.
3. To assess physiological and psychological measures before, during, and after the touch.
4. To assess the recipient's perception of the effect of the touch.

PROCEDURES FOR DEVELOPMENT

Using pertinent literature, the Touch Instrument incorporated those items believed to influence touch and how the touch is perceived by the toucher and the recipient. The receipient's perceptions include those factors identified in the literature that are thought to be positive and negative outcomes of touch, including some items from the previous work by Stolte (1976).

ADMINISTRATION AND SCORING

The Touch Instrument is intended to be administered in a checklist and questionnaire format. Parts I and II may be completed by the toucher or an observer (the demographic data, and items 28, 29, and 30 of Part I require the toucher's self-report). Items 7 through 14 of Part I may be obtained by interview and information from the patient's medical record. Part III is a questionnaire to be given to the recipient of the touch (preferably by someone other than the toucher).

Part I may take approximately 5 to 10 minutes to complete; Part II will vary in time, depending on when physiological and psychological effect is measured; and Part III may take the recipient approximately 10 minutes to complete.

The Touch Instrument is scored as follows: Part I is not scored but provides a description of the toucher, the recipient, and the touch given. Part II is scored by starting with the total number of physiological items being measured (e.g., 3 items). All items that are not included in the assessment will be designated by NA (not applicable). For every item that changed toward a more relaxed state, a 3 is recorded; for every item that did not change in either direction (stayed the same), a 2 is recorded; for every item that changed toward a tensed state, a 1 is recorded. The points are then summed (range of points from 3 to 9, if 3 items are evaluated) for each subject. A percentage score can be calculated by comparing the points recorded to the total number of possible points. The same scoring procedure applies to the psychological section. The higher the total score and percentage score for each of the two sections, the more positive the physiological and psychological reaction to the touch. The lapsed time after touch will be recorded without any additional scoring. Part III contains a semantic-differential scale with steps numbered 1 to 7 (1 depicting the most positive state). Subjects indicate how they feel about the touch they received by selecting a number on the scale for each of the 31 items. Items 2, 5, 7, 8, 9, 11, 13, 18, 22, 24, 27, 30 are scored in reverse order. The subject's responses are summed for a total number. The range of possible scores is 31 to 217. The lower the score, the more positive the perception of the touch received. Items 32, 33, and 34 are not scored but provide further information about the recipient of the touch.

RELIABILITY AND VALIDITY ASSESSMENTS

The Touch Instrument is intended to measure a state attribute. Therefore, it was not expected that a stability procedure (test–retest) would yield a high correlation in nurse–patient interactions unless replicated simulations were used. Therefore, a high test–retest coefficient was expected. A test–retest correlation was determined in simulated situations in which 15 nursing students received the same audiovisual situations. A Pearson product-moment (Pearson's) correlation coefficient of .82 ($p = .0001$) for scores on Part III was obtained from test to retest with a 2-week interval for a procedural touch simulation and a Pearson's correlation coefficient of .76 ($p = .001$) for a supportive touch simulation.

Interrater reliability was assessed for Parts I and II. Two master's-prepared nurses viewed the same nurse–patient interaction, which included a report of the physiological values for the patient. A 91% agreement was obtained for all items.

Internal consistency was assessed for Part III using Cronbach's alpha. Alpha coefficients ranging from .81 to .97 were obtained for the study, using simulated nurse–patient supportive and procedural touch interactions. In a study of 41 adult hospitalized patients an alpha coefficient of .97 was found. Internal consistency for Part II (physiological) revealed an alpha of .45. The alpha for the psychological section of Part II could not be computed due to zero variance. An additional study of five rural hospitalized patients revealed an internal consistency alpha of .95. The item-to-total correlations for the 31 items in Part III for both groups of hospitalized patients ($N = 46$) ranged from .40 to .87.

Content validity was determined for each part (Parts I, II, and III) through review of the literature and review by three nurse researchers in the area of touch. Each evaluator was provided with the conceptual basis of the measure, purpose, objectives, construction, administration, and scoring information about the instrument. Each judge was asked to review the entire instrument and determine on a scale of 1 to 4 the relevance of each item. Two judges evaluated the relevancy of each item, and a content validity index of .88 was obtained. The third judge provided written support for the instrument and suggested on item for inclusion (Item 32 of Part III). Minor modifications were made in the instrument based on comments offered by the other two judges.

Construct validity was evaluated using a contrasted-groups approach within a simulated setting. Seventeen nursing students were provided with two audiovisual situations in which the 17 subjects, in the role of patients, responded to items on Part III of the instrument. The first situation included a supportive touch provided by a nurse to a patient; the second situation included a painful procedural touch by a nurse to a patient. Paired-samples t tests revealed significant differences for responses to the two types of touch ($df = 16, t = -10.56, p = .0001$). The simulations were repeated 2 weeks later with the same subjects, and significant differences were again found ($df = 16, t = -14.16, p = .0001$).

Construct validity was also assessed, using a group of 41 hospitalized adult patients who were randomly assigned to an experimental group or control group. The experimental group received 2 to 5 minutes of supportive touch in a patient–nurse interaction during routine care. The control group received a verbal interaction without any touch. Blood pressure, respiration, and pulse, were monitored and a brief psychological assessment was conducted before and after the interactions. Patients were then requested to complete Part III, including a one-item patient-satisfaction visual analogue scale (Item 34); t tests for independent samples revealed significant differences between the experimental and control groups in their responses to Items 1 through 31 of Part III ($df = 39, t = -2.95, p = .005$) and patient satisfaction scores ($df = 39, t = 2.17, p = .036$). Although subjects in the touch group had more positive physiological assessment scores, there were no significant differences between groups for physiological or psychological assessment scores (Part II).

Concurrent validity was assessed by correlating Part III scores with the patient visual analogue item (34). Two Pearson's correlation coefficients were calculated for the nursing students' ($N = 15$) simulated nurse–patient interactions: $-.79, p = .0001$, for patient satisfaction and supportive touch and $-.61, p = .008$, for patient satisfaction and procedural touch. The Pearson's correlation coefficient between patient satisfaction and supportive touch (in the experimental group) and the patient satisfaction scores and no touch (control group) of the hospitalized patients were both nonsignificant.

DISCUSSION AND CONCLUSIONS

The Touch Instrument provides preliminary efforts in the development of an instrument that includes a comprehensive assessment of touch and items that measure the physiological, psychological, and perceived effects of the touch by the recipient. Further refinement of the instrument is planned. The low alpha levels relating to Part II and the nonsignificant difference between the hospitalized patient groups (touch and no touch) suggest a need to examine better ways to measure the physiological effects of touch. Another concern relates to social desirability, which may possibly confound subject perception scores. Although efforts were made in this psychometric study to assure patients that their responses were not going to be used in any manner other than for the development of the instrument and that there were no right or wrong responses, it is suggested that a measure of social desirability be included in future work. The patient satisfaction measure used for examination of concurrent validity in this study did not produce a significant correlation coefficient in the hospitalized patient groups. Therefore, future efforts may also include correlating measures of other concepts that have been suggested to be closely related to expressive touch (e.g., empathy, caring) with scores from this instrument. Plans also include further development of the instrument to provide a measure of the effects of the touch upon the toucher.

REFERENCES

Anderton, C. H., & Heckel, R. V. (1985). Touching behaviors of winners and losers in swimming races. *Perceptual and Motor Skills, 60,* 289–290.

Barnett, K. (1972). A theoretical construct of the concepts of touch as they relate to nursing. *Nursing Research, 21,* 102–110.

Belcore, L. P. (1981). The effects of doctors' touching patients during patient visits as measured by patients' reports of their attitudes towards physicians. *Dissertation Abstracts International, 42,* 2977B. (University Microfilms No. 8200410).

Bell, P. L. (1984). The effects of supportive touch on depression and anxiety among female residents of a nursing home. *Dissertation Abstracts International, 45,* 993B. (University Microfilms No. 8414812).

Bramble, B. (1985). The effect of one touch modality on state anxiety during a hospital admission procedure. *Dissertation Abstracts International, 46,* 1867B. (University Microfilms No. 8516713).

Brickel, C. M. (1979). The therapeutic roles of cat mascots with a hospital-based geriatric population: a staff survey. *The Gerontologist, 19,* 368–372.

Burnside, I. M. (1973). Touching is talking. *American Journal of Nursing, 73,* 2060–2063.

Clement, J. M. (1983). A descriptive study of the use of touch by nurses with patients in the critical-care unit. *Dissertation Abstracts International, 44,* 1060B. (University Microfilms No. 8319577).

Copstead, L. C. (1980). Effects of touch on self-appraisal and interaction appraisal for permanently institutionalized older adults. *Journal of Gerontological Nursing, 6,* 747–752.

DeTomaso, M. T. (1971). Touch power and the screen of loneliness. *Perspectives in Psychiatric Care, 9,* 112–118.

El-Kafass, A. A. (1983). A study of expressive touch behaviors by nursing personnel with patients in critical care units. *Dissertation Abstracts International, 43,* 3187B. (University Microfilms No. 8304646).

Fisher, J. D., Rytting, M., & Heslin, R. (1976). Hands touching hands: Affective and evaluative effects of an interpersonal touch. *Sociometry, 39,* 416–421.

Gergen, K. J., Gergen, M. M., & Barton, W. H. (1973, October). Deviance in the dark. *Psychology Today,* pp. 129–130.

Gioiella, E. C., & Bevil, C. W. (1985). *Nursing care of the aging client.* Norwalk, CT: Appleton-Century-Crofts.

Goldberg, S., & Lewis, M. (1969). Play behavior in the year-old infant: Early sex differences. *Child Development, 40,* 21–31.

Goodykoontz, L. (1979). Touch: attitudes and practice. *Nursing Forum, 18,* 4–17.

Goodykoontz, L. (1980). Touch: Dynamic aspect of nursing care. *The Journal of Nursing Care, 13*(6), 16–18.

Hallstrom, B. J. (1968). Contact comfort: Its application to immunization injections. *Nursing Research, 17,* 130–134.

Harlow, H. F. (1958). The nature of love. *The American Psychologist, 13,* 673–685.

Heidt, P. (1981). Effect of therapeutic touch on anxiety level of hospitalized patients. *Nursing Research, 30,* 32–37.

Henderson, V., & Nite, G. (1978). *Principles and practice of nursing* (6th ed.). New York: Macmillan.

Henley, N. M. (1977). *Body politics power, sex, and nonverbal communication.* Englewood Cliffs, NJ: Prentice-Hall.

Henley, N. M., & LaFrance, M. (1984). Gender as culture: Difference and dominance in nonverbal behavior. In A. Wolfgang (Ed.), *Nonverbal behavior* (pp. 351–371). New York: C. J. Hogrefe.

Hollinger, L. M. (1980). Perception of touch in the elderly. *Journal of Gerontological Nursing, 6,* 741–746.

Hubble, M. A., Noble, F. C., & Robinson, S. E. (1981). The effect of counselor touch in an initial counseling session. *Journal of Counseling Psychology, 28,* 533–535.

Huss, A. J. (1977). Touch with care or a caring touch. *The American Journal of Occupational Therapy, 31,* 11–18.

Jay, S. S. (1982). The effects of gentle human touch on mechanically ventilated very-short-gestation infants [Monograph]. *Maternal–Child Nursing Journal, 11,* 199–257.

Johnson, B. S. (1965). The meaning of touch in nursing. *Nursing Outlook, 13,* 59–60.

Jourard, S. M., & Friedman, R. (1970). Experimenter-subject "distance" and self-disclosure. *Journal of Personality and Social Psychology, 15,* 278–282.

Jourard, S. M., & Rubin, J. E. (1968). Self-disclosure and touching: A study of two modes of interpersonal encounter and their interrelation. *Journal of Humanistic Psychology, 8,* 39–48.

Kagan, J. (1971). *Change and continuity in infancy.* New York: John Wiley & Sons.

Kleinke, C. L. (1977). Compliance to requests made by gazing and touching experimenters in field settings. *Journal of Experimental Social Psychology, 13,* 218–223.

Kulka, A., Fry, C., & Goldstein, F. J. (1960). Kinesthetic needs in infancy. *American Journal of Ortho-psychiatry, 30,* 562–571.

Langland, R. M., & Panicucci, C. L. (1982). Effects of touch on communication with elderly confused clients. *Journal of Gerontological Nursing, 8,* 152–155.

Mason, A. (1985). Something to do with touch. *Physiotherapy, 71,* 167–169.

Montagu, A. (1986). *Touching the human significance of the skin* (2nd ed.). New York: Harper & Row.

Nguyen, T., Heslin, R., & Nguyen, M. L. (1975). The meaning of touch: Sex differences. *Journal of Communication, 25,* 92–103.
Nolan, M. F. (1985). Quantitative measure of cutaneous sensation. *Physical Therapy, 65,* 181–185.
Noller, P. (1978). Sex differences in the socialization of affectionate expression. *Developmental Psychology, 14,* 317–319.
Parkinson, M. H. (1986). Therapeutic interaction. In K. C. Sorensen & J. Luckmann (Eds.), *Basic nursing: A psychophysiologic approach* (2nd ed.) (pp. 71–102). Philadelphia: W. B. Saunders.
Pepler, C. J. (1984). Congruence in relational messages communicated to nursing home residents through nurse aide touch behaviors. *Dissertation Abstracts International, 45,* 2106B. (University Microfilms No. 8422312).
Porter, L., Refern, S., Wilson-Barnett, J., & May, A. L. (1986). The development of an observation schedule for measuring nurse–patient touch, using an ergonomic approach. *International Journal of Nursing Studies, 23,* 11–20.
Posthuma, B. W. (1985). Learning to touch. *Canadian Journal of Occupational Therapy, 52,* 189–193.
Pratt, J. W., & Mason, A. (1984). The meaning of touch in care practice. *Social Science Medicine, 18,* 1081–1088.
Preston, T. (1973). When words fail. *American Journal of Nursing, 73,* 2064–2066.
Quinn, J. F. (1984). Therapeutic touch as energy exchange: Testing the theory. *Advances in Nursing Science, 6*(2), 42–49.
Randolph, G. L. (1984). Therapeutic and physical touch: Physiological response to stressful stimuli. *Nursing Research, 33,* 33–36.
Royeen, C. B. (1986). The development of a touch scale for measuring tactile defensiveness in children. *The American Journal of Occupational Therapy, 40,* 414–419.
Silverman, A. F., Pressman, M. E., & Bartel, H. W. (1973). Self-esteem and tactile communication. *Journal of Humanistic Psychology, 13,* 73–77.
Stolte, K. M. (1976). *An exploratory study of patients' perceptions of the touch they received during labor.* Unpublished doctoral dissertation, University of Kansas, Lawrence.
Thayer, S. (1982). Social touching. In W. Schiff & E. Foulke (Eds.), *Tactile perception: A sourcebook* (pp. 263–304). New York: Cambridge University Press.
Thornbury, J. M., & Mistretta, C. M. (1981). Tactile sensitivitiy as a function of age. *Journal of Gerontology, 36,* 34–39.
Tobiason, S. J. (1981). Touching is for everyone. *American Journal of Nursing, 81,* 728–730.
Ujhely, G. B. (1979). Touch: Reflections and perceptions. *Nursing Forum, 18,* 18–32.
Watson, W. H. (1975). The meaning of touch: Geriatric nursing. *Journal of Communication, 25,* 104–112.
Watson, O. M., & Graves, T. D. (1966). Quantitative research in proxemic behavior. *American Anthropologist, 68,* 971–985.
Weiss, S. J. (1979). The language of touch. *Nursing Research, 28,* 76–80.
Weiss, S. J. (1986). Psychophysiological effects of caregiver touch on incidence of cardiac dysrhythmia. *Heart and Lung, 15,* 495–505.
West, B. A. (1981). Understanding endorphins: Our natural pain relief system. *Nursing, 11*(2), 50–53.
White-Traut, R. C. (1983). Maternal-infant interaction as a function of maternal stimulation of the premature infant initiated at twenty-four hours of infant age. *Dissertation Abstracts International, 44,* 1785B. (University Microfilms No. 8319011).
Willis, F. N., & Reeves, D. L. (1976). Touch interactions in junior high students in relation to sex and race. *Developmental Psychology, 12,* 91–92.

THE TOUCH INSTRUMENT

Part I. Description of Touch Given

Directions: Please place a checkmark in the space to the left of your response and fill in the blanks as indicated.

TOUCHER

1. Sex: ____ M ____ F
2. Age: ________
3. Marital Status:
   ____ Single
   ____ Married
   ____ Widowed
   ____ Divorced
4. Ethnic Group:
   ____ Asian
   ____ White
   ____ Black
   ____ American Indian
   ____ Hispanic
   ____ Other, specify
   ____

RECIPIENT

7. Sex: ____ M ____ F
8. Age: ________
9. Marital Status:
   ____ Single
   ____ Married
   ____ Widowed
   ____ Divorced
10. Ethnic Group:
   ____ Asian
   ____ White
   ____ Black
   ____ American Indian
   ____ Hispanic
   ____ Other, specify
   ____

[Items 5 and 6, description of the toucher, and items 11, 12, 13, 14, description on the recipient, are continued in respective columns on the next page.]

5. Highest Education Level:
   ____ Less than 12 years
   ____ High School graduate
   ____ Diploma in Nursing
   ____ Some college, no degree
   ____ Associate degree
   ____ Baccalaureate degree
   ____ Masters degree
   ____ Doctoral degree
6. Status of Toucher:
   ____ Family member, specify relationship________________
   ____
   ____ Friend
   ____ Student Nurse
   ____ R.N.
   ____ L.P.N.
   ____ Aide or Orderly
   ____ Physician
   ____ Other ________

11. Highest Education Level:
   ____ Less than 12 years
   ____ High School graduate
   ____ Some college, no degree
   ____ Associate degree
   ____ Baccalaureate degree
   ____ Masters degree
   ____ Doctoral degree
12. Medical Diagnosis:
   ____
13. Existing Sensory Problems
   ____
   ____
14. Current Medications Affecting Sensorium:
   ____

COMPLETE FOR EACH TOUCH GIVEN:

15. Setting in which Touch Occurred
    ____ Recipient's room
    ____ Recipient's bathroom
    ____ Hallway
    ____ Dining room
    ____ Other, describe________________________________
16. Type of Touch Given
    ____ Technical (involving a procedures), describe ________
    ____
    ____ Expressive (comforting), describe ________
    ____
17. Source of Touch Given (What touched the recipient?)
    ____ Hand ____ Arm ____ Shoulder
    ____ Other, describe ________________________________
18. Location of Touch Given—mark location with an X on the body figure below. Both a front view and a back view are pictured.

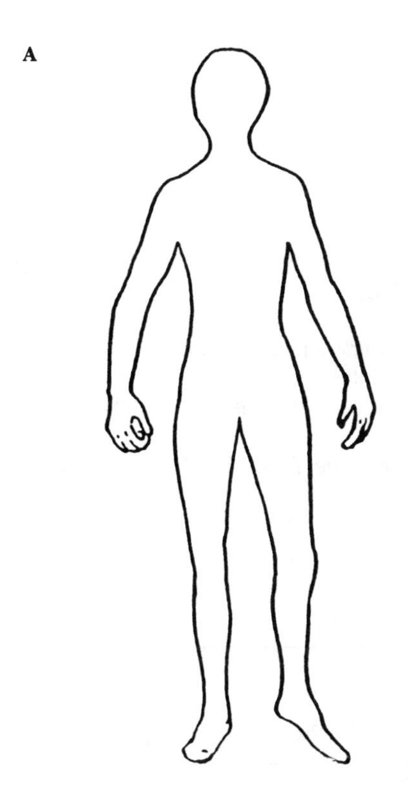

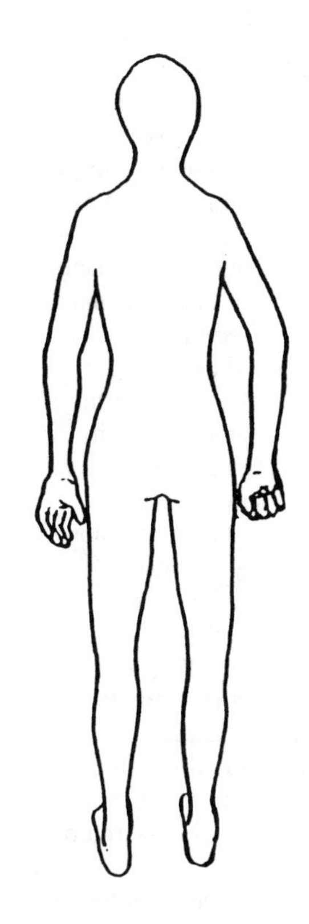

FIGURE 16.1 Body figure. **A:** Front View; **B:** Back View.

19. Duration of Touch Given
    ____ Less than 1 second
    ____ 1 second to 15 seconds
    ____ 16 seconds to 60 seconds
    ____ 61 seconds to 2 minutes
    ____ More than 2 minutes, approximate time ____________________
20. Initial Intensity of Touch Given
    ____ No indentation
    ____ Slight indentation
    ____ Moderate indentation
    ____ Strong indentation
21. Intensity Variation of Touch Given
    ____ No indentation
    ____ Slight indentation
    ____ Moderate indentation
    ____ Strong indentation
22. Action (specific gesture or movement) of the Touch
    ____ Stroke
    ____ Pat
    ____ Grasp, Squeeze
    ____ Other, specify____________________
23. Toucher's Position when Touch was Given
    ____ Standing, facing recipient
    ____ Standing, not facing recipient
    ____ Sitting, facing recipient
    ____ Sitting, not facing recipient
24. Recipient's Position When Touch Was Given
    ____ Standing, facing toucher
    ____ Standing, not facing toucher
    ____ Sitting, facing toucher
    ____ Sitting, not facing toucher
    ____ Reclining, facing toucher
    ____ Reclining, not facing toucher
25. When Was the Touch Given?
    ____ Approaching the recipient (occurs when first interacting with the recipient)
    ____ Interfacing with the recipient (occurs as interaction stabilizes)
    ____ Separating from the recipient (occurs as individual prepares to end the interaction and leave the area)
26. Other Communication Channels Accompanying the Touch Used by the Toucher
    ____ Eye contact
    ____ Verbal
    ____ Smiling
    ____ Frowning
    ____ Other body/facial gestures, describe ____________________
    ____
27. How was the Touch Reciprocated by the Recipient?
    ____ Was not reciprocated
    ____ Touch was returned, describe type and location
    ____
    ____ Verbal expression. What was said?____________________

____ Turned head toward toucher
____ Turned body toward toucher
____ Made direct eye contact
____ Smiling
____ Frowning
____ Other body/facial gestures, describe ____________________

____

The following items (23, 29, 30) require the response of the Toucher:
28. What was the intended action of the touch?
29. What was the expected sensation for the recipient of the touch?
30. Did the Toucher feel comfortable touching?
____ Yes
____ No
31. Additional Comments

Part II. Effect of Touch

Directions: Record the before touch measurement, the during touch measurement (if patient has a continuous monitor), the after touch measurement, and the length of lapsed time since touch was given.

	Before Touch	During Touch	After Touch	Lapsed Time After Touch
Physiological				
1. Blood Pressure	________	________	________	________
2. Pulse Rate	________	________	________	________
3. Respiratory Rate	________	________	________	________
4. Other, specify				
________	________	________	________	________
Psychological				
8. Orientation	___ Alert	___ Alert	___ Alert	___
	___ Confused	___ Confused	___ Confused	___
9. Willingness to cooperate	___ Yes	___ Yes	___ Yes	___
	___ No	___ No	___ No	___
10. Willingness to self-disclosure	___ Yes	___ Yes	___ Yes	___
	___ No	___ No	___ No	___
11. Other, specify				
________	________	________	________	________

12. Additional Comments:

Part III. Patient's Perception

Directions: There are many feelings that we have when someone interacts with us. Please read each of the following items and place a checkmark on the line of each item to describe how you felt about the interaction you have just had with the nurse. For example, on the Cared for/Neglected word pair, 1 = totally cared for; 2 = moderately cared for; 3 = slightly cared for; 4 = neutral; 5 = slightly neglected; 6 = moderately neglected; 7 = totally neglected. There are no right or wrong responses.

The interaction made me feel:

	Totally	Moderately	Slightly	Neutral	Slightly	Moderately	Totally	
1. Cared for	__ 1	__ 2	__ 3	__ 4	__ 5	__ 6	__ 7	Neglected
2. Upset	__ 1	__ 2	__ 3	__ 4	__ 5	__ 6	__ 7	Reassured
3. Comfortable	__ 1	__ 2	__ 3	__ 4	__ 5	__ 6	__ 7	Uncomfortable
4. Worthy	__ 1	__ 2	__ 3	__ 4	__ 5	__ 6	__ 7	Unworthy
5. Unhappy	__ 1	__ 2	__ 3	__ 4	__ 5	__ 6	__ 7	Happy
6. Courageous	__ 1	__ 2	__ 3	__ 4	__ 5	__ 6	__ 7	Scared
7. Unaccepted	__ 1	__ 2	__ 3	__ 4	__ 5	__ 6	__ 7	Accepted
8. Distrustful	__ 1	__ 2	__ 3	__ 4	__ 5	__ 6	__ 7	Trustful
9. Physically tense	__ 1	__ 2	__ 3	__ 4	__ 5	__ 6	__ 7	Physically relaxed
10 Good	__ 1	__ 2	__ 3	__ 4	__ 5	__ 6	__ 7	Bad
11. Unsure	__ 1	__ 2	__ 3	__ 4	__ 5	__ 6	__ 7	Confident
12. Helped	__ 1	__ 2	__ 3	__ 4	__ 5	__ 6	__ 7	Not helped
13. More pain	__ 1	__ 2	__ 3	__ 4	__ 5	__ 6	__ 7	Less pain
14. Less anxious	__ 1	__ 2	__ 3	__ 4	__ 5	__ 6	__ 7	More anxious
15. Pleasant	__ 1	__ 2	__ 3	__ 4	__ 5	__ 6	__ 7	Unpleasant
16. Better	__ 1	__ 2	__ 3	__ 4	__ 5	__ 6	__ 7	Worse

Item	1	2	3	4	5	6	7	
17. Secure	___ :	___ :	___ :	___ :	___ :	___ :	___	Threatened
18. Uncooperative	___ :	___ :	___ :	___ :	___ :	___ :	___	Cooperative
19. Willing to share feelings	___ :	___ :	___ :	___ :	___ :	___ :	___	Unwilling to share feelings
20. Understood	___ :	___ :	___ :	___ :	___ :	___ :	___	Misunderstood
21. Closer to the nurse	___ :	___ :	___ :	___ :	___ :	___ :	___	More distant
22. Alone	___ :	___ :	___ :	___ :	___ :	___ :	___	Supported
23. Safe	___ :	___ :	___ :	___ :	___ :	___ :	___	Unsafe
24. Less aware	___ :	___ :	___ :	___ :	___ :	___ :	___	More aware
25. Respected	___ :	___ :	___ :	___ :	___ :	___ :	___	Ignored
26. Calm	___ :	___ :	___ :	___ :	___ :	___ :	___	Annoyed
27. Discouraged	___ :	___ :	___ :	___ :	___ :	___ :	___	Encouraged
28. Warm	___ :	___ :	___ :	___ :	___ :	___ :	___	Cold
29. Restful	___ :	___ :	___ :	___ :	___ :	___ :	___	Restless
30. Less able to do things	___ :	___ :	___ :	___ :	___ :	___ :	___	More able to do things
31. More aware of what person was saying	___ :	___ :	___ :	___ :	___ :	___ :	___	Less aware of what person was saying

Directions - Please answer the following questions by placing a checkmark in the space preceding your response to each item.

32. Would you consider yourself a
    ________ toucher (I like to touch or be touched by other people)
    ________ nontoucher (I do not like to touch or be touched by others)
33. How many times have you been hospitalized?
    ________ None
    ________ 1 time
    ________ 2 times
    ________ 3 times
    ________ 4 times
    ________ 5 or more times
34. *Directions* - Please place an X on the line below indicating how satisfied you are with the care you are receiving at the current time.
    Very satisfied ____ Very dissatisfied

THANK YOU FOR YOUR PARTICIPATION

17
Refinement of the Sexual Adjustment Questionnaire

Margaret Chamberlain Metcalfe

This chapter discusses the Sexual Adjustment Questionnaire, a measure of a person's sexual adaptation following treatment for a serious illness.

Adjustment to one's ever-changing sexuality is a lifelong process as we pass through the many phases of our lives. However, the diagnosis of cancer, with its potentially disfiguring treatments that may cause temporary or permanent sexual dysfunction (Greenberg, 1984; Kolodney, Masters, & Johnson, 1979), causes rapid alterations in the ways one relates to others. Cancer is a disease that impacts on all components of an individual's life. The Sexual Adjustment Questionnaire was developed to measure the sexual behaviors of an individual diagnosed and treated for cancer (Waterhouse & Metcalfe, 1986). There are many ways one can define sexual adjustment; for the purposes of this study it was defined as the process of positive or negative sexual adaptation following treatment for cancer.

REVIEW OF RELATED LITERATURE

Cancer is a disease that impacts on all components of an individual's life. Adams (1980) had identified five elements of the disease process that may compromise the client's sexual health: the biologic processes of cancer, the personal process of accepting the diagnosis of cancer, the effects of treatment on sexuality, any permanent alterations caused by the disease and treatment, and the family process of accepting the diagnosis. Fisher (1983) states that in addition to assessing the organic dysfunction that cancer may precipitate, the health professional must also consider the psychological

The author wishes to acknowledge the support of Edith Anderson, Ph.D., R.N., F.A.A.N., and the College of Nursing, University of Delaware, for their support of this project. The secretarial assistance of Mary Ann Rapposelli is also gratefully acknowledged.

impact that accompanies these dysfunctions. She feels that there are three types of factors in one's personality that will affect reaction to a psychosexual problem: psychological, sociocultural, and sexual factors.

Sexuality may be affected by the perceived mutilation of cancer surgery as well as by the disease itself. Grinker (1976) states that the dread of exposing oneself to one's spouse as crippled, damaged, incomplete, or dying may cause sexual inhibition or abstinence. Intimacy and sexual bodily functions may be affected by shame and embarrassment. Mutilation may make exposure and nudity extremely painful. In a retrospective study examining the relationship between mastectomy and changes in sexual behavior, Frank, Dornbush, Webster, and Kolodney (1978) found that having a mastectomy interfered with sexual activity, specifically a decrease in the type and frequency of specific behaviors. In their sample, one third of the 60 respondents had not resumed sexual intercourse 6 months after discharge from the hospital. Jamison, Wellesch, and Pasnau (1978) sampled postmastectomy patients 22 months after surgery and found a sense of decreased femininity and of mutilation in the women. Additionally, one fourth of the sample reported a decrease in the frequency of intercourse and a decrease in their sexual satisfaction.

The literature review supports the thesis that cancer and its treatment cause changes in the individual's sexuality. There are few research studies that provide quantitative data on specific "aspects of sexuality that may be threatened by disease" (ONS & ANA, 1979). There is little additional research to guide the nurse in the most effective ways to assist the client to cope with changes in sexuality, possibly because we do not know exactly what components of sexuality are altered by the disease and its treatment (Anderson, 1985; Greenberg, 1984).

The literature was also reviewed for tools useful in assessing changes in sexuality and sexual functioning. The literature showed three major instruments that are useful in measuring these changes (see also Table 17.1).

The first instrument, the Hanson Assessment of Sexual Health (HASH) is an interview tool designed to assess the sexuality of persons with chronic illness that is medically managed. Reliability and validity of this tool have been tested and are within acceptable ranges (Hanson & Brouse, 1983); however, this tool is not specific for assessment of sexual functioning in cancer patients. The Sexual Function after Gynecologic Illness Scale (SFAGIS) was developed specifically to assess sexual functioning after treatment for cervical, uterine, or ovarian cancer (Bransfield, Horiot, & Nabid, 1984). This is a 30-item self-report scale that addresses 15 "content factors" that have repeatedly been mentioned in the literature pertaining to sexual functioning and gynecologic cancer; each factor is represented twice. The content factors are sexual desire, unavailability of a partner, fears about sexual activity, partners' fears about sexual activity, sexual satisfaction, initiation of sexual activity, affectionate behavior, frequency of sexual intercourse, frequency of organism, vaginal dimensions and muco-

TABLE 17.1 Summary of Available Sexual Assessment Tools

Name of Scale, Variable Measured, Reference	Description of Tool and Items	Administration and Scoring Procedure	Reliability	Validity	Positive Points	Negative Points
Hanson Assessment of Sexual Health (HASH). Variable = Sexuality in chronic illness. Hanson-Brouse (1983).	Interview guide. Four subscales: I. Demographic Information II. Functional Impairments of Chronic Illness III. Effect of Impairments of Chronic Illness on Sexual Functioning IV. Selected Sexual Implications of Chronic Illness	Administered through interviews in health clinic waiting room. No discussion of scoring method.	Internal consistency: Cronbach's alpha = .60 for five subscales on Part III. Not able to be calculated for other subscales.	Content validity	Addresses the patient's perception of the relationship between chronic illness and sexuality.	Not specific for cancer patients: does not measure changes over time.

Sexual Function After Gynecologic Illness Scale (SFAGIS). Variable = Sexual functioning after treatment for GYN cancer. Bransfield, Horiot & Nabid (1984).	30 item self-report tool. 15 content factors presented twice.	Self-report takes 20 minutes to administer Likert-type scale (0–4). Maximum score = 120 Minimum score = 0 High score = high level of sexual activity and freedom from sexual concerns. Low score = low level of sexual activity and many sexual concerns.	Spearman-Brown = split-half reliability coefficient of .80. Interitem consistency using K-R formula = .756.	Content and concurrent validity established.	Adequate reliability level.	Limited definition of sexual functioning useful only with GYN cancers. Does not measure changes over time. Weak validity testing.
Derogatis Sexual Functioning Inventory (DSFI). Variable = Sexual function/ dysfunction. Derogatis and Melisaratos (1979)	Multidimensional measure of 10 areas of sexual functioning. Used to identify sexual dysfunction in healthy persons. Self-report.	245 item self-report tool. Variable item format.	Test–retest reliability = 0.60–.92 on the subdomains. Internal consistency = .56–.94.	Used principal-component analysis on pooled data; rotated original solution and a normalized varimax criterion.	Conceptualized sexual functioning as having various components that can be measured separately and scores for each component summed to obtain total score on sexual functioning.	Not specific for cancer. Does not measure changes over time.

TABLE 17.1 Continued

Name of Scale, Variable Measured, Reference	Description of Tool and Items	Administration and Scoring Procedure	Reliability	Validity	Positive Points	Negative Points
Sexual Functioning Questionnaire. Variable = Sexual functioning in hypertensive clients. Watts (1982).	17 item self-report tool; measured 4 subcomponents of sexual functioning: desire, arousal, orgasm, satisfaction	17 item tool with responses measured on 5 point Likert-type scale. High score = positive sexual functioning.	Test–retest method = .83.	Content validity established.	Conceptualization of sexual functioning into subconcepts. Compares sexual functioning in medication treated hypertensive clients to nonhypertensive clients.	Not specific for cancer patients. Does not measure changes over time.
Sexual Adjustment Questionnaire Variable = Sexual adjustment. Waterhouse and Metcalfe (1986).	Self-report scale identifies 7 subcomponents of sexual adjustment.	16-page, 108-item tool. Administered in 3 sections over a 20-week period. Uses Likert-type scale.	Test–retest method = scores ranged from .5389 to .9374. $\bar{x}$ = .6721	Construct validity; 2-tailed t test.	Measures changes over time. Specific for cancer patients requiring surgical intervention.	Weak reliability and validity testing.

sal condition, potential for vaginal lubrication, intervention of a health care provider, desire for sexual information, changes in sexual activity after therapy, and compliance with a prescription for a dilator. Each item is measured on a 5-point Likert Scale. SFAGIS reliability was found to be adequate (r_{KR20} = .80, alpha r = .76). Face and content validity were established by experts who reviewed the tool, and concurrent validity was examined informally by comparing the client's score on the SFAGIS to anecdotal notes made by the client's physician. The SFAGIS appears to be a useful tool in assessing sexual functioning in gynecologic cancer patients, yet it is limited in its definition of sexual functioning (heterosexual intercourse), is specific to patients with gynecologic cancer, and measures the attributes of sexual functioning only at one point in time.

Another well-known instrument is the Derogatis Sexual Functioning Inventory (DSFI), which is a multidimensional measure of 10 areas of sexual functioning (Derogatis & Melisaratos, 1979). This 245-item self-report tool was designed to identify sexual dysfunction in physically healthy persons. This tool provides information on the overall sexual health of the individual, relative to heterosexual behavior, as well as data on various aspects of sexual functioning. The 10 subdomains measured are information, experience, drive, attitude, psychological symptoms, affects, gender role definition, fantasy, body image, and sexual satisfaction. Test–retest reliability on the DSFI ranges from .60 to .94. Factorial validity was reported on the DSFI using a principal-components analysis on pooled data from 380 subjects. Various rotations, using Kaiser's varimax criterion, yielded 21 dimensions.

The Watts (1982) sexual Functioning Questionnaire (SFQ) is designed for use in comparing the sexual functioning in medication-treated hypertensive clients to the sexual functioning in nonhypertensive persons. This is a 17-item tool with responses measured on a 5-point Likert-type scale. A high score on the SFQ indicates positive sexual function. Subcomponents of sexual functioning measured are sexual desire, arousal, orgasm, and satisfaction. Reliability was established at r = .83 using the test–retest method. The tool was reviewed by experts for content validity.

The tools above lack specific components that should be found in a single tool. For example, as Waterhouse and Metcalfe (1986) suggest, a tool useful in measuring sexual functioning in cancer patients should provide quantitative data, be specific to cancer and its treatment, and yet be general enough to apply to all cancers, measure changes over time, and be useful with large numbers of subjects.

CONCEPTUAL FRAMEWORK

The Sexual Adjustment Questionnaire (SAQ) was developed using the Oncology Nursing Society's outcome standard (ONS & ANA, 1979) on sexuality as a guide. This outcome standard states: "The client and partner can identify aspects of sexuality that may be threatened by disease and can enumerate ways of maintaining sexual identity" (p. 9). However, little is known about the impact of cancer on the various subdomains of sexual functioning. Implied in the term "sexual adjustment" is the process of adaptation, which provides the basis for Roy's adaptation theory. Roy has defined adaptation as "a process of responding positively to environmental changes" (Fawcett, 1984, p. 254). She conceptualizes humans as biopsychosocial beings, and since sexuality has a biological component (the physiologic mode), a psychological component (the self-concept mode), and a social component (the role function and interdependent relationships mode), one can say that any threat to sexuality will cause a lack of homeostasis and a need to adapt in each of these modes. Roy sees the individual's ability to adapt as a function of the degree of change occurring (focal stimulus) and the individual's state as the adaptation level (Fawcett, 1984). The individual's adaptation level comprises a zone that indicates the range of stimulation that will lead to a positive response. This zone is determined by the combined effect of three classes of stimuli: the diagnosis and treatment for cancer is the *focal stimulus;* the *contextual stimuli* are the individual's developmental stage, self-concept, body image, social/sexual interaction patterns, relationships, and all other influences on one's sexuality; the *residual stimuli* are the individual's beliefs, attitudes, and values relating to sexuality. The SAQ addresses aspects of these three classes, and its score indicates how much, if any, stimulation (education) is needed to encourage a positive sexual adjustment.

PURPOSE OF THE MEASURE

The SAQ was developed to quantify the effects cancer and cancer treatment have on selected aspects of the sexuality of an individual. There are many ways one can define sexual adjustment, but for the purposes of this study it was defined as the process of positive or negative sexual adaptation following treatment for a serious illness. This is a multidimensional process and involves changes in the individual's biopsychosocial sexual functioning. The dimensions of biopsychosocial sexual functioning measured include one's desire, activity level, relationships, arousal ability, orgasm, techniques, and sexual satisfaction. Sexual adjustment may be characterized primarily as being a trait attribute in that it is a relatively stable concept of the individual's personality (Waltz, Strickland, & Lenz, 1984). The stimulus of cancer and cancer treatment causes momentary instability in this attribute, necessitating adaptation to a different level of adjustment. Operationally, sexual adjustment is measured as the client's sexual feelings and functioning after treatment for cancer relative to his or her sexual feelings and functioning before the diagnosis of cancer. This yields a sexual adjustment "score"; one is determined to have a high level of sexual adjustment if there is little change between the prediagnosis and posttreatment values.

PROCEDURES FOR DEVELOPMENT

The SAQ represents an expansion and elaboration of Metcalfe's (1980) Sexual Interview Tool. It is a 16-page, 110-item tool that is administered in three separate sections, A, B, and C, with 38, 30, and 40 items, respectively.

The three sections of the SAQ assess sexual feelings and functioning at three different points in time. All three sections are administered posttreatment, although Section B assesses the prediagnosis period. Section A assesses current sexual feelings and functioning during the period 4 to 6 weeks after treatment. Section B assesses sexual adjustment prior to the diagnosis of cancer. It is administered approximately 2 weeks after Section A and asks subjects to remember sexual feelings and functioning before finding out that they had cancer. (Section B could have been designed for use between diagnosis and treatment, but it was felt this could have negative effects on the patient's self-concept and on posttreatment sexual functioning). Section C is administered 16 to 20 weeks posttreatment and again assesses current sexual feelings and functioning. (Section C was not used in this project.)

Initial Testing of the Tool

Face validity was established by having the SAQ reviewed by two nurse researchers who are experts in sexuality, by an expert nurse clinician in head and neck cancer, by a nurse biostatistician, and by a sociologist who is an expert in sexuality. All agreed that the SAQ appeared to measure sexual adjustment and that the subsections seemed to address the components of desire, relationship, activity level, arousal, orgasm, techniques, and satisfaction. Several of the consultants made suggestions for better wording of questions, for more accurate breakdown of the subsections, and for ordering of the main sections. These suggestions were incorporated into the tool before initial testing with subjects.

This revised form of the SAQ was then administered to a large group of healthy subjects and a smaller group of head and neck cancer patients to determine construct validity and test–retest reliability. To determine the construct validity of the SAQ, a contrasted-groups approach was utilized (Shelley, 1984). Based on the limited literature in this area, healthy subjects would be expected to have higher scores on many of the subsections, such as Desire, Activity Level, and Relationship, than would cancer patients. Healthy subjects would also be expected to demonstrate fewer changes in sexual feelings and functioning over time, an indication of a trait attribute.

Results

The SAQ was tested on a total of 84 healthy subjects and 8 head and neck cancer patients. Fifty-seven of the healthy subjects and 7 of the cancer patients completed all three sections of the SAQ (27 subjects dropped out after completing only one or two sections). Demographic data for each group suggest that the typical healthy subject was 43 years of age, white, working at a clinical or professional job, with a bachelor's or master's degree. The cancer patient typically was 51 years old, with some college education. Alcohol intake averaged 4–5 drinks per week in both groups.

Test–retest reliability was determined separately for each subsection of the SAQ, using the Pearson correlation coefficient. As can be seen in Table 17.2, maximum r values for each subsection ranged from .54 to .94. The overall mean reliability was .67; the mean of the maximum r values for each subsection was .78. As expected, reliability was generally highest between Sections A and C, except for the Activity Level susection, which had the highest reliability between Sections A and B.

To determine construct validity, results of healthy and cancer subjects were compared on each subsection, using a two-tailed t test. Table 17.3 represents the mean responses for each group. Significant ($p < .05$) differences were found only on the Activity Level subsection of Section A and the Relationship and Techniques subsections of Section C. These significant differences were in the predicted direction, healthy subjects having higher scores than the cancer patients.

Revision of the SAQ

Many difficulties were encountered in the initial testing of the SAQ: low response rate, the small number of cancer subjects compared to healthy subjects, and the relatively large dropout rate of the healthy subjects (Waterhouse & Metcalfe, 1986). A primary emphasis of this project has been to obtain a larger sample (N = 60) of both healthy and cancer subjects. (As the project is still in progress, these numbers have not yet been achieved.)

Some difficulties in data analysis may have been due in part to the variation in response choices between items in each of the subsections of the SAQ. For example, in the subsection on desire, Item 21 had seven possible answer choices and Item 22 had five. This prevented the use of summative scoring. The SAQ has been revised so that each item in each subsection has the same number of choices on a Likert-type scale and a summative score may be obtained for each of the subsections (Hinshaw, 1986). (See Table 17.4).

ADMINISTRATION AND SCORING OF THE SAQ

The SAQ uses a Likert-type scale that yields interval-level data. Each response has been given a number that ranges from 1 to 4, 1 to 5, or 1 to 6, depending on the subsection. All items within each subsection have the same number of responses. The score range on the SAQ is 7 to 145. High scores on the Desire, Activity Level, Arousal, Orgasm, and Satisfaction

TABLE 17.2 Test–Retest Reliability of the Sexual Adjustment Questionnaire

	Desire		Activity Level		Relationship		Arousal		Orgasm		Techniques		Satisfaction		
Section	*r*	*p*	*r*	*p*	*r*	*p*	*r*	*p*	*r*	*p*	*r*	*p*	*r*	*p*	Mean
A and B	.68		.54		.56		.61		.63		.90		.60		.65
(2–4 weeks between tests)		.000		.016		.008		.000		.000		.000		.000	
B and C	.70		.40		.60		.67		.67		.94		.67		.66
(10–12 weeks between tests)		.000		.148		.004		.000		.000		.000		.000	
A and C	.75		.11		.82		.84		.75		.88		.80		.70
(12–14 weeks between tests)		.000		.420		.004		.000		.000		.000		.000	
Mean	.71		.35		.66		.71		.64		.90		.70		.67

$*p < .05$.

TABLE 17.3 Mean Subsection Responses for Healthy and Cancer Subjects

Section	Group	Desire	Activity Level	Relationship	Arousal	Orgasm	Techniques	Satisfaction
A	Healthy	18.06	3.48	4.84	12.40	6.09	32.12	12.06
	Cancer	17.00	2.48*	3.83	11.43	5.00	31.00	11.43
B	Healthy	13.66	10.62	4.72	8.48	10.66	32.36	8.32
	Cancer	12.67	9.86	4.00	8.29	9.71	31.17	8.42
C	Healthy	18.00	3.58	4.91	12.07	8.67	32.40	12.18
	Cancer	16.67	2.67	3.60*	11.17	8.83	26.20	11.67

$^{*}p < .05$.

TABLE 17.4 Numbers of Items and Choices and Potential Score Ranges for Subsections

	No. of Items	No. of Choices	Minimum Score	Maximum Score
Desire	6	5	5	30
Relationship	3	6	0	15
Activity Level	3	6	0	15
Arousal	3	6	0	15
Orgasm	2	5	1	10
Techniques	9	6	0	45
Satisfaction	3	5	1	15
Total	29	—	7	145

subsections indicate more positive feelings or functioning in these areas. A high score on the Relationship subsection indicates a long-term relationship with a single partner; a high score on Techniques indicates a greater variety of sexual methods and activities employed.

A "Background Information" sheet is administered prior to Section A of the SAQ to collect demographic data (e.g., age, race, sex, educational level, general health, and general sexual health). Questions on past and present use of alcohol are also included because of the influence of alcohol use and abuse on sexual functioning. Information on the subject's medical diagnosis, surgical procedure, radiation therapy, and other pertinent information is recorded from the chart on a separate form.

An example of scoring in the Activity Level subsection:

How soon after surgery did you resume your previous sexual relationship(s) with another person(s)? — 3 / 29

In hospital	Less than 1 month	1–3 months	3–6 months	Have not yet	No partner

Have you been the one to initiate (start) sexual activity with your partner(s) since your surgery? — 2 / 30

Always	Almost always	Sometimes	Almost never	Never	No partner

How often do you have sexual activity (with or without a partner)? — 2 / 31

More than 4 times a week	2–3 times a week	1 time a week	1–3 times a month	Less than once a month	Not at all

Subsection Score = 7

This score would be added to the other subsection scores to obtain a total sexual adjustment score. It could also be compared to the prediagnosis

(Section B) score to determine if any change occurred in the person's sexual activity level since receiving treatment for cancer.

Sexual adjustment was defined as the client's sexual feelings and functioning *after* treatment for cancer, relative to sexual feelings and functioning *before* diagnosis of cancer. Therefore, a high level of sexual adjustment exists when there is little change in sexual feelings and functioning between the prediagnosis and posttreatment periods, or when sexual feelings and functioning change in a positive direction (as defined by the client).

Conversely, a negative level of sexual adjustment would exist when the posttreatment total score on the SAQ is less than that obtained on the prediagnosis measure. For example, if Subject E had a total score of 130 on the prediagnosis measure (Section B) and a score of 105 on the posttreatment scale (Section A), a significant negative change in the person's sexual adjustment would be noted. This would indicate a need for further assessment and intervention.

RELIABILITY AND VALIDITY ASSESSMENT

Sample

Thus far, the revised version of the SAQ, Sections A and B, has been administered to 24 healthy subjects, 6 male and 18 female. The sample ranged in age from 22 to 63 years; the majority (93%) were white, employed in a professional position, and had a bachelor's or master's degree. Alcohol intake averaged one to seven drinks per week in the study group. A very small number of females had experienced menopause (2), whereas 30% of the males reported some difficulty in achieving an erection.

Reliability

Reliability of the revised SAQ was determined by using a variety of procedures. Because sexual adjustment has been conceptualized as a trait attribute, test–retest reliability is appropriate only for healthy subjects (G. Padilla, personal communication, March 1987). Waltz et al. (1984) say that the test–retest reliability involves correlating scores from a test administered on two separate occasions, which may be from 2 weeks to 6 months apart. For this project, Section A of the SAQ was administered approximately 4 weeks after the initial administration of Section A. A Pearson product-moment coefficient was calculated for the total section as well as for each of the seven subsections. The value of the r for the total tool was .933, $p = .01$. The values of r for each of the subsections ranged from .53 to .90; all were significant at the $p = .01$ level. (See Table 17.5)

A second measure of reliability, Cronbach's alpha, was done to assess the internal consistency of the SAQ. An alpha coefficient was determined

TABLE 17.5 Test–Retest Reliabilities on Section A, Sexual Adjustment Questionnaire

	Desire	Rela-tion-ship	Activity Level	Arousal	Tech-niques	Orgasm	Satis-faction
r	.70	.90	.81	.66	.85	.63	.53
*p**	.01	.01	.01	.01	.01	.01	.01

*Two-tailed.

TABLE 17.6 Coefficient Alpha for Dimensions of Sexuality

	Desire	Relation-ship	Arousal	Orgasm	Tech-niques	Satis-faction	Total Test
Alpha	.84	.40	.60	.66	.60	–.03	.70

for Section A of the SAQ, as well as for each of the seven conceptual dimensions of the tool (desire, arousal, etc.). The alpha obtained for Section A was .70. The value of alpha on six of the seven dimensions ranged from .0 to .7. Alpha was not run on the dimension of Activity Level because of a large number of missing values. (See Table 17.6.)

The values of alpha obtained for five of the dimensions indicate internal consistency for those components of the tool; that is, response to one item in the dimension is a good indicator of performance on another item in that dimension. The alpha of zero was obtained on the Satisfaction dimension. This may be a reflection of the low variability of responses to this item or the homogeneity of the sample (Waltz et al., 1984).

Validity

Because the SAQ has been revised, it was necessary to have it reviewed for content and appropriateness prior to testing. The SAQ was reviewed by three experts from the areas of cancer nursing and sexuality. They were asked to rate each of the items for relevance/nonrelevance to the concept being measured. The index of content validity was .80 for Sections A and B.

DISCUSSION AND CONCLUSION

There is mounting evidence that the SAQ is a reliable and valid tool for use with cancer patients receiving surgery as a treatment for their disease.

There are, however, some limitations to the interpretation and generalizability of the data presented in this chapter.

The SAQ has been shown to have some degree of test–retest reliability. That the correlation coefficient values were all significant indicates that there was little change in sexual behavior over time. This finding supports the conceptualization that sexual adjustment is a trait attribute.

Although reliability of the SAQ has been established in this study and others (Waterhouse & Metcalfe, 1986; K. B. Haldeman, personal communication, March 5, 1988), the case for validity of the tool is not as strong. The index of content validity in the current study is .80. According to Lynn (1986), this is not an acceptable value. She feels that in order to say the tool has content validity at the .05 level of significance, all three experts must agree on their rating of the items. Future refinements of the tool will incorporate the suggestions of the reviewers, which mainly focused on the Relationships dimension. This may then improve the index of content validity of the SAQ.

Future testing of the SAQ for validity will be done using the contrasted-groups approach. With this type of validity, the researcher is interested in the extent that the measure is consistent with the theoretical basis of the construct (sexual adjustment) being measured (Shelley, 1984). For this measurement, a healthy sample could be contrasted with a group of cancer patients, who would be expected to have a lower level of sexual adjustment over time. A two-tailed *t* test would be done to determine the difference between means of the two groups on each of the subscales.

Item analysis and factor analysis are two other procedures that need to be performed on the SAQ. Item analysis would help determine if each item on the tool discriminates in the same manner in which the overall measure is intended to discriminate (Waltz et al., 1984). Factor analysis would determine if the conceptual dimensions (desire, arousal, etc.) are defined by items thought to define the dimensions on the basis of the index of content validity.

A problem encountered in the administration of the SAQ to a group of healthy subjects is the large number of missing cases and the large number of subjects who drop out of the study. Because the tool is intended for use with cancer patients, many of the items contain the phrase "since your surgery" or "since your diagnosis," which is not applicable to the healthy subjects used. The researcher attempted to avoid this problem by asking the subjects to ignore those phrases when answering the questionnaire, but this was not effective. Future attempts to determine reliability should involve cancer patients who are not currently receiving treatment for their disease and who may be considered "cured" of their disease.

The SAQ was initially developed for and tested on a sample of head and neck cancer patients; however, the questions are applicable to any cancer patient undergoing surgery as a treatment modality. To increase the generalizability of the SAQ, testing of the tool with other diagnoses is indicated. Reliability of the tool has been determined using a sample that is primarily white and middle to upper-middle class. Use of the tool with groups of a different race, culture, and socioeconomic status is also necessary to determine its appropriateness for other groups.

The SAQ as presently constructed is a complex tool. There are various ways it could be modified to make it a more clinically useful tool. For example, the format could be modified so that the tool would appear more like a checklist. This would make it a shorter tool and decrease the time it takes to answer. It might also be conceptualized as a repeated-measures tool, eliminating Sections B and C. However, that would eliminate the data regarding prediagnosis sexual functioning.

The SAQ has the potential to be a clinically useful tool. It could be used as part of a nursing history to obtain baseline information regarding sexual functioning. It would also give permission to the patient that sexuality and sexual concerns are valid topics of discussion with the nurse. It could also provide the nurse with some data from which to begin to plan patient teaching regarding the impact of the treatment on the patient and partner, as well as clarifying any previous misconceptions they had regarding sexual functioning.

There is a need for nurses to identify the ways in which cancer and the treatment for cancer affect the sexual functioning of the individual. Once we know this, we can begin to identify effective interventions that will help the patient adapt to alterations in sexual functioning. It is hoped that the SAQ will add to our body of knowledge in this area.

REFERENCES

Adams, G. K. (1980). The sex counseling role of the cancer clinician. *Frontiers of Radiation Therapy and Oncology, 14,* 66–78.

Anderson, B. L. (1985). Sexual functioning morbidity among cancer survivors: Current status and future research directions. *Cancer, 55,* 1835–1841.

Bransfield, D. D., Horiot, J. C., & Nabid, A. (1984). Development of a scale for assessing sexual function after treatment for gynecologic cancer. *Journal of Psychosocial Oncology, 2,* 3–19.

Derogatis, L. R., & Melisaratos, N. (1979). The DSFI: A multidimensional measure of sexual functioning. *Journal of Sex and Marital Therapy, 5,* 244–281.

Fawcett, J. (1984). *Analysis and evaluation of conceptual models of nursing.* Philadelphia: F. A. Davis.

Fisher, S. G. (1983). The psychosocial effects of cancer and cancer treatment. *Oncology Nursing Forum, 10,* 63–68.

Frank, D., Dornbush, R. L., Webster, S. K., & Kolodney, R. C. (1978). Mastectomy and sexual behavior: A pilot study. *Sexuality and Disability, 1,* 16–26.

Greenberg, D. B. (1984). The measurement of sexual dysfunction in cancer patients. *Cancer, 53,* 2281–2285.

Grinker, R. R. (1976). Sex and cancer, *Medical Aspects of Human Sexuality, 10,* 130–139.

Hanson, E. L., & Brouse, S. H. (1983). Assessing sexual implication of functional impairments associated with chronic illness. *Journal of Sex Education and Therapy, 9,* 39–45.

Hinshaw, A. S. (1986, July). *Process for developing instruments.* Paper presented at the Measurement of Clinical and Educational Outcomes Project Workshop, Hyannis, MA.

Jamison, K. R., Wellesch, D. K., & Pasnau, R. O. (1978). Psychosocial aspects of mastectomy: I. The woman's perspective. *American Journal of Psychiatry, 135,* 432–436.

Kolodney, R. C., Masters, W. H., & Johnson, V. E. (1979). *Textbook of sexual medicine.* Boston: Little, Brown.

Lynn, M. R. (1986). Determination and quantification of content validity. *Nursing Research, 35,* 382–385.

Metcalfe, M. C. (1980). Adjustments in sexuality made by head and neck cancer patients. In *Proceedings: Fifth Annual Congress of the Oncology Nursing Society* (No. 118).

Oncology Nursing Society and American Nurses Association (1979). *Outcome Standards for Cancer Nursing Practice.* Kansas City, MO: American Nurses Association.

Shelley, S. I. (1984). *Research methods in nursing and health.* Boston: Little, Brown.

Waltz, C. F., Strickland, O. L., & Lenz, E. R. (1984). *Measurement in nursing research.* Philadelphia: F. A. Davis.

Waterhouse, J., & Metcalfe, M. C. (1986). Development of the sexual adjustment questionnaire. *Oncology Nursing Forum, 13*(3), 53–59.

Watts, R. J. (1982). Sexual functioning, health beliefs, and compliance with high blood pressure medications. *Nursing Research, 31,* 278–283.

ID Number ________

Sexual Adjustment Questionnaire (2) Section A—(Female)

In this study I am interested in all aspects of your sexual thoughts, feelings and activities. I know this is a very sensitive area, but I will not be making any judgment about your sexual expression. I hope you will be as honest as you can be in answering the questions so that I will be able to help future cancer patients as they deal with their illness and surgery.

You will probably be more comfortable completing the questionnaire in private. Please read each question carefully. Circle the word which best describes your thoughts, feelings and/or experiences. Space has been left after each question for you to write comments, clarifications, or explanations if you wish.

For the purposes of this questionnaire:

SEXUAL ACTIVITY means *ANYTHING* you do related to sex. This can include, *but is not limited to,* intercourse, kissing, caresssing, masturbation, sexual fantasies, oral sex, etc. These activities may happen alone, between people of the same sex, or between people of opposite sexes.

SEXUAL RELATIONSHIPS(S) means any physical and/or emotional sexual association between two persons that has developed over a period of time.

Note: Items 1 through 19 are general background and demographic items which may be obtained from the author upon request.

CODE—
DO NOT
WRITE IN
THIS LINE

Please return the completed questionnaire in the enclosed envelope within a week. Thank you.

20. What is the importance of sexual activity in your life right now? ___ 20

Extremely Important	Very Important	Important	Slightly Important	Of no Importance

21. How soon after surgery did you resume sexual activity (alone or with another person)? ___ 21

In hospital	Less than 1 month	1–3 months	3–6 months	Have not yet

22. Do you enjoy sexual activity? ___ 22

Always | Almost always | Sometimes | Almost never | Never

23. Do you find that you are too tired for sexual activity? ___ 23

Always | Almost always | Sometimes | Almost never | Never

24. Do you have desire for sexual activity? ___ 24

Always | Almost always | Sometimes | Almost never | Never

25. Do you desire sexual activity more often than your partner(s)? ___ 25

Always | Almost always | Sometimes | Almost Never | Never | No partner

26. How long have you been involved with your current primary sex partner? ___ 26

Less than one month | Less than one year | 1–3 years | 3–10 years | More than 10 years | No partner

27. How many sexual partners have you had since your surgery? ___ 27

None | 1 | 2 | 3 | 4 | More than 5

28. Do you and your partner(s) talk about your sexual relationship? ___ 28

Very often | Often | Sometimes | Almost never | Never | No partner

29. How soon after surgery did you resume your previous sexual relationship(s) with another person(s)? ___ 29

In hospital | Less than 1 month | 1–3 months | 3–6 months | Have not yet | No partner

30. Have you been the one to initiate (start) sexual activity with your partner(s) since your surgery? ___ 30

Always | Almost always | Sometimes | Almost never | Never | No partner

31. How often do you have sexual activity (with or without a partner)? ___ 31

More than 4 times a week | 2–3 times a week | 1 time a week | 1–3 times a month | Less than once a month | Not at all

32. Do you have trouble becoming sexually aroused or excited? ___ 32

Always | Almost always | Sometimes | Almost never | Never | Have not tried

33. Do you notice dryness of your vagina during sexual intercourse? ___ 33

Always | Almost always | Sometimes | Almost never | Never | Have not tried

34. Do you feel any pain or discomfort during sexual intercourse? ___ 34

Always | Almost always | Sometimes | Almost never | Never | Have not tried

35. Are you able to reach a climax ("come") during sexual activity? ___ 35

Always | Almost always | Sometimes | Almost never | Never | Have not tried

36. Is it important for you to reach a climax ("come")? ___ 36

Always | Almost always | Sometimes | Almost never | Never

37. Do you kiss your partner(s) on the lips? ___ 37

Always | Almost always | Sometimes | Almost never | Never | No partner

38. How important to you is being held, touched, and caressed by your partner(s)? ___ 38

Extremely important | Very important | Important | Somewhat important | Not important | No partner

39. Are you held, touched, and caressed by your partner(s)? ___ 39

Always | Almost always | Sometimes | Almost never | Never | No partner

40. Do you spend time holding, touching, and caressing your partner(s)? ___ 40

Always | Almost always | Sometimes | Almost never | Never | No partner

41. Do you kiss your partner's(s') mouth using your tongue (French kiss)? ___ 41

Always | Almost always | Sometimes | Almost never | Never | No partner

42. Do you have intercourse facing your partner(s) (man on top or woman on top)? ___ 42

Always | Almost always | Sometimes | Almost never | Never | No partner

43. Do you have intercourse with your partner(s) positioned behind you? ___ 43

Always | Almost always | Sometimes | Almost never | Never | No partner

44. Do you use your mouth and/or tongue to stimulate your partner's(s') genitals and/or other parts of their body? ___ 44

Always | Almost always | Sometimes | Almost never | Never | No partner

45. How often do you masturbate to reduce sexual tensions? ___ 45

Daily | 3–4 times a week | 1–2 times a week | 1–3 times a month | Less than once a month | Not at all

46. Do you feel satisfied after sexual activity? ___ 46

Always   Almost always   Sometimes   Almost never   Never   No activity

47. Are you satisfied with the frequency of sexual activity in your life? ___ 47

Very satisfied   Somewhat satisfied   Neutral   Somewhat Unsatisfied   Very unsatisfied

48. Do you feel tense or frustrated after a sexual experience? ___ 48

Always   Almost always   Sometimes   Almost never   Never   No activity

49. Do you discuss any sexual concerns with your physician or nurse? ___ 49

Always   Almost always   Sometimes   Almost never   Never

50. Do you discuss your sexual concerns with anyone other than your partner(s)? ___ 50

Other family member   Friend(s)   Clergy   Other   Not at all   Other___________

51. Has having *cancer* changed your sexual relationship with your partner(s)? ___ 51

Very bad effect   Some bad effect   No effect   Some good effect   Very good effect   No partner

52. Has having *surgery* changed your sexual relationship with your partner(s)? ___ 52

Very bad effect   Some bad effect   No effect   Some good effect   Very good effect   No partner

53. Have you had difficulties with your sexual ability since your surgery? ___ 53

No activity   Very many difficulties   Many difficulties   Some difficulties   A few difficulties   No difficulties

Please describe any difficulties:

54. Did the *nurses* at the hospital discuss the effect surgery could have on your resumption of sexual activity? ___ 54

Yes; this was very helpful   Yes; this was somewhat helpful   Yes; this was not helpful   Did not discuss

55. Did the *doctors* at the hospital discuss the effect surgery could have on your resumption of sexual activity? ___ 55

Yes; this was very helpful   Yes; this was somewhat helpful   Yes; this was not helpful   Did not discuss

56. Do you believe that nurses should discuss sexual concerns with their patients? Please explain:

___ 56

Always   Almost always   Sometimes   Almost never   Never

57. Do you believe that doctors should discuss sexual concerns with their patients? Please explain:

___ 57

Always   Almost always   Sometimes   Almost never   Never

ID Number __________

Sexual Adjustment Questionnaire (2) Section B—(Female)

Thank you for completing the Background Information Sheet and Section A of the Sexual Adjustment Questionnaire. Although Section B may seem a lot like Section A, it deals with your sexual thoughts, feelings and activities *before you found out that you had cancer.* Please try to remember the time about 6 months before your cancer was diagnosed. You may not remember some things for certain, but please answer as you *think* you remember.

Again, I know that this is a very sensitive area, but remember that I will not be making any judgments about your sexual expression. I hope that you will continue to be as honest as you can be in answering the questions, keeping in mind my goal of helping future cancer patients to deal with their illness and surgery.

You will probably be more comfortable completing the questionnaire in private. Please read each question carefully, circle the word which best describes your thoughts, feelings, and/or experiences before finding out that you had cancer. Space has been left after each question for you to write comments, clarifications and explanations, if you wish.

For the purposes of this questionnaire:

SEXUAL ACTIVITY means *ANYTHING* you do related to sex. This can include, *but is not limited to,* intercourse, kissing, caressing, masturbation, sexual fantasies, oral sex, etc. These activities may happen alone, between people of the same sex, or between people of opposite sexes.

SEXUAL RELATIONSHIP(S) means any physical and/or emotional sexual association between two persons that has developed over a period of time.

CODE—
DO NOT
WRITE IN
THIS LINE

Please return the completed questionnaire to us within one week in the enclosed envelope. Thank you.

60. In the 6 months before you found out you had cancer, how important was sexual activity in your life?

___
60

Extremely important	Very important	Important	Slightly important	Of no importance

62. How often was sexual activity enjoyable? ___ 62

Always | Almost always | Sometimes | Almost never | Never

63. Were you too tired for sexual activity? ___ 63

Always | Almost always | Sometimes | Almost never | Never

64. Did you have desire for sexual activity? ___ 64

Always | Almost always | Sometimes | Almost never | Never

65. Did you desire sexual activity more often than your partner(s)? ___ 65

Always | Almost always | Sometimes | Almost Never | Never | No partner

66. How long had you been involved with your primary partner? ___ 66

Less than one month | Less than one year | 1–3 years | 3–10 years | More than 10 years | No partner

67. How many sexual partners did you have during the 6 months before you found out you had cancer? ___ 67

None | 1 | 2 | 3 | 4 | More than five

68. Did you and your partner(s) talk about your sexual relationship? ___ 68

Very often | Often | Sometimes | Almost never | Never | No partner

69. Were you having sexual relations with anyone? ___ 69

Very often | Often | Sometimes | Almost never | Never | No partner

70. Were you the one to initiate (start) sexual activity with your partner(s)? ___ 70

Always | Almost always | Sometimes | Almost never | Never | No partner

71. How often do you have sexual activity (with or without a partner)? ___ 71

More than 4 times a week | 2–3 times a week | 1 time a week | 1–3 times a month | Less than once a month | Not at all

72. Before you found out you had cancer, did you have trouble becoming sexually aroused or excited? ___ 72

Always | Almost always | Sometimes | Almost never | Never | Did not try

73. Did you notice dryness of your vagina during sexual intercourse? ___ 73

Always | Almost always | Sometimes | Almost never | Never | No partner

74. Did you feel any pain or discomfort during sexual intercourse? ___ 74

Always Almost always Sometimes Almost never Never No partner

75. Were you able to reach a climax ("come") during sexual activity? ___ 75

Always Almost always Sometimes Almost never Never Did not try

76. Was it important for you to reach a climax ("come")? ___ 76

Always Almost always Sometimes Almost never Never

77. Did you kiss your partner(s) on the lips? ___ 77

Always Almost always Sometimes Almost never Never No partner

78. How important to you was being held, touched, and caressed by your partner(s)? ___ 78

Extremely important Very important Important Somewhat important Not important No partner

79. Did you spend time being held, touched, and caressed by your partner(s)? ___ 79

Always Almost always Sometimes Almost never Never No partner

80. Did you spend time holding, touching, and caressing your partner(s)? ___ 80

Always Almost always Sometimes Almost never Never No partner

81. Did you kiss your partner's(s') mouth using your tongue (French kiss)? ___ 81

Always Almost always Sometimes Almost never Never No partner

82. Did you have intercourse facing your partner(s) (man on top or woman on top)? ___ 82

Always Almost always Sometimes Almost never Never No partner

83. Did you have intercourse with your partner(s) positioned behind you? ___ 83

Always Almost always Sometimes Almost never Never No partner

84. Did you use your mouth and/or tongue to stimulate your partner's(s') genitals and/or other body parts? ___ 84

Always Almost always Sometimes Almost never Never No partner

85. How often did you masturbate to reduce sexual tensions? ___ 85

Daily 3–4 times a week 1–2 times a week 1–3 times a month Less than once a month Not at all

86. Before you found out you had cancer, did you feel satisfied after sexual activity? ___ 86

    Always Almost always Sometimes Almost never Never No activity

87. Were you satisfied with the frequency of sexual activity in your life? ___ 87

    Very satisfied Somewhat satisfied Neutral Somewhat Unsatisfied Very unsatisfied

88. Did you feel tense or frustrated after a sexual experience? ___ 88

    Always Almost always Sometimes Almost never Never No activity

89. Had you ever discussed any sexual concerns with your physician or nurse? ___ 89

    Always Almost always Sometimes Almost never Never

90. Had you discussed sexual concerns with anyone other than your partner(s)? ___ 90

    Other family member Friend(s) Clergy Other Not at all Other________

Thank you very much for participating in this study. I sincerely hope your recovery from surgery is going well. If you would like to receive a summary of the results of the study, please check the box below and enclose your name and address on a separate sheet of paper.

ID Number ________

Sexual Adjustment Questionnaire (2) Section A—(Male)

In this study I am interested in all aspects of your sexual thoughts, feelings and activities. I know this is a very sensitive area, but I will not be making any judgment about your sexual expression. I hope you will be as honest as you can be in answering the questions so that I will be able to help future cancer patients as they deal with their illness and surgery.

You will probably be more comfortable completing the questionnaire in private. Please read each question carefully. Circle the word which best describes your thoughts, feelings and/or experiences. Space has been left after each question for you to write comments, clarifications, or explanations if you wish.

For the purposes of this questionnaire:

SEXUAL ACTIVITY means *ANYTHING* you do related to sex. This can include, *but is not limited to,* intercourse, kissing, caresssing, masturbation, sexual fantasies, oral sex, etc. These activities may happen alone, between people of the same sex, or between people of opposite sexes.

SEXUAL RELATIONSHIPS(S) means any physical and/or emotional sexual association between two persons that has developed over a period of time.

Note: Items 1 through 19 are general background and demographic items which may be obtained from the author upon request.

Please return the completed questionnaire in the enclosed envelope within a week. Thank you.

20. What is the importance of sexual activity in your life right now? ___ 20

Extremely Important | Very Important | Important | Slightly Important | Of no Importance

21. How soon after surgery did you resume sexual activity (alone or with another person)? ___ 21

In hospital | Less than 1 month | 1–3 months | 3–6 months | Have not yet

22. Do you enjoy sexual activity? ___ 22

Always | Almost always | Sometimes | Almost never | Never

23. Do you find that you are too tired for sexual activity? ___ 23

Always | Almost always | Sometimes | Almost never | Never

24. Do you have desire for sexual activity? ___ 24

    Always   Almost always   Sometimes   Almost never   Never

25. Do you desire sexual activity more often than your partner(s)? ___ 25

    Always   Almost always   Sometimes   Almost Never   Never   No partner

26. How long have you been involved with your current primary sex partner? ___ 26

    Less than one month   Less than one year   1–3 years   3–10 years   More than 10 years   No partner

27. How many sexual partners have you had since your surgery? ___ 27

    None   1   2   3   4   More than 5

28. Do you and your partner(s) talk about your sexual relationship? ___ 28

    Very often   Often   Sometimes   Almost never   Never   No partner

29. How soon after surgery did you resume your previous sexual relationship(s) with another person(s)? ___ 29

    In hospital   Less than 1 month   1–3 months   3–6 months   Have not yet   No partner

30. Have you been the one to initiate (start) sexual activity with your partner(s) since your surgery? ___ 30

    Always   Almost always   Sometimes   Almost never   Never   No partner

31. How often do you have sexual activity (with or without a partner)? ___ 31

    More than 4 times a week   2–3 times a week   1 time a week   1–3 times a month   Less than once a month   Not at all

32. Do you have trouble becoming sexually aroused or excited? ___ 32

    Always   Almost always   Sometimes   Almost never   Never   Have not tried

33. When sexually excited, are you able to get an erection? ___ 33

    Always   Almost always   Sometimes   Almost never   Never   Have not tried

34. Do you feel it takes a long time for you to get a firm erection? ___ 34

    Always   Almost always   Sometimes   Almost never   Never   Have not tried

35. Do you have problems in "coming" (ejaculating) or feel that you "come" too soon since your surgery? (If so, please explain) ___ 35

    Always   Almost always   Sometimes   Almost never   Never   Have not tried

36. Is it important for you to reach a climax ("come")? ___ 36

Always | Almost always | Sometimes | Almost never | Never

37. Do you kiss your partner(s) on the lips? ___ 37

Always | Almost always | Sometimes | Almost never | Never | No partner

38. How important to you was being held, touched, and caressed by your partner(s)? ___ 38

Extremely important | Very important | Important | Somewhat important | Not important | No partner

39. Are you held, touched, and caressed by your partner(s)? ___ 39

Always | Almost always | Sometimes | Almost never | Never | No partner

40. Do you spend time holding, touching, and caressing your partner(s)? ___ 40

Always | Almost always | Sometimes | Almost never | Never | No partner

41. Do you kiss your partner's(s') mouth using your tongue (French kiss)? ___ 41

Always | Almost always | Sometimes | Almost never | Never | No partner

42. Did you have intercourse facing your partner(s) (man on top or woman on top)? ___ 42

Always | Almost always | Sometimes | Almost never | Never | No partner

43. Do you have intercourse entering your partner(s) facing their back? ___ 43

Always | Almost always | Sometimes | Almost never | Never | No partner

44. Do you use your mouth and/or tongue to stimulate your partner's(s') genitals and/or other parts or their body? ___ 44

Always | Almost always | Sometimes | Almost never | Never | No partner

45. How often do you masturbate to reduce sexual tensions? ___ 45

Daily | 3–4 times a week | 1–2 times a week | 1–3 times a month | Less than once a month | Not at all

46. Do you feel satisfied after sexual activity? ___ 46

Always | Almost always | Sometimes | Almost never | Never | No activity

47. Are you satisfied with the frequency of sexual activity in your life? ___ 47

Very satisfied | Somewhat satisfied | Neutral | Somewhat unsatisfied | Very unsatisfied

48. Do you feel tense or frustrated after a sexual experience? ___ 48

Always Almost always Sometimes Almost never Never No activity

49. Do you discuss any sexual concerns with your physician or nurse? ___ 49

Always Almost always Sometimes Almost never Never

50. Do you discuss your sexual concerns with anyone other than your partner(s)? ___ 50

Other family member Friend(s) Clergy Other Not at all Other________

51. Has having *cancer* changed your sexual relationship with your partner(s)? ___ 51

Very bad effect Some bad effect No effect Some good effect Very good effect No partner

52. Has having *surgery* changed your sexual relationship with your partner(s)? ___ 52

Very bad effect Some bad effect No effect Some good effect Very good No partner

53. Have you had difficulties with your sexual ability since your surgery? ___ 53

No activity Very many difficulties Many difficulties Some difficulties A few difficulties No difficulties

Please describe any difficulties:

54. Did the *nurses* at the hospital discuss the effect surgery could have on your resumption of sexual activity? ___ 54

Yes; this was very helpful Yes; this was somewhat helpful Yes; this was not helpful Did not discuss

55. Did the *doctors* at the hospital discuss the effect surgery could have on your resumption of sexual activity? ___ 55

Yes; this was very helpful Yes; this was somewhat helpful Yes; this was not helpful Did not discuss

56. Do you believe that nurses should discuss sexual concerns with their patients? ___ 56

Always Almost always Sometimes Almost never Never

57. Do you believe that doctors should discuss sexual concerns with their patients? Please explain: ___ 57

Always Almost always Sometimes Almost never Never

ID Number __________

Sexual Adjustment Questionnaire (2) Section B—(Male)

Thank you for completing the Background Information Sheet and Section A of the Sexual Adjustment Questionnaire. Although Section B may seem a lot like Section A, it deals with your sexual thoughts, feelings and activities *before you found out that you had cancer.* Please try to remember the time about 6 months before your cancer was diagnosed. You may not remember some things for certain, but please answer as you *think* you remember.

Again, I know that this is a very sensitive area, but remember that I will not be making any judgments about your sexual expression. I hope that you will continue to be as honest as you can be in answering the questions, keeping in mind my goal of helping future cancer patients to deal with their illness and surgery.

You will probably be more comfortable completing the questionnaire in private. Please read each question carefully, circle the word which best describes your thoughts, feelings and/or experiences before finding out that you had cancer. Space has been left after each question for you to write comments, clarifications, and explanations if you wish.

For the purposes of this questionnaire:

SEXUAL ACTIVITY means *ANYTHING* you do related to sex. This can include, *but is not limited to,* intercourse, kissing, caressing, masturbation, sexual fantasies, oral sex, etc. These activities may happen alone, between people of the same sex, or between people of opposite sexes.

SEXUAL RELATIONSHIPS(S) means any physical and/or emotional sexual association between two persons that has developed over a period of time.

CODE—
DO NOT
WRITE IN
THIS LINE

Please return the completed questionnaire to us within one week in the enclosed envelope. Thank you.

60. In the 6 months before you found out you had cancer, how important was sexual activity in your life?

___ 60

Extremely Important	Very Important	Important	Slightly Important	Of no Importance

62. How often was sexual activity enjoyable? ___ 62

Always | Almost always | Sometimes | Almost never | Never

63. Were you too tired for sexual activity? ___ 63

Always | Almost always | Sometimes | Almost never | Never

64. Did you have desire for sexual activity? ___ 64

Always | Almost always | Sometimes | Almost never | Never

65. Did you desire sexual activity more often than your partner(s)? ___ 65

Always | Almost always | Sometimes | Almost Never | Never | No partner

66. How long had you been involved with your primary partner? ___ 66

Less than one month | Less than one year | 1–3 years | 3–10 years | More than 10 years | No partner

67. How many sexual partners did you have during the 6 months before you found out you had cancer? ___ 67

None | 1 | 2 | 3 | 4 | More than five

68. Did you and your partner(s) talk about your sexual relationship? ___ 68

Very often | Often | Sometimes | Almost never | Never | No partner

69. Were you having sexual relations with anyone? ___ 69

Very often | Often | Sometimes | Almost never | Never | No partner

70. Were you the one to initiate (start) sexual activity with your partner(s)? ___ 70

Always | Almost always | Sometimes | Almost never | Never | No partner

71. How often did you have sexual activity (with or without a partner)? ___ 71

More than 4 times a week | 2–3 times a week | 1 time a week | 1–3 times a month | Less than once a month | Not at all

72. Before you found out you had cancer, did you have trouble becoming sexually aroused or excited? ___ 72

Always | Almost always | Sometimes | Almost never | Never | Did not try

73. When sexually excited, were you able to get an erection? ___ 73

Always | Almost always | Sometimes | Almost never | Never | Did not try

74. Did you feel it took a long time for you to get a firm erection? ___ 74

Always | Almost always | Sometimes | Almost never | Never | Did not try

75. Did you have problems in "coming" (ejaculating) or feel that you "came" too soon? (If so, please explain) ___ 75

Always | Almost always | Sometimes | Almost never | Never | Did not try

76. Was it important for you to reach a climax ("come")? ___ 76

Always | Almost always | Sometimes | Almost never | Never

77. Did you kiss your partner(s) on the lips? ___ 77

Always | Almost always | Sometimes | Almost never | Never | No partner

78. How important to you was being held, touched, and caressed by your partner(s)? ___ 78

Extremely important | Very important | Important | Somewhat important | Not important | No partner

79. Did you spend time being held, touched, and caressed by your partner(s)? ___ 79

Always | Almost always | Sometimes | Almost never | Never | No partner

80. Did you spend time holding, touching, and caressing your partner(s)? ___ 80

Always | Almost always | Sometimes | Almost never | Never | No partner

81. Did you kiss your partner's(s') mouth using your tongue (French kiss)? ___ 81

Always | Almost always | Sometimes | Almost never | Never | No partner

82. Did you have intercourse facing your partner(s) (man on top or woman on top)? ___ 82

Always | Almost always | Sometimes | Almost never | Never | No partner

83. Did you have intercourse entering your partner(s) facing their back? ___ 83

Always | Almost always | Sometimes | Almost never | Never | No partner

84. Did you use your mouth and/or tongue to stimulate your partner's(s') genitals and/or other body parts? ___ 84

Always | Almost always | Sometimes | Almost never | Never | No partner

85. How often did you masturbate to reduce sexual tensions? ___ 85

Daily | 3–4 times a week | 1–2 times a week | 1–3 times a month | Less than once a month | Not at all

86. Before you found out you had cancer, did you feel satisfied after sexual activity? ___ 86

    Always   Almost always   Sometimes   Almost never   Never   No activity

87. Were you satisfied with the frequency of sexual activity in your life? ___ 87

    Very satisfied   Somewhat satisfied   Neutral   Somewhat unsatisfied   Very unsatisfied

88. Did you feel tense or frustrated after a sexual experience? ___ 88

    Always   Almost always   Sometimes   Almost never   Never   No activity

89. Had you ever discussed any sexual concerns with your physician or nurse? ___ 89

    Always   Almost always   Sometimes   Almost never   Never

90. Had you discussed your sexual concerns with anyone other than your partner(s)? ___ 90

    Other family member   Friend(s)   Clergy   Other   Not at all   Other________

Thank you very much for participating in this study. I sincerely hope your recovery from surgery is going well. If you would like to receive a summary of the results of the study, please check the box below and enclose your name and address on a separate sheet of paper. Thank you!

18
The Haber Level of Differentiation of Self Scale

Judith Haber

This chapter discusses the Haber Level of Differentiation of Self Scale, a measure of the degree to which a person maintains intellectual functioning as opposed to being controlled by emotional forces within relationship systems, particularly the family system.

In the past 20 years, a great deal of attention has been devoted to the study of families, both in nursing and in other disciplines. Much time has been spent in the development of family theory and related intervention models. However, the basic propositions of such theory have not been empirically tested. Consequently, there are few valid and reliable tools available that propose to measure specific aspects of family functioning.

The purpose of this study has been the development of a valid and reliable family assessment tool. The tool, the Haber Level of Differentiation of Self Scale (LDSS), is designed to measure specific aspects of the concept of differentiation of self, one of the eight concepts of the Bowen theory (Bown, 1978b).

REVIEW OF THE RELATED LITERATURE

Differentiation of self, which can be viewed as an index of self-functioning, characterizes people according to the degree of differentiation or fusion between intellectual and emotional system functioning. As such, it is defined as *the degree to which a person can maintain intellectual system functioning as opposed to being controlled by emotional forces within the relationship system.* This speaks to a balance between intellectual and emotional system functioning. The most relevant patterns and characteristics of differentiation occur in contexts of family and other interpersonal relationships (Bowen, 1978b).

A person's level of differentiation evolves out of the family relationship system, which creates an environment that either facilitates or inhibits movement in the direction of differentiation. A person's basic level of differentiation, which assumes a certain degree of undifferentiation in all people, is established by the time he or she leaves the family of origin. It exhibits itself most characteristically at times of anxiety and stress, especially chronic anxiety and negative stress, when emotional, social, or physical dysfunction is most apparent.

Bowen (1976a) proposes that although people at all levels of differentiation are vulnerable to anxiety and stress, those with higher levels of differentiation will have lower levels of dysfunction, especially during periods of chronic anxiety and stress that have a negative impact on the family system. This relates to Bowen's notion that people with higher levels of differentiation have fewer of life's problems; those that they do have tend to be less severe and are recovered from more quickly and completely.

As such, Bowen's (1976b, 1978b) description of differentiation of self and its conceptual relationship to anxiety and stress bears a similarity to what has been described by stress theorists as protector-vulnerability factors or as moderator variables of stress (Johnson & Sarason, 1978, 1979; Lazarus, 1977; Sarason, Johnson, & Siegel, 1979). As stress and anxiety increase from low to high levels, an increase in the level of differentiation will tend to moderate the effects of stress.

Despite the fact that the Bowen theory has been widely accepted by family clinicians in nursing and other disciplines, the literature reveals a paucity of research studies that empirically test the constructs of the theory.

Bowen (1978a, 1978c) has developed a Differentiation of Self Scale, which conceptually presents levels of differentiation as they correlate with a wide range of intellectual and emotional system functioning. The "scale" consists of profiles that characterize human functioning at each level of differentiation, ranging from 0 to 100. Bowen (1976b) states that the Differentiation of Self Scale, as he views it, is not meant to be a measurement tool. Rather, it represents an effort to clarify conceptually the ways in which people are different from each other in terms of intellectual and emotional system functioning.

Early attempts to measure differentiation of self (Moynihan & Ingraham, 1971; Winer, 1971) represent pioneering efforts to objectively measure Bowen's concept. However, small sample size ($N = 4$), inconsistent data patterns, and lack of statistical analysis minimize the contribution of these studies to the family research data base.

Subsequent efforts by Weinberg (1978), Kear (1978) and Garfinkel (1980) to develop an objective measure of differentiation of self were also unsuccessful. Each measure has varied conceptual and/or methodological problems in tool development, sample size, factor structure, and bias that preclude their usefulness as tools with which to measure the concept of differentiation of self. As such, a profound gap in the measurement literature provided the impetus for the development of the LDSS.

CONCEPTUAL BASES OF THE MEASURE

The LDSS is conceptually derived from Bowen's cornerstone concept, differentiation of self. Differentiation of self can be defined as the degree to which a person maintains intellectual functioning as opposed to being controlled by emotional forces within the relationship system. The well-differentiated person has a balance between intellectual and emotional system function and is characterized by emotional maturity.

PURPOSE OF THE MEASURE

The purpose of the LDSS is the assessment of intellectual and emotional system functioning of individuals within a family system. This provides a valid and reliable family assessment tool for nurses and other clinicians who work with families.

PROCEDURES FOR DEVELOPMENT

The starting point for the development of the LDSS was the reanalysis of the 41-item Kear (1978) Differentiation of Self Scale (DOSS) that was undertaken by Kim and Merrifield (1982). Their factor-analytic and reliability studies identified a 30-item instrument composed of five independent subscales, rather than the unidimensional scale that was proposed by Kear (1978). The Emotional Maturity (EM) and Emotional Dependency (ED) subscales of this instrument appeared to most accurately reflect Bowen's description of intellectual and emotional system functioning. However, because these two subscales contained only six questions each, as well as because of psychometric problems inherent in the Kear (1978) scale, a decision was made by the researcher to use the 12 questions contained in the two subscales as the basis for a larger item pool in the development of a new scale containing only two subscales, EM and ED. An item pool of 50 questions for each subscale was developed. The items for each subscale were organized around categories that seemed to most closely resemble the characteristics of differentiation described by Bowen as they related to the intellectual and emotional system functioning. The categories for the EM subscale included values and beliefs, goals, cognitive versus emotional processes, I-positions, assessment of self, and expectations of others. The categories for the ED subscale included decision making, need for approval, need for security, response to group pressure, feelings about self, and problem-solving ability (Haber, 1984).

Each category was expanded to a minimum of eight items by means of formulating additional items with similar wording. Each category contained an equal number of direct and reverse-score items to reduce response set.

The results of the pilot study of the 100-item tool yielded a 32-item Level of Differentiation of Self Scale (LDSS). The tool had a 19-item EM subscale and a 13-item ED subscale.

The data from subsequent construct validity studies indicated that the original subscale structure of the 32-item LDSS was not valid. Factor analysis demonstrated a factor-loading pattern consistent with a unidimensional structure. In two different factor analyses, 24 of the 32 LDSS items loaded on Factor I (EM). As such, the LDSS has been revised as a 24-item, unidimensional scale. This will be discussed in detail in the "Validity and Reliability" section of this chapter.

ADMINISTRATION AND SCORING

The LDSS can be administered in either an individual or group setting. It takes approximately 15 to 20 minutes to complete. The response format consists of a 4-point Likert-type scale. Subjects are instructed to answer each item according to how well it describes them. Response categories consist of numbers indicating Strongly Agree (4), Agree (3), Disagree (2), and Strongly Disagree (1). Responses indicating evidence of differentiation are scored in the above manner. However, responses to items indicating lack of differentiation are reverse-scored. Thus, the higher the total score, the higher the level of differentiation of self. Items 1–7, 9, 10, 12, 13–16, 18, 20, 21, 23, and 24 are direct-score questions. Items 8, 11, 17, 19, and 22 are reverse-score questions. Scores for the LDSS range from 24 to 96.

RELIABILITY AND VALIDITY ASSESSMENTS

The reliability and validity of the LDSS was established in three stages during the course of three studies utilizing three different samples.

The Pilot Study—Stage I

The pilot sample consisted of 257 volunteer subjects (151 female, 116 male) who were recruited from undergraduate and graduate classes at urban and suburban universities and community colleges and through personal contacts. Fifty-eight percent of the sample was female, 92% were Caucasian, and 58% were married. The average age of females was 32.9 years; of males, 33.1 years. Several religious preferences were reported: 38.2% Catholic, 29.5% Jewish, 20.5% Protestant, and 11.4% representing other religious prferences.

An item analysis was used to arrive at a final item pool with satisfactory reliability. Item-to-total correlations were computed for the 50 items of each subscale (EM and ED). Items on each subscale that correlated most highly (.30 or above) with the total score were selected for consideration.

Items that met this criterion were reviewed with regard to duplication and spread of content. The 19 questions that were selected for inclusion in the EM subscale yielded an alpha coefficient of .86. The 13 questions selected for the ED subscale yielded an alpha coefficient of .83, indicating a high degree of internal consistency among the items of each subscale.

Content validity of the pilot tool was established by a review panel consisting of two family theoreticians and practitioners of family therapy, as well as an expert in tool development. The judges determined that the items were representative of the content domain of the differentiation variable and that the psychometric properties of the tool were satisfactory. Construct validity studies were not undertaken at this time because the sample (N = 257) was not adequate to do a factor analysis that would yield stable results.

Stage II

The 32-item LDSS was administered to another volunteer sample of 168 married couples (N = 336) who completed the LDSS and two marital assessment tools.

The sample was similar to the pilot sample. All were high school graduates, the majority having obtained some college education. Over 32% of the females and 45% of the males had attended graduate school, and 59% of females and 77% of males held professional positions. Almost 99% of the sample were Caucasian. Average ages for males and females were 34.6 years and 32.2 years, respectively. The homogeneous nature of the sample, which was almost entirely Caucasian, highly educated, and middle class, was a drawback in terms of potential generalizability of the findings. However, the homogeneity of the sample was necessary in light of controlling for extraneous variability in the dependent variable, marital conflict.

Coefficient alpha was computed to establish the internal consistency reliability of the LDSS. The EM subscale yielded an alpha of .86; the ED subscale, an alpha of .80. This indicates that the internal consistency reliability, although slightly lower than the alphas of the pilot study, remained satisfactory.

A varimax rotated factor analysis was undertaken to establish the construct validity of the LDSS. The findings indicated that 17 of 19 items from the EM subscale demonstrated a factor pattern loading of .40 or higher on Factor I. The two remaining EM items did not load significantly on either factor. Six of the 13 items from the ED subscale also loaded on Factor I. Five ED items loaded significantly on Factor II. Two items did not load significantly on either factor. The results suggest that Factor I accounted for the major proportion of the common variance, 80.4%. The factor-analytic data suggested preliminary evidence of construct validity for the LDSS. Moreover, it indicated that the LDSS may, in fact, represent a unidimensional construct, consisting of 23 LDSS items. However, a decision regarding this issue was postponed until a third study, with a more heterogeneous sample, could be undertaken.

Stage III

The 32-item LDSS, as well as the State-Trait Anxiety Inventory (Spielberger, Gorsuch, & Lushene, 1970), the Life Experience Survey (Sarason et al., 1979) and the Behavior Checklist (Gordon & Mooney, 1950) were administered to 372 volunteer subjects (240 female, 131 male). Subjects were recruited from community groups, adult education classes, work settings, and community and four-year colleges. A goal of subject recruitment was to obtain a heterogeneous sample. Demographic data presented in Table 18.1 indicate a more proportionate representation of subjects with regard to ethnicity, religion, level of education, work status, and marital status.

The reliability of the LDSS was reestablished using coefficient alpha. The data reveal an alpha of .86 for the EM subscale and .83 for the ED subscale. These data are similar to, but higher than, alphas from the two previous studies. This provides further evidence for the high degree of internal consistency reliability among the items of each subscale.

Content validity of the LDSS was reestablished by use of the content validity index (CVI). Two judges, both experts in the area of Bowen family theory and therapy, independently rated the relevance of each item to each subscale using a 4-point rating scale ranging from very relevant to not relevant. The CVI for the EM subscale was .95; for the ED subscale, .92. This indicates a satisfactory level of content validity.

Hypothesis testing as well as factor-analytic studies were carried out for purposes of reestablishing construct validity of the LDSS. Three hypotheses were tested that reflected propositions related to the concept differentiation of self. All three hypotheses were supported, thus lending support to the construct validity of the LDSS.

Hypothesis 1 stated that there will be a negative relationship between differentiation of self and trait anxiety. Pearson correlation coefficients between the EM and ED subscales of the LDSS and the Trait Anxiety subscale of the STAI were both $r = -.52$, $p < .001$.

Hypothesis 2 stated that there will be a negative relationship between differentiation of self and state anxiety. Pearson correlation coefficients between the EM and ED subscales of the LDSS and the State Anxiety subscale of the STAI were $r = -.43$ and $r = -.46$, $p < .001$, respectively.

The data from hypotheses 1 and 2 provide support for Bowen's proposition that the higher the level of differentiation of self, the lower the vulnerability to acute and chronic anxiety.

Hypothesis 3 stated that there will be a negative relationship between differentiation of self and adult dysfunction. Pearson correlation coefficients between scores on the EM and ED subscales of the LDSS and the Behavior Checklist (BC) were $r = -.53$ and $r = -.42$, $p < .001$, respectively. These data provide support for the proposition that people with higher levels of differentiation are less vulnerable to psychological dysfunction.

A second varimax rotated factor analysis ($N = 372$) was undertaken. The findings, as presented in Table 18.2 indicated the 17 of 19 items from

TABLE 18.1 Demographic Data—Stage III (n = 372)

Variable	%
Sex	
Female	62
Male	38
Religion	
Protestant	29
Catholic	46.2
Jewish	15.6
Other	9.2
Ethnicity	
Caucasian	83
Black	10
Hispanic	5.1
Asian	1.9
Education	
High school graduate	14.1
Some college	33.0
College graduate	29.0
College plus	23.9
Work status	
Professional	49.5
Technical	38.0
Other	12.5
Marital status	
Married	50.3
Widowed	1.5
Separated	5.1
Divorced	7.0
Single	35.0
Family income	
10–20,000	12.4
21–30,000	19.1
31–40,000	19.4
41–50,000	9.1
51–60,000	7.8
60+	32.0
Mean age	
Male 35.6 yr	
Female 34.1 yr	

the EM subscale demonstrated a factor pattern loading of .40 or higher on Factor I. All 17 items are the same items that loaded on Factor I in the previous factor analysis.

The other two items of this subscale did not load significantly on either factor. Seven of 13 items from the ED subscale also demonstrated a factor pattern loading of .40 or higher on Factor I. Six of seven of these items loaded significantly on Factor I in the prior factor analysis. Six of 13 items of the ED subscale did load significantly on Factor II. All ED items loaded significantly on either Factor I or II.

Table 18.2 Means, Standard Deviations, and Highest Factor Loadings of the LDSS—Stage III

Original Item No.	Final Item No.	Mean	Standard Deviation	Com-mon-ality	Highest Factor Loading
1		2.63	.83	.33	.48**
2	1	3.15	.66	.34	.44*
3	2	3.24	.65	.45	.42*
4	3	3.22	.61	.40	.47*
5	4	3.00	.77	.31	.45*
6		2.45	.82	.26	.43**
7	5	2.76	.77	.38	.40*
8	6	3.20	.69	.37	.40*
9	7	2.85	.78	.40	.47*
10		2.42	.83	.31	.56**
11	8	2.81	.90	.37	.41*
12	9	3.21	.68	.27	.42*
13	10	3.35	.67	.46	.59*
14		2.65	.67	.40	.42**
15	11	3.06	.77	.44	.50*
16	12	3.02	.76	.42	.49*
17	13	3.04	.72	.49	.58*
18	14	2.93	.64	.54	.59*
19	15	3.08	.64	.44	.46
20		2.64	.73	.47	.68**
21	16	3.22	.62	.57	.60*
22		2.32	.68	.30	.35
23	17	3.09	.64	.51	.59*
24		2.62	.74	.34	.37
25		1.98	.61	.36	.53**
26	18	2.90	.71	.52	.54*
27	27	3.33	.72	.38	.52*
28	20	3.19	.66	.60	.70*
29	21	3.20	.67	.56	.66*
30	22	3.11	.73	.38	.48*
31	23	3.22	.65	.45	.62*
32	24	3.04	.65	.54	.58*

*Item loads on Factor I, .40 or greater.
**Item loads on Factor II, .40 or greater.

The results suggest a marked stability in the factor structure of the LDSS. Again, Factor I (EM) accounted for a major proportion of the common variance, 82.1%.

As a result of the consistent data pattern that emerged in the Stage II and Stage III factor analyses, a decision was made to revise the LDSS as a unidimensional, 24-item measurement tool. Additional data contributing to that decision was a high correlation, $r = .70$, $p < .001$, between the EM and ED subscales as well as a combined alpha coefficient of .91, an alpha that was higher than that obtained for either subscale individually.

DISCUSSION AND CONCLUSIONS

The LDSS currently consists of a 24-item, unidimensional family assessment tool that accurately measures specific aspects of intellectual and emotional system functioning of the Bowen theory concept, differentiation of self. The LDSS has demonstrated evidence of internal consistency reliability, content validity, and construct validity.

A limitation of tool development has been the volunteer and relatively homogeneous nature of the samples. As such, a recommendation for future tool development would include further testing of the LDSS using a probability sampling technique that includes a more diverse population. Another limitation of the studies to date is lack of a specific focus on dysfunctional families and/or families in crisis. Future studies could test the tool on clinical populations that include multiproblem families coping with chronic and/or catastrophic illness in a family member. Expansion of the data pool to include such populations would facilitate the conduct of additional and different reliability, construct validity, and meta-analysis studies. This can only enhance the psychometric soundness of the LDSS.

The LDSS is clinically relevant as an assessment tool for nurse clinicians working with individuals and families. The LDSS provides nurses with an index of intellectual and emotional system functioning. Clients can complete the tool at the time of their initial visit, and the score can be used as baseline data for treatment planning and future evaluation. For example, if low differentiation of self-scores are obtained, the nurse may have to design interventions that focus on the assignment of concrete tasks, in contrast to a more cognitive–exploration–discussion approach. Because such families tend to be more problem-prone, the nurse, as a result of the assessment, can be prepared for and attempt to prevent crises through the intervention plan. The overall goal is to increase the client's functional level of differentiation from the baseline level of differentiation. Consistent with this goal are interventions designed to facilitate an increased balance in intellectual and emotional system functioning.

In conclusion, it is the hope of this researcher that another valid and reliable measurement instrument has been added to the armamentarium of outcome measurement tools developed by nurse researchers who are interested in studying family phenomena.

REFERENCES

Bowen, M. (1976a). Family reaction to death. In P. Guerin (Ed.), *Family therapy: Theory and practice* (pp. 335–348). New York: Gardner Press.

Bowen, M. (1976b). Theory in the practice of psychotherapy. In P. Guerin (Ed.), *Family therapy: Theory and practice* (pp. 42–90). New York: Gardner Press.

Bowen, M. (1978a). Intrafamilial-dynamics in emotional illness. In M. Bowen (Ed.), *Family therapy in clinical practice* (pp. 103–113). New York: Jason Aronson.

Bowen, M. (1978b). On the differentiation of self. In M. Bowen (Ed.), *Family therapy in clinical practice* (pp. 467–528). New York: Jason Aronson.

Bowen, M. (1978c). Toward the differentiation of self in one's family of origin. In M. Bowen (Ed.), *Family therapy in clinical practice* (pp. 147–181). New York: Jason Aronson.

Garfinkel, H. N. (1980). Family systems personality profile: An assessment instrument based on the Bowen theory. *Dissertation Abstracts International, 41,* 2757-B. (University Microfilms No. 80-29,639).

Gordon, L. V., & Mooney, R. L. (1950). *Mooney Problem Checklist, Adult Form.* New York: Psychological Corporation.

Haber, J. (1984). The relationship between differentiation of self, complementary psychological need patterns, and marital conflict. *Dissertation Abstracts International, 45,* 2102-B. (University Microfilms No. 800521-3042).

Johnson, J. H., & Sarason, I. G. (1978). Life stress, depression and anxiety: Internal-external control as a moderator variable. *Journal of Psychosomatic Research, 22,* 205–208.

Johnson, J. H., & Sarason, I. G. (1979). Moderator variables in life stress research. In I. G. Sarason & C. D. Spielberger (Eds.), *Stress and anxiety* (Vol. 6, pp. 224–243). Washington, DC: Hemisphere.

Kear, J. (1978). Marital attraction and satisfaction as a function of differentiation of self. *Dissertation Abstracts International, 39,* 2505-B. (University Microfilms No. 78-19, 970).

Kim, W. H., & Merrifield, P. (1982). *A differentiation of self scale.* Unpublished manuscript, New York University, New York.

Lazarus, R. S. (1977). Psychological stress and coping in adaptation and illness. In Z. J. Pipowski, D. R. Lipsitt, & P. C. Whybrow (Eds.), *Psychosomatic medicine* (pp. 383–401). New York: Oxford University Press.

Moynihan, C., & Ingraham, B. (1971). Observing family function: Toward a definition of change. In J. Brady & C. Moynihan (Eds.), *Systems therapy* (pp. 10–16). Washington, DC: Authors.

Sarason, I. G., Johnson, J. H., & Siegel, J. M. (1979). Development of the Life Experiences Survey. In I. G. Sarason & C. D. Spielberger (Eds.), *Stress and anxiety* (Vol. 6, pp. 279–291). Washington, DC: Hemisphere.

Spielberger, C. D., Gorsuch, R. L., & Lushene, R. E. (1970). *Manual for the State-Trait Anxiety Inventory.* Palo Alto, Ca.: Consulting Psychologists.

Weinberg, L. H. (1978). Differentiation and fusion in marital relationships. *Dissertation Abstracts International, 39,* 1002B. (University Microfilms No. 78-12, 251).

Winer, L. (1971). Some efforts in defining and assessing change. In J. Brady & C. Moynihan (Eds.), *Systems therapy* (pp. 23–30). Washington, DC: Authors.

Code Number ________

THE HABER LDSS

Below you will find a set of statements followed by numbers from 1 to 4. Please read each statement carefully. After reading the statement, decide how well it describes you. If you strongly agree with a statement, circle 4. If, however, you strongly disagree with a statement then circle 1. Use the other numbers next to the statements to indicate whether you agree (3), or disagree (2). There are no right or wrong answers. Answer as honestly as possible. Please read and answer *all* items.

	Strongly Disagree (1)	Disagree (2)	Agree (3)	Strongly Agree (4)
1. I will change my opinion more on the basis of new knowledge than on the basis of the opinions of others.	1	2	3	4
2. I am capable of helping myself when I am in a crisis.	1	2	3	4
3. When I have a problem that upsets me, I am still able to consider different options for solving the problem.	1	2	3	4
4. I do not find it difficult to disagree with the opinions of others.	1	2	3	4
5. My life is guided by a clear set of goals that I have established for myself.	1	2	3	4
6. I usually rely on myself for help when I have a problem, unless it is appropriate for me to seek the help of others.	1	2	3	4
7. I do not find group pressure hard to resist.	1	2	3	4
8. It is hard for me to set long-range goals for myself.	1	2	3	4
9. I can decide on my own whether or not I have done a good job.	1	2	3	4
10. I have a well-defined set of values and beliefs.	1	2	3	4
11. A lot of my energy goes into being what other people want me to be.	1	2	3	4

12. I prefer to maintain and defend my own position rather than conform to the majority.	1	2	3	4
13. I am emotionally mature.	1	2	3	4
14. My ability to make decisions is not greatly affected by the disapproval of others.	1	2	3	4
15. My knowing that I have done a good job is more important than the praise of others.	1	2	3	4
16. I make decisions based on my own set of values and beliefs.	1	2	3	4
17. My decisions and actions are based on the approval I get from others.	1	2	3	4
18. My decisions are not easily influenced by group pressure.	1	2	3	4
19. I do not behave in a grown-up manner.	1	2	3	4
20. I am comfortable about my beliefs and values even when others challenge them.	1	2	3	4
21. What I expect of myself is more important than what other people expect of me.	1	2	3	4
22. I will change my opinions to avoid arguments with people.	1	2	3	4
23. When important decisions need to be made, I consider all possible options.	1	2	3	4
24. My own assessment of the job I have done is more important than the assessment of others.	1	2	3	4

APPENDIX: Measurement of Clinical and Educational Nursing Outcomes Project: Project Participants and Topic Areas

Participant	*Topic Area*
Rinda Alexander, R.N., Ph.D. Purdue University–Calumet Hammond, Indiana	Quality of Life of the Adult Terminally Ill with Cancer
Jane Anderson, R.N., Ph.D. University of Michigan Hospital Ann Arbor, Michigan	Readiness for Discharge
Johnella Banks, R.N., D.N.Sc. Howard University Washington, D.C.	The Effect of Relaxation Training, Sex Education, and Imagery on Self Concept and Knowledge of Adolescent Students
Deidre Blank, R.N., D.S.N. National Center for Nursing Research National Institute of Health Bethesda, Maryland	Theoretical Model Testing
Fran Board, R.N., M.S.N. University of Michigan Ann Arbor, Michigan	Maternal Nursing, Cognitive Aspects of Expertise
Irene Bobak, R.N., M.S., N.P. San Francisco State University San Francisco, California	Caseload Management
Marie Boguslawski, R.N., Ph.D. Mount Sinai Hospital New York, New York	To Determine the Results of Holistic Nursing Practice
Kay Branum, R. N., Ph.D. MGH Institute of Health Profession Boston, Massachusetts	Medical-Surgical-Critical Care
Mary Brucker, R.N., C.N.M. Rush University Chicago, Illinois	Nurse Midwifery

Sue Bryant, R.N., M.S. Charlottesville, Virginia	Affective Domain
Janet Burge, R.N., Ph.D. University of Alabama Huntsville, Alabama	Employer Expectancies of New Teachers in Baccalaureate Nursing Programs and Relationship to Teachers' Perception of Graduate Education in Preparing for Teaching Role.
Barbara Byfield, R.N., Ph.D. University of Maryland Baltimore, Maryland	Continuing Education
Ruth Caggins, R.N., M.A. Prairie View A & M University Houston, Texas	Measurement of Psychosociocultural Concepts within a Baccalaureate Curriculum
Marci-lee Catanzaro, R.N., Ph.D. University of Washington Seattle, Washington	Effects of Chronic Progressive Illness during Midlife
Barbara Cohen, R.N., Ed.D. Lehman College Bronx, New York	Coping with Stress, Students and Coping with Stress, Parents of Children with Chronic Renal Failure
Carol Collison, R.N., Ph.D. University of South Carolina Columbia, South Carolina	Family Environment
Gretchen Cornell, R.N., Ph.D. Northeast Missouri State University Kirksville, Missouri	Evaluation of Educational Quality
Margaret Dahlhauser, R.N., Ph.D. Tennessee State University Nashville, Tennessee	Objective Clinical Outcome Measurement Tool
Sandra Davis, M.S.N. University of Alabama Birmingham, Alabama	Clinical Competencies in Decision Making, Human Relationships, Leadership, Professional Practice, and Technical Expertise
Jacqueline Dienemann, R.N., Ph.D. George Mason University Fairfax, Virginia	Performance Evaluation of Nursing Faculty
Willa Doswell, R.N., Ph.D. NYC Health & Hospital Corp. New York, New York	Minor Life Stress

Marie Driever, R.N., Ph.D. University of Washington Seattle, Washington	Coping and Adaptation in Chronic Illness
Mary Duffy, R.N., Ph.D. University of California San Francisco, California	Women's Studies—Perceptions (World View) of Women Undergoing the Transition to Divorce
Roberta Emerson, R.N., Ed.D. Intercollegiate Center for Nursing Education Spokane, Washington	Affective Domain and Theoretical Model Testing
Belle Erickson, R.N., M.S. Villanova University Villanova, Pennsylvania	Achievement Test Formats
Keville Frederickson, R.N., Ed.D. Lehman College Bronx, New York	Gerontology, Women's Health (Mental)
Betty Ferrell, R.N., Ph.D. University of Southern California Los Angeles, California	Palliative Care
Linda Finke, R.N., Ph.D. University of Wisconsin EauClaire, Wisconsin	Registered Nurses Seeking BSN
Sara Fry, R.N., Ph.D. University of Maryland Baltimore, Maryland	Descriptive Ethics—Explanation of the Phenomenon of Morality Related to the Practice and Discipline of Nursing
Elizabeth Geden, R.N., Ph.D. University of Missouri Columbia, Missouri	Theory Development
Patricia Gerrity, R.N., Ph.D. LaSalle University Philadelphia, Pennsylvania	Educational Nursing Outcomes
Linda Glazner, R.N., Ph.D. Hunter College–Bellevue New York, New York	Occupational Health
Mary Grohar, R.N., Ph.D. St. Louis University St. Louis, Missouri	Direct Nursing Care (Cost Structure) and Graduate Program Clinical Course

Judith Haber, R.N., Ph.D. College of Mount Saint Vincent Riverdale, New York	Construct Validity of a Differentiation of Self Scale
Gloria Hagopian, R.N., Ed.D. University of Pennsylvania Philadelphia, Pennsylvania	Oncology; Radiation Therapy
Nancy Hedlund, R.N., Ph.D. The Queens Medical Center Honolulu, Hawaii	Healing: Tissue Healing, Elimination of Infection, Psychological Healing
Elizabeth Hefferin, R.N., Ph.D. VA Medical Center West Los Angeles, California	Promotion of More Individualized Outpatient Care and Self-Care Management, Promote Clinic Staff Awareness and Documentation of Patients' Life-Styles, Psychosocial Needs, and Problems
Marilyn Herrmann, R.N., M.S. Loma Linda University, Loma Linda California	Clinical Laboratory and Its Impact on Values, Attitudes, and Personal Qualities
Nancy Hester, R.N., Ph.D. University of Colorado Denver, Colorado	Pre/Early Adolescent Health
Gail Hilbert, R.N., D.N.Sc. Widener University Chester, Pennsylvania	Social Support, Chronic Illness
Elizabeth Howard, R.N., Ph.D. Simmons College Boston, Massachusetts	Use of a Mathematical Model to Scale Nursing Behaviors Expected of Students in a Nursing Curriculum
Ann Hurley, R.N., M.S., CNA New England Deaconess Hospital Boston, Massachusetts	Individuals Who Have Diabetes Mellitus
Alicia Huckstadt, Ph.D. Wichita State University Wichita, Kansas	Touch As a Supportive Nursing Intervention
Debra Hymovich, R.N., Ph.D., FAAN King of Prussia, Pennsylvania	Children, Siblings, and Parents of Children with Chronic Illness
Rebecca James, R.N., Ph.D. University of North Carolina Greensboro, North Carolina	Computer-Assisted Instruction

Patricia Jassak, R.N.C.S., M.S. Loyola University Medical Center Chicago, Illinois	Quality of Life for Families of Cancer Patients
Linnea Jatulis, R.N., M.S. Russell State College Troy, New York	Measurement of Outcomes of Community Health Nursing Visits to Families
Linda Jones, R.N., Ph.D. Louisiana State University Medical Center New Orleans, Louisiana	Chronic Illness
Barbara Kakta, R.N., Ed.D. Lewis University Romeoville, Illinois	Development of Two Evaluation Tools for Baccalaureate Nursing Education
Virginia Karb, R.N., M.S.N. University of North Carolina Greensboro, North Carolina	Learning from Text.
Pauline Komnenich, R.N., Ph.D. Arizona State University Tempe, Arizona	Collaborative Research
Joyce Laborde, R.N., Ph.D. University of North Dakota Grand Forks, North Dakota	Pain Measurement
Shirley Laffrey, R.N., Ph.D. University of California San Francisco, California	Outcomes of public health nurse interventions
Patricia Lane, R.N., Ph.D. Louisiana State University New Orleans, Louisiana	Perceptions about Intrusions of Territory and Personal Space.
Dorothy Lyons, R.N., Ed.D. Jacksonville State University Jacksonville, Alabama	Educational Measurement
Maureen McCausland, R.N., D.N.Sc. University Hospitals of Cleveland Cleveland, Ohio	Nursing Administration
Anna McDaniel, R.N., M.A., C.S. Marion College Marion, Indiana	Caring Behavior of Baccalaureate Nursing Students and Graduates

MaryAlice Jordan-Marsh, R.N., Ph.D. Harbor UCLA Medical Center Torrance, California	Health Habit Counseling
Jeanette Matrone, R.N., M.S., CNAA The Miriam Hospital Providence, Rhode Island	Collaborative Practice Decision Making
Judith Maurin, R.N., Ph.D. University of Utah Salt Lake City, Utah	The Health and Mental Health Needs of Homeless, Especially Families
Margaret Metcalfe, R.N., M.S. University of Delaware Newark, Delaware	Sexuality/Oncology
Nancy Miller, R.N., M.S. Beth Israel Hospital Boston, Massachusetts	Clinical Outcomes: Timing of Discharge Planning Interventions as an Indicator of Successful Discharge
Sheila Miller, R.N., M.S.N. West Virginia Wesleyan College Buckhannon, West Virginia	Curriculum Development Measurement Methods
Paula Minehan, R.N., Ed.D. Minehan Consultations Milton, Massachusetts	Change in Needs of Patients (Acuity/Intensity)
Sarah Mynatt, R.N., Ed.D. Memphis State University Memphis, Tennessee	Program Evaluation
Brenda Nichols, R.N., D.N.Sc. Northern Rivers College of Advanced Education Australia	Nursing Administrations Reimbursement Techniques
Francine Nichols, R.N.C., Ph.D. The Wichita State University Wichita, Kansas	Maternal Newborn
Leslie Nicoll, R.N., Ph.D. University of New Hampshire Durham, New Hampshire	Maternal–Child Health
Ngozi Nkongho, R.N., Ph.D. Lehman College (CUNY) Bronx, New York	Clinical Evaluation of Graduate Students. Gerontological Nursing Tools

Priscilla O'Connor, M.S.Ed., M.S. Hahnemann University Philadelphia, Pennsylvania	Cardiac Patient/Client; BSN–MSN Student Education
Elizabeth Parietti, R.N., Ed.D. State University of New York Binghampton, New York	Educational Preparation for Nursing
Linda Pedersen, R.N., M.N. Virginia Mason Hospital Seattle, Washington	Nursing Interventions (Educational) in Working with Chronically Ill Patients
Sydney Pendleton, R.N., Ed.D. University of Missouri Kansas City, Missouri	Nursing Theory
Ginette Pepper, R.N., Ph.D. V.A./University of Colorado Denver, Colorado	Evaluation of Pre-employment Interview (Criterion-based)
Michael Perlow, R.N., D.N.S. Murray State University Murray, Kentucky	Self-esteem
Dorothy Pezzoli, R.N., M.S.N., CRN V.A. Medical Center Northport, New York	Development of a Tool to Measure Cost-Effectiveness of Clinical Nurse Specialist
Mary Powell, R.N., M.S.N. University of Arkansas for Medical Sciences Little Rock, Arkansas	Baccalaureate Education
Russell Powell, R.N., C.C.R.N. Durham Veterans Administration Hospital Durham, North Carolina	Assessment and Measurement of Critical Care Nurses to Determine Needs for Continuing Education Focus
Edith Raleigh, R.N., Ph.D. Harper-Grace Hospitals Detroit, Michigan	Coping with Chronic Illness
Tanya Ratney, M. N., Ed.D. Fitchburg State College Fitchburg, Massachusetts	Community Mental Health
Richard Redman, R.N., Ph.D. State University of New York Buffalo, New York	Patient Classification Systems

Mary Ann Remington, R.N., Ph.D. Intercollegiate Center for Nursing Education Spokane, Washington	The Development, Implementation, and Evaluation of a Career Enhancement/Development Program for New Baccalaureate Nurses
Carol Rossel, R.N., Ed.D. Lewis University Romeoville, Illinois	Baccalaureate Nursing Education
Jeanette Sasmor, R.N., Ed.D., FAAN University of South Florida Tampa, Florida	Continuing Nursing Education
Linda Scheetz, R.N., Ed.D. Mount Saint Mary College Newburgh, New York	Clinical Outcomes (BSN Students)
Terry Schwab, R.N., Ph.D. University of Texas Health Sciences Center San Antonio, Texas	Communication and Conflict Management
Mary Vesta Marston-Scott, Ph.D., FAAN University of Illinois Chicago, Illinois	Compliance in Hypertension and the Fishbein Model
Kathleen Simon,. R.N., M.S. Boston University Boston, Massachusetts	Children's Responses to Stressful Events
Lani Smith, R.N., Ph.D. University of Southwestern Louisiana Lafayette, Louisiana	Cardiovascular Nursing
Bonnie Smola, R.N., Ph.D. University of Dubuque Dubuque, Iowa	Program Evaluation
Linda Steele, R.N., Ph.D. McKendree College Lebanon, Illinois	Evaluation of the Roy Model As a Curriculum Framework
Yvonne Sterling, R.N., D.N.Sc. Louisiana State University Medical Center New Orleans, Louisiana	Discharge Planning for Parents of Children Receiving Home Care

Donna Story, R.N., Ph.D. Luther College Decorah, Iowa	Caring Behavior of Nurse
Janyce Tarell, R.N., M.S. National Institute of Health Oakton, Virginia	Psychiatric Nursing; Clinical Outcomes in Patients Who Experience Schizophrenia
Odessie Taylor, R.N., Ph.D. Creighton University Omaha, Nebraska	Risk Factors for Falls in the Elderly
Karen Tetz, R.N., M.S. Walla Walla College Portland, Oregon	Ability of Student Nurses to Make Clinical Decisions
Martha Thomas, R.N., M.S.N. Western Washington University Bellingham, Washington	Measurement of ADN's Clinical Baseline Skills in Both Cognitive and Technical Areas for Use in an RN–BSN Program
Gladys Torres, R.N., Ed.D. State University of New York Brooklyn, New York	Fear of Success in the Workplace
Terry VandenBosch, R.N., M.S., C.S. University of Michigan Hospital Ann Arbor, Michigan	Pain/Suffering and Object Relations
Nancy Wells, R.N., M.N. University of Rochester Rochester, New York	Adult, Surgical
Kathleen Wheeler, R.N., Ph.D. Hunter–Bellevue New York, New York	An Observatory, Exploratory Study to Delineate the Precise Nature of the Empathic Process in the Nurse–Patient Relationship
Joan Wilke, R.N., M.S. University of Wisconsin Milwaukee, Wisconsin	Family Responses to Chronic Mental Illness; Working with Families with Young Adult Chronically Mentally Ill Family Members
Connie Wilkinson, R.N., M.P.H., CNA Seattle VA Medical Center Seattle, Washington	Falls in Institutionalized Elderly
M. Shelley Young, R.N., Ph.D. Montana State University Bozeman, Montana	Postcardiotomy Delirium

Index

N

O

P